Rules for Corporate Warriors

To
my children, Adam and Briana,
for their encouragement, patience
and love

Rules for Corporate Warriors

How to Fight and Survive Attack Group Shakedowns

Nick Nichols

with an introduction by
Dr. Patrick Moore
Greenpeace co-founder

The Free Enterprise Press
BELLEVUE, WASHINGTON
Distributed by Merril Press
2001

Rules for Corporate Warriors

First Edition
Published by The Free Enterprise Press

Typeset in Times New Roman by The Free Enterprise Press, a division of the Center for the Defense of Free Enterprise, 12500 N.E. 10th Place, Bellevue, Washington 98005. Telephone 425-455-5038. Fax 425-451-3959. E-mail address: books@cdfe.org. Cover art by Sally Wern Comport. Cover design by Mic Bishop.

Rules for Corporate Warriors is distributed by Merril Press, P.O. Box 1682, Bellevue, Washington 98009. Additional copies of this book may be ordered from Merril Press at $25.00 each. Phone 425-454-7009.

LIBRARY OF CONGRESS CATALOGING-IN-PUBLICATION DATA
Nick Nichols, 1947-
    Rules for corporate warriors : how to fight and survive attack group shakedowns / Nick Nichols. -- 1st ed.
        p. ; cm.
    Includes bibliographical references and index.
    ISBN: 0-939571-21-8
    1. Corporate image. 2. Green movement. 3. Radicalism. 4. Conservation of natural resources. I. Title.

HD59.2.N53 2001
659.2'85--dc21

2001040645

PRINTED IN THE UNITED STATES OF AMERICA

Contents

Introduction

I have often wondered how long it would be before someone wrote a book like this. *Rules for Corporate Warriors* is not just a full-blown diatribe against the political extremists who have hijacked the environmental movement, it is a detailed guidebook on how to fight and win battles and wars with these self-appointed moralists. It will become essential reading for anyone involved in defending their company or association from the campaigns of extortion, denigration, and false claims that have become so common in the world today.

It has long been my view that the legitimate debate over the environment has degenerated into ideological warfare, pitting leftist extremists versus ultra-right debunkers of every environmental concern. In this climate of zero tolerance it is nearly impossible for the general public to determine which environmental issues merit their attention. The media offers little help as its main function is to perpetuate conflict and thus to assist in propping up even the most farcical assertions. Add to this the fact that most journalists are liberal arts majors with little education in science and you have the formula for today's very one-sided coverage of environmental affairs. The extremists on the left are portrayed as righteous crusaders fighting for the survival of the Earth and all its creatures. Those on the right are demonized as corporate despots, Earth destroyers, baby killers, and Darth Vaders. Finally there is a book that offers bold advice on how to restore some balance to this one-sided situation.

Simply put, Nick Nichols makes the case for fighting back rather than capitulating, for learning the rules of engagement rather than playing into your opponent's hands. During my 15 years as a founder and director of Greenpeace from 1971-1986 I learned these lessons well. Attack hard and fast in hopes of a quick victory, giggle with glee as inept corporate and government officials dig themselves deeper into the mire. It seemed they had never heard the "First Law of Holes." If you find yourself in one, stop digging.

Back in those days we were fighting for just causes that were based on serious consideration of science, reason and ethical concerns. Campaigns to end nuclear testing, prevent the extinction of whales, clean up toxic discharges into the air and water, and end the mass slaughter of seal pups in their breeding grounds were won along with the hearts and minds of the public. But as the movement gained power it succumbed to political and social activists who learned to use environmental rhetoric to cloak agendas that have little to do with ecology. Our original vision of Spaceship Earth and one human family was stolen and transformed into a virulent attack on corporations, technology, trade, and science. Even the organization I helped found and lead has joined this insane anti-almost-anything bandwagon. It is time to turn the tables.

Perhaps the most classic case of this misguided "environmentalism" is the campaign against genetically modified organisms or GMOs. Most of the major environmental groups have taken a zero tolerance position, stating that this technology should be banned completely and never developed. There are huge real and realistically potential benefits for the environment and human health and nutrition from the development of GMOs. There are no known serious negative impacts from growing or ingesting the GMOs that have already been developed and distributed. Yet every half-baked sensationalism and contrivance from activists with no training in science gets airtime on the evening news. Even the Golden Rice, a GMO that may help prevent blindness in half a million children every year is rejected out of hand by these anti-humanists who put unfounded fear-mongering ahead of the world's poor.

I was recently involved in a situation that highlights the benefits of dealing with extremists in a forthright and determined manner. As part of its bid to be the site for the 2008 Olympics, Toronto appointed an Environmental Committee to develop an environmental policy for the Games. It turns out that Greenpeace and its allies have become very successful at getting on these committees in a number of cities and then using them to further their extremist campaigns. They are very effective partly because the bid process is very secretive and competitive. The Environment Committee for the Toronto 2008 bid ended up producing a policy that banned fossil fuels, 98% of Canadian wood products, PVC, tin, and cadmium from the Games. This was done without consultation with any of the affected industries. Between them the forest and PVC industries forced a private hearing with the Environment Committee, only a handful of which turned out and listened politely. It became clear that they were not about to change their policy and both industry groups decided to remain polite so as not to alienate the committee members. As if the committee had any sympathy with them in the first place!

Taking matters into my own hands I produced a detailed critique of the Environmental Policy and sent it to the entire committee plus political leaders and media, most of whom were not aware of the points we had raised in the hearing. Then I took the bold move of publishing an editorial in the *National Post*, Canada's best newspaper, on the eve of the Environmental Committee's meeting to decide on any changes to their policy. In the editorial I pointed out that the Olympic torch is fired with fossil fuel and more seriously that both fuel cells and hybrid-gas electric vehicles, the most promising technologies to make vehicles cleaner and more efficient depended on fossil fuels. I also pointed out that tin is an essential ingredient of bronze and that the committee had thereby banned the Bronze Medal. In addition, I explained, tin is a component of the solder that is used in all electronic circuitry such as computers, camcorders, cell phones, etc. Suddenly there were a lot of phone calls made from high places advising the committee that it was embarrassing the nation. Nearly all the policies were made more reasonable and the extremists were defeated. In the end Toronto lost the bid to Beijing but a valuable precedent has been set for future Games. If that critique had not been written and that editorial had not been published the committee would have changed nothing.

I don't agree with everything in *Rules for Corporate Warriors*. For example I believe that population, forest loss through agricultural expansion and climate change are very important and that the environmental movement should focus on these issues. But that's not the point, the point is that Nick Nichols' book will be of invaluable assistance to people who are beset by the juggernaut of misinformation, threats, and negative media generated by activists out to destroy their company or product. I look forward to a shift in corporate strategy and a return to debate based on science, logic, and a balanced approach to the sustainable development of our civilization.

Patrick Moore, Ph.D.
Vancouver, British Columbia
Canada
August, 2001

Foreword

I wrote this book out of sheer optimism.

As a crisis manager to major corporations, I have seen some good companies meekly give rope to their hangmen, and give it without the slightest thought of self defense.

I have seen some good companies try to repel attack group shakedowns and then bungle the job from lack of experience.

I have helped some good companies stand their ground in the face of vicious attacks and emerge triumphant and invigorated.

So, despite the current rash of "capitulation counselors" in the crisis management field – and risk aversive cowardice in the boardroom – I wrote this book in the firm belief that *something can be done*. We do not need to stand by while radical activists cripple the economic heart of our society.

Optimistic? Absolutely. Overly optimistic? I don't think so. I see a popular movement emerging to counter the anti-corporate radicals. I hope *Rules for Corporate Warriors* encourages both pro-business grassroots and besieged executives and corporate directors.

It may come as news to some that an organized movement is out to cripple our economic life. But just read the headlines any day in the *New York Times*, the *Washington Post*, or any other daily newspaper. You'll find that someone is accusing a big company of dastardly deeds, or suing a whole industry, or lobbying for vindictive regulations, or staging protests that can be withdrawn with the payment of a cash settlement.

It all adds up to a corporate takeover – the takeover of corporate control by interests that are hostile to the very existence of corporations. If that takeover becomes widespread, the consequences for all of us are dire.

Yes, there are many problems with corporations. There would be more without them. And so this book is intended as a roadmap that anyone can use to help vital businesses survive.

While this book focuses on the problems of corporate executives, it was written for the general reader, and so avoids jargon as much as possible. It also rejects the tangled grammar of the business world by saying exactly and only what it means.

Rules for Corporate Warriors is meant to give the average American an insider's look at the corporate world as it's never been seen before.

This book has been brewing in my mind for more than a decade. If I had written it when most of its ideas first came to me, the business world might be a different place today.

But history has caught up with some ideas that seemed incredible back then. The activist riots in Seattle and Quebec have convinced many that the anti-corporate left is a palpable threat to the free enterprise system.

Like most books, *Rules for Corporate Warriors* is the work of many hands. It is impossible to acknowledge everyone who has shaped my ideas, but a few deserve special thanks.

Senator Gaylord Nelson (retired) and his merry band of old-school conservationists taught me during my formative years in Wisconsin that it was possible to conserve natural resources, while protecting free enterprise and individual property rights. I can well imagine that the Senator would disagree with many of my conclusions. However, I suspect that he, too, has rolled his eyes and uttered a curse under his breath when extremists have invoked Mother Earth to justify their destructive and violent behavior.

Saul Alinsky's *Rules for Radicals* not only inspired the writing of this book, but also provided me with a blueprint for countering those who have launched malicious attacks against businesses and the productive, talented people who run them.

Winston Churchill taught his generation, and the few of those who remain attentive to history, that appeasement is the tool of cowards and the elixir of megalomaniacs who believe they have a divine right to prey upon their fellow human beings.

William D. Novelli, founder of Porter Novelli and Associates, and current CEO of AARP, taught me much of what I know about the practical aspects of communications management. I added the in-your-face attitude. Bill took a chance and gave me my first job in the private sector. Were it not for him, I would probably be caged in a government agency, sucking up my fair share of taxpayer dollars.

Many thanks for research assistance and manuscript review to Joseph L. Bast, Heartland Institute; Robert L. Bradley, Institute for Energy Research; George Landrith, Frontiers of Freedom Institute; Deroy Murdock, Loud and Clear Communications; Scott D. Phillips, MD, FACP, Toxicology Associates, Prof. LLC; Teresa Platt, Fur Commission USA; David Ridenour, National Center for Public Policy Research; David Rothbard and Craig Rucker of the Committee For A Constructive Tomorrow; Fred L. Smith, Competitive Enterprise Institute; John Bankston; Walt Buchholtz; William F. Patient; and Ron Yocum.

Special thanks for enduring support and encouragement go to Eric Dezenhall, John Weber, David Egner, Sheila Hershow, Missy Houston, Caroline Oppleman, Andy Shea and Corinne Simon.

I owe the greatest debt of thanks to my editor, Paul Driessen, whose vast knowledge and deep experience are reflected throughout the text. My thanks also to Alan Gottlieb, president of the Center for the Defense of Free Enterprise, for accepting the manuscript for publication by the Center's division, the Free Enterprise Press. More thanks go to Ron Arnold, editor-in-chief of the Free Enterprise Press, for guiding the book through the production process.

Any merits of this book belong to these fine people. Any errors of fact or judgment are mine alone.

Nick Nichols
Washington, D.C.
August 2001

Prologue

War and Appeasement
a history lesson for corporate executives

> Decided only to be undecided, resolved to be irresolute, adamant for drift, solid for fluidity, all-powerful to be impotent.
>
> —Winston Churchill

The year was 1935. Adolf Hitler was chancellor of Germany, Benito Mussolini ducé of Italy, Edouard Daladier premier of France, and Neville Chamberlain prime minister of Great Britain. Hitler had come to power on a wave of nationalism, arising out of a severe economic depression in Germany and resentment over how the country had been treated by the Versailles Treaty that ended World War I.

Chamberlain was well aware that Nazi Germany was rearming, in defiance of Versailles. But he argued that many of Germany's grievances were just, and urged concessions in the name of German self-determination. Knowing that both Britain and France were weak militarily, he was also afraid to antagonize Hitler, or anger Mussolini into aligning with the German dictator.

So when Italy invaded Ethiopia, Chamberlain counseled restraint. When German troops later re-entered the Rhineland's demilitarized zone, again in defiance of the terms of Versailles, he urged Britain and France to do nothing. When Hitler seized Austria in March 1938, to "reunite" the two countries, Chamberlain again rationalized the aggression as legitimately aggrieved nationalism.

But Der Führer still was not satisfied. He began demanding the "return" of the Sudetenland, a largely German-speaking area of western Czechoslovakia. So on September 30, 1938, Chamberlain and Daladier caved in to Hitler and signed the Munich Pact. The next day, German troops goose-stepped into Czechoslovakia, which had not even been invited to the talks that decided its fate.

Chamberlain flew home to Britain, where he praised the Munich Pact for "bringing peace with honor, peace for our time." Most Brits agreed, but a cigar-chomping, Old Testament-style prophet named Winston Churchill warned that Chamberlain's pusillanimous appeasement would soon lead to war.

"The German dictator, instead of snatching the victuals from the table, has been content to have them served to him course by course," Churchill thundered. "You were given the choice between war and dishonor. You have chosen dishonor, and you will have war."

Six months later, Hitler seized the rest of Czechoslovakia and began threatening Poland. Nervously, Chamberlain and Daladier promised to intervene if the German dictator made good on his threat. Next, Hitler sprung a surprise and concluded a non-aggression pact with Russia, leaving him free to proceed with his plans to subdue western Europe.

Within two weeks, on September 1, 1939, fifty-three German army divisions invaded Poland. Britain and France declared war against Germany, and Europe was plunged into chaos. By June of 1940, Hitler's *Blitzkrieg* or "lightning war" had subdued Norway and Denmark, then struck through Belgium and the Netherlands, to bypass the "impregnable" fortresses of the Maginot Line and conquer France. Britain now stood alone.

Miraculously, 336,000 British and French troops managed to escape the beaches of Dunkirk near the French-Belgian border and, on a flotilla of ferry boats and coastal vessels, were evacuated to England, to fight another day. Chamberlain was ignominiously ousted from power, and King George VI asked Churchill to become prime minister.

Hitler launched an ultimately unsuccessful air war against Britain. In June 1941, the supremely overconfident dictator sent his armies rolling into Russia. And yet, even then, across the Atlantic, America ignored all these ominous developments, as it had Japan's brutal invasion of Manchuria and China. We convinced ourselves that these faraway events could never affect us and remained blissfully unprepared for the war that was to come.

Then, Japan attacked Pearl Harbor on Sunday morning, December 7, 1941, and invaded Hong Kong, Singapore and the Philippines. The world was now at war, in what would prove to be the bloodiest, most costly conflict in history.

It was a war that could easily have turned out very differently. Indeed, were it not for a resolute Winston Churchill and Franklin Roosevelt, Hitler's arrogance and blunders, a determined England's island status and a far-away industrial power called America, *ve could all be schpeaking Deutsch und Japanese* today.

Roosevelt had ignored those who counseled isolationism and provided aid to Britain and Russia, ensuring that they could resist the Nazi onslaught during their darkest hours.

Churchill had rallied his country, with stirring radio speeches and his dogged refusal to yield an inch to Hitler. "Victory at all costs," he declared in his first statement as prime minister – "victory in spite of all terror, victory however long and hard the road may be; for without victory, there is no survival." After Dunkirk he had promised, "… whatever the cost may be, we shall fight on the beaches, we shall fight on the landing grounds, we shall fight in the fields and in the streets, we shall fight in the hills; we shall never surrender."

Eventually, in 1945, at a cost of more than a trillion dollars and 40,000,000 lives, the Allied forces defeated Germany, Italy and Japan. World War II at last was over.

Why am I giving you a World War II history lesson in a crisis communications book? Very simply, so that you corporate executives might heed George Santayana's sage observation of a century ago: "Those who cannot remember the past are condemned to repeat it."

Chamberlain and Daladier could not learn their history lesson.

Perhaps you can.

For the sad reality is that we now have a new generation of would-be overlords, who also dream of world domination – not through force of arms, but through pressure, intimidation, terror and laws bent to serve their purposes. They lead mobs of increasingly vocal, rapacious, confident militants – preying on weak companies and communities, ganging up on large ones, rampaging in the streets, demanding tribute, and preparing to unleash a new lightning war that (they hope) will overwhelm industries, life styles and social, economic, legal, political and religious institutions.

They began with legitimate grievances. But as they became more powerful, they also became ever more insatiable in their demands, bold in their assaults, intolerant in their views, disingenuous in their claims, and callously indifferent to the havoc and human misery they have left in their wake. Their disdain for business, capitalism and even humanity seems boundless, and they seek to replace progress and modern society with a false, utopian vision of a benign Mother Nature that never was and never can be.

In the face of this assault, all too many business leaders, middle managers, public relations counselors and politicians have somehow concluded that the wisest course of action is to appease the predators' hungry demands, address even their most illegitimate grievances, present them with tasty victuals course by course, and ensure "peace with honor" and "peace for our time."

You think this is an unfair, inaccurate characterization of what is going on? Read the first few chapters, and ponder their examples, conclusions and advice. They should make even the most committed corporate ostriches, isolationists and appeasers reconsider.

Will you corporate chieftains learn from history?

Or will you allow yourselves, your companies, your employees, your investors, our citizenry, our consumers, and our world civilization to be dragged into a new ideological abyss?

Read this book, and decide what choice you should make.

> The terrible military machine, which we and the rest of the civilized world so foolishly, so supinely, so insensately allowed the Nazi gangsters to build up year by year from almost nothing, cannot stand idle, lest it rust or fall to pieces. . . . So now this bloodthirsty guttersnipe must launch his mechanized armies upon new fields of slaughter, pillage and devastation.
>
> —Winston Churchill

Part One

The Problem

1

Power Corrupts

In searching for a new enemy to unite us, we came up with
the idea that pollution, the threat of global warming, water
shortages, famine and the like would fit the bill.... All these
dangers are caused by human intervention.... The real enemy
then, is humanity itself.

— Council of the Club of Rome,
announcing a new unifying principle[1]

A century ago, man's genius and industry had brought America previously
unimaginable achievement. But like all good things, it had come at a price.
Lakes, rivers, forests, prairies and mountains had been wantonly abused in
the quest for raw materials to meet the needs of a growing nation.

President Theodore Roosevelt issued a call to arms, in response to
growing public anxiety over cycles of slash and burn, scrape and run, plow
and erode timber cutting, mining, grazing and farming. His strong interest in
conservation led him to appoint Gifford Pinchot, the "father of American
forestry," as the first Chief of the U.S. Forest Service and proclaim Devil's
Tower in Wyoming as the first of many national monuments. It was the
beginning of a utilitarian "conservation movement," which stressed that
use need not conflict with preservation.

They set aside national parks, forests and refuges; implemented new conservation, multiple use and reclamation policies; and resurrected the seemingly forgotten biblical command that man was to be a steward of the earthly garden God gave us. Our citizenry gained new appreciation for nature and outdoor recreation.

Seventy years and two world wars later, we had achieved even greater heights in technology, medicine, opportunity and human well-being. Gone were the polio, cholera and other plagues that had ravaged communities for millennia. Gone were early nineteenth century concerns that New York City would soon drown in horse urine, manure and carcasses. But as before, these accomplishments came at the price of new air and water pollution problems, new land use and wildlife concerns.

Thus was born Earth Day and the modern environmental movement, new laws and regulations to prevent pollution and protect scenic areas, an emphasis on energy conservation and recycling, a deeper respect for our planet, and new ways of doing business and conducting our lives. The gains have been nothing short of remarkable.

Reaping the benefits

Urban air quality has improved dramatically, as smog alerts and ozone, carbon monoxide, lead, particulate, hydrocarbon and sulfur dioxide levels have plummeted. Nationwide, overall air pollution emissions decreased 64 percent between 1970 and 2000, and the number of days with unhealthy air quality ratings has plunged between 1990 and 2000 from 173 to 18 in Los Angeles, from 96 to 3 in San Diego, from 36 to 1 in New York City, and by similar amounts in other big cities.[2]

Our rivers, groundwater and other waterways are likewise far cleaner – resulting in the return of fish, eagles, otter and other species. Since the late 1970s, bald eagle populations in the Lower 48 States have doubled every six or seven years, and there are now more wild turkeys than when the Pilgrims celebrated their first Thanksgiving. Alligators have been re-moved from the endangered species list, and populations of bighorn sheep, buffalo, elk and deer are up dramatically.[3]

Gas mileage for 2001 model year cars and light trucks is 56 percent better than for average 1975 models, and they emit 95 percent less pollu-tion than vehicles belched out just 25 years ago.[4] Fuel cells, advanced gasoline and diesel engines, gasoline-electric hybrids, alternative fuels and other technologies promise continuing improvements on all these fronts.

America's use of raw materials also showed its ecological side. Recycling is now commonplace. Aluminum beverage cans are some 30 percent lighter than they were in the 1960s, and 80 percent lighter than the steel cans they replaced (and over 80 percent of these aluminum cans are recycled). High-rise buildings today require 35 percent less steel than 20 years ago. A fiber-optic cable made from 60 pounds of silica sand (the most abundant element on earth) carries hundreds of times more information than a cable made from 2,000 pounds of copper – and does it much faster. Timber harvesting and sawmill processing changes reduced wood waste from 26 percent in 1970 to less than 2 percent in 1993, and even less today.[5]

New clean coal technologies are dramatically improving power generation efficiency, while also reducing pollutant emissions. A huge new 1500 megawatt coal-fired power plant being built 100 miles north of Sydney, Australia uses waste coal that otherwise would have no economic value. The potential prototype for a new generation of generators in the United States, the plant uses a new fluidized-bed system that virtually eliminates the production of nitrogen and sulfur oxides, while also scrubbing out almost all the fine dust particles – making the plant almost as clean as one fueled by natural gas.[6]

Modern energy production methods also prove that energy and the environment are not competing priorities. Directional drilling and other technologies have advanced so far that getting as much as 16 billion barrels of oil out of the South Carolina-sized Arctic National Wildlife Refuge would disturb only 2,000 acres. That's one-twentieth of the land area of Washington, DC, or 20 of the buildings Boeing uses to manufacture its 747 jets, and the work would be done in the dead of winter, using ice pads that would melt in the spring.[7] More than 60 wells can now be drilled from a single offshore oil platform, and modern reclamation methods quickly restore mined lands to thriving forests, grasslands and ponds.

Equally amazing, America used 40 percent less energy per unit of economic output or gross domestic product (GDP) in 2000 than it did in 1973; its output of goods and services, adjusted for inflation, rose by 125 percent, while its energy use increased by only 30 percent, during this period. The United States still trails France, Germany, Italy, Japan, the United Kingdom and a dozen other major countries in energy efficiency. However, far greater transportation distances, far more intensive industrial activity, widespread air conditioning and much higher economic output account for much of this difference. America's continuing investment in modern technology and equipment is constantly improving both productivity and energy efficiency.[8]

Thanks to biotechnology, new plant breeds use less water, are more pest resistant, convert fertilizers more efficiently and have higher yields than crops did just 10-20 years ago. The result? U.S. farmers now grow 50 percent more corn on 10 percent less acreage than in 1980, using fewer pesticides and less nitrogen and phosphate fertilizer.[9] The amount of farmland treated by pesticides fell by over 7 million acres between 1996 and 1998, according to the U.S. Department of Agriculture – and the use of active pesticide ingredients declined by 8.2 million pounds between 1997 and 1998 – as a direct result of farmers planting genetically modified (GM) crops.[10]

The next generation of bio-engineered plant products promises even greater benefits: greater tolerance for salinity; resistance to tropical insects, diseases and viruses; increased ability to grow in poor soils; longer shelf life; and enhanced nutrition and vitamin content, healthy oils, and medicinal values. Researchers have already developed rice containing beta-carotene, which human bodies can convert to Vitamin A, preventing half a million cases of blindness every year. Genetically modified potatoes can now produce vaccines for hepatitis B, and GM bananas contain a vaccine against cholera.[11] Other plants could soon provide substitutes for petroleum-based products, feed stocks for new types of polyurethane, nylon with stronger and more flexible fibers, and biodegradable lubricants.

Timber companies are implementing innovative sustainable forestry practices, mining companies are restoring areas that had been abandoned a century ago by companies that do not even exist today, and chemical and paper companies are installing pollution control systems that enable them to convert former effluent ponds into thriving marshes and wetlands.

Numerous conservation organizations, many of them local, are actively working to restore lands, streams, lakes and rivers to natural conditions. Others are transforming urban "brownfields" (abandoned industrial sites) into parks and playgrounds: a Los Angeles site has become a soccer field; a blighted 42-acre island in Pittsburgh now boasts attractive town homes, offices, sports facilities and a marina; and a Washington, DC brownfield will soon be converted into a mall, featuring a Home Depot, K-Mart, supermarket, hotel and office buildings. Thousands of people have turned their own quarter-acre or neighborhood ponds and common areas into backyard habitats for bluebirds and flickers, herons and wood ducks, deer and opossums, bass and other wildlife.

Some of these improvements have been driven by new government laws and regulations. Many were spurred by public demand, marketplace competition, corporate cost-saving efforts, and changing attitudes by corporate officers, employees, shareholders and customers. Others can be at-

tributed to tax incentives, conservation easements, cooperative partner-
ships, and a willingness by many state and local governments to encourage experimentation.

But all can be traced to the technologies, educated workforce and enormous, sustained investments that only a wealthy nation can afford. They
have also been made possible by a legal, social and market economic system that fosters and encourages creativity, personal choice and decisions
based on sound science, a reasonable phase-in period for new regulations,
and a balancing of risks, costs and benefits, health and environmental quality, economic growth and opportunity, and other values that we hold in
high regard.[12]

The dark side of The Force

Unfortunately, in addition to these unquestioned benefits, modern environmentalism also brought us a less desirable byproduct: an emerging school
of ecological alarmism. This doctrine teaches that corporations and technology are fundamentally evil, and that population growth, pesticides and
resource depletion are bringing us to the edge of planetary catastrophe.

Ultra-preservationist groups such as The Wildlands Project claim that
our excellent system of nature preserves is not enough, can never be enough.
Most citizens are proud that 250,000,000 acres of America's government
lands – an area larger than California, Oregon and Washington combined
– have been designated as wilderness, park, preserve and refuge areas.
Most of us support the millions of additional acres that are managed under
other highly restrictive programs.[13] The crown jewels of America's landscape are already saved, and we want it that way. But most of us don't
want to put all our natural resources off limits. We want some areas for
timber and energy and mineral wealth. We want federal lands available for
productive use. The ultra-preservationist faction has no answer to the question, "How much is enough?" They insist on an ever expanding nature
system that removes people and all human activity – except theirs.

An even more extreme school – "deep ecology" – rejects
"anthropocentrism," rejects civilization, and views humans as having no
greater moral value than any other animal. (An ant is a rat is a child, in
their view.) Aspiring to a state of pristine nature, deep ecologists gloss
over the fact that, for animals in the wild, life is nasty, brutish and short,
ending mostly by violent death at the paws of predators. Bill Devall and
George Sessions' 1985 book *Deep Ecology* recommended that human
population be reduced by unspecified "humane means" to the land's "carrying
capacity," whatever they judge that to be. Scary.

Even churches, synagogues and mosques have been recruited to The Cause. A liturgy distributed by the National Religious Partnership for the Environment says: "God's creation is being abused and violated.... We are responsible for massive pollution of earth, water and sky." In response, congregants are to chant, "We are killing the earth, we are killing the waters, we are killing the skies." The liturgy and accompanying sample sermons are components of the NRPE's 10-year, $16-million program to make "care for God's creation a central priority for organized religion" and a "defining lifetime vocation."[14]

Gradually, these alarmist views began to dominate debate, and to metamorphose into environmental, food and consumer factions, most of which shared the same fundamental hatreds, ideologies and goals. These radical alarmists drove away those of us who believe deeply in conservation and environmental protection, but see technology, science, economic growth and industrial progress as a vital pathway (albeit an erratic and bumpy one) to human and ecological improvement, solutions to previously intractable problems, and even lower birth and fertility rates.[15] They deeply troubled those of us who believe humanity should be an uppermost concern, view people and their amazing ingenuity as "the ultimate resource," and are mostly optimistic about our future.

Today, the alarmist groups are more powerful, wealthy and dominant than ever. They have become increasingly dogmatic, strident and intolerant in their views; increasingly coercive in their approach. Their environmental concerns have transmogrified into hardened attitudes that are ever more utopian, authoritarian, purist, preservationist, animal-rightist and socialist – ever more anti-technology, anti-business, anti-capitalism, anti-civilization and, most disturbing of all, anti-humanity.

No longer problem solvers, they manufacture dissent. They have evolved into crisis creators and problem perpetuators. Their power, influence and even survival depend on what H. L. Mencken called an ability to "keep the populace alarmed (and hence clamorous to be led to safety), by menacing it with an endless series of hobgoblins, all of them imaginary."

Even worse, the most radical elements have turned to "direct action" methods that increasingly include violent protest, extortion, vandalism, arson, bombing and even vicious assaults on people to hammer home their angry messages.

Thus, today's environmentalists fall into three components: traditional mainstream environmental and conservation organizations; environmental attack groups of varying degrees of militancy; and criminal or terrorist elements that are frequently encouraged, supported, and given legitimacy by the pressure groups, some of which candidly acknowledge that the eco-terrorists make the militants look moderate and reasonable by comparison.

Money and power

In his book, *Undue Influence*, former Sierra Club activist Ron Arnold observes: "It is well known that numerous former executives from environmental organizations occupy positions within the federal bureaucracy. It is less well known that thousands of activist members of advocacy groups are employed by federal agencies – in positions that give them opportunities to exercise agenda-driven influence...."[16] Those regulators have power to impose costly new regulations, agree to collusive "consent decrees" in sweetheart lawsuits brought by their pressure-group comrades in arms, dispense millions in taxpayer dollars, and harass companies and fellow employees who dare to question their tactics.

But power has as much to do with money as it has to do with access to government bureaucracy, and the activists are always short of cash. Right? Wrong.

"This is a growth industry – a huge growth industry," says Daniel Beard, chief operating officer at the National Audubon Society. But it is also no exaggeration to say that the Environmental Conflict Industry is the last unregulated, unaccountable big business in America. "There is no clearinghouse for information about environmental groups," notes Tom Knudsen, Pulitzer Prize-winning investigative reporter for the *Sacramento Bee*, "no oversight body watching for abuse and assessing job performance."[17]

This huge growth industry is also wealthy beyond anything even King Croesus could have imagined.

- Knudsen says money is flowing to environmental groups "in unprecedented amounts, reaching $3.5 billion in 1999."[18]

- *Boston Globe* reporter Scott Allen calculated that the tree huggers' annual revenues amounted to $4 billion![19]

- In 1998 alone, the dozen largest U.S. environmental groups collectively had total revenues of nearly $1 billion, according to the Capital Research Center and Philanthropic Research, Inc.[20]

- In 1999, say S. Robert Lichter and Stanley Rothman, the *ten* largest environmental groups collectively had annual revenues in excess of $1 billion.[21]

● The total non-profit movement – NGOs or Non-Governmental Organizations – annually spends more than $1 trillion in 22 countries studied by the Johns Hopkins Comparative Nonprofit Sector Project. If viewed as a nation, the NGO sector would rank eighth in economic power.[22]

That's real money, even by Washington, DC standards. And much of it is used to fund lawsuits, lobbying, regulatory pressure, propaganda masquerading as education, and demonstrations and shakedowns aimed at forcing companies to accept the radicals' agenda.

Where does all this cash come from? Some of it does come from member dues and donations – the result of a constant barrage of expensive direct mail campaigns. But that's only a small part of the total. Much more flows from tax-exempt foundations that were created by the barons of big industry. And a lot comes from government agencies, and even the corporate world, often subsidized by federal tax dollars.

No, this is not a perverse April Fools joke.

Sugar Daddies

Take for example the Pew Charitable Trusts, which is actually seven family trusts created by descendants of Joseph N. Pew, founder of Sun Oil Company. The Pew trusts are currently a leading contributor to extreme environmental groups that spend much of their time attacking the oil industry. According to published reports, in 2000 Pew funneled $52.1 million into 44 environmentalist programs that its founder likely would have despised.[23]

The $4.8-billion foundation is not merely the second largest single money source for environmental and animal rights groups (behind the David and Lucile Packard Foundation), but also serves as a behind-the-scenes architect of major campaigns and a puppet master for many of these political advocacy groups. Its principal areas of interest are forest preservation, global warming and marine causes. Pew's Global Climate Change Center alone received over $5 million in 2000. The Trusts helped generate more than a million public comments in support of the Clinton Administration's decision to close millions of acres to road building and timber cutting – a move that former Idaho Congresswoman Helen Chenoweth-Hage condemned as just one example of how western rural communities "are being crushed by an inaccessible and faceless movement, wielding great power and influence."[24]

Pew and Packard are not the only big business foundations that bankroll the attackers. The W. Alton Jones Foundation ranks among the top ten contributors to environmental causes. Its founder, W. Alton "Pete" Jones, was CEO of Cities Service Oil Company. Yet another supporter is the Heinz Family Foundation (of H.J. Heinz ketchup fame). In 1988, Teresa Heinz was elected a trustee of the Environmental Defense Fund or EDF (now known as Environmental Defense or ED),[25] and later served as the organization's vice chair. Following the death of her husband, Senator John Heinz, she turned the two Heinz family endowments into major supporters of the extremist environmental agenda.[26]

The New York-based Foundation Center, which tracks non-profit money, describes more than 1,200 grant-making foundations that support the environmental and animal rights movements alone. It reports that 379 of them donated more than $356 million in 1992. Ron Arnold estimates that the foundations collectively provide perhaps as much as $2 billion annually to green and other anti-business pressure groups. Government grants may account for an additional $2 billion a year, Arnold says.[27]

In the United States, the Conservation Fund reports, environmental organizations "depend on foundations for programmatic ideas, information on productive networking with other groups, occasional technical support and the sense of legitimacy and prestige that comes with foundation grants." Moreover, the role of these foundations has shifted "from behind-the-scenes players to one where the foundations drive the priorities and agendas of the environmental movement and other groups for social change within the United States."[28]

James Sheehan, in his book *Global Greens*, notes that World Bank direct grants to "non-governmental organizations" totaled $37 million in 1996; the NGOs also receive millions in additional funds through consulting and administrative grants, "social funds," small grants, special grants and other World Bank programs.[29] No wonder many radical groups have muted their past criticism and now perceive the World Bank as a potentially powerful ally in their drive to implement their policies and effect social change.

Thanks to these steady infusions of cash, militant NGOs and their allies are becoming far more active and effective in Asia and Africa, on issues ranging from pharmaceuticals (patents, access and price) to clothing manufacturing, GM foods, chemicals and global warming. Almost $350,000 flowed from America to the three leading anti-biotechnology NGOs in Malaysia, just in 1998. Most of this money comes from American sources like the Foundation for Deep Ecology and Pesticide Action Network, but even U.S. Catholic Relief Services has provided funding for the Asian anti-biotech NGOs, as has the Swedish Government.[30]

Much of this money is also being channeled to leftist Australian NGOs, as networks among activists become stronger and U.S. foundations perceive

Australia as a "key node in the region." The money is being used to train activists and inculcate them in the philosophies of anti-corporate, anti-capitalist thought. Recent conferences in Sydney and elsewhere have emphasized these themes.[31]

Numerous U.S. government programs at the Environmental Protection Agency, Department of the Interior and elsewhere likewise fund activist and attack groups, directly or through grants to third party agencies and organizations. Millions went to Environmental Defense and other nonprofit lobbying groups, to help EPA promote its so-called "anti-sprawl" or "smart growth" policies, to exercise control over people's most basic rights to live where and how they choose.

Another report by Sheehan reveals that, between 1994 and 1998, EPA distributed $14 million to U.S. environmental advocacy groups, $12 million to colleges and universities, and $5.5 million to international environmental activists, for global warming and sustainable development programs. The grants are "cleverly designed to create the appearance of broad support for its global policy agenda," Sheehan notes. The EPA academic research grants go in large part to "studies likely to support its assumptions and theories,"[32] meaning that researchers who might buck "consensus" get nothing.

EPA also gave hundreds of thousands of taxpayer dollars to companies like the Eastern Research Group, to crank out "educational" literature for schools and communities, claiming for instance that recycling household trash can help reduce "greenhouse gases" and prevent "profound changes in the Earth's climate and ecosystems."[33] Other hefty EPA grants went to industry groups like the Alliance for Responsible Atmospheric Policy, which represents companies that hope to reap profits via government regulations on chlorofluorocarbons and greenhouse gases, under various rent-seeking schemes.[34]

EPA also advocates central planning for America's cities and suburbs. To promote its Washington-centered vision of "smart growth" controls on "urban sprawl," EPA distributed over $1.25 million to Green lobbying groups in 2000. Tracking down these government grants is not easy, notes Utah State University professor Randall O'Toole. "The difficulty is in narrowing down the [Internet search] criteria enough not to be overwhelmed by [the thousands of] grants, yet making the criteria broad enough to get all appropriate grants."[34]

In fact, it is difficult to get complete information about any of these grant-giving programs. The fat-wallet foundations and even government agencies operate through secretive grant applications. They act on their own exclusive agendas, determined by an elite few who are subject to little or no public scrutiny. The grant-making pipelines are convoluted and hidden. Those who know the secrets ain't talkin'. Paper trails go through shredders on their way to landfills or recycling centers. And computer hard drives mysteriously go blank.

The EPA actually admitted in federal court that former EPA Administrator Carol Browner personally ordered contractors to erase records on her computer storage drive on the last full day of the Clinton Administration. The hard drives of three of Browner's top aides were also erased. The action violated a preliminary injunction issued the same day by Federal District Court Judge Royce Lamberth at the request of the Landmark Legal Foundation, ordering Browner and EPA to preserve the records. The court was overseeing the foundation's September 29, 2000 legal challenge to last-minute regulations that the foundation says were illegally drafted by EPA in impermissibly close cooperation with radical environmental groups.[35]

Moreover, neither the grant givers nor the organizations they fund are really accountable to the public. As U.S. Congressman Richard Pombo (R-CA) has observed:

"Foundations have no voters, no customers, no investors. The people who run big foundations are part of a small, elite, insulated group, most of whom live in the eastern United States, hundreds or even thousands of miles from the areas affected by the environmental policies they support. They have no way of receiving feedback from those affected by their decisions, nor are they accountable to anyone for promoting policies which adversely affect the well-being of people or local economies."[36]

Adds Arnold: the Rockefeller Family Fund and the Environmental Grantmakers Association (EGA) are "expert at secretly routing" millions of dollars into activist groups and media campaigns, to create and promote initiatives like the "ancient forests" concept, which was devised as a way to ban logging on millions of acres in the Pacific Northwest. "We would never have realized that this years-long Ancient Forest campaign was a synthetic artifact of the EGA, had audiotapes of their 1992 conference not come to our attention."[37]

It was at this conference that the corporations and foundations involved in the Ancient Forest campaign acknowledged that this was a "class issue" of rich grantors versus poor workers, that their grants were destroying people's jobs, and that the workers were about to "capture the high ground" as the true guardians of sound environmental stewardship. The EGA's response? More secret money to the Wilderness Society, Fenton Communications and the MacWilliams Cosgrove Snyder PR firm, to expand the campaign and smear the grassroots groundswell known as the Wise Use Movement.[38]

Ralph Nader claims his college campus Public Interest Research Groups (PIRGs) are run by student volunteers and supported by voluntary contributions. In reality, they are managed by professionals and derive most of their funding from a clever and deceptive mechanism. From the outset in 1971, Nader realized his PIRGs could fail if they had to spend their time raising money. So, using persuasive eloquence and offers that would have impressed Mario Puzo's Don Corleone, he convinced college administrators to set up a "negative check-off" system. Under this system, students would have to mark a box if they chose *not* to fund the local PIRG; no check meant part of their student fees automatically went to Nader, whether or not they supported his programs, policies and agendas. Over the next decade, the millions of dollars in student fees allowed PIRGs to spread to over 120 campuses in two dozen states.

Since the mid-1980's, however, the Committee For A Constructive Tomorrow and other anti-PIRG organizations have filed lawsuits, provided background information to interested legislators, and coordinated campus referenda and petitions to state boards of regents. These efforts have prevented PIRGs from collecting more than $4 million annually through deceptive check-offs, and today this system survives on only 60 campuses in 10 states. But the PIRGs still remain a potent force on many campuses, especially in California.[39]

Corporate foundations and direct corporate giving programs also make major contributions, borne of a misguided desire to be "good citizens," or to persuade pressure groups not to launch a threatened protest or boycott. Chevron gave thousands to the Audubon Society, which fights oil drilling on America's public lands, even as it continues to extract natural gas from its own Rainey wildlife sanctuary in Louisiana. Chase Manhattan Bank gave $158,750 to ACORN, a radical group that "helps poor people seize power" (so says the group's Web page) and dragoons banks into offering low-interest, minority-targeted loans, using methods that First Union Bank chairman Edward Crutchfield calls "pure blackmail."[40]

A master of similar tactics is the Reverend Jesse L. Jackson. Whether they are labeled "negotiations" (Rev. Jackson's preferred term), shakedowns (dozens of commentators use this term) or protection racket (dozens more use that one), the tactics have worked since he first used them against Coca-Cola and Anheuser-Busch in the early 1980s. In the late 1990s, Jackson used them to obtain millions of dollars from Viacom, Ameritech, AT&T, Bell-Atlantic, GTE and other telecom companies, who got his message. As I understand it, the message goes like this: Play ball with me, or I will threaten your sale, merger and acquisition plans, label you racist, white supremacist hate groups, and generally make your lives miserable. Right? Wrong? Anyway, a lot of money went to his Citizenship Education Fund (once headed by a mistress who bore his illegitimate child in 1999), but his friends also benefited.[41]

In 2000, Jackson persuaded companies to give his entangled enterprises a cool $17 million. The year before, his Citizenship Education Fund alone got

$9,919,914, according to CEF's Form 990, their official IRS report for 1999. Where did the money go? Salaries, wages, benefits and employment taxes gobbled up $1,147,034. Travel and conference expenses ate up another $2,486,449. Unnamed consultants got $1,307,393. $223,296 went to various unspecified miscellaneous items. Oddly enough, the entries on the Form 990 for fund raising, printing and publications show zero expenditure. How can Rev. Jackson have such a high-dollar outfit with no cost of fundraising? And how can an educational group have no cost for publications?[42]

We just have to assume he's honest. If you have a non-profit organization with a tax-exempt status, you can do strange and wonderful things. For the Reverend Jackson, it's doing the Lord's work. Maybe it's one of those miracles. Anyway, the radical environmental, consumerist and anti-biotechnology groups have learned much from this master activist – and thus far have been held equally accountable for their actions and expenditures.

Some corporate grants clearly reflect the views of liberal CEOs. In publicly held companies the money is not "theirs" to spend as they see fit – particularly when it is being used to pay protection money to the likes of Rev. Jackson or Earth Island Institute. As syndicated columnist Deroy Murdock observes, this money "belongs to shareholders, whose portfolios can suffer after corporate-sponsored liberal groups score policy victories."

For other CEOs, corporate philanthropy is such a small part of the overall revenue stream that they "can't be bothered," says Robert Malott, former chief of FMC Corporation. "That's nonsense, because it has a great impact on who you are and what you stand for, both internally and externally."

Anyone who thinks this "hush money" is going to silence anti-corporate radicals, change their views or end their pressure and ever-escalating demands needs psychiatric counseling. "You're not going to buy off these groups," warns Hudson Institute president Dr. Herbert London. Their motive is to "engage in a form of redistribution and control the free market," and financing them merely makes it easier for them to go after more victims.[43]

Government grants are also used to influence what comes out of government-funded research laboratories. As journalist Ronald Bailey advises, "Always remember the rule of financial and business reporting – follow the money."[44] Lab directors are keenly aware that continued funding often depends on tying their work to analyzing and solving some looming crisis *du jour*, such as ozone holes or global warming.

Melvyn Shapiro, chief of meteorological research at the National Center for Atmospheric Research once told *Insight* magazine, "If there were no dollars attached to this game, you'd see it played on intellect and integrity. When you say the ozone threat is a scam, you're not only attacking people's scientific integrity, you're going after their pocketbook, as well." Shortly afterward, Shapiro stopped talking to the press and told his colleagues he'd been muzzled by his superiors, Bailey reports.[45]

Global warming is another area where scientists like the University of Virginia's Patrick Michaels and S. Fred Singer and Harvard-Smithsonian's Sallie Baliunas worry that ideology and policy too often drive the science. Billions of dollars in U.S. and U.N. research and "education" grants have been made available annually to scientists whose work tends to support government-approved conclusions. No skeptics or realists need apply, and science by hypothesis, experiment and rigorous peer-review has been skewed leftward by politics – to be replaced with "science" by scenarios, garbage in-garbage out computer models and press releases sent to papers deemed most likely to run alarmist Page One above-the-fold stories.

Direct mail: Phony crises generate cash

Many environmental attack groups are also experts nonpareil at raising money through direct mail – reaching out to people who are worried, guilt-ridden and susceptible to crisis-of-the-month appeals.

Militant environmental groups are masters at manufacturing crises, crafting simplistic slogans, and generating conflict, anger and hysteria. Many members of this Crisis Creation Industry devote a substantial portion of their budgets to expensive direct-mail and telemarketing consultants. The typical send-money/save-the-planet appeal reads something like this:

> "America's National Park System – the first and finest in the world – is in real trouble right now. Our magnificent parks are being compromised by adjacent mining activities, noise pollution, commercial development and other dangerous threats." Please help the National Parks and Conservation Association save our parks, by sending "$15 or more."[46]

Suppose you did send in fifteen bucks. How would your hard-earned money be spent? According to the *Sacramento Bee*'s Knudsen, NPCA's own 1998-99 federal tax form reveals that "just $7.62 (51%) would have been spent on parks, less than the minimum 60% recommended by the American Institute of Philanthropy, a nonprofit charity watchdog group."[47] The rest would have paid for more fund-raising and extravagant overhead, which for many Green Industry subsidiaries includes huge staffs, glitzy offices, ritzy hotels, fancy parties and events, and executive salaries that top $200,000 at the ten largest U.S environmental groups. When NPCA fired its president several years ago, it awarded him a severance payment of $760,335.[48]

Another impoverished David, The Wilderness Society, in valiant battle against corporate Goliaths, spent $1.5 million in 1999 to send out 6.2 million letters in a single membership campaign. Of course, the saintly society could never admit this. So its annual report claimed that $1.3 million (87 percent) of this total was spent on "public education." A $94,411 telemarketing bill underwent a similar conversion, in which 71 percent was magically transformed into an educational expenditure.[49]

Defenders of Wildlife deftly employs the same clever accounting tactics – entering millions of dollars in direct mail and telemarketing expenses into the "public education" column of its ledger. The group boasts that it spends its members' and donors' money wisely, conscientiously keeping its overhead and fund-raising costs to a mere 19 percent. But deny Defenders its slick accounting ploy, and this number balloons to over 50 percent. "That was high enough to earn Defenders a "D" rating from the American Institute of Philanthropy," notes Knudsen.[50]

Challenged to defend its slick accounting methods, Defenders gave Knudsen several examples of "educational" statements from a "Tragedy in Yellowstone" solicitation letter:

- "Unless you and I help today, all of the wolf families in Yellowstone and central Idaho will likely be captured and killed."

- "The American Farm Bureau's reckless statements are nothing but pure bunk."

- "For the sake of the wolves ... please take one minute right now to sign and return the enclosed petition."[51]

Now I'm not a teacher, and I haven't examined much of what passes for classroom materials in today's schools – but somehow the educational value of these statements escapes me.

All together, The Wilderness Society mailed 6.2 million membership solicitations in 1999, totaling almost 350,000 pounds. All together, says Knudsen, Green groups sent more than 160 million pitches swirling through the U.S. Postal Service that year.[52]

No one knows how many trees were processed into pulp, how much bleach and other chemicals were used to recycle the waste paper into new paper stock, how many barrels of ink were devoured to print all the "crisis-related shrill material," or how many gallons of gasoline were burned to deliver these 160 million emotional appeals to your home and mine. No one knows how many stuffed dolphins, bumper stickers, calendars, "wolf adoption papers," cameras, umbrellas or holiday note cards greased the way for whatever donations came in – often at a rate of about 1 percent of total pitch letters sent out, says Knudsen. No one knows how many decals, self-sticking personal address labels and bumper stickers fouled up paper recycling systems. But it's doubt-less enough to make a true conservationist blush.

Independent analysts and CPAs might also see a further problem here. Donations to these environmental groups are generally tax-deductible, on the grounds that what they do is educational. However, when fabricated "crises" and blatant appeals for cash are peddled as "public education" – and much of the groups' efforts focus on lobbying, political activism, organizing protests and shaking down corporations – serious questions arise about deductibility and the legitimacy of continued 501(c)(3) status of these environmental attack groups.

If for-profit companies engaged in such accounting sleights of hand, the IRS, FTC, state watchdog agencies and a host of activist groups would be all over them, charging mail fraud, tax evasion, and false advertising. But appar-ently it's OK for The Wilderness Society, Defenders, NPCA, Audubon and similar groups to engage in such questionable practices. They are doing it for "the public interest," to "save Planet Earth" – not out of some base, greedy corporate drive to increase the bottom line.

Another clever fund raising technique is employed by the Humane Society of the United States (HSUS), which many people assume is somehow related to the local Humane Society branches that operate animal shelters. It is not. The HSUS devotes itself to animal rights, anti-hunting and anti-wildlife man-agement initiatives. It provides no money to local shelters and does not run any shelters of its own, even though it has over $100 million in assets and an annual budget of more than $55 million.[53]

The largest single item in that annual budget? Fund raising: more than $16 million, much of it for direct mail. "People donate money to the Humane Society of the United States and they think they're helping local shelters, but the money doesn't come to us," according to one shelter manager, who asked to remain anonymous. Another big ticket item is salaries for its CEO and president – almost $450,000 a year in 2000, plus perks amounting to tens of thousands more.[54]

Recently, a California environmental activist, backed by the AFL-CIO, actually sued Nike over its campaign to respond to attacks designed to create public outrage over working conditions in its overseas plants. The litigants claim Nike's campaign amounts to false advertising under the state's con-sumer protection laws. They want the court to force the company to end its public relations campaign and surrender millions of dollars in profits they say were illegally gained with the help of the allegedly false advertising. Nike says its statements are true and are protected by the First Amendment and constitu-tional free speech guarantees.[55]

So far the court has ruled in Nike's favor. But if the company ultimately loses the case, the same arguments could certainly be used against environmental and consumerist groups that engage in shrill, misleading direct mail campaigns. Things could get very interesting, especially if the court decision is based on false advertising arguments.

Litigation and in-kind contributions

It's apparent that the Environmental Crisis Industry has a veritable Midas touch. After having raked in billions of dollars every year through member, corporation, foundation and government generosity, it still has a couple more fund-raising tricks up its sleeve.

Radical environmental litigation generates millions for their war chests. During the 1990s, the U.S. government shelled out nearly $32 million in attorney fees for environmental cases filed against federal agencies – often for nothing more than missed deadlines. The environmental groups' attorneys charged us taxpayers $150 to $350 an hour to "represent" us abused citizens against inept regulators and evil corporations.[56]

In a number of cases, the lawyers' bills included claims for time spent lobbying, talking to the news media, flying and driving to and from meetings and courthouses, and even preparing the bills. In 1993, the U.S. Circuit Court of Appeals in Washington was so outraged by a Sierra Club Legal Defense Fund lawyer's "flagrant over-billing" that it reduced her award to zero.[57]

Finally, the radical environmentalists also get billions worth of in-kind help, including consistent media support for their ideology and agenda – the kind of free media money can't buy. To cite just one example, a Media Research Center analysis of television network coverage of President Bush's rejection of the controversial Kyoto climate change treaty revealed that:

- The view that human-induced global warming is leading to catastrophic climate change received six times as much attention as the views of scientific skeptics who argue that such gloom-and-doom scenarios are either exaggerated or wrong.

- There were only seven references to the existence of global warming skeptics, and six of those were on the Fox News Channel. The three broadcast networks (ABC, CBS and NBC) totally excluded the views of global warming skeptics from their coverage.

- Opponents of the Kyoto treaty and other new restrictions on industrial activity were outnumbered 20 to 3 by spokesmen for environmental groups.

- By a two-to-one margin, the networks also skewed the debate over President Bush's decision not to regulate carbon dioxide emissions in favor of his critics.[58]

Then, to top it off, partisan environmental groups receive handsome donations of invaluable professional fund raising help. For over a decade, the Advertising Council has designed and placed ads on their behalf. Its latest series solicits donations for Sierra Club, NRDC, Union of Concerned Scientists, Friends of the Earth, U.S. Public Interest Research Group and dozens of similar organizations, fourteen of which have launched attack ads targeting the Bush administration. Even *USA Today* has sharply criticized the council, saying: "The conclusion is inescapable: In spite of its reputation for high-quality public service ad campaigns, the Ad Council's standards for political neutrality are situational at best."[59]

> "Not only do journalists not have a responsibility to report what skeptical scientists have to say about global warming – they have a responsibility NOT to report what these scientists say."
>
> —Ross Gelbspan, former Boston Globe editor[60]

Modus operandi

All these billions underwrite a steady stream of attacks on corporations, communities and technology. What is most striking about the aggression is how often the same radical groups employ the same tactics, devices, exaggerated claims and outright lies. Two United Kingdom researchers, Mark Neal and Christie Davies, examined a number of predatory campaigns and divided them into a dozen categories.[61] Among them are:

- **The cluster fluster.** "This involves finding clusters of a disease or problem in one particular place, and identifying this as abnormal or suspicious." Anyone who's seen *Erin Brokovich* or *A Civil Action* is familiar with this technique. In reality, clusters often occur naturally and randomly; taken alone, they are not hard evidence of a genuine health or environmental hazard.

- **The exaggerated hazard.** Exaggerating risks is a surefire way to grab Page One headlines. When later evidence revealed that Alar, dioxin and asbestos were not the hazard activists had claimed they were, that news got buried in the business pages or simply ignored. It's a lot like refusing to consider DNA evidence or proof of perjury in a death row appeal – but, hey, the accused is just some greedy corporation, so who cares? Therefore, once a law is in place, the radicals' rule of thumb is, never revisit the alleged risks or scientific evidence, never modify, moderate or eliminate even the most unnecessary rules.

- **The denial of dosage.** This tactic ignores the fundamental rule of toxicology that the dose makes the poison: exposure to small amounts of a potent toxin is not harmful, and may even build immunity to a chemical. Radical environmentalists have a field day, because we can now detect chemicals in concentrations of one part per quadrillion. In their view there is no safe threshold level and, since large amounts of arsenic, table salt or di-hydrogen monoxide are harmful – even deadly – small amounts must also be dangerous.

- **The appeal to nature and purity.** Nature is benign and pure, the argument goes, whereas products of mankind's genius and technology are evil, impure and dangerous. From infant formula to irradiated food, from artificial sweeteners to breast implants and genetically modified organisms, this stratagem has been employed successfully on a host of occasions.

Two other battle-tested tactics are employed in virtually every attack. In the Demonize Dissent ploy, companies and their executives are vilified as evil, uncaring profit-seekers – and independent experts who disagree with the militant attack groups are pilloried as having been "bought off." (Advocates and experts bankrolled by the eco-militants, of course, are exempted from these standards.) The Cherish the Children stratagem employs frightful scenarios and heart-wrenching images of what might happen to little kids (or "future generations"), usually coupled with earnest, solemn "authorities" who have "devoted their lives to fighting corporate greed and corruption."

Obviously, there's a method to their madness. Employing the same tactics time and time again works, so why mess with success? Until the targets of these attacks learn to fight back more effectively – or strike first as the predators are massing for an assault – these tactics will continue to be key weapons in the predators' arsenal.

An exhaustive report by several Washington-area public interest groups has uncovered a "tangled web" of activist groups, private foundations and companies, whose joint advocacy efforts are coordinated by Fenton Communications, a Washington, DC public relations firm. The notches on the stalkers' hired guns include victories in their campaigns against Alar, plastics, breast implants and bovine growth hormone.

Using the same tactics to generate pseudo-science and public health scares are Consumers Union, the Natural Resources Defense Council (NRDC), Ralph Nader's Public Citizen, the Command Trust Network, Environmental Media Services (a Fenton friend), Center for Science in the

Public Interest, National Environmental Trust, Health Care Without Harm, Physicians for Social Responsibility, the Union of Concerned Scientists and many others. All have garnered vastly increased fame, power and fortune as a result of these efforts.

Various companies and other rent seekers also jump onboard, to reap the benefits of these campaigns, at least temporarily. They include organic food growers and retailers, Penguin Books, Ben & Jerry's, "progressive" politicians, companies and radical groups involved in the international "trade and tariff" wars and, of course, class-action-oriented law firms – which just happen to be Fenton Communications clients, as are many of the predator groups.[63] Friendly celebrities and media outlets have their own reasons for joining in the fun. They can be fed misinformation, disinformation, hyperbole, phony horror stories and spin – and relied upon to repeat them uncritically.

Bankrolling the schemes, to the tune of millions of dollars a year, are the Tides Foundation, Pew Charitable Trusts and W. Alton Jones Foundation, among others. The cross-pollination of advisors, directors, registered agents and employees among these various entities is truly a wonder to behold. In a perverse way, it's comforting to know that greed, profit and power are prime motivators outside the corporate world.[64]

With the same tactics, plot lines, producers and actors appearing again and again, it is hardly surprising that the ensuing policy battles look like reruns and remakes of the low-grade television programs that today pass for investigative journalism. They all depend on an American public that can often be misled by their sophisticated, well-staged, grandiose and colorful media gestures, which are cleverly crafted and presented to capture maximum media attention.[65]

- In the social sphere, we have endured air-rage over claims that long flights cause blood clots in legs, and protracted fights over the number of children in poverty, the impact of welfare reform, the rise of illegitimacy, and the plight of the homeless.

- In the realm of food safety, there've been battles over fast foods (featuring charges of cover-ups, and demands for a centralized "food czar" to "protect us" against industry), bovine somatotropin (BST milk, also known as rGBH milk, for recombinant growth hormone), mad cow disease, and Bt corn (dying butterflies, the "Bambi of insects").

- A host of chemicals have been linked variously, tenuously and hypothetically to cancer, leukemia, endocrine disruption, autism, lowered sperm counts, early puberty in young girls, and as yet indeterminable problems that might arise in this or future generations because trace amounts of assorted chemicals have been detected in blood and urine.

● In the energy arena, nuclear power has spawned claims about cancer, meltdowns and higher infant mortality rates, while fossil fuels have generated speculation about asthma from air pollution, a decline in caribou mating due to drilling, and catastrophic global warming due to emissions of greenhouse gases.

Of course, in the lexicon of predator groups, attacking companies, progress and humanity are always white knight crusades to "save" whales, owls, indigenous peoples, priceless natural treasures and our very planet. Politicians, journalists and public relations counselors whose own careers, revenues and ideologies benefit from the attacks always present the controversies as legitimate grievances, important issues or communications problems – in which the predators always wear white hats, and their victims are always garbed in black.

Don't be fooled. Few of the major issues manufactured, packaged and promoted by the predatory NGOs involve legitimate concerns or simple communication challenges. Fewer still represent the best interests or priorities of "average people." They are based on a value system and marketing program that must villainize industry, technology, science, progress and wealth to succeed. The radical activists may be masters in camouflaging their attacks, but the real issue is money and power – your money and power, and how to get it.

In this ongoing crusade to dismantle free enterprise and "save the planet," compromise, truce, "making nice" and cooperation are little more than useful short-term tactics in pursuit of the NGOs' larger self-interests and long term agendas. In the long run, having you over for dinner becomes simply having you for dinner. And as in all wars, the tally of innocent victims eventually numbers in the millions.

> Power tends to corrupt, and absolute power corrupts absolutely.
>
> — John, Lord Acton

> SED QUIS CUSTODIET IPSOS CUSTODES?
> But who will guard the guards?
>
> — Juvenal

Chapter 1 Notes

1. Club of Rome, Alexander King and Bertrand Schneider, *The First Global Revolution*, New York: Pantheon Books (1991), page 115.
2. Pacific Research Institute, *Index of Leading Environmental Indicators 2001*, pages 18-22. (Go to www.pacificresearch.org/issues/enviro for full text.) See also Bjorn Lomborg, *The Skeptical Environmentalist: Measuring the real state of the world*, Cambridge, UK: Cambridge University Press (2001); written by a former Greenpeace official, this exhaustively researched and footnoted book critiques "phantom problems" concocted by environmental groups.
3. Robert E. Gordon, Jr. and George S. Dunlop (National Wilderness Institute), "Creature Comfort," *Policy Review*, Washington, DC: Heritage Foundation (Summer 1990).
4. Department of Energy, *Transportaion Energy Data Book*, Ward's Motor Vehicle Facts and Figures 2000, pages 46, 48.
5. Lynn Scarlett and Jane S. Shaw, *Environmental Progress: What Every Executive Should Know,* Bozeman, MT: Political Economy Research Center (1999), page 3. See also Lynn Scarlett, "Doing More with Less: Dematerialization – unsung environmental triumph?" in Ronald Bailey (editor), *Earth Report 2000: Revisiting the True State of the Planet*, New York: McGraw-Hill (2000).
6. Brian Bishop, "Australia and the future of coal," *Environment & Climate News*, April 2001, page 9.
7. Paul K. Driessen, "California's crisis means ANWR should be opened," *Environment & Climate News*, May 2001, page 11 (available online at www.heartland.org).
8. Bruce Bartlett, "Conservation hallucinations," *Washington Times*, May 28, 2001. For more details, see the National Center for Policy Analysis Web site at www.ncpa.org and OECD reports at www.oecdwash.org
9. Michael Fumento, "Fear not the farms and the fertilizer," *Washington Times*, May 2, 2001.
10. Beatrice Trum Hunter, "Biotech Reduces Pesticide Use," *Consumers' Research*, April 2001.
11. Gregory Conko, "Hope, not hype, in the golden grains: Biotech gives hope for feeding world's poor," *CEI Update*, vol. 14, No. 3, Competitive Enterprise Institute, April 2001.
12. For extensive discussions of these and similar efforts, see Terry L. Anderson and Donald R. Leal, *Free Market Environmentalism*, Bozeman, MT: Political Economy Research Center (1991); and Terry L. Anderson and Peter J. Hill, *Environmental Federalism*, Lanham, MD: Rowman & Littlefield (1997).
13. L. Courtland Lee and Paul K. Driessen, "Mining law reform: Where are the geologists?" *Professional Geologist*, September 1994.
14. "Organizations at a Glance: The National Religious Partnership for the Environment," *Environmental Stewardship Review*, Grand Rapids, MI: Acton Institute for the Study of Religion and Liberty (1999), page 6. For a

comprehensive counterpoint to NRPE philosophy, see Michael B. Barkey (editor), *Environmental Stewardship in the Judeo-Christian Tradition: Jewish, Catholic and Protestant wisdom on the environment*, Grand Rapids, MI: Acton Institute (2000); Interfaith Council for Environmental Stewardship, www.stewards.net.

15. Ben Wattenberg, "Miscast fertility forecasts," *Washington Times*, March 8, 2001, page A16. Wattenberg cites United Nations reports, which note that birth and fertility rates are declining dramatically in developed and developing regions alike, including Brazil, Mexico, Indonesia, Korea, Thailand and Turkey.
16. Ron Arnold, *Undue Influence*, Bellevue, Washington: The Free Enterprise Press, (1999), page 1. See also the Capital Research Center's annual publication, *Patterns of Corporate Philanthropy*.
17. Tom Knudsen, "Fat of the land: Movement's prosperity comes at a high price," *Sacramento Bee*, April 22, 2001.
18. *Ibid*.
19. Scott Allen, "Environmental donors set tone activists affected by quest for funds," *Boston Globe*, October 20, 1997.
20. Robert Huberty, Capital Research Center, Washington, DC, personal communication, January 23, 2001; and Philanthropic Research, Inc's GuideStar online database guide to over 700,000 nonprofits (www.guidestar.org).
21. S. Robert Lichter and Stanley Rothman, *Environmental Cancer: A Political Disease?* Yale University Press, New Haven, CT, 1999; table 4.4.
22. Lester M. Salamon, et al., *The Emerging Sector Revisited*, Johns Hopkins University, 1998. Cited in Arnold, *Undue Influence*, page 66.
23. Arnold, *Undue Influence*, page 122 ; Robert Lerner and Althea K. Nagai, "The Pew Charitable Trusts: Revitalizing the 'spirit of the 60s,'" Capital Research Center , November 1995 (available at www.capitalresearch.org/ap/ap-1195b.html).
24. Douglas Jehl, "Charity is new force in environmental fight," *New York Times*, June 28, 2001.
25. "Six Prominent Individuals Elected Trustees of EDF," Environmental Defense Fund Newsletter, Vol. XIX, No. 1, January 1988.
26. Scott Allen, *op cit*.
27. Arnold, *Undue Influence*, page 66.
28. Institute of Public Affairs, "Philanthropy drives green agenda in the U.S.," *NGO Watch Digest*, April 2001, pages 6-7.
29. James M. Sheehan, *Global Greens: Inside the International Environmental Establishment*, Washington, DC: The Capital Research Center (1998), pages 150-152.
30. Institute of Public Affairs, "U.S. money funds anti-biotech campaign in Malaysia," *NGO Watch Digest*, April 2001, page 5. See also Don D'Cruz (editor of *NGO Watch Digest*), *Show me the money: Anti-biotech NGOs in Asia*, Institute of Public Affairs, Melbourne, Australia, June 2001.
31. *Ibid*.
32. James M. Sheehan, "Federal Government Doles Out Millions in Greenhouse Pork," *CEI UpDate*, Washington, DC: Competitive Enterprise Institute (August 1998), pages 1-2.

33. U.S. Environmental Protection Agency, "Pay-As-You-Throw: A Cooling Effect on Climate Change," May 1996.

34. Sheehan, "Federal Government Doles Out Millions," pages 1-2.

35. "EPA funds anti-growth lobbyists," *Environment & Climate News*, Heartland Institute, January 2001, page 11.

36. David Pace, "Former EPA Officials Erased Files," *Washington Times*, April 28, 2001.

37. Arnold, *Undue Influence*, page x.

38. Ron Arnold and Alan Gottleib, *Trashing the Economy: How Runaway Environmentalism Is Wrecking America*, Free Enterprise Press (1993), pages 241-242, 599-600.

39. *Ibid.*, pages 41-44, 148, 241-242.

40. Craig Rucker, CFACT vice president, personal communication, January 29, 2001.

41. "Jackson's protests benefit his family, friends," by Chuck Neubauer and Abdon M. Pallasch, staff reporters, *Chicago Sun-Times*, February 4, 2001

42. IRS Form 990, Citizenship Education Fund, 1998, pages 1 and 2.

43. Deroy Murdock, "Jesse Jackson's black hole for corporate cash," *Chief Executive*, June 2001, page 20.

44. "'Fund-raiser' extraordinaire," editorial in the *Washington Times*.

45. Ronald Bailey, *Eco-Scam: The False Prophets of Ecological Apocalypse*, New York: St. Martin's Press (1993), page 174.

46. *Ibid.*, pages 120-121.

47. Tom Knudsen, "Fat of the land: Movement's prosperity comes at a high price," *Sacramento Bee*, April 22, 2001.

48. *Ibid.*

49. *Ibid.*

50. *Ibid.*

51. *Ibid.*

52. *Ibid.*

53. Tom Knudsen, "Green machine: Mission adrift in a frenzy of fund raising," *Sacramento Bee*, April 23, 2001.

54. Rich Landers, "HSUS always seems to have another angle," *Spokesman Review* (Spokane, WA), May 17, 2001.

55. *Ibid.*; the *Washington Post* and *U.S. News & World Report* also did exposes on the HSUS in recent years.

56. "Nike corporate 'greenwashing' campaign on trial," *NGO Watch Digest*, April 2001, page 6.

57. Tom Knudsen, "Litigation central: A flood of costly lawsuits raises questions about motive," *Sacramento Bee*, April 24, 2001.

58. *Ibid.*

59. Media Research Center, *Clamoring for Kyoto: The Networks' One-Sided Coverage of Global Warming*, May 7, 2001 (also available online at www.mediaresearch.org/specialreports/fmp/2001/globalwarming.html).

60. "Ad Council sacrifices credibility to politics," editorial comment, *USA Today*, May 3, 2001.

61. Ross Gelbspan, "Of icecaps and islands: Effects of global warming," speech before Institute for Policy Studies, Washington, DC, July 12, 2000.

62. Mark Neal and Christie Davies, *The Corporation Under Siege: Exposing the Devices Used by Activists and Regulators in the Non-Risk Society*, London: The Social Affairs Unit (1998), pages 37-41.

63. Bonner Cohen, John Carlisle, *et al.*, *The Fear Profiteers: Do "Socially Responsible" Businesses Sow Health Scares to Reap Monetary Rewards?* Arlington, VA: Lexington Institute (2000).

64. For a fascinating look at how corporations use and abuse laws and regulations to improve their bottom lines, see Richard B. McKenzie, "Using Government Power: Business against free enterprise," Washington, DC: Competitive Economy Foundation (1984). CFE is now chartered as Citizens for a Sound Economy (www.cse.org).

65. Cohen, Carlisle, *et al.*, pages 65-67.

66. *Ibid.*, page ii.

2

The War on Corporations

I'm mad as hell and I'm not going to take it any more.

— Peter Finch as Howard Beale in Paddy Chayefsky's
1976 United Artists release, "Network"

So the radical attack groups have money and power.

So what?

So there's a clear pattern to their well-orchestrated attacks.

What of it?

So some companies and shareholders get burned once in a while.

Serves 'em right. So their profits get clipped a little, and maybe they even have to trim their fat executive salaries a bit. Why should anyone else give a hoot?

These statements summarize the attitudes of many Americans, and probably a majority of people in the print and electronic media. It is certainly true, moreover, that attacks on corporations first and most obviously take a toll on the companies, their bottom line, share prices, dividends and employment levels. These are also the effects that ill-advised corporate representatives mention most often, and media reports typically highlight.

The victims

However, the attacks affect all of us in ways that rarely get noticed. While companies may be the immediate victims (the targets of choice), the "collateral damage" is often severe. Remember the August, 1998 truck bomb that destroyed the U.S. embassy in Nairobi, Kenya? It killed 12 Americans – the intended targets – but at least 240 other victims (and most of the severely injured) were native Kenyans. Disregard for innocent bystanders is common among self-styled liberators, revolutionaries and saviors, and the ripple effects of pressure group politics can be widespread and significant.

Consider:

New laws and regulations, implemented in response to intense political pressure, often carry high price tags but bring only minimal, theoretical benefits. The cost is reflected in the inflated prices we pay for virtually everything we consume.

That, in turn, affects profits and share prices. With nearly all pension plans and half of all Americans now holding stock in companies and mutual funds, it can severely affect people's efforts to save for college, a new home or car, and retirement.

Falling profits and investor interest can have a devastating effect on employees, who can lose their jobs, their health, life and disability insurance, their cars, homes and savings.

Large corporations have the resources to adapt and change, but small businesses often find they simply cannot weather the assaults and must close their doors, or turn their market share over to the big boys and learn to exist along the peripheries.

Alleged intimidation, harassment, extortion and legal challenges mean consumer choice is reduced, and even life-saving drugs and devices may be unavailable for years, or forever. As Fred Smith, president of the Competitive Enterprise Institute, has put it: if the product could save 1,000 people a year, how many died while it was kept off the market?

Lawsuits, protests and other actions that prevent power plant construction and oil or gas development helped quadruple electricity and natural gas prices between 1999 and 2001, and caused blackouts in California in 2001. For millions of minorities, poor people and elderly retirees on fixed incomes, the results were devastating.[1]

Properly handled and used, anti-termite pesticides are safe and effective. But bans on their use have resulted in billions of dollars in needless property losses annually.[2]

Even after the West Nile virus killed eight people in the northeastern United States, vocal protests by a few activists threatened to curtail aerial pesticide spraying and put many more lives at risk, especially among vulnerable groups, like children and the elderly.[3]

Inflexible enforcement of the Endangered Species Act, to protect potential beetle habitat downstream of an earthen dam, cost three California women their lives. They drowned when the dam broke, after years of government refusals to permit repair of the deteriorating structure, despite repeated pleas by locals and engineers' reports that the dam was unsafe.[4]

Militant environmentalist pressure to keep snowmobiles out of a forest area persuaded a ranger to dig a 15-foot deep, unmarked pit behind an artificial embankment. A snowmobiler rode into the pit, broke his back and almost died.[5]

Tirades against irradiated food decrease the shelf-life of meats and vegetables, reduce the availability of food in poor neighborhoods, and increase the risk of deadly salmonella poisoning, particularly for children and old people.[6] Antagonism and terrorism against biotechnology is having even more serious effects.[7]

Over-hyped concerns about alleged dangers have helped convince growing numbers of parents not to have their children vaccinated against measles, mumps and other diseases, greatly increasing the risk that the children will get sick and infect their classmates.[8]

Bans on DDT have caused millions of deaths from malaria in developing countries every year since the early 1970s.[9]

Because of pressure by chemophobic activists, scarce research money, scientists and laboratory facilities are diverted to study the hypothetical problem of "endocrine disruption," and away from vital research into cancer, diabetes and heart disease.[10]

Bombings and other violent acts by extremists opposed to biotechnology and animal research could force universities to pump more money into security, leaving less for research and setting medical, agricultural and other research efforts back many years.[11]

Intense environmentalist opposition to dams in India and Africa force millions of the world's most destitute people to continue living without electricity, basic sanitation or safe drinking water. Untreated human and animal sewage is discharged into rivers, causing millions of children to die every year from dysentery and similar diseases.[12]

Animal rights activists are even demanding severe restrictions on military training, to protect endangered and other species within areas that have been specifically set aside for gunnery practice and maneuvers.[13] Apparently, they are far more concerned about wildlife than about combat readiness or the deaths of insufficiently trained solders. No doubt, they realize that neither they nor their close friends and family members will ever serve in the armed forces, which today are composed primarily of volunteers from black, Hispanic and blue collar white communities.

Meanwhile, in Buffalo, New York, more than 10,000 people signed petitions demanding harsh punishment for three teenagers who plead guilty to the heinous torture and blinding of a pet donkey. Four months earlier, the Buffalo district attorney's office had received "two or three" calls expressing outrage, after five teens tortured and beat another teen to death, then burned his body and tossed it into a dumpster.[14] Sociologists and ethicists could have a field day, debating the implications of this bifurcated concern over human and animal life.

The list could go on and on. But the bottom line is simple. Resources, benefits, costs and risks are redistributed. The resources and benefits flow to a few activist groups, while the vast majority of people face far greater costs and risks, enjoy far fewer benefits and have access to far fewer resources. Property is destroyed and people get hurt or die, out of misplaced concerns for the environment. Scientific research is set back by years. Human life is accorded far less respect than animal or even plant life.

One begins to suspect that something about our values system, perspective and humanity has gone seriously awry.

The attack groups and their victims

If "military justice is to justice as military music is to music" – the title of a 1970 book by Robert Sherrill – what can we say about environmentalist ethics? A closer look at the tactics and "ethics" of several predator groups will begin to shed dramatic light on the devastation they cause and victims they leave behind.

Greenpeace and Green pals: Greenpeace began in Canada as a ragtag bunch of mostly Quakers bearing witness against nuclear testing. It mutated into a $175-million-a-year international struggle junkie organization bearing false witness in spectacular fundraising stunts against corporations, and did little to save nature. Internal squabbles ejected both rational and radical, leaving an odd blend of extremists and moderates in control. Greenpeace allied itself with the Nader mafia for doorbell fundraising and extremists like Earth First, the Rainforest Action Network and Ruckus Society for direct actions against corporations.

Even co-founder Dr. Patrick Moore now calls elements of Greenpeace and its allies anti-science, anti-technology, anti-trade, anti-business and anti-human. Of the green movement's early days, Moore wrote,

> "Violence against people and property were the only taboos. Non-violent direct action and peaceful civil disobedience were the hallmarks of the movement. Truth mattered and science was respected for the knowledge it brought to the debate. Now this broad-based vision is challenged by a new philosophy of radical environmentalism....Many environmentalists have taken a sharp turn to the ultra left, ushering in a mood of extremism and intolerance....They perpetuate the belief that all human activity is negative, whereas the rest of nature is good."[15]

In 1995, Greenpeace launched a sophisticated $2-million public relations assault on Shell Oil Company. Britain's Environment Ministry had granted the company permission to sink its Brent Spar offshore oil storage platform in the deep Atlantic. But the Rainbow Warriors ranted that Shell intended to use the ocean as a waste dump for tons of toxic and radioactive waste, and 35,000 barrels of oil. They organized a consumer boycott, slipped militants onto the platform, and sent videos and press releases to gullible news outlets.[16]

Shell's timid, overly-technical and unimaginative response was no match for the Greens' onslaught. Its reputation blackened, the company abandoned its plans for deep-sea disposal. Eventually, Greenpeace admitted that there had been no oil or wastes on the structure, and apologized to Shell in writing. The admission and apology barely made the business pages. Observed Moore:

> "Tens of millions of dollars and much precious time were wasted over an issue that had nothing to do with the environment and everything to do with misinformation, hysteria and an opportunity for Greenpeace to ... conduct a high-profile fundraising campaign."[17]

For years, Greenpeace and other militant groups promoted dubious claims about whaling and fishing, often staging raucous, even violent protests against businesses that sold products from countries like Greenland, Iceland and the Faeroe Islands. "Eventually, the incessant lies, distortions and confrontational pressure tactics generated so much misplaced international outrage that the economic foundations of these countries were nearly destroyed. In Greenland, they also led to a tragic rash of suicides by young native men, who saw their futures and way of life destroyed," says independent documentary producer Magnus Gudmundsson.[18]

The Rainbow Warriors were unrepentant, blaming the suicides on the local adult community – and saying they never intended to destroy any traditional fishing economies. But the issue is not intent. The issue is results. Exxon never intended to have the *Exxon Valdez* run aground in Alaska. Does that excuse the company from blame or compensation?

By then, Greenpeace was off on new escapades, and had no time to discuss ethics. While shadowing a freighter whose cargo included 1.7 tons of plutonium for fast-breeder nuclear power plants in Japan, one of the Warriors' boats got too close and collided with the *Akatsuki Maru*'s escort ship in the English Channel. The incident underscores how easily these cat-and-mouse games could turn to disaster, if such a collision had caused the freighter to sink.[19]

In the Pacific, Greenpeace organized mass demonstrations to protest French nuclear tests in 1995. The protests quickly degenerated into arson, looting and riots in Papeete, the capital of Tahiti. The airport was severely damaged, demonstrators pounded police shields with pipes and chains, and several rioters repeatedly kicked one policeman on the ground.[20]

Moving to the Atlantic Ocean, Rainbow Warriors boarded an oil rig and attempted to halt exploratory drilling. Shutting down operations on one of these rigs can cost a company a million dollars a day. Greenpeace was already facing a £1 million damage claim for its occupation of a similar rig the previous week. A Marathon Oil Company official said: "Greenpeace is all about soundbites and selective science. The rest of us have to live in the real world." He might also have mentioned the hypocrisy of the organization railing against oil development, while its pension fund invested heavily in oil and chemical company stocks.[21]

Greenpeace networks with radicals via conferences and computer links, but also maintains much closer ties to certain extremist groups. Many of these connections run through one person: Mike Roselle – former Rainbow Warrior national campaign coordinator, until recently a member of Greenpeace's board of directors, and still a driving force behind several groups that promote his preference for much more direct action.[22]

Roselle co-founded the Ruckus Society, which teaches would-be protesters how to engage in raucous civil disobedience. Roselle serves on the board of the Rainforest Action Network. RAN pursues a hard-edged anti-capitalist "social change" agenda to take power from businesses and industries that support modern civilization. It played a key role in organizing the Seattle World Trade Organization protests that quickly degenerated into violence and widespread property damage.[2]

Roselle also co-founded the ultra-radical group Earth First. Notorious for spiking trees to stop logging, this group also publishes a journal that advocates sabotage against businesses and equipment. Roselle is known for his shoot-from-the-lip quotes, such as, "We think that we have the right to use force in certain cases, that if things are so important, that we have to be very forceful."[23]

Greenpeace can always count on these extremist groups to up the ante in any confrontation, and all the groups are highly skilled in separating their organizations' legitimate practices from their members' illegitimate or violent actions. Nobody don't know nothin'. Nobody specifically told anyone to do anything illegal. And nobody can say Greenpeace is responsible for what misguided individuals might do.

Friends of the Earth: When India established tiger and animal preserves like the Royal Chitwan National Park, environmentalists applauded their actions. They turned a blind eye to tens of thousands of native people who were forcibly expelled from the areas, given no compensation, and told they would be fined, jailed or even shot on sight if they hunted in the parks. Villagers who actually killed a tiger, even in self-defense, would be fined $1,200 US; families of villagers killed by tigers would receive $120 US in compensation.[24]

But when India proposed building a dam on the Namada River in Gujarat Province, to provide electricity, safe drinking water and basic sanitation to millions who have never had any of these basic amenities, it was a different story. From his posh Washington, DC office, Friends of the Earth president Brent Blackwelder preached: "Dams serve only greed," and "it's not possible" for people in developing nations to have the lifestyle of the average American. Besides, "who would want to wish that on the rest of the world? Many American are very unhappy," because "there's no sense of community anymore."[25]

From the ultra modern bathroom in her London flat, another smug environmentalist spoke out against the dam, and even the notion that the local people might actually want the dam, electricity, clean water or a rudimentary bathroom. She complained that the dam would "change the path of the river, kill little creatures along its banks and uproot tribal people in the area."[26] The documentary *Against Nature* and other interviews vividly capture the irony and hypocrisy of the extreme Green animosity toward a dam that the locals support almost unanimously.

Local villagers angrily retorted that they did not want to be "kept in a museum" and forced to continue scooping up wet cow dung with their bare hands, to dry and burn for fuel, as they have for generations. They said they would merely like to see their babies grow up, instead of watching them die before their fifth birthday. They condemned opposition to the dam as "a crime against humanity," and pointed out that the dam meant they would get new farmlands, schools and homes with electricity.[27]

(Ironically, *Against Nature's* creators held Marxist views, and were angered that fundamentalist environmental policies have harmed destitute people in developing nations. The militant environmental leaders presented so unflatteringly in the film, for their part, were incensed that the program's producers had supposedly mislead them into thinking they would be portrayed as valiant crusaders against the evils of capitalism. Otherwise, they sniffed, they never would have been so candid about their misanthropic attitudes.)

The Wilderness Society and friends: Smokey the Bear forestry practices – preventing and putting out fires – kept America's national forests lush and green for half a century. However, they also turned the forests into dense, overgrown thickets that now are susceptible to savage crown fires.

Parts of Arizona's Kaibab National Forest, for example, went from 81 trees per acre in 1876 to 690 and even 1,800 trees per acre by 1994. The trees in these overgrown stands are thin, overstressed and little more than superb kindling for a raging inferno. Visiting these areas, says *Sacramento Bee* journalist Tom Knudsen, is to "enter a world of living matchsticks."[28]

A 1999 report by the U.S. General Accounting Office concluded that "over-accumulation of vegetation" is "the most extensive and serious problem" facing national forests in the interior western states. The Forest Service calculates that 39 million acres are at high risk of fire, says GAO.[29]

Today, there is a growing recognition that fire plays an important role in the natural process, clearing out underbrush and scraggly, diseased and dead trees. Few recognize that we cannot simply switch overnight from Smokey the Bear policies to primeval "let it burn" attitudes.

Unbending Green ideology and the constant drumbeat of political correctitude by much of the news media nonetheless demand that the overnight switch be made.

No timber harvesting would be permitted, even to thin out dense thickets or vast stands of trees killed by disease, drought or beetles; and that fires would be allowed to burn if they were caused by lightning or other acts of Mother Nature, rather than by humans.

The operative Green guideline appears to have been borrowed from the Vietnam era: We have to destroy it, in order to save it.

Pleas and petitions, concern and common sense, by foresters and citizens alike, fall on deaf ears. Using endless lawsuits, regulatory appeals and vicious attacks on all who urge selective timber harvesting, The Wilderness Society, Sierra Club, Environmental Defense and other environmental zealots have stopped virtually every proposal to reduce the fire hazards dead in their tracks.

The results have been predictable. Monstrous, unnatural fires explode in these areas, burning hundreds or thousands of acres at a time, immolating goshawk and spotted owl habitats, boiling away trout and salmon streams, incinerating every living organism in the soil, triggering massive soil erosion, destroying homes, wiping out entire ecosystems, broiling eggs and fledglings in their nests, and leaving thousands of birds and mammals to starve for lack of forage and habitat.

"There was not a green tree left," said Tammy Randall-Parker, a biologist with Arizona's Coconino National Forest, after a devastating 1996 fire. "What the scientists said could happen – did happen, right in front of my eyes."[30]

"We're not sure if some of these burned areas will ever recover their native biological diversity," said Wallace Covington, a professor of forest ecology at Northern Arizona University and a nationally recognized fire scientist. "What happened is much worse, ecologically, than a clearcut – much worse. And that fire is the future. It's happening again and again. We're going to have skeletal landscapes. Certainly, over evolutionary time, new species will emerge. But these are major devastations."[31]

And still these same environmental groups pursue their unrelenting campaigns to buy up more private forest lands (using taxpayer dollars or taxpayer subsidies), and have more federal lands "protected" as monuments, refuges and wilderness areas – to be managed under the kind of tender loving care that only Attila the Hun could appreciate.

Center for Biological Diversity: Sometimes, environmentalist litigation goes well beyond wasteful, irritating, abusive, fee-generating ploys or clever gambits to prevent development. In some cases, government or environmentalist legal actions have had perverse effects that seriously harm the environment and the public interest.

It's well known that the threat of endangered species designations frequently prompts landowners to cut trees or otherwise remove habitat that might attract birds, mammals or even insects whose presence could quickly lead to prohibitions of any economic uses of the land. In some instances, the threat has resulted in more direct action against listed plants or animals, under the "shoot, shovel and shut up" rule of land management. Many conservationists, however, have dedicated their lives and fortunes to changing this.

Joe and Valer Austin, for example, invested more than $1 million to return their picturesque El Coronado Ranch in Arizona's Chiricahua Mountains to ecological health. They constructed thousands of erosion control structures, reduced herd size and grazing, worked to restore endangered species, welcomed scientists to observe their progress and earned numerous awards.

Nevertheless, acting under the principle that no good deed should go unpunished, the Southwest Center for Biological Diversity (now known as the Center for Biological Diversity) sued the Austins and Forest Service for not doing more. The court, however, ruled that the suit had been brought in bad faith and ordered the center to pay the Austins' $56,909 legal bill. But that hardly addressed the long-term damage caused by the lawsuit.

"Everything we were trying to do to convince other ranchers and landowners that endangered species are not a liability has been lost," Joe Austin said. "The Southwest Center proved me wrong. The Center proved to everybody that having an endangered species is a liability. In fact, many people think you should just get rid of them. That is the exact thing I didn't want to happen."[32]

But that's the exact lesson many landowners will learn from the case. It's also part of the enormous and generally unrecognized price our nation, wildlife and habitats are paying for the militant environmentalists' ever-escalating demands and addiction to billion-dollar budgets that only incessant cries of "crisis" can sustain.

Consumers Union: In the battle for the hearts, minds and pocketbooks of citizens, attackers frequently exploit the rules and abuse science, to disparage products that are used by millions of consumers. A good example is the plastic baby bottle. This product, usually made with polycarbonate plastic, was introduced into the marketplace to meet the needs of parents who wanted a bottle that was inexpensive, shatter-proof, light-weight enough that a child could hold it, and clear, so a parent could see what's in the bottle.

Then came the attackers, led by the Consumers Union, the group that publishes *Consumer Reports*.

Large numbers of American consumers consider *Consumer Reports* to be an unbiased, non-partisan publication that aims to protect them from the heartless, profit-grubbing product manufacturers that care only about the almighty dollar, and nothing about consumer safety. If you share that view, dismiss it. Consumers Union is no different than other attack groups. It has a political agenda. It plays by different rules.

In May 1999, *Consumer Reports* attacked plastic baby bottles. An article titled "Baby alert: New findings about plastics" claimed that a chemical called bisphenol-A might leach from polycarbonate baby bottles into the formula consumed by newborns (see Chapter 5, page 118, *Wildcard #4*): "We bought six different bottles and heated plastic from each in simulated infant formula. The plastic from each of the bottles leached into our test formula a chemical called bisphenol-A, which in lab animals has produced physiological effects similar to those produced by estrogen. During such 'endocrine disruption,' chemicals interfere with or mimic the actions of hormones, possibly upsetting normal development."[33]

The article went on to report that, based on *Consumer Reports'* research, "a typical baby who drank formula sterilized by heating in the bottle would be exposed to a bisphenol-A dose of about 4 percent of an amount that has adversely affected test animals in studies by Frederick vom Saal, a professor of biological science at the University of Missouri, Columbia."[34] Many parents were terrified – not by any proof or even actual scientific evidence, but by the possibility that the chemical might have some unspecified effect on some aspect of "normal development."

Okay. It's time for a reality check.

First, industry and independent research studies, conducted by the rules, have shown that bisphenol-A does, in fact, exhibit weak estrogenic activity in laboratory studies. But these effects are much lower than natural sources of estrogen, such as breast milk. A comprehensive industry review of available research found no evidence that bisphenol-A selectively affects reproduction or development, and no evidence that it causes cancer or other adverse effects on the mammary gland or other reproductive organs of either female or male rats and mice.[35]

Second, *Consumer Reports* failed to inform its readers that, at the time of its publication, Frederick vom Saal's research had not been replicated by other researchers, who tried to obtain the same results using similar research techniques. A year after the *Consumer Reports* article on plastic baby bottles, vom Saal presented new, unpublished, non-peer-reviewed data supporting his previous findings on bisphenol-A.[36] Whether or not this new data will put the issue of replication to rest, it clearly did not confirm that humans are at risk from low doses of bisphenol-A in products such as baby bottles. Moreover, because vom Saal had bred his mice to be especially susceptible to chemicals, and then had killed all the mice before other researchers could examine them, fully analyzing his data and conclusions is virtually impossible.[37]

Third, *Consumer Reports* failed to inform consumers about a critical point: The fundamental theory – that small doses of chemicals that mimic hormones can harm humans – remains a theory, unproven by scientific standards. In fact, one study often used to validate this theory was withdrawn by its author prior to the *Consumer Reports* article on plastic baby bottles. According to an August 1997 Associated Press story, "a senior Tulane researcher quietly withdrew the paper, saying there may have been a mistake. And last week, the university announced 'an internal inquiry into the circumstances' of the whole episode."[38]

With all of this controversy about the research on bisphenol-A, what did *Consumer Reports* recommend to parents? "Dispose of all clear, shiny baby bottles, unless the manufacturer tells you they're not made of poly-carbonate."[39] A rather draconian recommendation, when you consider the facts. Unless, of course, a political agenda demands scapegoats. Plastics. Chemicals. Manufacturers.

Perhaps next, Consumers Union will adopt Homer Simpson's ideas of wrapping babies in bubble wrap and filling swimming pools with Jello, to reduce the risks of injury and drowning.[40]

Fenton Communications: Those who might still be inclined to believe *Consumer Reports* would benefit from a routine Internet search that focuses on the publication's past attacks.

Those who take the time to conduct the search will discover that the same *Consumer Reports* "scientist" who authored the attack on baby bottles had also helped launch the attack over a decade ago on Alar, a chemical that regulates the growth of apples.

The assault on Alar, which cost the apple industry more than $100 million, was later discovered to have been based on highly questionable science. The Alar attack was orchestrated by Fenton Communications and significantly amplified by the CBS news magazine "60 Minutes," which called Alar "the most potent cancer-causing agent in our food supply."

In reality, the chemical is safe, and humans would have to consume 500 gallons of apple juice a day for 70 years to match the dosage given to the experimental mice.[41]

In subsequent interviews, David Fenton bragged, "The idea was for the 'story' to achieve a life of its own, and continue for weeks and months, to affect policy and consumer habits.... The PR campaign was designed so that revenue would flow back to NRDC from the public." Did it ever.[42]

The Consumers Union attack on plastic baby bottles was featured on the ABC news magazine "20/20." David Fenton and his firm have also played a major role in the "ancient forest" campaign to shut down the timber industry in the Northwest, by planting misleading stories with numerous media outlets.[43]

Environmental Protection Agency: The professional activists and their media and government allies are also experts at using government regulations to whipsaw companies and attack products.

In 1998, the U.S. Environmental Protection Agency's (EPA) Office of Prevention, Pesticides and Toxic Substances (OPPTS) issued testing guidelines aimed at "harmonizing" the toxicology testing methodologies used under the Federal Insecticide, Fungicide and Rodenticide Act (FIFRA), and the Toxic Substances Control Act. In plain English, it sought to modify the government's rules for testing the potential health effects of chemicals.

Known as the Series 870 Health Effects Test Guidelines, these ground rules require that researchers test chemicals on laboratory animals at three different dose levels, and state that the highest dose level should be chosen, with the aim of inducing adverse health effects, but not death or severe suffering (we wouldn't want the animal rights folks to go completely bonkers).

Most board-certified toxicologists will tell you that, conceptually, these rules are appropriate. Once a scientist finds a dose that causes a negative health effect, it becomes fairly easy to identify exposure levels below which health effects are not expected. It's a bit trickier to extrapolate the research findings from lab animals to humans, but regulators and scientists do just that. They often build in 100-fold margins of safety that militate against extrapolation errors.

So, how are these research rules used and abused by attackers to victimize consumer product companies and consumers? As an illustration, let's test my favorite chemical, di-hydrogen monoxide on Ralph the Rat. First, Ralph is forced to drink a teaspoon of the chemical. Nothing happens. Then, Ralph is forced to drink a tablespoon. Still, nothing happens. Finally, Ralph is forced to drink a cup of di-hydrogen monoxide. Ralph chokes. He vomits. He temporarily loses bladder control and his kidneys show signs of stress.

For legitimate researchers, these findings suggest that Ralph can be exposed to a tablespoon of di-hydrogen monoxide without suffering adverse health effects. But what do these results mean to The Coalition to Ban Di-hydrogen Monoxide? Pay dirt.

Coalition leaders proceed to convince a local television reporter to blow the lid off this deadly chemical. Their message? "This stuff caused severe kidney and bladder problems in laboratory animals. Do you want your child exposed to it?"

Does the reporter question whether children are exposed to enough of this toxic brew to cause the effects that Ralph the Rat experienced? No, because Rodney the Reporter and Ralph have about the same IQ when it comes to toxicology. What about the parents who see the report on television? What's their response? "You can't trust anything these days. Pretty soon, the only thing we'll be able to feed our kid is water."

That's being overly optimistic.

If you think this is off the rails, consider the fact that junior high school student Nathan Zohner convinced 86 percent of the people he interviewed for a science fair project that they should support a ban on di-hydrogen monoxide.

Zohner told the people he interviewed that this dangerous chemical "can cause excessive sweating and vomiting, it is a major component in acid rain, accidental inhalation can kill you, it can cause severe burns when in gaseous form, it contributes to erosion of the natural landscape, it decreases the effectiveness of automobile brakes and it has been found in tumors of terminal cancer patients."[44]

If you were a parent, wouldn't you be concerned? Scared half to death?

What the petition failed to mention is that di-hydrogen monoxide is water. Plain, common H_2O! Zohner won grand prize in the Greater Idaho Falls Science Fair for his project, titled "How Gullible Are We?"

(You're allowed to plead the Fifth Amendment against self-incrimination on that one.)

The Series 870 Guidelines that industry toxicologists live by virtually guarantee that many of the chemicals tested will be shown to produce a negative health effect on laboratory animals, because that's what the testing is *designed* to do.

In the right hands, the results of these tests can be used to set safe exposure standards for people. In the hands of the neo-Luddites, nannies, neurotics and other full-time crisis mongers, the results represent ammunition to destroy the target *du jour*, frighten consumers away from using products that actually are perfectly safe, and destroy people's right to free, informed choices.

What happens when the rules aren't sufficient to satisfy the attackers' appetite for marketplace carnage? They use their political power to change the rules.

The EPA's June 2000 decision to restrict residential use of the insecticide chlorpyrifos (sold under the brand name Dursban®) is a case in point. The agency justified its decision by pointing to a laboratory study reporting brain damage in the offspring of female rats fed high doses of chlorpyrifos; doses high enough to *sicken* the mother rat.

According to Steven J. Milloy, a biostatistician who publishes *junkscience.com*, "Normally, fetal effects secondary to maternal toxicity are considered an experiment artifact. But the EPA is treating these effects as though they were real, and predictive of human effects."[45] In other words, if the testing makes mommy rat physically sick, it isn't scientifically kosher to conclude that the health effects in baby rats are linked to the stuff you forced mommy rat to eat. Baby rat's problems may have been caused by the fact that mommy rat was puking her brains out while she was pregnant.

While the EPA's interpretation of this particular laboratory test may be highly questionable, the real kicker in the chlorpyrifos decision is that the manufacturer of the insecticide had provided the agency with research results from tests conducted on paid human volunteers.

The results demonstrated safe exposure levels in humans that countered the EPA's interpretation of the rat data. Uh-oh! What to do?

The anti-pesticide crowd at the EPA, supported by environmental attack groups (which were in turn partially supported by EPA), changed the rules and declared that human testing is "unethical" and unfit for regulatory consideration. So, the research showing safe levels of human exposure for chlorpyrifos was swiftly taken off the regulatory table, and the highly questionable rat data became the only "evidence" on which to base a 180-degree regulatory turn with far-reaching implications.

The result of EPA's anti-pesticide zealotry? Millions of consumers have now been denied products that have been used for decades to control disease-carrying insects, termites and other pests.

Worse, the decision comes as a voracious, recently imported termite species is spreading like a biblical plague throughout the South and beyond. These Formosan termites make the suburban bugs most of us are familiar with look like harmless midnight noshers. They even attack asphalt, rubber, plastic foam and thin sheets of soft metal – and "their multi-million member colonies can render a solid house uninhabitable within a matter of 24 months."[46]

Will the EPA and the anti-pesticide zealots be held accountable for the spread of disease, or property damage from termites? For the answer, proceed to Chapter 10 and review *Ethics Edicts 5* and *9*.

Cheatem & Ruinem, Mass Tort Attorneys-At-Law

By now, virtually everyone is familiar with America's fastest growing and most lucrative industry: mass tort class actions against big corporations. Our nation is being pounded by a tidal wave of lawsuits that share essential common traits:

- a few high profile injuries or illnesses;

- the existence of other plausible victims;

- statistical data showing that an industrial activity took place in or near the area where this broadly defined class of victims lived or worked;

- aggressive lawyers who can demonize the corporate defendants and assert that mere coincidence proves cause and effect; and, most importantly,

- the presence of at least one deep-pocket defendant that can make the predators (and any states, counties and cities they can persuade to sign on to their schemes) rich beyond their wildest dreams.

Examples abound. A couple farmers living near power lines got leukemia; therefore, power lines cause cancer. Women who had silicon breast implants got sick; therefore, the implants cause disease. Several non-smoking flight attendants got lung cancer; therefore, secondhand smoke causes cancer. People who use cell phones got brain tumors; therefore, cell phones cause brain tumors. Shipyard workers who smoked heavily and worked with a particular type of asbestos that easily punctured their lungs got cancer; therefore, all types of asbestos cause cancer.[47] Therefore, the corporate slime must pay.

Even a little packaging business that owned an insulation company for *93 days* nearly *40 years ago* can find itself in the litigators' cross hairs, as they seek ever more deep pockets to augment targets that have already gone into Chapter 11.[48]

Just over the horizon, directly in the path of the onrushing tidal wave, is the mass tort industry's next victim: the paint, chemical and petroleum companies whose current subsidiaries or predecessors used lead in their paints. The Cluster Fluster argument? These evil companies "preyed on" and poisoned little children, who got lead poisoning, learning disabilities, poor standardized test scores and other "ailments" because they lived in high-risk poor neighborhoods where they may have chewed on lead paint at some time when they were younger.

The "scum-bag" paint companies should pay to have every bit of lead-based paint removed from every wall, door frame and window sill in the United States, says Ronald Motley, the South Carolina "killer lawyer" who has made a career out of stalking corporate defendants with pockets billions of dollars deep. If the school districts and cities receiving their "fair share" of the fat payout choose to use their loot for something other than remediating the supposed problem, that's their choice. What's important, in their view, is not that the problem be fixed, but that corporate America pay, and that the lawyers, their plaintiff classes, allied predator groups and cooperative communities get paid their pieces of silver or pound of flesh.[49]

However, individual symptoms (or even clusters of symptoms) by themselves do not constitute proof that a substance (even a toxic substance) caused the symptoms. And random collections of people who have assorted symptoms and happened to live near a site where potentially toxic substances were used do not constitute a legally defined "class" with standing to sue. At least that's the opinion of many legal experts and even some courts.

Rocketdyne made these points when it won its case against Masry & Vititoe, the L.A. mass tort firm that's home to the real Erin Brockovich. However, a setback here and there has not deterred the *juris* predators. As Edward Masry candidly observed, "Let's face it, there's a lot of money in [toxic tort suits], and I'd be lying if I said I don't like the money."[50]

The bottom line? Corporate America would be well advised to heed Michael Freedman's caution: "One thing the defendants won't do, if they have any brains, is dismiss Motley's lawsuits as preposterous. The tobacco companies made that mistake."[51]

Natural Resources Defense Council, CalPIRG and friends: 2001 was the year the lights went out in California, tarnishing the Golden State's reputation and bludgeoning its economy. Rolling blackouts froze ATM machines, disrupted traffic lights, left people stranded on elevators, forced children to study in darkened classrooms, and gave residents a taste of what it's like to live in the Third World.

During a single two-week period in January, California lost an estimated $2.3 billion in wages, sales and productivity.[52] Within just a few months, the state's utility companies lost over $12 billion, and one major utility was forced into bankruptcy, because state laws forced them to buy electricity at prices far higher than they were allowed to charge their consumers. Thousands of workers were laid off, as businesses of all sizes cut energy consumption and expenses to stay afloat.

As the crisis worsened, the state's politicians, environmentalists and consumer activists went into overdrive, looking for scapegoats. Instead of meeting with aides and utility executives to find solutions, Governor Gray ("Grayout") Davis and other state politicians wasted precious weeks playing the role of demagogues-in-chief, raging that "price gougers," "pirates" and "out-of-state profiteers" were somehow responsible for the disaster.[53]

A glance in the mirror would have revealed who was really to blame.

More than anything, what caused the California energy crisis was a head-on collision between rhetoric and reality. Between a love of hot tubs and a hatred of power plants to heat the water. Between vague, esoteric, utopian paeans to renewable energy – and the harsh reality of a growing population, surging economy and skyrocketing demand for electricity.

Way back in 1978, newspaper headlines extolled Governor Jerry Brown's "new energy path," citing a Lawrence Livermore Laboratory study that claimed an energy surplus, slowing economy and stabilizing population meant the state could phase out nuclear and fossil fuel power plants, and focus instead on conservation and renewable energy. Amory Lovins, Tom Hayden, Ralph Nader and assorted other end-of-growth, energy-suppression pundits echoed the same themes for years. The new mantra: Millions for guilt, not one cent for energy.

In 1992, the Natural Resources Defense Council's Ralph Cavanagh released *An Energy Efficiency Blueprint for California*, which a doting reviewer claimed subsequently led to "an atmosphere of mutual trust and respect" between utilities and Greens and a "collaborative process" (initiated by Cavanagh) that would let everyone "win by getting on the conservation bandwagon." Within four short years, the grand and glorious bandwagon had carried California to passage of a much ballyhooed electricity "deregulation" bill.[54]

Cavanaugh received the Heinz Award in Public Policy for his "unparalleled success" in persuading the state to adopt his "deregulation" package. Meanwhile, Gray Davis was elected governor, capping off a career in which, since 1978, he had also been Governor Brown's chief of staff, a state senator, president of the senate and lieutenant governor.

Unfortunately, there were a few problems. California's economy hadn't stabilized; it had actually increased by 10 million people and 4 million households since 1980. Its economy hadn't stopped growing; in fact, it had blossomed 34 percent between 1990 and 2000 alone. Its power generation infrastructure hadn't kept pace; in fact, the state hadn't issued permits to build a major new electrical generating plant in nearly 12 years, or even allow the construction of any new high voltage transmission lines – even as electricity demand shot up 22 percent in ten years.[55]

California politicians, regulators, environmental militants, news media and citizens blithely ignored all these developments. Instead of modifying their ideologies and policies, they forced power plants to switch to natural gas – then led the charge to ban drilling for gas on onshore and offshore lands all over the United States. Meanwhile, the state continued to import electricity from its energy colonies in the Pacific Northwest and

Four Corners Region, which for years had had ample surplus energy to export to their voracious neighbor. It was a typical colonialist arrangement: California got the electricity, while the colonies got to deal with the pollution.

Perhaps worst of all, the state enacted an electricity deregulation law that can only be characterized as a hoax. The law did not deregulate anything. In fact, it imposed complex new rules and forced the utilities to sell off nearly all their power plants, buy all their electricity on a daily "spot" market, and sell the juice at prices that had been capped at a rate 10 percent lower than they had been in 1996, regardless of what happened to wholesale purchase prices.

In essence, California had done what it has long been most famous for. It created a celluloid reality that – like the *T rex* in *Jurassic Park*, Forrest Gump's meeting with LBJ and Private Ryan's D-Day invasion – seemed *so real* you couldn't convince anyone it was done with smoke, mirrors, computers and other studio magic. *Then* the state went a step further, and used that celluloid reality to justify passage of laws and regulations that affect millions of consumers both in California and far beyond its borders.

When worried utility execs saw that natural gas and electricity prices were starting to inch upward in early 2000, they petitioned the state Public Utilities Commission for permission to enter into long term contracts that would lock in energy prices, before they went any higher. CalPUC and Governor Davis told them to take a hike.[56]

Within months, prices had quadrupled, the surplus in California's energy colonies was gone, demand for electricity in the once golden state had far outstripped available supply – and the Chicken Littles of environmental extremism had come home to roost.

When a few courageous corporate executives, politicians and university professors suggested that consumer prices should be raised, to encourage conservation and investment in new generating facilities, the California Public Interest Research Group went into a rage and sent activists into city streets, carrying placards that screamed, "Don't Raise Rates!" And in the midst of the crisis, when initiatives went before voters and city councils in two communities to build more power plants, the proposals went down in flames.

To the inhabitants of Hollywood-land, celluloid reality really does seem to be more realistic than real reality. If not more realistic, at least infinitely preferable. The question is, Will celluloid reality, ideology, rhetoric and corporate scapegoating continue to trump reason, sound science and rational economics – spreading the California disease far beyond its borders? Or will enough politicians, corporate executives, journalists and citizens finally begin to recognize that the radical environmentalist emperor has no clothes?

To paraphrase Edmund Burke, the only thing necessary for the triumph of evil, ideology and stupidity is for good men to do nothing.

Today, the need for good people to take action has grown even more acute, as ultra radical Greens and animal rightists increasingly turn to terrorism to impose their agenda of anarchy on society. Meet the *spetzsnaz* (special ops commandoes) of the radical Green army.

Earth Liberation Front: Once upon a time, elves made shoes in the wee morning hours for gentle, impoverished cobblers, and Alfs were cuddly little TV characters. No longer. Today, they are the *Al Fatah,* the eco-terrorist vanguard of the radical environmental movement. Elves ply their criminal trade for the ultra-militant Earth Liberation Front (ELF), while Alfs carry out their hit-man rampages on behalf of the Animal Liberation Front (ALF).

As Ron Arnold points out in the preface to his book, *EcoTerror: The violent agenda to save nature*, the Unabomber killed and maimed in the name of the environment. But he "was only an isolated symptom of years of hate for industrial civilization that had been incited by the powerful environmental lobby." As a result, "a systematic underground movement of violence against industry [now threatens] the base of our entire society."[57]

Across America's western states, radical predators in the Earth Liberation Front and similar groups like the Strawberry Liberation Front and Anarchist Golfing Association have expanded their years-long campaign of arson, bombings and mayhem – even burning university laboratories and spiking trees with ceramic nails (which magnetic devices can't detect), so that saw blades explode, potentially maiming any unfortunate mill worker who happens to get in the way. Eco-Storm Trooper mouthpiece Craig Rosebraugh defends their actions this way:

> "Rich industry leaders are all Earth rapers. They all profit off the destruction of life and liberty (whether it be animal, natural world, or worker). ... The only language these people understand is money. We must inflict economic sabotage on all Earth rapers if we are ever to stop the madness we live in. To do so is not a crime, it is a necessity."[58]

> "People are tired of spending an incredible amount of time and energy to try and have campaigns legally that basically get nowhere at all. Individuals in the ELF want to see results. They want to pick up where the law is leaving off."[59]

> "These are not just random acts of what the government calls 'violence.' They have a very clear political and social motive, and that's to end these abusive industries."[60]

A series of investigative reports by *The Oregonian* revealed that over 100 major acts of eco-terrorism caused more than $43 million in damages around the West, between 1980 and 1999. A single fire-bombing at the Vail, Colorado ski area caused $12 million in damages; other attacks destroyed testing labs, genetically engineered crops, helicopters, corporate headquarters and even a ranger station.[61] A member of Earth First (probably an avid reader of David Foreman's *Monkeywrenching* guide to eco-terrorism) proudly admitted:

> "I shot holes in the oil reservoirs on gear boxes of windmills. When the wind blows after a day or two, it burns up the gears and destroys the gear box. I've thrown rocks and steel into wells, to plug them. There are hundreds of galvanized steel water tanks all over the place. I've shot holes in them and pulled out float valves. I want to run ranchers out of business."[62]

The saboteurs have also expanded their operations eastward, bombing Michigan State University's Agriculture Hall and torching new luxury homes on Long Island, because they oppose "urban sprawl." In a "Style Section" story that is all too typical of the attitude the major media have for these crimes, the *Washington Post* commented, "If you think *you* hate suburban sprawl, you're an amateur."

The story went on to quote Rosebraugh as saying: "I think this economic sabotage does have a clear role in the environmental movement, and that is to cause as much economic damage to the entities as possible." The perpetrators, it noted, are typically young, "college-educated, highly motivated idealists. As terrorists go, they are fairly puckish. The press release claiming credit for the Long Island arson apologized to the firemen for waking them so early."[63]

"Fairly puckish." That's certainly one way to put it. A few years ago, the late David Brower observed that "Earth First makes Friends of the Earth look reasonable. What we need now is an outfit that makes Earth First look reasonable."[64] Wherever he is now, Brower must be absolutely delighted that the Earth Liberation Front and its merry band of arsonists are making such an ardent effort to do precisely that.

One can only wonder how the *Post,* Rosebraugh or Brower might respond if Rosebraugh's Portland, Oregon home or vegan bakery were burned down by one of the eco-terrorists' many victims, in a fit of poetic justice. Or if the victims began trashing and torching Sierra Club, Greenpeace, Earth First and FOE offices? Would they say such puckish behavior has a legitimate role in the battle against environmental extremists – which is to make them realize that the innocent victims are mad as hell and aren't going to take it anymore?

Kenyan agronomist Florence Wambugu spent three years with Monsanto, developing a genetically modified sweet potato that is resistant to a virus that nearly destroyed this important crop in her country. She is incensed that Earth Liberation Front anti-biotechnology "hooligans" destroyed the Monsanto labs where this wonder crop was created. The new GM potato "requires no pesticides and holds the promise of feeding some of the 800 million chronically undernourished people in the world," she emphasizes – whereas traditional organic farming in African and other developing countries has consistently resulted in low yields and hungry people.[65]

GM food crops like Golden Rice and new varieties of sweet potatoes, corn and wheat could enable many countries to become agriculturally self-sufficient and economically better off. But apparently the Gaian crusaders would rather the malnourished simply starve. Population control by any means is a virtue, you understand.

However, the eco-*Al Fatah* remains most active in the western United States.

In California, new Mediterranean fruit fly infestations kept appearing in odd and unexpected places. The patterns of infestation are so bizarre that some members of an advisory panel have concluded that anti-agriculture extremists are purposely breeding and releasing Medfly larvae. This scenario might seem the height of paranoia and conspiracy theory, except for one fact: Former Los Angeles mayor Tom Bradley and various newspapers received letters during 1989 from a group that called itself the Breeders and claimed it was spreading Medflies to protest irrigation, pesticide use and other modern agricultural practices in the state.[66]

Mark Urlaub, director of the U.S. Department of Agriculture's bio-security program, has also confirmed that the Medfly infestation "could well have been an intentional introduction."[67]

More recently, ELF arsonists destroyed the University of Washington's Center for Urban Horticulture and the Clatskanie tree farm in Oregon. The two simultaneous terror attacks caused over $5 million in property damage and incalculable millions in lost research. Among the items destroyed at the Horticulture Center by these zealous crusaders for Franken-free-forests were:

● A hundred specimens of endangered stickseed plants that one researcher was trying to restore through tissue culture, to reintroduce to the wild;

● Over 30 years of research documenting the regrowth of vegetation around Mount St. Helens since its eruption in May 1980;

- Research that could help plants break down cancer-causing toxins in soil;

- Hundreds of rare, out-of-print, irreplaceable scientific books, reports and studies on ecology, genetics and ecosystem improvement; and

- Research on wetlands rehabilitation and plants that aid in reduced water use in urban landscapes.[68]

An ELF news release claimed the group has caused more than $40 million in damages in North America just since 1997, through arson and other acts.

It warned, "As long as the universities continue to pursue this reckless 'science,' they run the risk of suffering severe losses. Our message remains clear: we are determined to stop genetic engineering."[69]

And now the stakes have gone even higher. In May 2001, the Earth Liberation Front began using its Web site to instruct legions of would-be Unabombers how to burn down buildings.

The highly detailed how-to manual is dedicated to the credo, "always strive for guaranteed destruction," and claims its formulas and devices have all been "carefully crafted" and "tested many times."

The guide presents four basic rules for successful arson and has chapters on topics that will all but guarantee a rise in violence and terrorism:

- Where to put incendiary devices to ensure that buildings will be completely destroyed;

- Fuel requirements for buildings of varying sizes;

- Assembling fail-safe incendiary devices;

- Creating a "clean room" to minimize the likelihood of getting caught;

- Constructing electrical timers from wind-up and digital equipment;

- Using light bulbs and model rocket igniters to set off the incendiary devices; and

- The "finer points" of constructing and placing bombs guaranteed to do the job right.[70]

One has to wonder how many (inevitable) deaths it will take, before our legislators and law enforcement officials finally begin to use every means at their disposal, to root out these criminals and put them away until they are too old and feeble to terrorize anyone else.

If we are vandals, so were those who destroyed forever the gas chambers of Buchenwald and Auschwitz.

—Craig Rosebraugh[71]

Genetic engineers, neo-Darwinists and the biotech industry are the new Nazis. The Nazis in the 1930s only experimented on the Jewish race; the new Nazis are experimenting on the entire human race.

—Keith Parkins[72]

Animal Liberation Front: "Even if animal research produced a cure [for AIDS], we'd be against it," Ingrid Newkirk, chief ethicist for People for the Ethical Treatment of Animals (PETA), has said.[73]

In an apparent effort to put this philosophy into practice, animal rights activists claimed they had infiltrated Huntingdon Life Sciences (HLS) research labs in Britain and the United States in 1997 – and obtained "shocking video" of laboratory workers mistreating animals. An ALF communiqué to investors and securities traders said the videos show workers "taunting and abusing" animals, subjecting them to "invasive procedures and chemical tests," while punching beagle puppies in the face, shoving and throwing monkeys into cages, and performing a dissection on a monkey that "was still alive, though partially sedated."[74]

Having worked and spoken with many animal researchers over the years, I cannot imagine that they would abuse the animals on which their studies depend. What about PETA? It disseminated the Animal Liberation Front's press release about a 1992 arson of the Michigan State University mink research laboratory that destroyed work *to reduce the need for live animals in research.* Rodney Coronado was convicted in that arson and sentenced to nearly five years in federal prison. U. S. Attorney Michael H. Dettmer prosecuted Coronado and emphasized in his sentencing memorandum that PETA founder Ingrid Newkirk arranged to have a package of documents stolen by Coronado from MSU sent to her – and made the arrangement days *before* the MSU arson occurred. Are PETA and ALF linked?

ALF's phony charges of widespread, endemic abuse have devastated Huntingdon's reputation, however. Various banks, brokerage houses and investors are shying away from HLS and other companies that use animals in research. The real losers will be the millions of diabetics, paraplegics, AIDS patients and others for whom animal research offers the only hope for a cure. Of course, that is of little concern to the terrorists.

We are non-violent. We are non-violent. How many times have you heard eco-militants spout this line? Some undoubtedly are, of course. Others simply count on reliably less non-violent types to do their dirty work. Still others utilize the famous defense of "it depends on what the meaning of non-violent is."

For David Barbarash, "spokesman for the North American Animal Liberation Front press office," the phony distinction is crucial: "We do not consider the destruction of property, of things, to be committing violence. How does one do violence against something which is not alive?" In case you missed his message, he continues, "Let's hit them where it hurts the most. Figure it out. Be secure. Be tribal. Go for the jugular."[75] He wraps up his tirade, by reverting to one of the animal rights crowd's favorite analogies, Nazis and the Holocaust:

"We don't view experimentation on animals any different than we view what the Nazis did to the Jews in Germany."[76]

This truly lunatic fringe of the animal rights movement would up the ante substantially. It is escalating its own use of violence, raising the question of how soon the violence will become the standard operational procedure for all the wackos who want to send humanity back to its caves. Some of these lunatics are simply as violent as they come.

Several of them came very close to committing felony murder on Mother's Day 1999, when they torched the Childers Meat Company in Eugene, Oregon. Firefighters entered a roaring inferno and, by pure luck, chanced upon a second firebomb that had been placed next to a natural gas line. Had the deliberately delayed device ignited, firefighters would likely have died. The ALF Web site later claimed the fire had been set to protest the meat industry's poor treatment of cows.[77] We are non-violent, we are non-violent – my eye.

In Britain, animal rights groups have sent letter bombs to UK businesses that have ties to animal use in research and testing; three bombs exploded, causing facial injuries to two adults and leg wounds to a six year-old girl. A "stop Huntingdon" group posted the names and addresses of company managers on its Web site, along with the message "HLS workers are animal killers: Go Get 'Em." Eleven employees subsequently had their cars firebombed, and a senior manager had caustic chemicals sprayed in his face. In February 2001, UK-based Huntingdon's managing director was bludgeoned with baseball bats in his own driveway. Several months later, police arrested three men in connection with the brutal attack, one of them at an animal sanctuary run by a television script writer and animal welfare campaigner.[78]

At about the same time, the head of Scotland's National Farmers Union received death threats because he advocates culling cattle herds (rather than merely vaccinating them) to control the spread of foot-and-mouth disease. Other animal rights thugs in London are posting stickers with the names, addresses and photographs of senior pharmaceutical industry officials whose companies use HLS. The Web site urges visitors: "Animal Killer. Let him know what you think of animal cruelty."

The U.S. campaign against Huntingdon now lists shareholder addresses and corporate customers on its Web site.[79] Shortly after this information was posted, animal rights anarchists smashed windows and vandalized ATM machines at a bank in Long Island, because of its supposed connection to HLS. Other AR storm troopers trashed a Bed Bath & Beyond store in Salt Lake City, because BB&B is connected to a company that deals with a financial company that deals with Huntingdon.[80] And you still think you couldn't possibly be their next target?

Meanwhile, the former dean of the Ben-Gurion University medical school resigned as chairman of the Israeli government's Council on Animal Experimentation, after receiving threats to sabotage his car and hurt members of his family.[81]

A German animal rights group threatened to publish a 400-page directory of researchers who use animals in experiments. Several Web sites and college activists at the University of Oregon and elsewhere have published lists of researchers; and one animal rights Web site has posted a directory of fur farms, along with detailed bomb-making instructions.[82]

Hard-core animal-rights wackos are even going after seeing-eye dogs for the blind. Claiming that guide dogs are being abused by the very people who depend on them for their safety and mobility, a couple of activists stalked a blind woman in Seattle, looking for a chance to grab her dog and turn it loose. In the wackos' view, even owning a dog constitutes abuse.[83]

The grim possibility that eco-terrorists were behind the Medfly devastations also makes other recent warnings more credible. The director of the U.S. Department of Agriculture's bio-security program has said terrorists might try to infect animals with diseases like "mad cow" and foot-and-mouth, which have devastated Britain's farming industry.

It would be "almost impossible" to prevent terrorists from bringing diseases like these into the United States, warn experts, and several animal rights activists have been quoted as saying they hope the diseases do infect livestock in this country.[84] PETA co-founder Ingrid Newkirk, for instance, has said:

> "I openly hope [foot-and-mouth] comes here. It will bring economic harm only for those who profit from giving people heart attacks and giving animals a concentration camp-like existence. It would be good for animals, good for human health and good for the environment."[85]

While no group has yet claimed responsibility for the foot-and-mouth outbreak, the British news service Ananova reported in April 2001 that the outbreak "could have been started deliberately by someone who stole a test-tube of the virus from a laboratory."

The *Sunday Express*, a British newspaper, reported that a container of the virus "went missing from a secret government lab at Porton Down two months before the crisis began."[86]

A similar outbreak in the United States would be a major threat to America's $55 billion-a-year livestock industry. "If, in fact, the outbreak of foot-and-mouth disease in the United Kingdom was the work of animal rights terrorists, it rapidly achieved the goal of having a devastating effect on that nation's economy," National Anxiety Center director Alan Caruba pointed out. The infestation could also destroy trade relations among many countries.[87]

Obviously, a dangerous line is being crossed with increasing frequency, and the stakes are getting higher. Clearly, more needs to be done to stop these attacks, incarcerate the offenders, exact financial reparations from them and deter future violence.

However, the ideologically driven extremists are rarely caught, and some commentators appear to go out of their way to explain, even excuse, the outrages of the most extreme elements of the neo-barbarian movement – or at least to apply strained principles of situational ethics to their behavior. "Obviously murder is something that is far beyond any political philosophy," said one journalist. "But [Ted Kaczynski] had a bike. He didn't have any plumbing, he didn't have any electricity."[88]

Some believe the reason ELF, ALF and other eco-terrorists are so rarely brought to justice is that they operate in "cells," small cohesive groups in which members maintain their anonymity even with each other, something like the Irish Republican Army. The terrorists' spokesman often doesn't know the identity of other group members, and any one of them could e-mail a call for "direct action" against companies, organizations and people that he targets as "enemies of the Earth" for somehow profiting from using animals or other natural resources. Anyone with an axe to grind and an environmental philosophy to "justify" his criminal behavior would then have an excuse to say they're working on behalf of ELF to save the planet.

Ron Arnold and others who have tracked cases for years are convinced that such cells don't exist, and law enforcement should be looking for something even more elusive. They believe the campaigns are loosely planned hit-and-run incidents, with the crimes carried out by geographically isolated clusters of individuals who share anti-industry beliefs but do not know people in other clusters. Arnold calls the clusters "action groups."

The action groups (also known as "phantom congregations") may not even be aware they are actually going to commit crimes until a highly mobile and sophisticated activist shows up – an activist Arnold calls the "traveling evangelist." These evangelists may follow a pre-planned route, but they also veer off on routes of opportunity when someone on the road tells them of a good target with reliable activists nearby.

The traveling evangelist thus comes into contact with one action group after another over the course of a long journey, trains and motivates them, and perhaps leads them on rampages across one or more states, leaving a trail of arson, vandalism and other destruction in their wake.

Trying to connect the dots is usually beyond the capability of the county sheriff who gets saddled with the detective work. By the time he's figured out the fire was arson, the perpetrators have dispersed back into the community, and the traveling evangelist is three states away, leading another rampage.

Because there is currently no *national clearinghouse* that federal, state and local jurisdictions can turn to for tracking eco-terrorist crimes, solving these crimes is difficult or impossible. Establishing such a clearinghouse must be made a high priority, before the violence gets even worse.

A psychological profile

The bulk of evil on a world scale is committed by ideologues and their followers. People are capable of bottomless cruelty to those outside the tribe.

—Michael Stone[89]

Slowly, gradually, it becomes painfully obvious to even the most obtuse among us that these radical attack groups are dangerous, extremely sophisticated, well-financed multi-national NGO conglomerates. They stand four-square in opposition to the fundamental mission of any business: to grow, prosper, and introduce new products, services and technologies; in short, to advance science and progress, for the betterment of societies and people the world over.

But according to the radical NGO worldview (as presented by Miss Ann Thropy and other representatives of the militant groups), people are the problem, technology is an evil curse, and progress must be thwarted by any means available.

"We must make this an insecure and uninhabitable place for capitalists and their projects. This is the best contribution we can make towards protecting the earth."[90]

"Green politics demands a whole new ethic in which violent, plundering humankind abandons its destructive ways, recognizes its dependence on Planet Earth, and starts living on a more equal footing with the rest of nature.... It is industrialism itself which threatens us."[91]

"Free enterprise really means rich people get richer. And they have the freedom to exploit and psychologically rape their fellow human beings in the process. Capitalism is destroying the earth."[92]

"Modern industrial civilization, as presently organized, is colliding violently with our planet's ecological system. The ferocity of its assault on the Earth is breathtaking, and the horrific consequences are occurring so quickly as to defy our capacity to recognize them, comprehend their global implications, and organize an appropriate and timely response.... We must make rescue of the environment the central organizing principle for civilization ... Minor shifts in policy, marginal adjustments in ongoing programs ... are all forms of appeasement, designed to satisfy the public's desire to believe that a wrenching transformation of society will not be necessary."[93]

"Among the abnormal conditions present in modern industrial society are excessive density of population, isolation of man from nature, excessive rapidity of social change and the breakdown of natural small-scale communities, such as the extended family, the village or the tribe. The positive ideal that is proposed is Nature. That is, wild nature: those aspects of the functioning of the Earth and its living things that are independent of human management and free of human interference and control."[94]

As former Senator Malcolm Wallop puts it, these "anti-capitalist extremists will not stop until they create an idyllic world in which profits and wealth are no longer valued."[95] George Reisman, professor of economics at Pepperdine University's Graziadio School of Business and Management in Los Angeles, is equally scathing in his criticism:

"The environmental movement ... is elitist. It is the movement of neo-feudal mentalities who desire a world of broad open spaces for themselves, spaces that are essentially ownerless, and who care nothing for the plight of crowded, starving masses, who are to be denied the benefit of access to those open spaces, which are to be closed to all development."[96]

Sociologist Lewis Coser would call them "struggle groups" that may actually seek to "attract enemies, in order to help maintain and increase group cohesion. Continued conflict being a condition of survival for struggle groups, they must continually provoke it ... so the groups' search for enemies is aimed not at obtaining results for their members, but merely at maintaining their own structure as a going concern."[97]

In a more lighthearted vein, humorist P.J. O'Rourke describes the militants as humorless Perennially Indignant protesters who "don't care if a policy works. In many ways it's better for them when a policy fails."[98] Otherwise, they wouldn't have a problem to rail about, businesses to attack, a justification for their own existence, or a reason to be Perennially Indignant.

Eric Hoffer once observed, "Mass movements can rise and spread without a belief in God, but never without a belief in a devil."[99] While we draw no conclusions about the religious faiths of these attackers, we certainly know their determination to exorcise multiple devils from our society – including the devils of Biotechnology and Big Business.

George Mason University psychologist John Riskind sees disturbing parallels between eco-extremists and the militants and autocratic states profiled in University of Pennsylvania professor emeritus Aaron Beck's book, *Prisoners of Hate: The Cognitive Basis of Anger, Hostility and Violence*. Beck examines the "primal thinking" and "hostile framing" that cause extremists to perceive themselves as engaged in a holy war against dangerous, evil, even subhuman creatures who deserve to be punished. Such thinking locks the extremists' minds in "prisons of hate," in which the false image is mistaken for the real person, thus justifying any actions. Riskind continues:

> "Beck has vividly depicted the extremist mentality that closely parallels Eric Hoffer's portrait of 'The True Believer.' The extremist outlook on the world is one where his own cause is viewed as the only righteous, moral and correct reality. Other people, with different views, are seen as reprehensibly wicked and immoral. There are no shades of gray in the worldview of extremists. Thus, the tension between good and bad leads logically, in their minds, to a moral crusade in which any action against the evil-doers is justified."[100]

It is a true case of "cynical duplicity and moral bankruptcy making the world safe for hypocrisy," as the late scientist Robert White-Stevens once put it. A psychoanalyst might well conclude that these constant fits of hysteria over exaggerated risks reflect a serious, perhaps incurable neurosis, which flows from the radicals' habit of constructing current situations in terms of an inaccurate description of a kernel of truth from a single poorly remembered past event. Rarely held accountable for their abusive actions, the environmental attack groups live primarily by what the great political thinker Max Weber called "the ethics of absolute ends" and ignore the "ethics of responsibility" that govern most of society.

But regardless of the explanation, the predators are allegedly abusing their nonprofit, tax-exempt status, partaking of the huge foundation, corporation and government trough of money and power – some using threats, possible extortion, lawsuits, government edicts and violence to extract additional funds from unwilling victims. Every new victory, every capitulation gives them more power, wealth and prestige, additional resources and allies, and a greater sense of invincibility and inevitability – enabling and emboldening them to seek out new prey.

Even more frightening, however, are their frequent dehumanizing, anti-civilization rantings, recalling earlier utopian justifications for actions that betray just how thin is the veneer of our civilization.

And yet, these spine-chilling comments are rarely reported by the mainstream press, and virtually never subjected to the vitriol and calumny that would greet an "insensitive" comment by a corporate officer or conservative legislator.

"Loggers losing their jobs because of Spotted Owl legislation is, in my eyes, no different than people being out of work after the furnaces of Dachau shut down."[101]

"There are too many people in the world, and banning DDT is as good a way to get rid of them as any."[102]

"I know social scientists who remind me that people are part of nature, but it isn't true. Somewhere along the line – at about a billion years ago, and maybe half that – we quit the contract and became a cancer. We have become a plague upon ourselves and upon the Earth. Until such time as *Homo sapiens* should decide to rejoin nature, some of us can only hope for the right virus to come along."[103]

Perhaps Prince Philip of Great Britain, international president of the World Wildlife Fund, will come to the rescue. He has said that if he were to be reincarnated, he would like to return as a "particularly deadly virus, to lower human population levels."[104]

Over the past decade, to their advantage and our collective disadvantage, these predatory groups have effectively become a fourth branch of government. They sit on corporate boards and increasingly play important, sometimes decisive roles on government advisory panels and commissions. They regulate the regulators, and yet are subject to none of the checks and balances, none of the accountability, none of the rules and regulations, that rein in the other branches, if ever so slightly.

Even their most disingenuous claims and charges, their most absurd arguments, their most outrageous lies and conduct, go largely unchallenged, uncensored and unpunished. Even now, despite this wave of arson and destruction, many journalists still portray the predators, and many otherwise intelligent people still envision them, as heroic champions, working selflessly to bring greedy corporations to justice, and save our planet.

Fighting back

It is a bleak picture, to be sure – a depressing state of affairs that has been tediously recounted far more articulately than here, in far greater detail, throughout an entire genre of books, articles and speeches. This book will not add further to that total, or advocate appeasement or abject surrender to frustration, pessimism and the Dark Side of the Force. Nor will it suggest that we emulate the Polish cavalry, which in September 1939 charged German Panzer tanks and infantry on horseback, to die bravely, gloriously, with honor – and in vain.

In an impassioned speech to the American Enterprise Institute, Supreme Court Justice Clarence Thomas observed that it is extremely hard and risky to challenge "sacred policies." Frank discussion on these taboo issues is not permitted, and anyone who insists on engaging in "debates of consequence" on them, he continued, must be "willing to endure attacks that range from mere hostile bluster to libel." In all too many instances, however, we simply "allow our critics to intimidate us ... we censor ourselves. This is not civility; it is cowardice, a well-intentioned self-deception, at best."[105]

It is time to end the self-censorship, cowardice and appeasement. We must recognize what is going on, and what is at stake. We must develop winning strategies and tactics for fighting back. Most importantly, we must find the fortitude Justice Thomas talked about, to fight back, and win – at the corporate, local, state, national and international level.

[Those Costa Rican] fishermen are full of shit. We should have used real bullets on the damn bastards, not paint bullets. These fishermen are pigs. They're raping the environment for the sake of a buck.
—Peter Brown, Sea Shepherd Conservation Society[106]

If you live by the sword, you may die by the sword. But if you live by the olive branch, you may still die by the sword.
—Eric Dezenhall

Chapter 2 Notes

1. See discussion of Natural Resources Defense Council and the California energy crisis (page 47).
2. See section on the Environmental Protection Agency (page 39).
3. See Chapter 10, Ethics Edict 8 (page 224).
4. National Center for Public Policy Research (NCPPR), *National Directory of Environmental and Regulatory Victims* (1998), page 15, citing congressional testimony by Rep. Wally Herger, before the U.S. House of Representatives Committee on Resources, April 10, 1997.
5. NCPPR, *National Directory of Environmental and Regulatory Victims* (2000), page 30.
6. See Chapter 5, Wildcard #1 (page 115); Chapter 6, Balkanization (page 129).
7. See discussions of Animal Liberation Front (page 50) and Earth Liberation Front (page 46).
8. Kathryn M. Edwards, MD, "State Mandates and Childhood Immunization," *Journal of the American Medical Association*, December 27, 2000. For more on health and biomedicine, see www.ncpa.org/pd/regulat/reg-7.html.
9. See Chapter 4 (page 101).
10. For example, the U.S. Environmental Protection Agency has established a Committee on Environment and Natural Resources to "identify key scientific questions and uncertainties," inventory ongoing research and evaluate possible new research programs related to endocrine disruption in animals. Other agencies are doing likewise.
11. Ellyn Ferguson, "Terrorism could divert research money to security," Gannett News Service, June 5, 2001. Catherine Ives, director of Michigan State University's Agricultural Biotechnology Support Project, estimated that her institution spent nearly $1 million to improve security and rebuild the fourth floor of Agriculture Hall after arson destroyed her office in January 2000, according to Ferguson.
12. See discussion of Friends of the Earth and the Namada Dam project (pages 33-34).
13. AnnMarie Bonardi, Amanda Bower, *et al.*, "A farewell to arms?" *Time*, May 21, 2001.
14. "There's no accounting for outrage," *Buffalo News*, May 18, 2001.
15. Patrick Moore, "Hard choices: The future of environmentalism," *Earth Day 96*, Heartland Institute (1996), www.heartland.org/earthday96/choices.htm.
16. Patrick Moore, "Environmentalism for the Twenty-first Century," Fraser Institute (1999), www.fraserinstitute.ca/forum.
17. Patrick Moore, *op. cit.*
18. Magnus Gudmundsson, personal communication, January 16, 2001.
19. "Greenpeace boat shadows Japanese plutonium ship despite collision," *Atlanta Journal*, November 9, 1992
20. "Violent N-bomb protest in Tahiti: Demonstrators and police clash," *Seattle Post-Intelligencer*, September 7, 1995; "Tahiti hit with violent protesting: Hundreds of teens surround airport," *Atlanta Journal*, September 8, 1995.

21. Gillian Harris, "30 Greenpeace activists arrested as rig protest starts," *Times of London*, April 1, 2000; Simon Reeve, "Green group's cash in 'dirty' firms," *Times of London* , Sunday, October 29, 1995.
22. Ron Arnold, *Eco-Terror: The violent agenda to save nature*, Bellevue, WA: Free Enterprise Press (1997), pages 73-78, 237-246, 255-256, 263-264, 273-274. See also www.greenpiece.org and www.ranamuck.org
23. Direct quote from interview with Mike Roselle in *The Man In The Rainbow*, a documentary film by Magnus Gudmundsson.
24. Personal e-mail communication from Barun Mitra, The Liberty Institute, New Delhi, India, November 9, 1999.
25. Brent Blackwelder, speaking in *Against Nature*, Martin Durkin producer, London: Channel 4 Television Corporation (1997).
26. Lisa Jordan, director of the Bank Information Centre, speaking in *Against Nature*.
27. Dr. Ila Patachk, member of the Gujarat Women's Action Group, *ibid*. Dr. Anil Patel, "Gujarat – Its Environment and Challenges," seminar paper delivered October 19, 1999; provided courtesy of the Liberty Institute, New Delhi, India.
28. Tom Knudsen, "Playing with fire: Spin on science puts national treasure at risk," *Sacramento Bee*, April 25, 2001.
29. *Ibid.*; Lance Morrow, "The perfect firestorm: The fires have ignited a culture war over logging and the best way to save the American wilderness," *Time*, September 11, 2000, pages 42-45; Robert H. Nelson, *A Burning Issue: A case for abolishing the U.S. Forest Service*, Lanham, MD: Rowman and Littlefield (2000); Robert H. Nelson, "Western Wildfires: Seeing the forest through dense, dead and diseased trees," *CEI On Point*, No. 71, Competitive Enterprise Institute, September 14, 2000.
30. Tom Knudsen, "Playing with fire," *op. cit.*
31. *Ibid.*
32. Tom Knudsen, "Litigation central: A flood of costly lawsuits raises questions about motive," *Sacramento Bee*, April 24, 2001.
33. "Baby alert: New findings about plastics," *Consumer Reports*, May 1999.
34. Ibid.
35. www.bisphenol-a.org/hazard.html, July 27, 2000.
36. "Low Dose Bisphenol-A Effects Confirmed," *Endocrine/Estrogen Letter*, June 2, 2000.
37. Steven Milloy, "Lingering infestation of science moles," *Washington Times*, May 30, 2001.
38. "Widely reported study now deemed flawed," The Associated Press, August 21, 1997.
39. "Baby alert: New findings about plastics," *Consumer Reports*, May 1999.
40. *The Simpsons*, March 11, 2001.
41. Bonner Cohen, John Carlisle, *et al.*, *The Fear Profiteers: Do "Socially Responsible" Businesses Sow Health Scares to Reap Monetary Rewards?* Arlington, VA: Lexington Institute (2000), page 7.
42. *Ibid.*, page 9.

43. Ron Arnold and Alan Gottleib, *Trashing the Economy: How Runaway Environmentalism Is Wrecking America*, Free Enterprise Press (1993), pages 241-242.
44. "Science Fair winner tests gullibility," *The Post Register OnLine*, www.idahonews.com, April 27, 1997.
45. "EPA's way of pulling the pesticide plug," Steven J. Milloy, junkscience.com, June 12, 2000.
46. Anita Bartholomew, "Bugzilla!" *Reader's Digest*, March 2001, pages 84-89.
47. See Dixie Lee Ray with Lou Guzzo, *Environmental Overkill: Whatever happened to common sense?* Washington, DC: Regnery Gateway (1993), pages 151-152.
48. Monte Burke, "An affair to remember: Crown Cork owned an asbestos company for 93 days in the 1960s – long enough for today's tort lawyers to pick it clean," *Forbes*, June 11, 2001, pages 60-62.
49. Michael Freedman, Turning lead into gold: Lawyer Ronald Motley beat the tobacco and asbestos companies. Now he's out to demonize the Dutch Boy," *Forbes*, May 14, 2001, pages 122-126. See also "Shield Sham: The cell phone cancer scare has spawned protective devices for the wary. Never mind whether they actually work," *ibid.*, pages 228-230.
50. Michael Fumento, "The real gal: Erin Brockovich has spent an awful lot of time crusading for the little guy – and trying to line the pockets of the law firm she works for," *Forbes*, May 28, 2001, page 64.
51. Michael Freedman, "Turning lead into gold," page 126
52. Spencer Abraham, Secretary of Energy, "A national report on America's energy crisis," Remarks to U.S. Chamber of Commerce, National Energy Summit, March 19, 2001.
53. Rene Sanchez, "California power crisis may dim Davis's bright political prospects," *Washington Post*, February 4, 2001.
54. Sarah van Gelder, "Transforming a mega-utility I: Why NRDC chose collaboration over confrontation – an interview with Ralph Cavanagh," *In Context: A Quarterly of Humane Sustainable Culture*, Fall 1992.
55. Paul Driessen, "Recipe for disaster: What really caused California's energy crisis? What can we do now?" Committee For A Constructive Tomorrow, Briefing Paper #109, April 2001; William Tucker, "California Unplugged: Environmentalists dreamed of soft power. The state woke up in the dark," *The American Spectator*, April 2001, pages 30-43.
56. *Ibid.*
57. Ron Arnold, *EcoTerror: The violent agenda to save nature – The world of the Unabomber*, Bellevue, WA: Free Enterprise Press (1997), page ix.
58. ELF statement published by Humanitarians for Animal Rights Education, www.haregrp.net, following an August 7, 1999 attack on the property of a Michigan vet working with fur farmers.
59. ELF spokesman Craig Rosebraugh, quoted in "Disruption is activists' business," *Los Angeles Times*, April 25, 2000.

60. Craig Rosebraugh, comment in the newsletter of his organization, Liberation Collective; quoted in the *Willamette Week Online*, www.wweek.com/html/cover120397.html, December 3, 1997.
61. Bryan Denson and James Long, "Crimes in the Name of the Environment," *The Oregonian*, September 1999 (available at www.landrights.org/ALRA.Oregonian.eco-terrorism.htm).
62. Michael Parfit, "Earth Firsters wield a mean monkey wrench," *Smithsonian*, Vol. 21, No. 1, April 1990, pages 184-204.
63. Frank Ahrens, "An Elemental Clash Of Earth and Fire," *Washington Post*, January 13, 2001, Page C1.
64. Doug Bandow, "Ecoterrorism: The Dangerous Fringe of the Environmental Movement," Heritage Foundation Backgrounder (April 1990), page 8. Cited in Ben Bloch and Harold Lyons, *Apocalypse Not: Science, Economics and Environmentalism*, Washington, DC: Cato Institute (1993), page 5.
65. Megan Rosenfeld, "Food Fight: PBS tackles issue of modified crops," *Washington Post*, April 24, 2001.
66. Robert S. Root-Bernstein, "Infectious terrorism: it is time to think seriously about how biological agents could be deployed against innocent citizens," *The Atlantic*, May 1991, page 44.
67. Chris Baker, "Farms targets for terror? Livestock illness seen as weapon," *Washington Times*, May 8, 2001.
68. Michelle Malkin, "Setting fires in the 'Frankenforest,'" *Washington Times*, May 29, 2001; Eric Sorenson and Peytonn Whitely, "Group confirms it set UW fire: School officials blast attackers, vow to rebuild," *Seattle Times*, June 2, 2001.
69. Sorenson and Whitely, *op. cit.* See also a series of articles by Scott Sunde and Paul Shukovsky on environmental and animal rights terrorism, *Seattle Post-Intelligencer*, June 18, 2001. For detailed information on eco terrorism and vandalism, go to www.cffar/vandalwatch, a Web site maintained by the Center for Food and Agricultural Research.
70. *Setting fires with electrical timers: An Earth Liberation Front guide*, May 2001 edition, www.earthliberationfront.com/main.shtml; see also Joseph Frazier (Associated Press), "Underground group publishes arson manual on Web site," May 31, 2001. Frazier's article contains a moronic statement by an FBI spokeswoman, who said she did not know if the site was legal, and "there is a very fine line between freedom of speech and censorship." One assumes she meant, between freedom of speech and incitement to arson and riot.
71. Craig Rosebraugh, quoted in "Sparks fly at forum on activism," *Hoosier Times* (Indiana), June 30, 2000.
72. Commentary by self-styled Internet guru Keith Parkins, www.heureka.clara.net/gaiagenetics.htm; quoted in Thomas R. DeGregori, "Environmentalism, animal rights activism, and eco-Nazism," American Council on Science and Health, www.uh.edu/~trdereg (University of Houston).
73. Ingrid Newkirk, *Vogue*, September 1989.

74. "Huntingdon's Secrets Exposed," www.AnimalLiberation.net, communiqué, May 8, 2001.
75. *Boston Globe*, Oct. 30, 1999; North American ALF Press Office press release, Oct. 24, 1999; letter to Earth First Journal, 1994; reproduced by the Ecoterror Response Network, www.cdfe.org/indict.html.
76. David Barbarash, quoted in Seth Lewis, "Tale of Terror: Animal-rights activists on verge of 'major coup,'" CNSNews.com, May 23, 2001.
77. Lisa Baker, "Near Misses: Oregon's eco-terrorists push the envelope," *Brainstorm*, November 1999.
78. William Underhill, "War On Science," *Newsweek*, May 7, 2001; Matt Adams, "Police arrest three over attack on head of Huntingdon Lab," *The Independent* (London), May 24, 2001.
79. William Underhill, "War On Science," *Newsweek*, May 7, 2001.
80. Al Baker, "Environmental groups claim to have vandalized banks," *New York Times*, June 14, 2001; Rich Vosepka, "Underground animal rights group claims responsibility for vandalism," Associated Press State & Local Wire, June 12, 2001.
81. Seth Lewis, "Tale of Terror: Animal-rights activists on verge of 'major coup,'" CNSNews.com, May 23, 2001; Rosie Murray-West, "Banks warned on animal protests, *London Daily Telegraph*, May 2, 2001; Meg Milne, "Police called in over death threat sent to farming boss," *Sunday Express*, May 20, 2001.
82. Society of Environmental Journalists, "U.S. animal rights attacks slow but steady," May 2, 2001; see www.sej.org/pub.
83. Diane Brooks, "Blind man guides way for Layla's Law: Service dogs now protected," *The Seattle Times,* May 10, 2001.
84. Chris Baker, "Farms target for terror? Livestock illness seen as weapon," *Washington Times*, May 8, 2001.
85. Alan Elsner, "Animal rights leader hopes disease comes to US," Reuters, April 2, 2001.
86. Ananova, "Stolen foot-and-mouth virus released deliberately," www.ananova.com/news/story/sm_223605.html, April 8, 2001.
87. "A new terrorism has come of age: Animal rights and eco-terrorism pose multi-million dollar losses to nations," news release, National Anxiety Center, May 24, 2001. See also David Brown and Richard Savill, "Foot and mouth: Eco-terrorists may be to blame, says NFU head," *London Daily Telegraph*, May 15, 2001.
88. *Time* reporter Elaine Shannon talking about the Unabomber, April 7, 1996, C-SPAN "Sunday Journal." Contrast that absence of condemnation with Today Show co-host Bryant Gumble's April 25, 1995 remark: "The bombing in Oklahoma City has focused renewed attention on the rhetoric that's been coming from the right and those who cater to angry white men."
89. Janet McConnaughey, quoting Columbia University psychologist Dr. Michael Stone, in "Forensic psychiatrist working to develop a depravity scale," Associated Press, May 11, 2001.
90. David Foreman, *Ecodefense: A Field Guide to Monkeywrenching* (a how-to guide to arson, spiking trees, "decommissioning" heavy equipment, and other acts of sabotage), Tucson, AZ: Ned Ludd Books (1987).

91. Jonathon Porritt and David Winner, British Ecology Party, quoted in Ray and Guzzo, *Environmental Overkill: Whatever happened to common sense?* Washington, DC: Regnery Gateway (1993), page 203.
92. Helen Caldicott, Australian pediatrician, author and member of the Union of Concerned Scientists. Quoted in Elizabeth Whelan, *Toxic Terror*, Ottawa, IL: Jameson Books (1985), pages 53-54.
93. Albert Gore, Jr. *Earth in the Balance: Ecology and the Human Spirit*, New York: Plume (1992), pages 269-274.
94. Theodore Kaczynski, "Unabomber Manefesto" Paragraphs 47, 183.
95. Malcolm Wallop, chairman, Frontiers of Freedom Institute, "Memo to Business: The Greens intend to place profits on the endangered list," *Investor's Business Daily*, January 8, 2001, page A24.
96. Arnold, *Undue Influence*, page 304.
97. Lewis Coser, *The Functions of Social Conflict*, New York: The Free Press, 1956. Quoted in Ron Arnold, *Ecology Wars: Environmentalism As If People Mattered*, Bellevue, Washington: Free Enterprise Press (1987), page 91.
98. P.J. O'Rourke, *Parliament of Whores: A lone humorist attempts to explain the entire U.S. government*, New York: Vintage Books (1991), page 191.
99. Eric Hoffer, *The True Believer*, New York: Harper & Row (1951), page 89.
100. John Riskind, George Mason University, personal communication, January 30, 2001.
101. David Brower, founder of Earth First! Speaking in British Columbia. Quoted in Ray and Guzzo, *Environmental Overkill*, page 204.
102. Dr. Charles Wurster, former scientist for the Environmental Defense Fund, quoted in Robert Whelan, et al., *The Cross and the Rain Forest: A Critique of Radical Green Spirituality*, Grand Rapids, MI: Acton Institute (1996), page 87.
103. David Graber, former research biologist for the National Park Service, Los Angeles Times Book Review, October 22, 1989, page 9.
104. Quoted in Whelan, et al., *The Cross and the Rain Forest*, page 65.
105. Clarence Thomas, "Be Not Afraid: Justice Thomas on courage and civic priciples," excerpts from his February 13, 2001 speech before the American Enterprise Institute, *Washington Times*, February 15, 2001.
106. Mick Kronman, freelance reporter for *National Fisherman* and *Underwater USA* magazines, as related to Teresa Platt of the Fishermen's Coalition, May 20, 1992, and reported in Ron Arnold and Alan Gottleib, *Trashing the Economy: How runaway environmentalism is wrecking America*, Bellevue, WA: Free Enterprise Press (1993), page 190.

3

Corporate Cowardice

An appeaser is one who feeds a crocodile, hoping it will
eat him last.

—Winston Churchill

Spend three decades managing crises for politicians, policy makers and
product manufacturers, and you will conclude, as I have, that four powerful myths exert near-biblical influence over the way we react to public
controversies about the food we eat, the goods we purchase and the materials
we use in our daily lives:

**Myth #1: Environmental and consumer groups are always motivated
by the altruistic desire to protect people, wildlife and the planet.** *Baloney.
Professional environmental and consumer activists are just like the rest
of corporate America. They are part of a multi-billion-dollar business
and are motivated by power, politics, money and the desire for self-per-
petuation.*

Myth #2: Reporters are objective and stick to the facts. *Untrue.
News, too, is a multi-billion-dollar business. Ratings points and circulation
numbers are the coin of the realm. Despite efforts by many journalists
to protect the dignity of their chosen profession, truth, facts and balanced
reporting blow out the tail pipe of the media if they don't contribute to
the bottom line. 24-hour news cycles, competition to get on Page One,
and the tendency to hype stories and cross the line between news and
advocacy or entertainment also tarnish objectivity.*

Myth #3: "Spin" and "finding common ground" are the public relations wonder drugs that will heal all wounds. *Horse puckey. Honest disagreements, misconceptions and compromises are one thing – attacks by predators bent on gelding, blackmailing or destroying a company quite another.*

Myth #4: Corporate executives are tough, calculating street fighters driven by blood-thirsty competition. *Hogwash. Sure, corporations are driven by competition for profits. But the present-day corporate culture produces more Neville Chamberlains than Winston Churchills. If companies were populated by street-fighting Winstons, Greenpeace and organizations like it would have been de-fanged, disarmed and dismantled a long, long time ago.*

The internal language of American business is the lexicon of warfare. Companies "launch" campaigns, "outflank" the competition and "battle" for market share. CEOs marshal their corporate warriors for the sole purpose of achieving "the mission" – increased profits.

When business executives communicate among themselves, they often talk like Winstons. But in today's corporate culture, especially in dealing with very real external threats, many executives act like Nevilles.

Many of the men and women who run American companies today grew up during the turmoil of Vietnam, Earth Day and Watergate. They watched as corporations were fingered for everything judged immoral at the time: napalm, Agent Orange, pollution and political corruption. They listened as the leaders of the fledgling environmental movement quoted Rachel Carson's "Silent Spring," and Ralph Nader condemned companies for making profits, depleting natural resources, manufacturing products that maimed unsuspecting consumers, and generally promoting technological progress, rather than a return to "nature" and a "simpler life." (That's the same Ralph Nader who, according to *The Washington Post*, "is worth at least $3.8 million and is heavily invested in technology stocks.")[1]

From the moment today's class of corporate leaders entered the business world, many were told that their company's mission was to become a "good corporate citizen." They listened as public relations consultants preached zero risk, conflict avoidance, political correctness and business ethics out of one side of their mouths, and "spin control" out of the other. Some bought this public relations propaganda. Others, to their credit, did not.

When a company comes under attack, it quickly becomes evident whether corporate leadership is from the "Neville" or "Winston" school of management. Their zero-risk mindset paralyzes the Nevilles in the midst of a crisis. The true Winstons understand that zero-risk does not exist, particularly when someone is trying to slit your corporate throat.

The mega-myths just described have distorted public policy, consumer behavior and corporate conduct since Ralph Nader was riding around in a baby carriage.

But now, the impact of these fictions on an already volatile marketplace has become even more insidious, thanks to the:

- blastoff of cyber-communications and cyber-attacks;
- proliferation of predatory special interest groups that exist solely for the purpose of launching marketplace attacks;
- break-neck competition among an ever-increasing number of news outlets, battling for fame, market share and profits; and
- the emasculation of corporate America by public relations Nevilles and zero-risk managers.

What are the results?

Consumers are routinely frightened out of their wits by phony health scares. They throw away perfectly safe products. Their attention is diverted from real health hazards, and their trust in government safety regulations is slowly but surely being replaced by cynicism and disbelief.

Government officials chase one wacky doomsday theory after another, dropping bags of taxpayer dollars in their wake, as the rest of us try to separate real hazards from those that are the figment of someone's paranoia or political agenda. Cancer-causing teethers and apples. Sperm-destroying baby bottles. Killer taco shells. Brain-frying cell phones and power lines. Mutant-producing soy beans. Or, maybe not!

No wonder the reprise to Tom Harris's best seller *I'm OK, You're OK* is called *I'm Afraid, You're Afraid.*[2]

It's perfect for today's culture of overblown fear, which paradoxically thrives in what is arguably the safest era in human history.

Corporations that have produced safe products for decades find those same products lynched in the court of public opinion by attackers seeking publicity, reporters lusting for ratings points and government bureaucrats looking for more turf to govern.

Who wins in this perverse game of cat and mouse? The activists. The Luddites. The news-as-entertainment industry.

And the Neville Chamberlains of public relations and middle management, who spend their days writing corporate ethics statements and posing for pictures extolling their saintly virtues, while their clients and companies are being pillaged by those who play by a different set of rules – rules for radical predators.

Capitulation counseling

It gets worse. In December 2000, Edelman Public Relations hired former Greenpeace international communications director Jonathan Wootliff to be managing director of its global non-governmental organization (NGO) practice, based in Brussels.[3] Another ardent environmental activist, Leslie Dach, coordinates what former U.S. Senator Malcolm Wallop calls the firm's new "capitulation counseling" practice.

CEO Richard Edelman intends to position his company as a leader in coordinating and promoting consumer activists and the growing role of NGOs in global governance and corporate management. In his view, NGO organizations like Greenpeace are now "superbrands, in the same lexicon as Microsoft, Coca-Cola, *et cetera*." They now "face the same dynamics as business, which is to say that they have to continue to build their brands."

As Wallop puts it, the firm and its superbrand clients "have found a way to promote their green agenda and get corporations to pay for it," by teaching the fine art of preemptive capitulation. However, "extortion, once successful, never ends. Once a company capitulates to activists, other groups smell blood in the water and launch another attack."[4]

Make no mistake about it. Capitulation counselors may say they practice "engagement," "dialogue" or "beneficial relationships." They may say *wei-ji*, the Chinese word for crisis, means "danger" and "opportunity" – emphasizing the supposed opportunity, while ignoring the real dangers. But peel away the rhetorical veneer, and you're left with surrender – not to watchdog groups over honest differences of opinion, but to sophisticated predators whose ultimate goal is overthrowing business, industry and capitalism.

That is not to say there is never any room for appeasement, by whatever name. As historian Donald Kagan has observed:

> "Appeasement is a perfectly respectable and often useful instrument of policy. It can be effective when applied from a position of strength, when it is a freely taken action to allay a grievance and create goodwill. It is an unsatisfactory and dangerous device when it is resorted to out of fear and necessity, for then it does not reduce resentment but shows weakness and induces contempt."[5]

The critical question, then, is knowing when to allay a legitimate grievance, and when to get out the long knives.

At a London seminar shortly after he hired Wootliff, Edelman actually praised former Greenpeace leader Peter, the fourth Lord Melchett, who was tried on theft and criminal damage charges for his role in destroying a crop of genetically modified plants – and acquitted by a jury that didn't think it was a crime. On the Brent Spar oil platform protest, Edelman said, "I think driving a car into the waters of the North Sea...was a perfect example of how you make something understandable. Well done, Peter."

Well done, Peter? Is this the same Greenpeace we got to know in Chapter 2? The same one whose members have harassed industry after industry, mounted numerous market-destroying scare campaigns and been arrested hundreds of times?[6]

(Lord Melchett is reportedly leaving Greenpeace to become a consultant for organic food giant Iceland Foods.[7] Having led an anti-biotechnology crusade for years, generating unfounded fears of conventional and genetically modified foods and creating a broad market for organic products – all through a tax-exempt organization funded in no small part by "natural" food producers – Melchett will now profit more directly from the political situation he helped create.)

Who loses in this high-stakes game? Corporate CEOs and shareholders, employees and their families, consumers who lose the option to choose perfectly safe products, and the world's disenfranchised poor, whose lives are never touched by the progress, products and basic amenities we take for granted.

As one historian has observed, "Neville Chamberlain's ego led him to believe that his personal negotiations with Hitler were a statesman-like contribution to world peace. In fact, he did little but give way to Hitler's bullying, and ratify and assist the aggression he claimed to be stopping. In addition, Chamberlain's well publicized meetings with Hitler encouraged the more extreme Nazis, while demoralizing the few influential Germans who opposed Hitler's methods."[8] The lesson for corporate executives should be obvious.

Understanding the competition

Any company executive worth a grain of salt knows that *understanding the competition* is a cardinal rule of marketing. Millions are spent by companies conducting research and gathering intelligence about other products and other businesses. For many multi-national companies, the budget for keeping an eye on their top competitors would probably exceed the operating budget of some third-world countries.

However, there is one class of competitors that is not well researched, analyzed or understood by chief executive officers (CEOs) and the people they command: the professional attackers – individuals and groups who make their living by attacking products and the companies that make them.

A business executive who ignores these full-time attackers does so at extreme peril. And many do.

How does a CEO get up to speed on how these marketplace adversaries operate? This book is a good start, but among the best backgrounders are the books of Saul D. Alinsky.

Alinsky (1909 – 1972) was raised and educated in the back streets of Chicago. His formal schooling in criminology took place at the Windy City's namesake university. Why should corporate executives care about Alinsky? Because his true genius was as an organizer and motivator of people who, for whatever reason, found themselves at odds with the *establishment*. Alinsky showed them how to take power away from the powerful, and how to use society's rules against its rule makers.

Alinsky taught his followers how to bring the mighty to their knees. He humbled Mayor Richard Daley, Sr. by threatening to hijack all the toilets at O'Hare Airport – thus the term "sit-in." He caused chaos at Eastman Kodak's Rochester, New York headquarters, by leaking word that he intended to bring one hundred low-income people to a Rochester Symphony Orchestra concert, but only after they had been well-fed at a three-hour baked bean dinner.

A cursory review of Alinsky's books may lead some to conclude that he was America's foremost, albeit radical, prankster. However, a more thorough review of his philosophy, strategies and tactics should convince anyone with a brain that Saul D. Alinsky's legacy will be felt long into the 21st century.

In 1971, Alinsky published *Rules for Radicals*. It became the bible for thousands of activists, many of whom were in diapers at the time of his death. It serves as an inspiration for this book, because there is no better source on how modern-day attackers conduct guerrilla warfare against corporations. There is likewise no better point of departure for developing a new corporate mindset, and a more effective battle plan for stopping the attacks.

> Some people have constructed a vision of the world in their mind that differs greatly from the real world. And they cannot bring themselves to give up that vision. Nor will they allow others to shatter their vision with facts. The real question is: Why do we take them seriously? Are we so easily impressed or intimidated by their airs of superiority?
>
> —Thomas Sowell[10]

Chapter 3 Notes

1. "Nader's Worth At $3.8 Million," Mike Allen, *The Washington Post*, June 19, 2000.
2. Melinda Muse, *I'm Afraid, You're Afraid: 448 Things to Fear and Why*, Hyperion Books (2000).
3. "Inside PR, Executive Edition," Volume 7 Number 8, December 4, 2000, page 7.
4. Malcolm Wallop, chairman, Frontiers of Freedom Institute, "Memo to Business: The Greens intend to place profits on the endangered list," *Investor's Business Daily*, January 8, 2001, page A24.
5. Donald Kagan, *On the Origins of War and the Preservation of Peace*, New York: Doubleday (1995), p. 260.
6. "Fact Sheet: Greenpeace and Violence Incidents," Center for the Defense of Free Enterprise, news release, February 2001.
7. Anthony Trewavas, "Lord Melchett: The payoff and the hypocrisy," Glasgow Herald, March 11, 2000. (See www.greenpiece.org/herald.html and www.altgreen.com.au/misc/honours00.html) Trewavas is director of the Institute of Cell and Molecular Biology at the University of Edinburgh.
8. Len Deighton, *Blood, Tears and Folly: An Objective Look At World War II*, London: PIMLICO (1995), p. 145.
9. Saul D. Alinsky, *Rules for Radicals: A pragmatic primer for realistic radicals*, New York: Vintage Books, 1971.
10. Thomas Sowell, "Vanquished Facts," *Washington Times*, August 23, 2000.

Part Two

The Solution

4

Corporate Courage

In a fight almost anything goes. It almost reaches the point
where you stop to apologize if a chance blow lands above
the belt.

—Saul D. Alinsky

There is a fundamental difference between business executives and their activist group adversaries. Business people tend to focus their time, energy and resources on developing detailed goals and objectives to shape their response to marketplace attacks. The attackers skip right to the strategies and tactics required to launch their attacks.

Corporate crisis management teams often consume scores of hours and hundreds of croissants debating goals and objectives that describe *where they want to be* when the battle is over, rather than *how they are going to get there* (strategies and tactics). In essence, they confuse motion with action, and assume the attackers will launch predictable attacks and behave in accord with corporate battle plans. That's rarely the case.

I recall one firm's crisis team spending its entire first meeting debating the criteria for disbanding the team. That's optimism bordering on hilarity. By the time they arrived at a discussion of tactics (several meetings later), their adversaries had fired several rounds from various directions, all aimed at the company's vital organs.

The *goal* is to anticipate, prepare for and survive the attack.

The *objective* is to destroy the enemy, or at least his ability and will to wage war.

The *strategy* is to fight back, and create real risk for the attackers.

Now, what *power plays* and tactics will you use to get where you want to be? That's where the focus ought to be – and why this book starts with power plays and the tactics they inspire, and then deals with strategies, the message, the media and, finally, ethics.

Power plays and tactics are about one thing and only one thing. Winning. The attack groups know that. The organization with the most effective power plays and tactics will whip those who, for whatever reason, come up short on the tactical front when the battle is joined.

Attack groups are primarily interested in taking power from the establishment for their own benefit and the benefit of the selected groups they have anointed as victims. They portray themselves as Davids battling Goliaths, as protectors of the "public interest," as advocates for consumers, the poor, indigenous peoples, little animals, the rainforest, the planet.

In reality, David has become Goliath, and a review of the tactics and policy agendas of many attack groups suggests that they are primarily interested in acquiring more money and power, to advance their political ideology, expand their organizations, and exert greater control over corporate decisions and people's lives. In other words, good old-fashioned greed. Their continued success reflects their own skills and audacity, corporate passivity and incompetence, and the attack groups' synergistic alliances with predatory lawyers, activist foundations, journalists, judges, government regulators and even companies that stand to benefit (temporarily) from the latest attack.

These attack groups are part of what Thomas Sowell calls the "anointed" political and intellectual elites. They engage in what is commonly passed off as "thinking" about important social, economic and environmental issues, and they are very effective in promoting their ideas and vision, particularly among upper crust urbanites. It is these urban intellectuals who often have the poorest understanding of where energy, consumer products and quality of life actually come from; share the deepest guilt about "despoiling" nature; detest corporations with the greatest intensity; and are most vocal in promoting their vision and worldview.

"Those who accept this vision are deemed to be not merely factually correct but morally on a higher plane," Sowell observes. "Put differently, those who disagree with the prevailing vision are seen as being not merely in error, but in sin."[1]

However, on closer examination, the anointed elites' analyses often turn out to be nothing more than assertions of politically correct claims, followed by evasions of mounting evidence against the assertions and vitriolic assaults on anyone daring to challenge their assertions.

To understand these attackers, you must understand that they rarely have any interest in compromise and moderation. As a result, efforts to appease the attackers with anything short of corporate surrender are useless. In fact, the attackers see any concessions by their targets as signs of weakness that merely invite demands for further concessions, as they pursue the goal of total victory that will cripple or destroy their enemies.

Consider how The Green Party USA presents itself. "The Green Party alternative is a people's party: a party for the working class majority; a party for all people oppressed by racism, sexism, heterosexism[2] or any form of domination; a party for everyone who loves peace, justice, a clean environment, and a participatory democracy."[3]

Now, take a closer look at the Green Party's political platform and program for the 21st century. Ralph Nader's party has advocated the following policies:[4]

1. The abolishment of the "aristocratic" U.S. Senate.

2. Abolishment of the U.S. Supreme Court's power to declare legislation passed by Congress unconstitutional.

3. Re-appropriation of several prime-time hours a day of commercial broadcast time for "real" public service broadcasting.

4. The break-up of any company with more than 10 percent market share, unless the firm makes a compelling case to the government that a break-up is not a good idea.

5. The "voluntary" conversion of small and medium businesses to "democratic public enterprises" or co-ops.

6. A 100 percent tax on all income over 10 times the minimum wage, which as I write this book, is about $5.15 an hour. So, a person can make up to $51.50 an hour. Any amount above that goes to the government.

To sweeten the deal, the Green Party's political platform for the new millenium includes:[5]

1. A six-hour workday with no cut in pay. (The government issues a supplemental paycheck to make up the difference.)

2. Free education through graduate school.

3. Government-financed universal healthcare.

4. Guaranteed family income of at least $26,000 per year for a mother with three children, with an extra $3,250 per each additional child. (So much for population control.)

Who do you suppose would benefit from these proposals? Professional attackers. Political organizers. Full-time activists. In other words, members of the Green Party. In short, their true purpose is: advancing their political ideology, self perpetuation, good old-fashioned greed.

Karl Marx had a word for what the Green Party is advocating. The socialist movement's color may have changed, but the agenda hasn't. A quick survey of modern history suggests that when political parties take over the media, expropriate private property and abolish democratic institutions like the United States Senate, bad things happen to human beings, whether they are the "Haves" or the "Have-Nots."

Victims of the Quest for Utopia

As the 1997 opus, *The Black Book of Communism*, points out, Communist regimes murdered between 85 million and 100 million people during the twentieth century – a number far in excess of those slaughtered by the Nazis. These victims died in systematic programs of class, racial and ideological genocide – crimes against humanity on an incredible, monumental scale.[6]

And yet, as former Communist François Furet argues in *The Passing of an Illusion*, Stalin was able to mask the terror of the Soviet state, and even widen its appeal to many Americans and Europeans, by cloaking his butchery in the mantle of anti-fascism.[7]

The Soviet empire's abuse of the environment has likewise become legendary, as the truth about pollution throughout the former USSR has come out. When the "iron curtain" was finally torn down, we saw environmental devastation in Russia and Eastern Europe on scales unknown to the rest of the world: coal being burned with no emission controls whatsoever; lakes and rivers turned into lifeless cesspools of chemical and fecal pollution; deforestation on so great a scale it was visible to astronauts in outer space.

Against this backdrop, one cannot but be amazed by the late Earth First activist Judi Bari's bald assertion that, "If we don't overthrow capitalism, we don't have a chance of saving the world ecologically. I think it is possible to have an ecologically sound society under socialism. I don't think it's possible under capitalism."[8] Apparently, she never had the opportunity to visit Poland, Smolensk or the former East Germany to witness their version of EarthCare firsthand.

Those who roll their eyes and argue that these Green Party USA ideas could never take root in the U.S. should note that Nader's presidential candidacy in 2000 picked up enough votes from liberals to elect Texas Governor George W. Bush as president of the United States. Nader and other Green leaders knew that Vice President Al Gore was closer to their beliefs than Bush was. But the Greens had no interest in electing Gore and taking more moderate steps toward their radical goals – just as the most determined attackers of corporations have no interest in compromise.

Gore's efforts to appeal to Nader to accept moderation and drop out of the presidential race were as useless as appeals by corporations to radical attackers to accept reasonable concessions and halt their assaults. Attackers are in the business of attacking and winning – not compromising.

Next, take a long, hard look at what the Greens Party has accomplished in Europe. The "greens" now share power in many European countries, and their favorite whipping boys are the corporate executives who ignored the Green Movement when something could have been done about it.

European corporations opted for appeasement. The only remaining question is, who is going to be whipped next?

American businesses had better wake up and smell the menacing dogs before their execs find themselves in the same boat as their brethren across the Atlantic. Corporate executives who understand the threat posed by attackers like the Green Party, Greenpeace, Sierra Club, Health Care Without Harm, Environmental Working Group, Earth First, the Animal Liberation Front (ALF) and Earth Liberation Front (ELF) must also recognize that efforts to launch a counter-attack will require a dramatic shift in how they conduct battlefield operations.

- **First**, they must reject the peddlers of appeasement and spin.
- **Second**, they must accept the reality that their adversaries are playing by a different set of rules.
- **Third**, they must recognize their attackers' strengths and weaknesses.
- **Fourth**, they must be prepared to embrace and exploit the attackers' own rules and tactics to achieve an advantage on the battlefield. Business people often complain that all they want is a level playing field. That should *not* be the goal. The goal should be superiority on the playing field.

The Power Plays that follow are powerful weapons that companies, industry groups and determined citizens can use to beat back their attackers and survive in the 21st century.

Power Play 1: Flash your brass knuckles. Let the attackers worry about how you will use them – and whether they are real or illusory.

When Greenpeace activists want to drive a consumer products company toward appeasement, what do they do? They tell the firm's executives that thousands of Rainbow Warriors will put skull-and-crossbones stickers on the company's products at retail stores, worldwide. Then, just to make the point, they select a single retail store near the company's headquarters; send in a couple of paid organizers and slap stickers on a few products within camera range of local television crews.

What does the company do? It plays "Let's Make a Deal," because the corporate leaders assume that Greenpeace has hundreds of thousands of members around the planet with nothing better to do than spend time on the sticker brigade. Is there any evidence that Greenpeace is capable of carrying out such a threat? No. In fact there is plenty of evidence to suggest that the Rainbow Warriors are in crisis – wounded but still dangerous.

According to Britain's *The Sunday Times,* "Greenpeace International has lost more than 1.6 million members and has seen its income plummet by £30 million" ($45 million).[9] Its executive director left, the entire board of Greenpeace USA resigned, and one of its own founders, Dr. Patrick Moore, has repeatedly attacked the organization for being "dominated by leftwingers and extremists who disregard science in the pursuit of environmental purity." That does not mean Greenpeace should be taken lightly. It does mean flashing your brass knuckles is a far better tactic than pre-emptive appeasement.

Power Play 1 can be a powerful weapon in the hands of a company that is prepared to defend its product.

What should the company do? Inform Greenpeace that its threatened attack on a perfectly safe product is nothing short of extortion, and that the company intends to: 1) notify law enforcement authorities and retailers of the threat; 2) continue its *ongoing* investigation in preparation for litigation; 3) make the company's financial and legal resources available to any retailer who elects to prosecute Greenpeace and its members for destroying private property; and 4) alert pro-business, pro-progress activist groups that can effectively pillory Greenpeace for its hypocrisy, fraud and misdeeds.

Will your middle managers and public relations consultants lose bladder control when they hear about the company's response to Greenpeace? Oh, yes. Will the retail stores appreciate the show of force? Far more than they would appreciate your company caving in to the threat. Is it possible that Greenpeace will re-think its tactic? Yes, especially if Greenpeace's lawyers are informed that the firm doesn't take kindly to extortion. And your customers will cheer!

Keep in mind that most attackers assume corporations have extensive legal, financial and investigative resources. Let Greenpeace worry about whether those resources will actually be used. Let them worry about how long the company has been investigating, whether there is a whistle-blower in their midst, and what the firm's investigators have uncovered.

Power Play 1 also comes into play when attackers exploit the investor relations trump card. "Do what we say or we'll introduce a resolution at your next shareholders meeting and force you to do it." Think about this threat before you sound the signal for retreat.

Who maintains an ongoing relationship with your shareholders? Your company, not some ragtag band of attackers. How will a majority of your shareholders react when they get wind that some activist group is trying to dictate corporate policy? How will they respond if you roll over and bark at the moon every time some activist group makes a demand? You already know the answers to those questions.

What to do? Be prepared to introduce a company-sponsored resolution that rejects the demands of the activists. Tell the attackers you will meet them at High Noon at the stockholders meeting. Bring in independent experts to ridicule the attacker's resolution. Tell your investor relations people you want to kick butt and take names, or their butts and their names will no longer be associated with your company.

Prepare a clear, simple message for the media. Make sure it spells out, in no uncertain terms, why the attackers' resolution is a terrible idea, why it's impractical and why it's bad for shareholders, customers, employees, families and children. Bring in clergy, consumer advocates and other independent experts to back up your points and take on the attackers. If the assault has international ramifications, an impoverished African, Bangladeshi or Chilean family (live or on tape) would make it crystal clear who's wearing the white hats.

You're uncomfortable with this? Ask the good folks at Novartis whether they achieved any benefits from giving in to the activists on genetically engineered foods. Novartis is one of the world's leading agricultural biotechnology companies and the parent company of Gerber.

It may boggle the mind, but Novartis Consumer Health actually sent a letter to Greenpeace informing the Rainbow Warriors that, effective June 30, 2000, it stopped producing food containing genetically engineered ingredients.[10] The letter was leaked to *The New York Times*. (Who could have done that?) *Times* reporter Andrew Pollack succeeded in getting Novartis to confirm the decision and then wrote, "The move could put Novartis in a delicate spot, because its agricultural division continues to sell genetically modified seeds...Novartis is a member of a coalition of agricultural biotechnology companies that is spending $50 million to defend the safety of such crops."[11]

To add insult, Greenpeace issued a news release taking credit for the Novartis cave-in, attacking the company's genetically engineered Bt corn variety and highlighting the fact that Novartis was caught speaking out of both sides of its corporate mouth. The news release quoted Greenpeace activist Charles Margulis: "Novartis sells genetically engineered seed to American farmers, then turns around and tells those farmers it won't buy the food produced from the seed.... Novartis simply must stop duping farmers and contaminating the environment – and the food supply – by ending its production and sale of genetically engineered seeds."[12] Talk about a short honeymoon.

So Novartis gets a black eye. Farmers get the shaft. Greenpeace gets infusions of cash from gullible citizens, agenda-driven foundations and profit-seeking producers of "organic foods." Biotech R&D suffers. Monarch butterflies – which recent studies prove would not have been harmed by Bt genes in corn – get treated to aerial sprayings of pesticides (or Bt powder!), to control corn borers. And consumers get to pay more for corn.

Among the many self-proclaimed "experts" working tirelessly to "save" farmers and consumers from the "threat" of genetically modified plants is Vandana Shiva, professor of physics at a university in India. This anti-biotech activist believes organic farming could eliminate the widespread starvation that, in her view, is a direct result of the fabled "green revolution."

While on a tour of biotechnology company Rice-Tec's facilities and experimental fields in Texas, Ms. Shiva commented: "The plants look unhappy. The rice plants at home look very happy."

To which a Rice-Tec representative replied: "We harvested the rice in August. Those are weeds."[13]

Ford Motor Company has also learned about courtship, commitment and one-night stands, Rainbow Warrior style. The company invested billions developing natural gas, hybrid, electric and fuel cell vehicles that get far better mileage and emit far less pollution; streamlining its assembly line processes to reduce energy demands and effluents; and taking the lead on dozens of other environmental initiatives. It spent millions more in a multi-year effort to enhance its corporate image on safety and ecological issues.

Chairman William Ford, Jr. even gave a major speech at a Greenpeace business conference in October 2000, underscoring his company's commitment to doing even more for the environment.

What did the company get for its efforts? Almost a year to the day after its acrimonious divorce from Novartis, Greenpeace launched a vitriolic attack on Ford Motors, for having failed to parade arm-in-arm with the churlish Warriors in support of the Kyoto global warming treaty. Ford doesn't buy the radicals' theory that a climate Armageddon is about to befall us – or that we must accept the wrenching social and economic impacts that the Kyoto Protocol will cause. (See Chapter 11.) Greenpeace, on the other hand, sees Kyoto as merely the "first step" in slashing energy use and economic development even more drastically.

So the organization disavowed by founder Patrick Moore organized a hate-Ford email campaign and protests at the company's dealerships, demanding that it endorse Kyoto. Greenpeace climate campaign czar Kert Davies ranted that "Ford's green rhetoric is like a hood ornament – it may look pretty, but it does nothing for performance. Ford's current position leaves them in the same camp as GM, ExxonMobil and the other corporate polluters of the world."[14] And Ford ended up like a male praying mantis at the end of a courtship ritual – getting eaten alive by its former lover.

What's the lesson here? What happens to companies that cave to the demands of attackers is entirely predictable. More demands. Public misrepresentations of the "deal." Critical news coverage. Another attack.

The end result? CEOs who engage in appeasement are often treated like the real Neville Chamberlain who was ousted from Parliament to cries of, "Depart, I say; and let us have done with you. In the name of God – go!" And their employees, shareholders and customers get left to fend for themselves on the beaches of Dunkirk.

Power Play 2: Execute the unexpected.

If you remember none of the other rules in this book, remember this one. Follow *Power Play 2,* and you will cause confusion, fear, chaos and retreat within the attacker's ranks.

What do attackers expect a corporate target to do when an attack is launched? They expect company executives to stop acting like a team, and start acting like green infantry troops in a full rout, all focused on self-preservation.

If the company reacts at all, the attackers expect the target to respond slowly and defensively. They expect the firm to communicate convoluted messages laced with scientific terms; messages devoid of emotion. They assume the company will refuse media requests for a spokesperson and issue a bland statement, instead. If by some odd twist of fate a corporate representative does go before the news cameras, the attackers expect to see a silver-haired male in a pin-stripe suit from the "50s" generation. Get the picture? In short, the attackers do not expect any down-side risk to their behavior.

What won't the attackers expect? Rapid action. A message with a wallop. Aggressive media relations. An effective, credible spokesperson. A serious counter-attack. A serious downside risk to their behavior.

Think of an attack as a boxing match, and your corporation as the defending champ. The challenger has studied videotapes of all your fights, and trained to respond to your usual moves. The best way to throw him off is to adopt new tactics, hit him before he can hit you, and counterpunch furiously against his blows. Gentle words won't persuade him to back off. You need to knock him flat on his back – and preferably, break his jaw.

Speed is everything in boxing – and it is just as vital in mounting a rapid response to an attack on a corporation. If a boxer stands in the ring and absorbs blows while he tries to think of a brilliant strategy to respond, he will be too battered and bloody in a very short time to do his attacker any harm. Same with a corporation.

I have often seen corporate executives mull over my firm's advice for days or even weeks, while their company is subjected to withering attacks that brand it a villain in the public's mind. Finally, after the lawyers and consultants and Neville Chamberlains have all weighed in – and the corporation's crisis has gone from bad to worse – the executives take our advice. Too late. Unfortunately, a counterpunch that could be a knockout blow in Round Two of the fight becomes a glancing blow in Round Eight. Too many unanswered blows by an attacker will weaken even the strongest corporation.

The War Room that Bill Clinton's presidential campaign created in the 1992 election can serve as a model of the swift and powerful "counterattack machine" that corporations need in times of crisis. The Clinton campaign resolved to let no attack go unanswered.

The Clintonites' goal was to respond to attacks within the same news cycle, blunting the power of the attacks as much as possible, and making sure that readers and viewers would hear the Clinton defense at the same time they heard the attack. This made Clinton – aptly nicknamed Slick Willy by his opponents – like a fast-moving boxer executing a strategy of stick-and-move. In the memorable words of Muhammed Ali, Clinton's strategy was to "float like a butterfly and sting like a bee."

Stopping the attackers is all about *creating risk*. Creating risk usually requires tactics that violate the enemy's expectations. Tactics that stop attackers in their tracks can range from frat-boy high jinks to legal prosecution, and everything in between. It doesn't matter on which end of the continuum tactics fall. If they are legal and will achieve the mission, they are worth executing.

I recall an attacker's outdoor news conference that was completely neutralized by a mime and a fortuitous fender-bender.

It happened in a public park across the street from the target's Washington, D.C. offices. The camera crews showed up to record the attacker lambasting industry for filling up landfills and burying civilization in garbage. The mime, hired from a local talent agency, jumped in front of the cameras with mime-like weirdness when the speaker started her harangue. And just as the attacker was about to deliver her main message, two cars on an adjacent street happened to collide, setting off a cacophony of horn blowing and obscenities. The resulting circus proved to be well outside what the media-hound activists expected or were prepared to cope with.

Was the mime tactic immature and juvenile? You betcha. But no more immature than some of the stunts the attackers pull.

The result was no news coverage and a very frustrated adversary. There was one added benefit. Everyone involved in executing the caper really enjoyed the experience (see *Power Play 4*).

Given the success achieved by this particular tactic, was there an outbreak of mime attacks at future news conferences? No. The mime, according to credible sources, was unceremoniously retired from active service.

Perhaps next time, pro-business grassroots organizations might hang a banner in front of PETA's Norfolk, Virginia headquarters. I think it could say: "People Haters!" or "Research Wreckers!" or "Moral Lepers!" or even "Malicious Medical Meddlers!"

It would provide a marvelous backdrop for speeches and protests calling attention to the radicals' ethical dilemma. The news media would find it hard to resist, and revelations like those chronicled in Chapter 2 (as well as countless more that doubtless lurk just beneath the surface of this vast iceberg) would likely spawn many more investigations and stories.

Even among the generally very liberal journalistic elites are many whose desire is to uncover the truth, advance their careers and sell newspapers and ad time. A few clever tactics and well-placed tips could work wonders.

Clearly, the only real limits to unconventional tactics like these are the imaginations and fortitude of companies that might be thinking about venturing into these uncharted waters.

How would the corporate Nevilles react to a battle plan that included nasty banners or a weird, discourteous mime? Their reaction would go something like this: "These tactics are out of the question. They are beneath the dignity of our company."

Not surprisingly, the Nevilles prefer defeat with "honor."

During the 1997 global climate change negotiations in Kyoto, Japan, Friends of the Earth (FOE) presented the Global Climate Coalition with a "scorched earth" award. The Committee For A Constructive Tomorrow (CFACT) and Competitive Enterprise Institute (CEI) turned the trophy into a "scorched economy" award, which it presented to FOE at a press conference, forcing the green radicals to participate in a well-publicized debate that was attended by hundreds of journalists and conferees. The debate dramatically revealed the complete absence of science behind the greens' alarmist claims.[15]

Another thing activists rarely experience is an attack by the news media, or by one of their own. When Greenpeace founder Dr. Patrick Moore started criticizing the Rainbow Warriors and their fellow travelers for contaminating the environmental agenda with leftist politics, the activists became completely unglued.

According to an article about Dr. Moore by Anthony Browne, published in *The Observer* on May 21, 2000, "Greenpeace has declared that he has 'gone off the rails.' The Forest Action Network has even dedicated an Internet web site to proving that 'Patrick Moore is a big fat liar' featuring pictures of him with a Pinocchio nose."

Browne quotes Chris Genovali, of the Western Canada Wilderness Committee, on his reaction to Moore's criticisms: "Each time I read something by this megalomaniacal crackpot, I get the urge to hurl."[16] You be the judge about who has gone off the rails in this instance.

One final example of *Power Play 2* in action comes from the City of Brotherly Love. When the Republican Party pulled up stakes following its Y2K convention, left behind were about 360 protesters who had been charged with misdemeanor or felony offenses. When their lawyers asked the Philadelphia D.A. to drop all criminal charges and eliminate bail for the jailed demonstrators, they received quite a shock. Philadelphia District Attorney Lynne Abrahams told the lawyers to "get a life, it ain't gonna happen."[17]

During convention protests, 15 police officers were injured and nearly 30 city vehicles were vandalized. Unlike Seattle and Washington, DC, where charges against many demonstrators were dropped, Philadelphia vowed to practice tough brotherly love by throwing the book at those taken into custody.

When was the last time a corporation pressed charges against protesters for destroying property and putting lives in jeopardy? Nevilles.

Power Play 3: Exploit your strengths. Offset your weaknesses.

Many people in corporations have been indoctrinated with a decision-making model that is slow, methodical, incremental and, above all, risk-averse. This model works pretty well when a company is managing complex technical issues, developing new products or launching new marketing initiatives. It stinks when a firm is under attack and decisions must be made rapidly.

Asking people who were baptized, confirmed and ordained in the zero-risk culture to make rapid, high-risk/high-gain decisions in response to an attack, often without complete information, is just plain stupid. Ordering them to execute tactics that are confrontational rather than collegial may be akin to ordering a Cub Scout troop to do battle with a street gang.

Executing tactics that are foreign to your people may breed fear, confusion and chaos, and may also result in a collapse of internal communications. You can't turn Nevilles into Winstons. Don't even try.

That doesn't mean kowtow in submission. It does mean using people outside your company who know how to kick butt and take names.

My favorite example of a *Power Play 3* violation comes from the world of politics. Remember when some half-wit decided to give presidential candidate Michael Dukakis a ride in a tank, to visually demonstrate the candidate's commitment to our national defense? The ride was well outside the liberal Democrat's personal experience. When the footage was aired on network television that night, Dukakis looked like one of those spring-loaded clowns that pop out of a jack-in-the-box. What a disaster!

If you discover that the actions required to achieve the mission are beyond the competence of your front line soldiers, it may be time to hire a few mercenaries to get the job done.

There are highly credible people in the real world who like nothing better than going toe-to-toe with the attackers. These are people who have a deep and abiding respect for science, free enterprise and the rule of law. They also have a deep and abiding disdain for the Luddites, nannies, neurotics, professional victims and con artists who prey upon consumers, taxpayers and corporations. If you keep these pit bulls well fed, and give them the respect they deserve, they will save the Nevilles of your organization from the embarrassment of staining their shorts the next time you issue an order that requires hand-to-hand combat.

There is, of course, an alternative to going outside the corporation for Type-W (Winston) personalities. You can hire a few to keep in reserve for those special occasions when circumstances require an unconventional response to an external threat. This small cadre of Type-Ws will serve the company well when the attackers come calling. Besides that, they are fun to watch in the corporate environment.

It's not difficult to spot Type-Ws in a boardroom. They look like caged jackals when the topic turns to "ethics." They stab their croissants with those little white plastic knives when someone mentions public relations. They doodle little Rorschach images when the lawyers start pontificating. And their eyes glaze over and roll back when someone suggests sitting down with the attackers to "meet them half way."

Throw the Type-Ws some raw meat on occasion and they will protect you not only from the spin doctors and zero-risk choir boys, but also from the professional attackers seeking the opportunity to draw first blood.

Power Play 4: If you are forced to plunder and pillage, make sure your offensive works and your people enjoy it.

Attack groups often stage media events that involve circus-style antics. Banners are unfurled on chemical plant smoke stacks. Placard-wielding demonstrators disrupt a stockholders meeting on roller blades. Activists in goofy costumes chant anti-business slogans while scaling the walls of a corporation's headquarters. Why all the hoopla? Because the attackers understand *Power Play 4*. These stunts not only make for great television, but also for happy, satisfied protesters. When Ted Hayes, a long-time Los Angeles activist, visited a Ruckus Society boot camp, he told a *Los Angeles Times* reporter: "It's a party. It's middle-class kids having a ball."[18]

Business people held responsible for executing tactics must enjoy the action. If the tacticians don't enjoy their work, the tactics will ultimately fail.

Suppose the activists were confronted by poor people from a small Louisiana town, who were kept jobless because white, middle-class protestors stopped the construction of a plastics plant? How do you suppose they and the news media would react? Maybe the experience would take the joy out of protesting for the self-anointed radicals. For your employees, on the other hand, it would put some fun back into working for a corporation and helping to protect the less fortunate by giving the local playground bully a good bloody nose.

The Louisianans could even present the protestors and their white, middle-class organization with an award, engraved plaque and certificate suitable for framing. The award might be a huge screw labeled Greenpeace, twisted into a black or Hispanic doll. The certificate could say, "Congratulations Greenpeace: The world's greatest promoter of poverty and environmental racism." A press release could explain the award in greater detail.

The obstructionist Nevilles will say that wacky, confrontational tactics like those used by activists could never be pulled off by silver-haired corporate executives in pinstripe suits.

Sure, and that's why hundreds of these same silver-haired, up-tight alpha males participate in so-called wilderness "team building" exercises where they fly through the trees on zip wires, crawl through the mud on their bellies and splatter each other with paint guns.

Remember, the arsenal of possible tactical weapons is limited only by your creativity and *cajones*. If some are too wacky for your tastes, establish ongoing relationships with grassroots groups that are more comfortable with them – or employ tactics that are more up your alley, but still more effective than pre-emptive capitulation and other Nevillean methods.

Here are a couple of real-life examples of enjoyable tactics at work. In 1999, environmental activists converged in Louisiana to protest that state's chemicals industry. Their tactic? Confront the governor with a plate of "toxic" fish. Catch the state's top executive on camera refusing to eat the filets.

Thanks to effective intelligence gathering, the tables were turned on the attackers. The activists were met by an aide to the governor who graciously accepted the plate of fish, and right on camera proceeded to eat their lunch. Literally. The attackers were dumbstruck. Bystanders laughed. The news media had a field day.

In 1995, the Equal Employment Opportunity Commission demanded that the Hooters restaurant chain replace 40 percent of its waitresses with men. Company executives, observed columnist Deroy Murdock, "hooted" at the suggestion – and arranged a press conference and advertisements, featuring a hairy-chested male waiter dressed in hot pants and blond wig. In one hand, he held a plate of chicken wings, in the other a sign that read: "Washington – get a grip!" A humiliated EEOC dropped the case.[19]

Even members of Congress are not immune to clever tactics or laughter. In 1978, Congressman John Seiberling of Ohio staged a series of field hearings around Colorado to promote his plan to designate millions of acres as wilderness and permanently ban farming, ranching, logging, oil drilling, mining, wheelchairs, and all forms of motorized access and recreation. Coloradans in general, and local citizens in particular, opposed his ham-handed scheme, but Seiberling was adamant. He brought a small army of environmental activists to a motel near Durango, where he had arranged a televised press conference.

As the congressman took his seat in front of the cameras, some 50 local citizens (many of them the size of NFL linemen) filled the front of the narrow room. Seiberling looked up to make his opening remarks, and not a friendly face did he see. His smirk disappeared, but he launched ahead, then took the first question. "Why are you trying to lock up our land and destroy our community?" The "eco-imperialist" from Ohio mumbled a non-answer, and pointed to another local, who said: "You didn't answer my friend's question. After you do, then I've got another question." From there, the press conference went downhill. A couple days later, Mr. Seiberling slipped while crossing a mountain stream. Guess how many people rushed forward, to help him out of the frigid water and get him some dry clothing?

Power Play 5: Keep sending in new plays from the bench.

Whether they are activists or corporate executives, the average human being can only remain interested in an activity for so long. Attacks on industry have lasted for decades. For example, environmental activists have been seeking to eliminate chlorine chemistry and the industries that depend on it for more than a decade. How have they maintained their enthusiasm for this long-standing campaign to remove "Cl" from the Periodic Table of Elements? New tactics. Different targets.

The activists attacked paper companies who use chlorine to bleach their products. They tried to convince governments to stop using chlorine to disinfect drinking water. Then they discovered that chlorine is used to make vinyl (polyvinyl chloride) plastic, so they attacked vinyl. They claimed that vinyl isn't recyclable. They said vinyl produces dioxin. They charged that vinyl contains heavy metals. They alleged that compounds used to soften vinyl are dangerous. The activists have attacked vinyl toys, medical devices, containers and construction materials. Get the picture?

Moving targets and changing tactics have prevented boredom in the ranks of the attackers. They've also kept industry off balance and on the defensive. The same rule applies to corporations, their allies and the attackers' many grassroots opponents.

Not surprisingly, the allegations against vinyl and chlorine aren't supported by science and real-world experience. In fact, the real health threat appears to be linked to the advice offered by the activists, not to the products being attacked. In 1991, Peru experienced its first cholera outbreak in 100 years and thousands of people died,[20] after government officials listened to radicals and the U.S. Environmental Protection Agency and decided to stop chlorinating its water supply. Pounding the table a few times with these facts, showing photos of real people with real names, and playing a videotape of bereaved family members would be a dramatic change of pace for any company.

Here's another switch that worked. For years, the Competitive Enterprise Institute and industry challenged the prevailing myths about dioxin. Then in 1999, CEI seized the opportunity to take a different tack, when the oh so politically correct and environmentally conscious folks at Ben and Jerry's proudly announced that their fine ice cream would henceforth be sold in dioxin-free packages.

There are two problems with this, television reporter John Stossel and the Competitive Enterprise Institute pointed out. Few people eat the packages, and the high-fat, heart-attack-in-a-carton ice cream itself is loaded with dioxin – at levels far higher than EPA considers safe.[22]

Ben & Jerry's promotional literature says "dioxin is known to cause cancer, genetic and reproductive defects and learning disabilities... The only safe level of dioxin exposure is no exposure at all." However, according to a 1999 study, a single serving of B&J's World's Best Vanilla Ice Cream contains almost 200 times more dioxin than the "virtually safe [daily] dose" determined by the EPA. Actually, dioxin is a by-product of industrial processes and is also created naturally through combustion of plant materials. Even EPA now acknowledges that concerns about its health and carcinogenic dangers were vastly overblown.[23]

The Rainforest Action Network (RAN) and several other environmental groups also got surprised not long ago by a trick play sent in from the bench. They had chosen March 28th, 2001 as a national day of action against Staples. Their goal was to picket, harass, intimidate and perhaps "ethically shoplift" the Office Superstore, to "persuade" it to stop selling products made from any kind of paper that might trouble ultra-sensitive radicals.

Not only did they get little media attention, despite RAN's $3 million in annual revenues,[24] they also couldn't get gullible high school and college kids to protest and harass people at the 100 stores their press release had promised they would invade.

Worst of all, dozens of citizen activists showed up at Staples stores all around the county to show their *support* for the office supply company's principled stance against the extremists, and its excellent, environmentally sound operations. These newly minted activists bought thousands of dollars worth of paper and other products, while verbally applauding employees. They also gave store managers notes and letters saying the environmental groups' claims were misleading and unethical, Staples' efforts on behalf of customers and the environment were laudable, and the company's refusal to cave in to extortion was something to be emulated.

But the truly amazing thing about this effort was its spontaneous grassroots nature. It came about because a few people sent email messages to their friends, neighbors and members in small local groups. These people contacted others, and the word spread. These once apathetic citizens have now formed a Stop RAN coalition, to counter the radical predators and support the industries they attack, using public education, media contacts and direct consumer action (buying the companies' products, while boycotting companies that cater to the militants).

Imagine what might have transpired, had these citizen activists been well organized or supported financially by a type-Winston company or foundation.

Imagine what might transpire, if opponents of drilling in the Arctic National Wildlife Refuge were suddenly confronted by some of the people who actually live there. Inupiat Eskimos like Democratic state senator Donald Olson, M.D. strongly support development and emphasize that the oil companies "have had 30 years of environmentally sensitive dealings" with North Slope Natives. They resent "having shackles put around" them, "being held as economic hostages by people from the Lower 48," and being "relegated to Third World conditions, where people have to melt ice to bathe ... and use 5-gallon containers for sanitation," because they do not have toilets, running water or a sewer system.

Eskimos near the Prudhoe Bay oil field have seen their standard of living increase dramatically, and those in ANWR want theirs to improve, as well.

The Eskimos acknowledge that Gwich'in Indians claim development would threaten their lifestyle. But the Indians live hundreds of miles away, the Eskimos point out, and once leased 1.8 million acres of Gwich'in tribal lands for oil development. (No oil was found.) The Eskimos also note that environmental foundations and pressure groups have given the Gwich'ins thousands of dollars and helped them raise thousands more, to place ads in major newspapers, appear in television ads and testify on Capitol Hill in opposition to ANWR oil exploration.[25]

Producing your own Eskimo TV ads, enabling Eskimo mayors and corporate chairmen to speak at news conferences and congressional hearings, and featuring them in news releases and articles, are just the kind of unexpected plays you should keep sending in from the bench.

So, where can you find enough additional fresh ideas to keep up your counterattack against these predators, and keep your team motivated? Read on. Then build coalitions with think tanks and grassroots groups, and check out Web sites like www.counterprotest.net, www.cei.org, www.cfact.org and www.heartland.org, which track issues like these and have links to many other Web sites and organizations.

Power Play 6: Make them sweat your threat.

When Saul Alinsky sought to gain concessions from Chicago Mayor Richard Daley, Sr., he threatened to send protestors to tie up the toilets at what was then the world's busiest airport, O'Hare International. The operative word here is "threatened." The tactic was never executed because, within 48 hours of the threat being delivered, the nation's most powerful mayor capitulated.

When past attacks on industry are analyzed, it becomes clear that marketplace damage is usually inflicted by a target industry's customers, not by government regulators or consumers in general. Customer decisions that translate into damage are often in response to mere threats from the attackers, not the actual carrying out of those threats.

When Greenpeace attacked phthalates (softeners in plastics) used in vinyl baby toys, damage in the form of lost markets was inflicted by toy companies, like Mattel. The toy makers caved to Greenpeace threats. American consumers did not panic. U.S. regulators concluded that the amount of phthalates ingested by small children "does not even come close to a harmful level."[26] But the corporate Nevilles and Barbies apparently found the Greenpeace threat too terrifying to stomach. They couldn't wait to capitulate.

The application of *Power Play 6* is, in fact, a form of psychological warfare. The objective is to create risk in the mind of the target; to force a reaction that will undermine the target's tactical position on the battlefield, allowing the attacker to take new ground.

There is only one effective defense against *Power Play 6*. No reaction. When Mattel's corporate leadership responded to the Greenpeace threat with appeasement, the company's decision to stop selling certain vinyl baby products created a snowball effect throughout the industry and among regulators worldwide. Greenpeace reaped the rewards.

How could a company use *Power Play 6* to create risk for an attacker? Leak word to the adversary that the company has a mole inside the organization. Watch them squirm. Or, put the word out that the company is investigating financial links between the attacker and corporate competitors. For activist groups that act as hired guns for predatory business competitors, the threat that someone is about to blow their cover can have a chilling effect on future attacks. How do you suppose the Rainforest Action Network (RAN) would react if they learned that a pro-business think tank was preparing a major media, legal, Internet and congressional offensive, showing that they had been abusing their tax exempt status?[27]

Because many business executives resist issuing direct threats to activist groups, there is a compelling need for credible independent parties to do the job for them. Develop relationships with these organizations, support them financially and with accurate information and insights, and don't be a Neville about utilizing their credibility and capabilities.

Not unlike government agencies, companies and trade associations have been infiltrated with people who commune with attack groups. The trick is to find them. Once the leakers are identified, resist the temptation to terminate them with extreme prejudice. Sure, keep proprietary information out of their reach, but when it's time to deliver misinformation or a credible threat to the other side, bring the pigeons into the inner circle. Then, let the games begin.

My associates and I often take advantage of *Power Play 6* when we work with the less savory types in the news media. Through actions or behind-the-scenes meetings, lawyer to lawyer – not mere words – we convey the message that our client is preparing to take legal action if the reporter knowingly and recklessly disregards the truth (see Chapter 6, *Dissuasion*).

Power Play 7: Turn the enemy's rules into your weapons.

Professional attackers are exceptionally effective at forcing companies to abide by "the rules." They are also very skilled at infiltrating government regulatory agencies and applying political pressure on the regulators responsible for developing and enforcing to the nth degree the rules and regulations that companies are required to follow.

So how well do the professional attackers follow their own ethical guidelines and standards, or the basic rules corporations and the rest of society are expected to follow?

Consider the rules Greenpeace claims to live by, taken from the organization's 1998 annual report: "Our core, immutable values are shared not just with staff and activists, but with supporters. They include independence, non-violence, bearing witness and commitment to peace and the well-being of the natural world. These are our principles."[28]

The organization's public commitment to non-violence attracts many of its youthful supporters and liberal donors to the movement. What would happen if these idealistic members and contributors found out about the group's pension fund investments in oil and chemical companies, and its close connection to the arrest-prone Rainforest Action Network and Earth First? Somehow, this doesn't seem to reflect a very sincere or deep commitment to truth, non-violence, peace, ethics or the well-being of the natural world.

Assuming the group's idealistic members and contributors aren't hardcore ideologues, they might feel uncomfortable just being associated with people who may be this cozy with the likes of Earth First and the Rainforest Action Network. Greenpeace coffers have actually shrunk significantly, as a result of such negative publicity.

What's needed is a Winston who is prepared to demand that Greenpeace not only apologize for any dishonest, unethical, immoral behavior – but also condemn Earth First, the Earth Liberation Front and similar groups for their violent acts. Then take it a step further, and demand that Greenpeace confess its involvement, apologize for past acts, pay reparations, and kick the offenders out of the organization.

Finally, build a business and political coalition that can force Greenpeace to publicly sign a statement, avowing that the group will henceforth obey all laws and hold itself to high standards of honesty, ethics, public disclosure of its operations, and commitment to the needs of humanity, animals and the environment.

The statement could be patterned after the well-known "Sullivan Principles" and the ten-point code of corporate conduct known as the "CERES Principles" (Coalition for Environmentally Responsible Economies). The CERES Principles were forged and promoted by the very activists who, in league with Greenpeace and Earth First, are attacking business as unethical and insensitive to the environment. Surely, they would have no problem committing themselves to more ethical behavior in the future?

Using the same strategy, persuade other environmental attack groups to publicly condemn ELF, ALF, Earth First and similar terrorist organizations; detect and eject any members who advocate or practice violence; root out and terminate any programs that may be funneling money into the violent groups; and cooperate fully with the FBI and other law enforcement groups, to find, arrest, prosecute and jail the terrorists.

What would these intensive, protracted counterattacks accomplish? Non-violent members will get the message that their contributions might end up in the hands of groups that practice violence to "save Mother Earth."

The radical organizations would get the message that the rules have changed, and there's a new sheriff in town: Clean up, or pay the price.

Truly pacifist tree huggers might take their money and support elsewhere. District attorneys might be persuaded to investigate and actually prosecute the groups, legislators and agency heads to hold hearings and enact new rules.

More injured parties might decide to sue for compensatory and punitive damages. Journalists might become less gullible, carry less water for the radicals or even uncover still more damning evidence.

Maybe the real pacifists would join the more conservative National Audubon Society. But before they do that, they certainly ought to read an article published in the *Los Angeles Times Magazine* quoting Brock Evans, who at the time was Audubon's vice president for national issues: "I honor Earth First for having the guts to do the things they do. And, ultimately, we all help each other."[29]

Highlighting the disingenuous and violent activities of Greenpeace activists may also have the effect of driving the group's natural allies off the battlefield. For example, when Lord Peter Melchett, Greenpeace director in the United Kingdom, was arrested in 1999 for vandalism and property destruction aimed at field trials of genetically modified crops, his actions and continuing calls for attacks on British farmers embarrassed other environmentalists to the point that he was condemned by Friends of the Earth.[30]

Actions by the Rainbow Warriors against plant biotechnology also resulted in a high-profile resignation by a noted Greenpeace activist. In his resignation letter, William C. Plaxton, professor of biology and biochemistry at Canada's Queen's University wrote: "...as a plant biochemist and NSERC-funded scientist, I can no longer back an organization such as yours that has recently undertaken such a blanket condemnation, fear-mongering and non-scientific attack against the production and use of genetically modified plants."[31]

What about honesty and ethics in another arena? Do attack groups hold themselves to the same rules of *science* that they expect their corporate targets to follow? Recent news reports quoted one Greenpeace organizer's response to that question. "Our purpose is not to be scientifically correct," he said. "That's the corporation robber-baron's job. Our job is to move the needle and effect radical change."[31]

This attitude also seems to be the guiding principle of many attack groups. Don't bother us with platitudes about facts, honesty, ethics and scientific integrity. What's important in public policy are feelings, ideology, nailing corporate executives to the wall, ending capitalism and reining in our "rampant consumption."

In other words, we favor bad science underwriting spurious regulations.

What specific steps might companies and citizens take to expose the duplicity and make the attackers live up to their own rules? First, find and support articulate spokespersons, and begin building a library of photographs, video clips, statements and sound bites.

Next, utilize news stories, email, Internet Web pages and chat rooms, disenchanted ex-radicals, think tanks, grassroots citizen groups, friendly legislators and regulators, and other resources to ferret out more information, anticipate where the next attacks might come from, and provide fuel and ammunition for your own attack or counterattack.

Next, broadcast what you learn far and wide, via all these avenues and in speeches, talk shows, news releases, interviews, classroom materials and corporate reports.

Support organizations that can prepare independent analyses, file legal actions and field protesters. Insist that legislators conduct investigations and hold hearings.

Bottom line? Corporate Winstons should always look for opportunities to use *Power Play 7* against their activist adversaries. The attackers may not play by the corporate book of rules, but they can be forced to play by rules that often conflict with their public actions – rules the public generally expects all of us to live by.

Power Play 8: Heap scorn, ridicule and humor on those who deserve it.

Humor is almost impossible to defend against. If your adversary becomes the target of jokes by the likes of Jay Leno or David Letterman, you've probably won the war. Funny counter-protests can be even better.

Anti-corporate activist groups generally aren't very good at using humor to scorn their targets directly. That's probably because they tend to be pretty humorless people.

People who consider themselves historically significant (I'm saving the planet, what are *you* doing?) tend not to tolerate laughter when it is directed at them. So ridicule is often a very effective tactic against attackers because it is likely to elicit an irrational, angry response. That's good. So the better the jokes get against them, the merrier it is for everyone else.

The problem for corporate executives is that it's hard for them to dish out a good dose of ridicule. Not unlike their attackers, CEOs are not known for their comedic abilities. I've met quite a few CEOs in my time. Most were genuinely decent and honorable people. But I can't recall a single CEO who would rank high on the "wacky" scale. The job of running a big company just doesn't demand that skill.

But that doesn't mean companies under attack are incapable of subjecting their attackers to a stinging dose of humor if it's justified. It just means the company may have to recruit some wacky mercenaries to execute the tactic.

A great source of "wacky" is a citizen group called the American Land Rights Association, based appropriately in Battle Ground, Washington, and run by a burly eco-battle veteran named Chuck Cushman. He says, "Our job is to make bad plans controversial, to show that people oppose them for good reason, and to do it non-violently." His people also have a hell of a lot of fun doing it.[33]

Cushman's favorite story revolves around a remote field station in the vast Malheur National Wildlife Refuge, baking in the desert some fifty miles south of Burns, Oregon. The federal facility – actually a converted military base – had been used for years by a regional green group as the site of their annual strategy session.

One year, local ranchers got word that the enviro meeting would feature Andy Kerr, leader of Oregon Natural Resources Council. The rumor went that Kerr was to reveal a plan for congressional designation of five million acres in southern Oregon as an official wilderness area. In addition, the striking geological feature known as Steens Mountain would be turned into a national park. That grandiose land grab would mean the removal of every rancher in the region. The ranchers were upset. *Really* upset.

Suzie Hammond, whose Steens Mountain ranch was on Kerr's hit list, called Cushman: "Chuck, can you come down here and turn all this anger into something peaceful?" Chuck got in his car with no idea what to do.

When he arrived at the appointed staging area in Burns, he found nearly 100 cars full of ranchers, loggers, miners and just plain folks, all ready to head for the field station, and confrontation. Two loaded logs trucks rumbled up and two full cattle trucks joined them. Chuck got an idea.

When they arrived at the field station an hour later, they found that some 200 enviros were assembled inside a windowless metal building near the road, with guards at the door to prevent Chuck's contingent from entering. The field station manager dashed from from her office toward the metal building as soon as she saw the rancher convoy pouring into the parking area. When she recognized Cushman in the lead, she called to him, "Thank God it's you. At least things won't get violent."

Cushman sized up the metal building where Andy Kerr was about to announce which Congressman had agreed to introduce the wilderness bill. He asked the cattle truck drivers to back one truck up to the left of the building, the other to the right. The one on the left contained mama cows. The one on the right held their babies. The babies wanted their mamas. The stereo effect was incredible.

Cushman lets go with his famous laugh as he recalls, "The Associated Press story began, 'Through the din of bawling cattle....' Inside, the greens were furious. Outside, everyone was doubled over with laughter. We ruled the media that day. But I can't take credit for this one. Back in Burns a rancher had told me the stunt would work better if we did it this way. Boy, was he ever right. Somehow that wilderness bill never got introduced, and we never found out who agreed to introduce it. The politicos all ran for cover. Chased by the din of bawling cattle. Ho Ho Ho!"

Boot camps for rich white radicals. One of the many barbs that Cushman hurls at environmentalists has caused considerable consternation within the movement and is certainly a topic worth exploiting. Specifically, the charge that environmental activists are, for the most part, "white, bourgeois liberals." This one really hits home, and the activists are hypersensitive to the criticism.

Just prior to the 2000 Democratic Party Convention, *Los Angeles Times* reporter Nicholas Riccardi wrote a lengthy story about a boot camp organized by the Ruckus Society to prepare the protesters for their assault on the Democrats. The organizers sought media coverage of their preparations, perhaps for the purpose of telegraphing their intentions (see *Power Play 6*). However, when it came time for the protest trainees to discuss diversity, the media was barred from the discussion.

According to Riccardi, "the activists regularly retreat from the news media to discuss race, class and power – overlapping topics that touch a raw nerve in some of the participants. Ruckus and many groups that make up the new, roving protest movement are overwhelmingly white, a jarring sameness in a cause that aspires to global significance."[34]

Environmental injustice. Harry Alford, president of the Black Chamber of Commerce, charges environmentalists with "pimping the black community to further their own agenda of a pristine earth at the expense of jobs" in minority communities. Real "environmental justice," he says, would recognize that jobless poor families also have no health insurance, so they often don't see doctors to check out symptoms that could mean breast cancer, pneumonia or other potentially fatal diseases. So more mothers and kids die.[35] Adds John Meredith, son of civil rights leader James Meredith: "Overregulation is the new millennium's preferred brand of institutional racism – and it's being perpetrated in the name of saving the environment."[36]

The growing crusade against urban sprawl also threatens the social and economic gains of minority Americans. Aggressive anti-sprawl policies cause housing costs to soar, severely impair access to affordable housing by low- and moderate-income families, and drastically curtail the rights of minority and other landowners to sell or develop their property or even cut trees on it.

In Richland, South Carolina, black farmers who have owned their land for 100 years or more have grown increasingly angry over a county zoning plan that has slashed the value of their property, just as demand for it is rising. The son of one black landowner, a Baptist minister and Democratic state representative, says "This is a net loss of wealth for poor people." In his view, it is an unconstitutional taking without just compensation. The Sierra Club is unmoved. Its local director says blacks who want to sell their land are "not true farmers," and their views do not need to be taken into account.[37]

Famines R Us. Earth First founder David Foreman argued that "the worst thing we could do about famines in Ethiopia is to give aid – the best thing would be to just let nature seek its own balance, to let the people there just starve."[38]

A lovely sentiment, worthy of a Klansman or Nazi Party member. I wonder what Harry Alford, John Meredith and other decent businessmen, civil rights leaders, politicians and columnists might have to say about that one.

Let them burn dung. Intense opposition by Green Marie Antoinettes to hundreds of hydroelectric dams throughout the developing world has forced peasant women and girls to collect wet cow dung with their bare hands, then dry and burn it in cooking fires.

Not surprisingly, nearly ten million people – half of them infants and children – die slow, agonizing deaths every year from dysentery and other water-borne diseases. Tens of millions of others contract often fatal lung diseases like tuberculosis every year from breathing the infected air, according to the World Health Organization.[39]

How would the attackers and their supporters respond if black leaders, comedians, politicians and columnists cross-examined, ridiculed and vilified them for sponsoring policies that are actually killing women and children in India, Ghana and other developing countries? I suspect they would go ballistic and head for the hills.

Making the world safe for mosquitoes. Malaria was eradicated in the United States in the 1950s, and from the rest of the developed nations and much of Asia and Latin America by the mid 1960s. But the disease is making a ferocious comeback in much of the developing world. Forty percent of the world's population now lives at risk of contracting malaria, and four people die from it every minute, two million every year, most of them children. It is an especially potent killer in Africa, where it is also so debilitating that it severely limits economic growth and strains the health care systems of entire nations.

The disease has spread as a result of population growth and movement, deteriorating health care systems, poor housing, increased resistance of some strains to anti-malarial drugs, and a drastic reduction in the use of DDT as a weapon. "In many parts of the world," a report in *Science News* notes, "this toxicant remains the best hope for reining in malaria. According to the World Health Organization (WHO), each year another 400 million people come down with the parasitic disease. This newly infected group equals the combined populations of the United States, Canada and Mexico."[40]

In response to the exploding epidemic, WHO, UNICEF, the World Bank, Competitive Enterprise Institute and other humanitarian groups began tackling the disease, through organizations like Roll Back Malaria and Africa Fighting Malaria (which coordinates the Save Children from Malaria campaign). Corporations and foundations also joined the effort, all of them advocating the retention of DDT for malaria control in poor areas where the disease is rampant, because DDT is far less expensive and far more effective than substitutes.

But when a number of countries began using DDT once again to bring the epidemic under control, a vocal and powerful consortium of environmental groups (including the World Wildlife Fund) issued an "urgent call" for a total, permanent, global ban on the use of DDT.

The developing countries and anti-malaria groups were outraged. Charging that the Green militants were condemning millions of people to death, they embarrassed the extremists and forced them to moderate their original proposal, back off from their demands for a phase-out date for the chemical, and agree that DDT should not be banned in countries with serious malaria problems.[41]

However, the extreme anti-DDT lobby refused to moderate its other demands. As a result, many American donor groups still refuse to fund any humanitarian efforts that include DDT, even in countries like Mozambique, where the disease is rampant. Even worse, the United Nations Environmental Program, under the Convention on Persistent Organic Pollutants, requires that the chemical may not be imported or exported. Thus, any nation that wants to use DDT must build a manufacturing facility, which many cannot afford to do.

Moreover, any nation actually using DDT must comply with strict, burdensome reporting requirements. Together, these requirements are likely to discourage many countries from using this life-saving pesticide, regardless of the human death toll that will inevitably result.

Consequently, the most effective and least expensive insecticide remains largely unavailable, largely out of a longstanding, but misplaced belief that it carries unacceptable health and environmental risks. The facts, however, do not support these dire concerns.

- The original decision to ban DDT is directly linked to actual and hypothetical environmental effects of excessive government spraying programs in the 1950s and 1960s. (The thinning of eagle and falcon eggs, due to excessive spraying, is well documented.) The use of pesticides and other chemicals is much more carefully controlled today, and the homes of an entire tropical country can be treated with the same amount of DDT that once might have been used on a single farm or community.[42]

- Millions of Allied soldiers, all the inhabitants of Naples and Tokyo, and former Nazi concentration camp inmates were sprayed with DDT, to prevent typhus or rid them of lice, notes Dr. Kelvin Kemm, co-founder of Africa Fighting Malaria. No cancers or other harmful effects have ever been detected above normal rates in these groups or other humans.[43]

Facts like these, however, rarely persuade environmental attack groups. A comment once made by Dr. Charles Wurster, former chief scientist for the Environmental Defense Fund, is illustrative. Asked if he thought a ban on DDT might result in the use of far more dangerous chemicals and an explosion of malaria cases in Sri Lanka, he replied: "Probably – so what? People are the cause of all the problems. We have too many of them. We need to get rid of some of them, and this is as good a way as any."[44]

How often have the manufacturers of pesticide products used this information to ridicule the attackers and call them to account? How often have they encouraged leaders of the America's black or south Asian communities to speak out? Have they ever helped organize protests or press conferences overseas – or by immigrants from these countries here in the United States? Have they ever helped African or Asian community leaders produce videotapes of these events for news media in the U.S. and Europe?

When the Environmental Working Group and World Wildlife Fund next gather to rail against pesticides, maybe they should be confronted with caskets representing the millions of people who die each year from malaria because DDT is no longer available to kill the mosquitoes that spread the deadly disease. When Friends of the Earth members rally to protest World Bank funding of a dam in India, caskets, body bags and photographs of disease-ridden babies and children could remind them of the millions who die every year from TB and water-borne diseases, as a result of their inhumane policies.

Scornful humor is another largely untapped opportunity to turn the tables on the radicals, challenge the views of the anointed elites and force the world to confront the truth, instead of comfortably hiding behind the bald assertions of politically correct misanthropes.

Power Play 9: Never let up. Keep the pressure on.

When attackers apply constant pressure on industry, the effect is often devastating. Business executives have short attention spans on the battlefield. They want the conflict to end as quickly as possible, so that they can return to the corporate home front and conduct business as usual. When predators sustain their attack for a long period of time, the target often capitulates.

The pest control industry is the poster child of *Power Play 9*. The attack on pesticides by activists, their friends in government, and the news media has been relentless. It's the environmentalist equivalent of The Hundred Years War. These folks are tenacious, if nothing else.

When the EPA used the Food Quality Protection Act to justify a complete review of 39 registered organophosphate pesticides, the pesticide manufacturers attempted to cut their losses and avoid another public relations disaster. First, they "voluntarily" withdrew chlorpyrifos from residential use. Then Novartis, the company that makes diazinon (and Bt corn), "voluntarily" cancelled its registration for all indoor uses of the product, even though Novartis says the EPA found no specific health risks linked to registered uses of the product.[45]

The company justified its action by claiming that the investment required to conduct new research requested by the EPA was not supported by sales to the indoor market sector. "We regret that Novartis has had to make the business decision," a company spokesman said. "We regret the loss of this valuable tool, particularly for our colleagues in the ornamental and structural pest control markets."[46] The pesticides industry might have added: We regret that thousands of homes will be infested with termites, including the now virtually unstoppable Formosan termites, costing homeowners and their insurers hundreds of millions of dollars in property losses every year.

How can companies subjected to constant attacks avoid tedium and the urge to retreat? New tactics. New people. New messages. Period.

Many of the industry people engaged in the battle over pesticides remained in the trenches for years, under constant bombardment, with no relief, weaponry or tactics in sight. Nothing to look forward to but the constant threat of incoming fire. No wonder they're shell-shocked.

Battle tanks, fighter planes and attack helicopters made trench warfare and fixed defensive positions obsolete – and a surefire guarantee of defeat. Just ask Saddam Hussein after Desert Storm, or the French soldiers who served along the Maginot Line when Hitler outflanked them. If necessity is truly the mother of invention, the pesticide manufacturers and legions of other industries will soon devise new weapons and tactics, break out of their trenches, and launch counterattacks across all the front lines. If they do not, utter defeat will be sure to follow.

Power Play 10: Locate your target. Lock onto it. Villainize it. Strike hard. Don't let up.

In marketplace conflict, there are certain commandments that are universal. *Power Play 10* is one of them. There is no point in crafting strategies and tactics unless there is a target upon which to focus the attack. Activists understand this commandment and usually live by it.

Biotechnology. When the European Luddites initially attacked agricultural biotechnology, they directed their weaponry at Monsanto and the company's top leadership. If the attack had been aimed at the entire industry, the activists' forces would have been spread too thin and industry could have executed a *diffusion* strategy (see Chapter 6). Monsanto was singled out and villainized. Other food biotech companies and their customers became targets only after the attack gained momentum, and the coalition to kill "Frankenfoods" expanded its membership and its ability to strike multiple targets.

A key criterion for target selection is the target's vulnerability. Despite its size, reputation and supreme confidence, Monsanto was particularly vulnerable in the early days of the European genetically modified food fight. Three words sum up its vulnerability: Ambitious. Arrogant. American.

Monsanto set out to take Europe by storm with a biotech *blitzkrieg* designed to maneuver around consumers and powerful political forces that might be threatened by the new technology: *e.g.*, farmers and food merchants. The company's strategy in Europe reminded many of what the British said about American soldiers during World War II: "The problem with the Yanks is that they are over-sexed, over-paid and over here!"

The attackers could not have asked for a more inviting target. Once the company was fast-frozen into the villain role, it was not difficult to frame the issue. The issue became "Monsanto." This 800-pound Yankee gorilla was not only trying to force Europeans to eat alien food, but was also trying to destroy Europe's small family farms. And what if this gene-tinkering got out of hand and destroyed the environment to boot?

The attackers' success in exploiting Monsanto's vulnerabilities to frame the issue also had a polarizing effect. European companies with a stake in advancing agricultural biotechnology concluded that this was Monsanto's fight alone. They stayed in their trenches and bunkers, rather than risk consumer outrage. By the time they discovered that their future was also in jeopardy, the first major battle of the Frankenfoods war had been lost.

Locate the target, lock onto it, villainize it, strike hard and don't let go. Build coalitions to increase your fire power and staying power. Could industry use this approach against the attackers? Sure, if it's willing to cage the Nevilles and turn loose the Winstons.

As Mark Neal and Christie Davies observe in their book, *The Corporation under Siege*, the radical activists are:

> "crusaders against modernity, for whom the fate of the actual environment is subordinate to the pursuit of strongly held symbolic goals.... [They do] not live in our ordinary human world of risk, cost and balance – but in a world of metaphysical absolutes.... [Theirs is] a primitive pagan belief system in which the earth and the sea are treated as if they were themselves both sacred and human.... [They] use science when it suits them, but only in an opportunistic way and in a context that is strongly anti-scientific.... [They] divide the world into demons, innocent victims and bystanders, and heroic demon-slayers.... [who are to be] treated as sources of oracular wisdom and not subjected to the same kind of harsh cross-examination as the 'representatives of capitalism.'"[47]

The radical activists appear to be convinced that they have a right to mislead judges, legislators, journalists and the public at large; to engage in deceit, violence, vandalism and terrorism; and to pursue any other means they deem necessary to achieve their goal – of attacking and destroying corporations, modern technology and the very wealth of society on which we all depend. Indeed, many seem to see themselves as a blessed elite who alone have been ordained with purity, decency, wisdom and the right to dictate to everyone else what is proper and how we should live.

This makes many of the attack groups operating today vulnerable to *Power Play 10*. And yet, industries victimized by these groups rarely use it to their advantage. I recall counseling a client to issue a statement fingering Greenpeace directly for lying about research results during an attack on a particular chemical. The reaction from those responsible for approving the statement was a flat-out refusal to name names. Conflict avoidance at any cost. Marquess of Queensberry Rules for a full-blown riot.

Let's take a look at *Power Play 10* in action.

Sweat shops. Next time a radical student group and some Hollywood celebrity rant and rave about child labor, sweat shops and what Nike or Old Main pay their workers, perhaps a counter-protest by Guatemalan or Bangladeshi immigrants could give them a dose of reality. Many of these people are terribly frustrated that their views are rarely included in the news stories and policy debates on these life-or-death issues. They desperately want to speak out but rarely get the opportunity to do so.

By aligning yourself with their grassroots groups and supporting their efforts, you could help end their frustration and make them a potent political force. Your active involvement could also make the next WTO, FTAA or World Bank confab radically different from the anti-globalization melees that have characterized recent trade meetings.

A girl dressed in rags and carrying a single crust of bread could remind the protesters and media that what U.S. companies pay their workers is typically two or three times the average wage in those countries. (The "slave wages" Nike subcontractors pay workers in Vietnam are twice what teachers earn.) A little girl dressed like a hooker could emphasize that prostitution (not school or a cushy $8-an-hour job in Bloomies) is often the alternative for children who must still support families that otherwise would be destitute and starving.

Talk about a media circus! Color, controversy, good versus evil, great visuals and sound bites, women, children and old folks. It would be a guaranteed lights, camera, action – and a refreshing new angle on the evening news and Ted Koppel's *Nightline*.

An expert like Columbia professor Jagdish Bhagwati could point out that unions are misleading and exploiting gullible undergraduates, who then rail against the "exploitation" of workers in developing countries. "The unions have a clear agenda," Bhagwati has noted. "By raising wages in labor-intensive industries abroad, they hope to moderate competition." That's a polite way of saying they hope to reduce or destroy the only competitive advantage these developing countries often have: cheap labor. Which means the "slave wages" are transformed into no wages.[49]

A couple of black children, bedecked in arm and leg shackles, could add another lesson to this educational seminar. Children from poor countries like Benin, Mali and Mauritania are sold into servitude in the Middle East and wealthier African nations like Gabon, Ghana and Ivory Coast. The abominable practice has reached epidemic proportions: the International Labor Organization estimates that 80 million African children between the ages of 5 and 14 work as slaves or virtual slaves.[50]

Lured by false promises of lucrative salaries abroad, they are held captive, forced to work 12-hour days on plantations or as domestic servants, given inadequate food and shelter, and subjected to repeated beatings and sexual abuse.[51] Young women are put on the auction block, to be sold as domestic servants, for as little as $8. But the women are not slaves, the brokers in human merchandise insist. "We're agencies. You pay us to have them, but once you've taken them home, it's up to you if you pay them." And what might be a decent wage? "She could do all your washing, cleaning, cooking and look after your baby," said one broker. "If you paid her $30 a month, she would be extremely happy."[52]

Assuming the girls and women actually do get paid $30 a month, and get one day a week off (and pigs fly) – this works out to 12 hours a day, 288 hours a month – or a princely ten cents an hour. With opportunities like these to be had, it's no wonder unions and the Hollywood crowd can feel so morally superior to business executives. What self-respecting African or Asian woman would want to work in a sweatshop for a loathsome multi-national corporation, when such enticing alternatives beckon?

The counter-protesters could also ask, where are Jesse Jackson, the NAACP and other black organizations? The WTO protesters with their clamorous, virulent, violent demands for justice for the poor people of developing countries? The Hollywood cause *du jour* glitterati? What is it about environmental extremists, that motivates them to say things like:

> "We in the Green movement aspire to a cultural model in which the killing of a forest will be considered more contemptible and more criminal than the sale of 6-year-old children to Asian brothels."[53]

By all means, pay fair wages, even wages in excess of what teachers and other professionals make in developing countries where you have facilities. Encourage and implement constant improvements in labor and workplace conditions. But stand up for the truth and never allow yourself to be browbeaten into confessions of guilt, for having brought some measure of opportunity and hope to the world's destitute.

The logger and oil driller protective services. Rainforest Action Network would be another easy target for a Power Play 10. This radical organization carries a lot of hidden negatives just waiting to be exposed. Aside from a long string of unlawful acts including trespass, obstruction, and theft of goods ("ethical shoplifting" against Home Depot to convince them to stop selling wood), RAN gets substantial funding from media mogul Ted Turner – who cuts timber on his Montana ranch and has oil exploration agreements with Pennzoil on his New Mexico ranch. RAN complains viciously against Boise Cascade Corporation's timber cutting, and Texaco's oil drilling, but never so much as whispers about sugar daddy Ted Turner doing the very same things.

Next time RAN launches an attack, make *them* the issue, let loose with a few salvoes and torpedoes of your own, and use your coalitions with businesses, grassroots groups and political organizations to conduct a wide-ranging campaign against these militant radicals.

The essential question is: Who among the group's future victims will be willing to counterattack, and give RAN and other radicals a taste of their own medicine? And what medicine? Not turning their own unlawful acts against them, of course. But lawsuits, exposés, vocal protests by communities they've ruined, congressional investigations and other foul-tasting medicine could work wonders.

When American paratroops were completely surrounded by a vastly superior Nazi force at Bastogne, during the Battle of the Bulge in 1944, the German commander asked them if they were ready to surrender. General Anthony MacAuliffe sent back the famous one-word response: "Nuts!" A week later, General George S. Patton broke through to save the GIs.

American industry needs this attitude now.

> Because half a dozen grasshoppers under a fern make the field ring with their importunate chink, whilst thousands of great cattle, reposed beneath the shadow of the British oak, chew the cud and are silent, pray do not imagine that those who make the noise are the only inhabitants of the field; that, of course, they are many in number; or that, after all, they are other than the little, shriveled, meager, hopping, though loud and troublesome, insects of the hour.
>
> —Edmund Burke

Chapter 4 Notes

1. Thomas Sowell, *The Vision of the Anointed*, New York: Basic Books, HarperCollins Publishers (1995), page 2.
2. How heterosexism differs from household variety sexism is beyond the intellectual scope of this author.
3. www.greenparty.org., "Toward Ecological Democracy," reviewed July 17, 2000.
4. www.greenparty.org., "GPUSA National Green Program Draft," reviewed July 17, 2000.
5. *Ibid.*
6. Stephan Courtois, Nicolas Werth, et al., *The Black Book of Communism: Crimes, Terror, Repression*, Boston: Harvard University Press (1999).
7. Francois Furet, *The Passing of an Illusion: The Idea of Communism in the Twentieth Century*, Chicago: University of Chicago Press (2000).
8. Quoted by Walter Williams, *State Journal-Register*, June 25, 1992. Comedian Chevy Chase echoed Bari during an *American Investigator* interview on Earth Day, April 24, 2000, saying capitalism would not necessarily be a good way to help the poor, "because sometimes socialism works." Asked to name an example where socialism has worked, Chase cited Cuba. (http://www.freerepublic.com/forum/a39040a67687d.htm).
9. "Greenpeace withers as its members quit," Jonathan Leake, *The Sunday Times*, July 30, 2000.
10. "Gerber Parent Novartis Eliminates Genetically Engineered Food From All Products," Greenpeace press release, August 3, 2000.
11. "Novartis ended Use of Gene-Altered Foods," Andrew Pollack, *The New York Times*, August 4, 2000.
12. "Gerber Parent Novartis Eliminates Genetically Engineered Food From All Products," Greenpeace press release, August 3, 2000.
13. Dennis T. Avery, "Anti-science activists entertain but don't enlighten," Hudson Institute, December 8, 2000.
14. Gary Skulnik, Greenpeace news release, "Greenpeace targets Ford Motor Company over environmental record, June 25, 2001.
15. James M. Sheehan, *Global Greens: Inside the International Environmental Establishment*, Washington, DC: Capital Research Center (1998), pages 52-53.
16. "Judas' of the eco-warriors spreads his gospel of doubt," Anthony Brown, *The Observer*, May 21, 2000.
17. "Philadelphia D.A. Won't Drop Charges," Reuters, August 9, 2000.
18. "Boot Camp for Roving Protesters," Nicholas Riccardi, *Los Angeles Times*, July 28, 2000.
19. Deroy Murdock, "Taking on the federal bullies," *Chief Executive*, September 2000, page 20.
20. "Cholera in Peru," *Lancet*, Vol. 337, March 2, 1991. See also Michelle Malkin and Michael Fumento, *Rachel's folly: The end of chlorine*, Competitive Enterprise Institute (March 1996).

21. "Cholera epidemic traced to risk miscalculation," Christopher Anderson, *Nature*, Vol. 354, November 28, 1991.
22. Competitive Enterprise Institute, Press Release: "Public Interest Groups File Deceptive Advertising Complaint with FTC Against Ben And Jerry's: Charge Ad Campaign Misleads Consumers On Dioxin Content of Ice Cream," December 16, 1999.
23. Michael Gough and Steven J. Milloy, "Dioxin in Ben and Jerry's ice cream," Junk Science Web site, November 1999, http://www.junkscience.com/dec99/benjerr2.htm .
24. GuideStar online database guide to over 700,000 nonprofits (www.guidestar.org).
25. Deroy Murdock, "Eskimos: Open ANWR Now: Their desire to open ANWR deserves the immediate attention of policymakers and journalists alike," *National Review Online*, May 17, 2001; Jonah Goldberg, "Ugh, Wilderness! The horror of ANWR, the American elite's favorite hellhole," *National Review*, August 17, 2001. See for example Alaska Conservation Foundation $10,000 grant to Gwich'in Steering Committee, FY 1998 Grants List, August 25, 1998; Kongsgaard-Goldman Foundation, $28,000 in grants to Gwich'in Steering Committee, 1995-2000, www.kongsgaard-goldman.org/grantdetail.cfm?Organization=Gwich; Brainerd Foundation, $331,000 in grants to Gwich'in Steering Committee, 1998-2001, www.brainerd.org/grant; Wilderness Society, $2,000 to Gwich'in Steering Committee 1998.
26. "Toys Safe to Melt in the Mouth? Mattel Plans to Replace Soft Plastic With Organic Playthings," Caroline E. Mayer, *The Washington Post*, December 8, 1999.
27. Frontiers of Freedom Institute, a non-profit think tank, did just that in June 2001. Their complaint was sent to the commissioner of the Internal Revenue Service, asking that RAN's tax exempt status be revoked. RAN went ballistic.
28. "1998 Annual Report," www.greenpeace.org.
29. "The FBI vs. the Monkeywrenchers; The Eco-Guerrillas of Earth First Say They're Saving the Planet; The Government Calls Them Criminal Saboteurs," Michael A. Lerner, *Los Angeles Times Magazine*, April 15, 1990.
30. "Greenpeace USA Struggles to Raise Funds" FSN and wire service reports, July 18, 2000.
31. www.greenpiece.org, July 27, 2000.
32. "Greenpeace USA Struggles to Raise Funds . . .," FSN and wire service reports, July 18, 2000.
33. Personal communication with Chuck Cushman, July 17, 2001.
34. "Boot Camp for Roving Protesters," Nicholas Riccardi, *Los Angeles Times*, July 28, 2000.
35. National Center for Public Policy Research, "The time is now for a new environmental justice policy," *National Policy Analysis*, No. 296, June 2000.
36. National Center for Public Policy Research, "Earth Day no celebration for black Americans," Project 21 News Release, April 14, 2000.

37. John K. Carlisle, "Is smart growth anti-poor and anti-black? *Environment & Climate News*, March 2001, page 8. See also Bernard J. Frieden, *The Environmental Protection Hustle*, Cambridge, MA: MIT Press (1979).

38. David Foreman, letter to the editor, The Nation, December 12, 1987. Quoted in Robert Whelan, et al., *The Cross and the Rain Forest: A Critique of Radical Green Spirituality*, Grand Rapids, MI: Acton Institute (1996), page 75. Whelan notes that a Nazi propaganda magazine once boasted, "your Fuhrer is an ardent opponent of any torture of animals, in particular of vivisection," and "will fulfill his role as the savior of animals from ... torment and pain ... by making vivisection illegal." Hermann Goering subsequently decreed that anyone who practiced vivisection "shall be lodged in a concentration camp," until other punishments were pronounced. He later sent a fisherman to a concentration camp for cutting up a frog as bait. (*Ibid*, page 73).

39. *Against Nature*, Martin Durkin producer, London: Channel 4 Television Corporation (1997).

40. "The Case for DDT: What do you do when a dreaded environmental pollutant saves live?" J. Raloff, *Science News*, Vol. 158, No. 1, July 1, 2000, page 12. See also Richard Tren and Roger Bate, *When Politics Kills: Malaria and the DDT Story*, Washington, DC: Competitive Enterprise Institute (2000).

41. Richard Tren and Roger Bate, *op. cit.*; "Resurgence of a killer," ExxonMobil advertorial, *Washington Times*, April 26, 2001.

42. Roger E. Meiners and Andrew Morriss, *Pesticides and Property Rights*, Bozeman, MT: Political Economy Research Center, PERC Policy Series issue PS-22, May 2001. Steve Chapman, "When environmental protection costs lives," *Washington Times*, January 6, 2001; Paul Driessen, "Is the DDT ban intended to control global population?" *Environment & Climate News*, April 2001, page 12. Ignoring extensive scientific findings exonerating DDT, EPA Administrator William Ruckelshaus agreed with an Environmental Defense Fund petition and signed an order banning the pesticide in 1972, at the same time that he was a director and fund raiser for EDF.

43. Dr. Kelvin Kemm, "Anti-DDT policies crash-landing on African continent," *Citizen Outlook*, Committee For A Constructive Tomorrow, Spring 2001. See also www.fightingmalaria.org.

44 Quoted in Elizabeth Whelan, *Toxic Terror*, Ottawa, IL: Jameson Books (1985), page 67; and Dixie Lee Ray, with Lou Guzzo, *Environmental Overkill: Whatever happened to common sense?* Washington, DC: Regnery Publishing (1993), page 77, citing hearings before the House of Representatives Committee on Agriculture.

45. "Diazinon may be Falling Off the Pesticide Shelf Next," AgWeb.com, August 3, 2000.

46. "Novartis Responds to EPA's Preliminary Assessment of Diazinon," Novartis News Release, July 24, 2000.

47. Mark Neal and Christie Davies, *The Corporation Under Siege: Exposing the Devices Used by Activists and Regulators in the Non-Risk Society*, London: The Social Affairs Unit (1998), pages 10, 25, 55.
48. Deroy Murdock, "CEOs on the globalization warpath," *Chief Executive*, June 2000, page 20. Radicals demanding pay scales equal to those in the U.S. also ignore the vast difference in cost of living between the United States and developing countries like Vietnam.
49. Jagdish Bhagwati, "Why Nike is on the right track," *The Financial Times*, May 1, 2000.
50. Steve H. Hanke, "Africa and economics," *Forbes*, May 28, 2001, page 96. In Sudan, thousands of Christian and other non-Muslim children have been rounded up and sold into slavery, to a thunderous yawn by most U.S. Green, civil rights and other "human rights" activists.
51. "The slaves of Africa," *Washington Times* editorial, May 1, 2001.
52. Christina Lamb (London Sunday Telegraph), "Destitute women sell selves as slaves: 'Agencies' oversee sale, take their pay," *Washington Times*, April 30, 2001.
53. Carl Amery, member of German Greens Party, quoted in *Mensch und Energie*, April 1983.

5

Playing the Wildcards

If you can't spot the pigeon in a poker game, then you're probably it.

—"Jack & Jill," James Patterson

When a company is under attack by the forces of evil, there are several important variables that will influence the outcome of the battle – variables that are well understood and exploited by modern-day activists.

Whether consumers yawn or take up arms in response to an attack on a product or a company is determined, in large measure, by:

Benefits.

Time.

Wildcards.

Benefits and time are fairly easy to understand.

Underscore the benefits.

If consumers value the benefits offered to them by a product, they are less likely to go bananas when some attack group claims the product hurts the environment or poses a health risk to people. Try to convince Americans to give up their cars. That's not going to happen. They appreciate the benefits of mobility, convenience and safety brought to them by the automobile.

What does this say about stopping the attackers? It says ...

Make certain that customers, consumers, employees, investors, and other important audiences are constantly reminded of the benefits that your company and its products bring to the table.

Ever wonder why you see those television ads about how plastics *make it possible*? How gold *makes it possible*? Now you know. The plastics and gold industries understand what it takes to stop the attackers in their tracks. Consumers and others are constantly reminded about the safety and convenience that only plastics can provide, and about the reflective, conductive, anti-corrosion and non-reactive properties that only gold can offer.[1]

Respond quickly.

What about time? It's a double-edged sword.

Act quickly, and you'll likely get a positive response. Delay, and the damage escalates. From the time the attack is initiated to the point when the target company launches a counter-attack, the potential for negative media coverage and anger and hysteria among important target audiences increases dramatically. Once an effective counter-punch is thrown, anger diminishes rapidly.

Shakespeare's warning (in *Henry VI*) that "delays have dangerous ends" is true. If company executives spend three weeks debating with spin doctors and lawyers about how to respond to an attack, chances are that, by the time they finally launch counter-measures, the damage will already have been done.

Understand the wildcards.

The third variable that can influence the outcome of a marketplace battle takes the form of ten wildcards that can significantly influence the magnitude of audience anger and hysteria in response to an attack.

These wildcards consistently come into play during marketplace assaults.

They can have a profoundly positive or negative effect on a company's ability to respond to threatening events.

Think of them as symptoms whose presence or absence often dictates the message, strategies and tactics for managing volatile situations, and stopping the attackers.

Wildcard #1: Give people control, or die.

The potential for anger and hysteria declines as the opportunity to exercise control increases.

What is the one thing human beings strive for? Control – over their lives and their environment. That's why control is often the single most powerful wildcard influencing a person's response to an attacker's allegation. When people are confronted with an alleged hazard – regardless of its severity – the more control they have over their personal exposure to the hazard, the less likely they will be to react with anger or hysteria.

Consider smoking. How many smokers walk the streets in a state of hysteria over the risks associated with smoking? How many non-smokers exhibit anger over their exposure to someone else's smoke? It all gets down to control. Non-smokers often have no choice when they are exposed to someone else's puffs. The result? Bans. Lawsuits. Legislation.

When the Ford-Firestone tire crisis hit the headlines, when did drivers really go bonkers? Drivers got real ugly when they were told to keep driving on what the media called "killer" tires because replacements were in short supply. Not much of a choice there.

Beware of orchestrated outrage. Take the case of food irradiation. Is all the supposed public anxiety over irradiated food real – or merely another illusory product of the Crisis Creation Industry? After the *Washington Post* ran an informative, even-handed article on the issue, the author's email "ran almost 3 to 1 against food irradiation." But when reporter Robert Wolke recounted the mail, after eliminating form letters generated by an "Action Alert" from Ralph Nader's Public Citizen, the mail score reversed and became "3 to 1 in support of irradiation."[2]

However, Wolke also noted that many consumers do not want to be fed irradiated foods without their knowledge or freedom to choose. Of course, since the Department of Agriculture already requires labeling of irradiated foods, implementing this life-saving food safety method should not be difficult.

Always evaluate an attack from the perspective of control. Where control is available, communicate its availability with vigor. Where control is absent, seek ways to introduce it.

Local wells may have been contaminated as a result of a chemical leak from your facility. Leaks happen. Are you going to force your neighbors to choose between drinking polluted water and selling their homes? If you get all hung up in a debate about whether donating water is an admission of guilt, chances are you will have a lot more to worry about than plugging the leak. Providing the neighborhood with bottled water until the problem is solved may mitigate public anger and reduce your need to post a "plant closing" sign at the front gate.

This wildcard is well suited as a weapon against activists who are constantly calling for product bans and measures to stop new technology from entering the market. When all is said and done, these nannies and neurotics are so arrogant as to believe that they know what's best for the rest of us. What they are really trying to do is deny us our freedom to control how we live our lives – while they gain fame, fortune and power in the process.

Sound like a message? Sure. Now, try and find someone in the corporate world to deliver it. They're out there just waiting to be told that it's all right to nail these nannies when they deserve it. But, instead, they are being told to avoid confrontation at all costs.

Wildcard #2: If you did it, solve it. If you didn't do it, don't take the rap.

The degree of audience anger in response to a hazard or threat will be influenced by who gets tagged as the villain, and who is viewed as the problem-solver.

This wildcard often comes into play when attackers claim that a facility is releasing toxic stuff into the environment, or in situations involving product contamination.

The crisis involving syringes in Pepsi® cans is a classic example of this wildcard at work. Consumers reacted with anger to the news that someone put syringes in the cans. They did not perceive Pepsi-Cola as the villain, because the company cooperated with law enforcement agencies; offered a media tour of a bottling plant to demonstrate that there was no way syringes could get into cans, either deliberately or accidentally; and provided people with information about how to protect themselves and their loved ones.

Turns out the company was being attacked by folks who thought Pepsi-Cola would engage in appeasement and pay big bucks to anyone who found a syringe in a can – even if they had to slip one into a can first, so they could "find" it. I believe there's a word for that in the law books. Extortion.

Once a company is widely viewed as the source of a problem, it has little choice but to become the source of the solution. If a company is being wrongly positioned as the source of a problem, it must act rapidly to challenge the allegation and demonstrate its innocence, before opinions are hardened.

Do not let some PR Neville convince you that you will somehow lend credibility to the allegation, by responding to an attacker's attempt to tag your company with a problem it didn't create. That's hogwash and should be treated as such. If you don't set the record straight, the attacker's allegation will be accepted as the truth.

Wildcard #3: Knowledge is divine. Ignorance is demonic.

With rare exception, the more knowledgeable people are about a problem or hazard, the less likely they are to overreact in the marketplace. Conversely, the more unfamiliar a problem is, the greater the potential for a market-threatening freak-out.

Consider the reaction of parents when *60 Minutes* reporter Ed Bradley told them: "The most potent cancer-causing agent in our food supply is a substance sprayed on apples to keep them on the trees longer and make them look better."[3] Parents who knew nothing about the use of Alar reacted with anger and hysteria over what turned out to be a bogus cancer scare that was not supported by science and the facts. Non-organic apple (and apple juice) sales plummeted, traditional apple growers lost millions, and Alar was pulled off the market. Organic apple growers, meanwhile, profited handsomely.[4]

Is it possible for a company under attack to prevent market damage by simply educating its key audiences? Not likely. It takes less time for the attackers to launch a well-planned assault and use the news media to create fear, anger and hysteria, than for their corporate victim to convey knowledge. If the public isn't already educated, fear and anger will be way ahead of you.

Efforts focused solely on educating key audiences following an attack are often interpreted as public relations gimmickry. Many times they are.

Educating key audiences – about the benefits offered by a product or service, modern production processes and safety practices, the true nature of alleged hazards, and the connection between your product or service and the lifestyles consumers enjoy – is essential to creating a balanced perspective, limiting the potential for damage and wining the battle.

However, the education process must be treated as an ongoing communications function, rather than a tactical response to an attacker's allegations.

Educate key audiences about benefits and risks in advance of an attack. And, at the risk of beating a dead horse, never let inaccurate or misleading claims about a product, service, process or corporate policy go unchallenged. Over time, those bogus claims will be perceived as true. It is difficult enough to educate people about risk. It is much more difficult to correct misinformation and myths that have become part of the audience "knowledge" base.

So if you use chemicals, plastics, genetically modified grain or food additives in your products, start educating consumers and journalists early. And have a top-notch "dark" Web site ready to launch the moment there is a predator attack or crisis.

Wildcard #4: Hurt a kid or zap a town, and you'd better put on your bullet-proof vest.

When evaluating the market damage potential of an attack involving an alleged hazard, remember this: Even though the likelihood of harm may be statistically insignificant, if it affects vulnerable people or may produce a cataclysmic result, the potential for anger and hysteria is quite significant.

A dangerously defective toy will engender more anger than a dangerously defective power tool, even though the tool can do more damage. It is important to know who is really using your product (*e.g.*, model airplane glue); it is equally important for those who run manufacturing facilities to know their neighbors. If your plant is located near a day care center, be prepared for the doo-doo to hit the fan if a kid gets hurt or some local group with a political agenda claims your smoke is causing an outbreak of asthma.

Ever wonder why attack groups consistently focus on products used by young children? Now you know. A product that is alleged to hurt babies stands a greater chance of being lynched than one that is used by middle-aged, silver-haired alpha males.

Consider why activists have been so successful in attacking nuclear power. For years, the nuclear power industry claimed that the chances for a meltdown were extremely remote. And for years, anti-nuclear forces have charged that if a meltdown occurred, thousands would perish immediately. That, of course, is scare-mongering at its worst. The debate over nuclear power was won long before Chernobyl. The winners succeeded by preaching catastrophe. The losers relied on science and logic.

The activists may not have the last laugh, though. The chaos visited upon California by its 2000-2001 energy crisis is breathing new life into nuclear energy. Intel CEO Craig Barrett told Bloomberg News that energy shortages and rolling blackouts threaten Intel's operations and ruin the quality of its products. "Nuclear power is the only answer," he said, "but it's not politically correct." Sun Microsystems founder and chairman Scott McNealy echoed Barrett's comments: "politicians have got to...come up with a better energy policy that includes nuclear power. As long as California is a Third World country, we won't build $2-billion manufacturing plants here."[5] Rolling blackouts, pink slips, darkened schools and the loss of warm water for hot tubs can concentrate the mind wonderfully.

Wildcard #5: Cancer always trumps heart failure. Chemicals always trump Mother Nature's toxins.

Some hazards and risks create more fear than others. A product that is alleged to cause cancer will attract more loathing and hysteria than a product that is alleged to cause heart failure.

The mere suggestion that something may have caused cancer in laboratory rats is often sufficient to produce a market-threatening public reaction. Attackers know that. But what do legitimate scientists have to say about the rat tests? Dr. Bruce Ames, professor of Biochemistry and Molecular Biology at the University of California, Berkeley, writes: "These standard tests of chemicals are conducted chronically, at near-toxic doses – the maximum tolerated dose – and evidence is accumulating that it may be the high dose itself, rather than the chemical *per se,* that is the risk factor for cancer."[6]

Consumers have also developed a neurosis over synthetic chemicals – Chemophobia. Pollsters have found that 10 percent of the population will predictably associate anything that sounds like a chemical with cancer. One research firm asked over 1,000 adults whether Pandemonium Chloride could cause cancer. Roughly ten percent said, "you betcha."

What does Dr. Ames say about the risks posed by synthetic chemicals? He writes, "Another misconception is that human exposures to carcinogens and other toxins are nearly all due to synthetic chemicals. On the contrary, the amount of synthetic pesticide residues in plant foods are insignificant compared to the amount of natural pesticides produced by plants themselves. Of all dietary pesticides, 99.99 percent are natural: They are toxins produced by plants to defend themselves against fungi and animal predators."[7]

It is worth noting that Dr. Ames developed the "Ames Test" that analyzes chemicals to determine if they cause mutations in bacterial DNA. The ability of a chemical to cause these mutations correlates strongly with chemicals that have been shown to cause cancer in laboratory animals. In the early days of the environmental movement, Dr. Ames was a hero among activists, because he held the opinion that many cancers were caused by industrial and consumer products. He changed his opinion as more research became available. He's not considered their hero today.

Why are people bonkers over chemicals? Perhaps this irrational fear stems from years of propaganda from activist groups that have liberally used the "cancer" label as a weapon to achieve their political objectives. Also, our school systems and news media have produced entire generations of scientific illiterates, who are particularly vulnerable to these scare tactics, as has been ably documented in books like *Facts, Not Fear: A Parent's Guide to Teaching Children about the Environment* and *Voodoo Science: The Road from Foolishness to Fraud.*[8]

When responding to an attack involving a hazard that is known to strike fear in the heart of humanity, do not fall victim to the *oddsmaker syndrome*, by informing people that "the risk is only one in ten million." Each individual may assume that he or she will be that one unlikely victim. It is far better to equate risk to exposure: "You would have to drink 400 cans of Swill Cola each day for 23 years before you receive the dose given to these lab rats over a seven week period."

It doesn't do to leave a live dragon out of your calculations if you happen to live near one.

—J.R.R. Tolkien, *The Hobbit*

Wildcard #6: Fairness is a value that must never be violated.

The potential for public anger will increase if an attack raises fundamental issues of fairness. If a small number of people have risks imposed on them for the benefit of the population at-large, the end result may be a market-threatening reaction.

This wildcard is most relevant in siting manufacturing, waste processing or power producing facilities that allegedly pose hazards to the immediate neighborhood, while benefiting the community as a whole. This particular wildcard has come into play so often that it has been awarded a pop-culture moniker – NIMBY (Not In My Backyard), and the lesser known sobriquets: BANANA (Build Absolutely Nothing Anywhere Near Anything) and NOPE (Nowhere On Planet Earth).

Public official: *We're going to site a municipal waste-to-energy facility about two miles down the road, so that thousands of people won't have to pay more for garbage pick-up. Don't worry. Be happy.*

Homeowner: *Over my dead body. Take your garbage to the country club and bury it under the 18th green. My lawyers will speak to your lawyers and, by the way, expect a friendly visit from Earth First.*

To neutralize potential damage from a "fairness" attack, seek legitimate ways to compensate those who are being asked to take risks, or live with added traffic or other inconvenience, for the benefit of others. Compensation should be offered in advance of any organized reaction to the risk. If compensation is accepted, communicate the fact broadly to neutralize anti-facility reactions from people who have too much time on their hands and need a cause.

Public official: *By the way, to compensate you for this inconvenience, this neighborhood will receive free electricity and garbage pick-up for as long as the facility is in operation.*

Homeowner: *Where do I sign up?*

Wildcard #7: Immorality guarantees Armageddon.

When perceptions about a product, service or corporation move into the realm of immorality, the potential for public anger increases exponentially. If your company spills oil or some other pollutant into a nearby river, trying to *spin* the spill to deflect responsibility, or attempting to cover it up, will virtually guarantee moral indignation from an unforgiving public that may also demand fines or even jail time for corporate officers.

Corporation X has been in business for 75 years. In the early days, discharging stuff into the river was the way things were done. Things have changed. Nothing has been intentionally dropped in the drink for over 20 years, except by a few midnight dumpers who deserve every year they spend behind bars. But environmentalists claim that some of the company's stuff is still in the river and it's extremely hazardous.

The company's response? "Everyone did it in those days. We're not even sure it's dangerous. Force us to clean it up and we won't be profitable. No profits and we'll pack our bags and head out of town."

Results? Community goes bonkers. Products are boycotted. Regulators get ugly. Lawyers get rich. Employees are shamed. Their kids are shunned.

To neutralize this wildcard, embrace the moral high ground and demonstrate a strong commitment to righting the wrong. Never use "lost profits" as an excuse for inaction. A huge segment of the population (even in our capitalist culture) views profit-taking as immoral. A company must be the first to publicly acknowledge both mistakes and rational solutions.

Corporate mistakes announced by others (regulators, attackers, the news media) imply cover-up. So if your company screwed up, admit it, apologize for it, and outline actions you are taking to prevent it from happening again. But never let anyone push you into thinking your company must take responsibility for something it didn't do.

Wildcard #8: If you can't be trusted, expect to be busted.

If a company is perceived to be dishonest, the magnitude of anger in response to an attack will increase. Businesses generally enjoy limited public trust, compared to activist groups, government agencies and self-anointed victims. Thus, companies are not only vulnerable to attack, but they are also at a distinct disadvantage when they must respond to an attack. This wildcard underscores the need for corporations to identify independent, credible allies to deliver the company's message in the court of public opinion. Consider this scenario.

Woman: *After my cancer surgery I asked them to put in breast implants. That's when all my problems started. They've ruined my health. I won't let that happen to other women.*

CEO: *There is no scientific evidence that our breast implants cause health problems. Beyond that, I have no comment.*

A corporation's trust bank must be protected at all costs and demonstrated at every opportunity. "No comment" responses are the kiss of death. "No comment" means "guilty as charged." It sends a message that the company is not prepared to be forthright and doesn't care about the problem.

If the corporate exec really has no helpful information to convey, be prepared to refer reporters and consumers to experts capable of answering questions or offering constructive comments and perspectives. Above all else, avoid leaving the impression that your company doesn't give a damn about the alleged problem.

Time erodes credibility. Taking three weeks to respond to a serious allegation is a sure-fire way to lose trust. Companies are often assumed to be guilty until proven innocent, and untrustworthy until proven honest. A credible ally may be the only means of effective communications when times get tough.

Mayo Clinic: *We investigated breast implants in hundreds of women and found no evidence that they cause serious health problems.*

Cultivate relationships with independent researchers, think tanks, respected authors, other experts, and local and national grassroots groups. Work with them, support their work, do so far in advance of the day you might actually need them, and maintain your friendly association long after the immediate crisis has ebbed. Above all, never mislead them, give them any reason to question your integrity or honesty, or attempt to "buy" or pressure them into drawing particular conclusions or otherwise influence the very independence that makes them credible and valuable.

Wildcard #9: Your great, great grandchildren had better be safe.

If an attacker claims a hazard will affect babies of the future, the potential for hysteria and anger will increase. Hazards that are here today and gone tomorrow are far more acceptable than those that threaten our great grandchildren and their offspring. Environmental groups are constantly seeking opportunities to invoke this wildcard and guilt-trip the public about what we are doing to future generations. Think about global warming, PCBs, nuclear waste and pesticides.

Polly Morphus: *Plastics aren't biodegradable. That plastic coffee cup will be here 500 years from now. We are going to bury our children in garbage, unless we stop using plastics.*

Never allow a phony "future generations" argument to go unchallenged. Never appear cavalier about a legitimate claim that the future is at stake. If a hazard may seriously affect future generations, the only effective response is to communicate a strong commitment to solving the problem.

Scientist: T*he Foundation for Our Children's Future found that we have enough landfill space for the next 136 years. University of Arizona garbage expert Bill Rathje says even hot dogs thrown into modern landfills are still recognizable 20 years later – so finding a plastic coffee cup would hardly be surprising. And studies show that our town could address these concerns by building a clean waste-to-energy plant that burns trash to generate electricity for homes, schools and businesses. As a bonus, it would also increase recycling rates by 14 percent and reduce trash collection and recycling costs by 21 percent. That's good for us, and for our children.*

Wildcard #10: Negative news coverage is like plutonium. If it reaches critical mass, you can kiss your butt goodbye.

The reach, frequency and tone of media coverage will have a profound impact on how audiences will respond to an attack against a company.

Media exposure is among the most volatile of the wildcards. As the Alar attack demonstrated so dramatically, market damage can be expanded exponentially by a single twenty-minute segment on CBS's *60 Minutes*, or by multiple stories in less powerful print and broadcast media.

With marketplace assaults, news coverage can take on the characteristics of a six round bout between Mike Tyson and Woody Allen. (Round #1) Computer nerd finds math flaw in widely used computer chip. He takes his discovery to the news media. (Round #2) Chip maker announces that most computer users won't notice the flaw, since their computer use is so basic. (Round #3) Computer users react with outrage at the perceived insult and the idea that they should accept a flawed chip in their hardware. (Round #4) Computer makers announce they will no longer use flawed chip. (Round #5) Chip maker announces recall. (Round #6) Crisis pundits deliver knock-out blow, declaring that the crisis has been mismanaged.

If an attack has the potential for significant media exposure, the primary objective must be to reduce the half-life of media coverage, avoiding any action that extends the life of the story. Equally important, your crisis management team must also be able to parry the sophisticated below-the-belt tactics so often used by predator groups.

Under attack conditions, there are two reasons that justify seeking additional media coverage: 1) to challenge misinformation and bogus claims, and 2) to achieve a quantifiable market advantage. Corporate victims of public attacks often compound the damage by venting their anger at adversaries through the media, or by attempting to spin the story to deflect responsibility for solving whatever problem they caused. The result is extended coverage and increased damage.

> There is no such thing as objective reporting. I've become even more crafty about finding the voices to say the things I think are true. That's my subversive mission.
>
> —Dianne Dumanoski, Boston Globe environmental reporter, and co-author of "Our Stolen Future "

Chapter 5 Notes

1. See www.AmericanPlasticsCouncil.org (plastics in your life) and www.GoldInstitute.org (uses of gold).
2. Robert Wolke, Radioactive Fallout, *Washington Post*, February 21, 2001.
3. "A Is for Apple," CBS News, *60 Minutes*, February 26, 1989, transcript.
4. For a detailed examination of the Alar debacle, read Chapter 1, "The Alarm over Alar," in Michael Fumento, *Science Under Siege: Balancing Technology and the Environment*, New York: William Morrow & Company, Inc. (1993). See also Bonner Cohen, John Carlisle, *et al.*, *The Fear Profiteers: Do "socially responsible" businesses sow health scares to reap monetary rewards?* Washington, DC: National Center for Policy Analysis (2000), pages 2-14.
5. Kenneth Smith, "Greenouts: New economy starving for electricity," *Washington Times*, February 15, 2001.
6. "Science and the Environment," Bruce N. Ames, *The Freeman*, September 1993.
7. *Ibid.*
8. Michael Sanera and Jane S. Shaw, *Facts, Not Fear: A Parent's Guide to Teaching Children about the Environment*, Washington, DC: Regnery Publishing Company (1996); Robert Park, *Voodoo Science: The Road from Foolishness to Fraud*, London: Oxford University Press (2000).
9. Micah Morrison, *American Spectator*, July 1991, quoting Diane Dumanosky at an *Utne Reader* symposium.

6

How to Win

The goal of public relations is to make people feel good about something. The goal of crisis management is to stop the attackers; to make them go away, whether they feel good or not.

—Nichols • Dezenhall

Crisis management strategies are very different from traditional public relations techniques.

They often fall into the high-risk/high-gain category and should never be employed in situations that do not pose a serious marketplace threat to a product, company or entire industry.

In practice, the risks attendant to most crisis management strategies can be minimized with the use of motivated surrogates capable of waging battle on the front lines, while camouflaging their behind-the-scenes allies.

Surrogates are individuals and groups who will benefit if the attackers fail.

Here are fifteen power strategies that have proven extremely effective in the hands of corporate Winstons bent on stopping the attackers in the midst of a marketplace assault.

Annexation: Positioning attackers as outside the cultural and political mainstream.

Despite the freak-show *milieu* of daytime television talkies, many reporters and political influentials are averse to carrying water for the wackier elements of our society. For they too are concerned about their own professional credibility. But the helter-skelter dynamics of today's media environment conspire against journalists who take the time to do background checks on their sources. Too many of their competitors are prepared to publish first, with a hope and a prayer that their source doesn't show up on *Oprah* as a Pee Wee Herman act-alike.

Annexation is a high-risk/high-gain strategy that merits consideration if the attacker is indeed a card-carrying member of the lunatic fringe. The risk is that efforts to raise awareness that the attacker is a few fries short of a Happy Meal® may be perceived by others as a personal slur. This risk can be reduced by using surrogates to deliver the message.

Remember Power Play 2: *Execute the unexpected.* Attack groups seldom, if ever, find themselves on the receiving end of an assault by other activists. When it happens, they usually run for their foxholes.

Medical and pharmaceutical research firms have enjoyed success in annexing radical animal-rights activists by mobilizing AIDS victims and other patient advocacy groups to counter-attack. People with serious illnesses depend on medicines and treatments that can be developed only through animal research. They don't take kindly to attempts by the bug, rat and bunny lovers to shut down research labs and harass the researchers.

Imagine the reaction from the animal rights activists when their staged media events are disrupted by Act Up, breast cancer victims, surgical and transplant patients, diabetics, hemophiliacs, quadriplegics, Alzheimers and cystic fibrosis sufferers, and numerous others who depend on medical research with animals to survive. Imagine a video of Christopher Reeves visiting an animal research facility in his motorized wheel chair, talking about his hope that continued research will ultimately find a cure for spinal cord injuries. The message sent by the patient advocates? "These animal rights militants care more about lab rats than people."

In fact, that's precisely the message that Chris DeRose has conveyed on at least one occasion. "If the death of one rat cured all diseases, it wouldn't make any difference to me," he told the *Los Angeles Times*. DeRose is the founder of the radical animal rights group, Last Chance for Animals, a spokesman for the eco-terrorist Animal Liberation Front, and for a time was actually employed as a producer-host for animal-issue segments on Paramount's television show, *Hard Copy*.[1]

Annexation. Include it in your arsenal of weapons.

> It is characteristic of all movements and crusades that the psychopathic element rises to the top.
>
> —Robert Lindner, psychoanalyst

Balkanization: Splitting potential attackers into mutually hostile groups that are vulnerable to divide-and-conquer tactics.

Balkanization is one of the oldest and most effective crisis management strategies. The Romans used it against the tribes of Europe. The British used it against the Scots. And John Belushi used it against Dean Wormer and his pals in "Animal House." The individual members of a coalition of attackers may, in fact, have very different agendas. Good intelligence-gathering will ferret those differences out. If the attackers have different needs, pick the one that seems most rational and play "let's make a deal." That's not appeasement; it's a sure-fire way to start a feud that may split the coalition and blunt the attack.

Food biotech companies seeking to bring their products to the U.S. market were initially opposed by a diverse coalition of environmentalists and anti-technology neurotics. The gene splicers succeeded in balkanizing the opposition, by playing to the interests of moderate environmentalists with the promise of pest-resistant plants that required fewer and less powerful pesticides.

Until recently, opposition to designer foods in the U.S. was the province of the finger-waving fringe – the folks who yearn for the good old days when mass starvation, pestilence and plague were the primary forms of population control. Folks like the authors of *Earthbound*, a collection of essays on so-called environmental ethics, where one kind-hearted essayist said: "Massive human diebacks would be good. Is it our duty to cause them? Is it our species' duty, relative to the whole, to eliminate 90 percent of our numbers?"[2]

To which Earth First's David Foreman added: "I see no solution to our ruination of Earth, except for a drastic reduction of the human population

... It may well take our extinction to set things straight."[3] Even the late Jacques Cousteau agreed, saying, "In order to stabilize world populations, we must eliminate 350,000 people per day. It is a horrible thing to say, but it's just as bad not to say it."[4]

Regrettably, the European neurosis over genetically modified foods has now infected the U.S. market – thanks, in part, to industry's anemic response to its Luddite attackers in Europe. Meanwhile, in 1998, officials from a major biotech firm with operations in India actually told a New Delhi journalist, who supported biotechnology research as a way to improve his country's agricultural output, that they didn't need his help. "We have everything under control," they told him.[5]

In fact, the attackers have now succeeded in executing a *Balkanization* strategy against industry, pitting biotech companies against farmers and against food marketing firms with no will to fight. Their brilliant, sophisticated battle plan is discussed in Chapter 10, *Ethics Edict 2*. The biotechnology and food marketing industries, by contrast, resorted to antiquated strategies and expensive television spots that addressed the wrong issues and targeted the wrong audiences. As a result, the food marketers are rapidly adopting anti-biotech policies in response to pressure and conflict campaigns generated by the radical attackers.

The lesson? Crisis management strategies can work for both sides on the battlefield.

Is it too late to turn the tables on the attackers? Of course not. Can industry sow the seeds of discord and split the packs of predators? Certainly. John Meredith, son of civil rights leader James Meredith, has said:

> "As a black American, I consider this opposition [to biotechnology] as elitism in its cruelest form, since the poorest members of the population, blacks in particular, are going to suffer because of it.... We are being denied the benefits other Americans take for granted. Produce that has a longer shelf life and more nutritional value at lower prices would be a godsend to urban blacks, who must usually rely on corner markets that don't get the same quality stocks as the Fresh Fields in the suburbs....

> "Then there is the problem of the African homeland. Sub-Saharan Africa has an infant mortality rate of 9.2 percent, and three million children who have survived are blind, due to a lack of Vitamin A in their diets. Biotechnology can now provide rice and tomatoes rich in Vitamin A. It can create crops that are resistant to insect predators, need less fertilizer and water, and reduce soil erosion. Existing crops like cassava and papaya can be genetically modified to beat back the viruses and insects that devastated them in the past."[6]

Radical attack groups are against all these advances. Why did it take the biotech companies so long to enlist people like John Meredith, think tanks, respected scientists, and poor people's advocates from India and Africa in this vitally important battle?

Are there so few Winstons in these companies?

If a house be divided against itself, that house cannot stand.

—New Testament

Cauterization: Destroying, discarding or denouncing the subject of a crisis catalyst, to prevent the spread of marketplace damage.

There are times when the target of an attack – a.k.a. the villain – becomes a gangrenous sore that threatens to destroy all in its path. When this occurs, there's no point in applying more salve and another bandage. Burn it out. Cut it out. Gouge it out. Do whatever is necessary to rid yourself of this infestation, before it gets rid of you.

Residents of the White House have turned *cauterization* into an art form often practiced on Chiefs of Staff. It works.

A fast-food restaurant chain puts its burgers in a yellow foam box. Burgers stay fresh. Burgers stay warm. Burgers stay clean. Environmentalists claim the burger box contains chemicals that will destroy the planet, and the box is filling up dumps. Not true, but the restaurant chain is put on the defensive.

Consumers feel guilty about using the box. So, Burger, Inc. gives the box the boot. Tree huggers declare victory. Consumers force a smile, as they eat cold hamburgers. Burger, Inc. gets public kudos.

Everyone lives happily ever after – except of course the people who made the yellow foam box, and the neighbors who watch the local landfill get loaded up with tons of paper wrappers and cardboard burger boxes.

A note of caution. While *cauterization* may save your hide in the short-term, it may also weaken your corporate immune system, leaving other products vulnerable to future attacks by activists who may assume that if the company cauterized once, it will do it again.

Who ever said life was fair?

—John Fitzgerald Kennedy

Differentiation: Distinquishing an organization or product from others affected by an attack.

Guilt-by-association is alive and well in our culture. Products and companies fall victim to it when they fail to differentiate themselves from the villain – real or imagined. The objective of *differentiation* is to shunt the risk away, toward a less-defined, or more appropriate target category. The trick to executing this strategy is rapid, aggressive communications. Don't wait 'til the next full moon to set the record straight. By then, it may be too late.

The prescription allergy drug market has become one of the most profitable and fiercely competitive in the booming sector of medical marketing. Take for example the neck-and-neck competition between two antihistamine products. When news broadcasts reported the FDA's proposal to remove one of the products, citing potentially deadly side effects, the competition wasted no time in reaching out to the millions of allergy sufferers.

Within days of the FDA's announcement, an opportunistic competitor launched an aggressive advertising campaign promoting the safety of its product – leading allergy sufferers to a clear choice. The ad language was taken directly from the FDA statement and informed allergists and allergy sufferers that not all antihistamine drugs are dangerous.

Not everyone at whom dogs bark is a thief.

—Proverb

Diffusion: Raising audience awareness that an alleged hazard or risk is spread across a wide spectrum of products, thereby preventing the attackers from focusing their assaults.

This strategy can be very effective when motivated adversaries make gross generalizations about an alleged hazard. For example: "More than 3,000 chemicals may be implicated," said Polly Morphus, director of the Coalition to Stop Progress Immediately (CSPI). Given no clear villain, the public will not support this attack. How could the public possibly stop using 3,000 chemicals? The crisis management tactic in this instance? Employ *diffusion* to reinforce the notion that the hazard, if it exists at all, is ubiquitous.

A small number of people – encouraged by their doctors and lawyers – claim to be sensitive to virtually every synthetic chemical in the environment. They want government disability funding. They want the rest of us to stop wearing perfume and deodorant in public places. They want subsidized, chemical-free housing. You get the picture. By blaming every synthetic chemical, and acting pretty wacky in the process, they have failed to give potentially sympathetic consumers a clear call to action and a villain to ban and berate. The *diffusion* message received by consumers? "These folks are allergic to life!"

> For the great majority of mankind are satisfied with appearances, as though they were realities, and are often more influenced by the things that seem than those that are.
>
> —Niccolò Machiavelli, *The Prince*

Dissuasion: Convincing potential attackers that it is against their best interest to launch an attack.

This strategy is often used with the news media, when advance warning is received that a potentially libelous story is in production. It is also used in the wake of an onerous story, to create a chilling effect on other tabloid journalists. *Dissuasion* tactics often include the implied threat of legal action. To be credible, the threat must be preceded by an aggressive, sustained effort to communicate the facts, not only to the reporter, but also to the reporter's legal counsel. You can't prove that a reporter knowingly or recklessly disregarded the truth if no effort was made to provide the truth (see *New York Times v. Sullivan*), unless you happen to have video or other documentary evidence to make your case.

The July 13, 2000, front page headline of *The Washington Post* declared: "Cancer Study Deemphasizes Gene's Roles." The lead paragraph of the article warned: "The vast majority of cancers are caused not by inherited defects in people's genes...but by environmental and behavioral factors such as chemical pollutants and unhealthy lifestyles, according to the largest cancer study ever to enter the 'nurture versus nature' debate."[7] There is only one problem with this lead. The study, which was published in *The New England Journal of Medicine*, did not contain a single reference to "chemical pollutants."[8] Not one. Zip. Nada.

An editorial that accompanied the study also failed to finger "chemical pollutants." Instead, it listed tobacco, alcohol, radiation, occupational toxins, infections, diet and drugs as environmental cancer hazards. Occupational toxins may well include some chemicals. But does this reference in an editorial that is not part of the study, itself, merit lead paragraph attention?

Is this a situation that merits *dissuasion*? You betcha. Call the reporter and ask him to cite the reference to "chemical pollutants" in the study. If he can't, demand a retraction. If he doesn't agree, it's time to request a meeting with his editor and, perhaps, the *Post's* lawyer. Don't settle for a letter-to-the-editor. Demand the retraction and the letter. Even if the *Post* refuses, there's a pretty good chance the reporter will actually read the next medical study he writes about, before including his personal opinion or an attacker's interpretation in the lead paragraph.

NBC's "Dateline" *vs.* General Motor's pickup truck: news team used an incendiary device to make sure truck's gasoline tank exploded after crash. CNN and Time vs. Operation Tailwind: publishers retracted and apologized for a report that U.S. Special Forces had used deadly sarin nerve gas against a village where they thought American defectors were hiding and on nearby North Vietnamese troops. The decade of the '90s was marked by a steady decline in journalistic ethics (things haven't improved in the new millennium), and by a steady increase in litigation against media that have crossed the line.

Businesses that fail to recognize this state of affairs, and refuse to include *dissuasion* in their arsenal of weapons, risk becoming fodder for the ratings war that now pervades the business of delivering the "news."

> The facts remain – among them the truth that many journalists continue to believe that they are involved in a calling so high as to entitle them to rights not given ordinary citizens, among them the right to deceive without consequences.
>
> —Dorothy Rabinowitz, editorial board, *The Wall Street Journal*

Diversion: Influencing the story angle of an attack in a way that diverts risk and audience outrage from the intended target to another subject.

More than any other time in our history, today's public controversies are often the result of shoddy journalistic research, an attacker's political agenda or the cultural desire to avoid personal responsibility. *Diversion* can be a very effective strategy under these circumstances, but only if it is executed before the controversy takes root.

An exposé about allegations that a product is carcinogenic could be *diverted* to become an exposé that focuses on the abuses of science, the scare tactics used by motivated adversaries, or the mercenary behavior of the plaintiffs' bar. Timing is key. Get to the battlefield before the attack.

Death rates linked to drunk driving were giving the alcohol industry a bad name. The industry was being blamed for the irresponsible behavior of individual drivers. After all, it's not easy to point the finger of blame at the dead and disabled. Why not villainize a faceless corporation, instead? To divert blame without pointing the finger at the victims, the alcohol industry launched its responsible drinking campaign. This had the positive effect of positioning the industry as part of the solution, and focusing public and regulatory attention back on the individuals where it belonged.

You don't get anything clean without getting something else dirty.

—Cecil Baxter

Expiation: Communicating remorse and making reparations for an alleged wrongdoing.

This is the "if ya done it, admit it and prove you're sorry" strategy. It's the easiest to execute, and the most difficult to adopt in a corporate board-room – particularly if questions of liability are on the table.

By fighting accusations that are true, a company's image and bottom-line may sustain far more damage than would have occurred if fault were admitted from the start. A note of caution. *Never* admit to something you didn't do, even if the short term consequences are appealing. Word will get out that your company is an easy mark.

Sexual harassment cases have become a regular topic for the news media. Harassment claims can be extremely damaging to publicly traded companies. Consider how two companies treated harassment allegations at their U.S. offices.

Managers at Company X and Company Y are accused of sexually harassing employees. After Company X finds itself exposed on the cover of a leading business magazine, it indefinitely suspends the accused individuals while completing its internal investigation, openly expresses regret, develops procedures for reporting sexual harassment, and trains managers to recognize and handle harassment claims.

Company Y creates the perception that it is seeking to blemish the reputation of the accusers, and draws even more media attention to its treatment of employees.

Bottom-line? Company X disappears from the media's radar screen. Company Y is harangued by the media and court cases ensue.

Always do right; this will gratify some people and astonish the rest.

– Mark Twain

Fraternization: Initiating friendly relations with the attackers.

If you can't beat them, perhaps you should join them (at least temporarily). There are times when business objectives are better served by a cease-fire and peace talks, than by all-out combat.

The *fraternization* strategy is often implemented when preemption and inoculation strategies have failed to produce results. As with all other crisis management strategies, timing is key. It's difficult to make nice to someone after successive strikes to the head with a two-by-four. Equally important, be extremely cautious about who you call a friend. Remember, your new friend may have other items on the agenda long after the immediate crisis has subsided. Remember, these guys are specialists in the Crisis Creation Industry, and new crises are their product, their business. So most of the time, it's better to build your own coalition or fraternity, than to join theirs.

Your company is accused of discrimination. Boycotts are threatened. Investors are getting nervous. Litigation is popping up all over. Corporate executives approach a well-respected leader of the aggrieved community who has been critical in the past, inviting the leader to help them vanquish the villains and ensure that the wrong is not repeated. Leader agrees (usually at a price). The media report that the problem is being fixed. Note: It *better* be fixed!

Also remember, there is a huge difference between bringing in a credible outsider to help solve a real problem, and caving in to an outsider who is threatening to fabricate a problem for your company. The first is fraternization. The second is extortion. Any company that caves in to extortion will get what it deserves.

Better to have him in the tent pissing out than out of the tent pissing in.

—Lyndon B. Johnson on J. Edgar Hoover

Inoculation: Providing key audiences with information and assurances that will counter the bogus claims and misinformation that may be communicated by an attacker in the future.

The objectives of *inoculation* are to: 1) frame the issue; 2) neutralize the impact of adversarial communications; and 3) ensure that key audiences are not caught off guard by the attack. *Inoculation* is the most commonly used crisis management strategy. However, it is effective only when executed *in advance* of an attack. It is often executed in tandem with other strategies.

Environmentalists spent the late '80s and early '90s taking Americans on a Chicken Little ride to the dump. We're running out of landfill space! We're burying our children in garbage! Most of their scary claims proved to be hogwash, but at the time consumers were downright frightened by the sight of their own garbage cans.

Disposable diapers were often fingered as the culprits at the top of the landfill. The disposable diaper industry successfully inoculated against these false claims in a series of initiatives launched on the consumer front. Parents were reminded of the product's benefits and educated about the diaper industry's resource conservation efforts, as evidenced by the development of thinner, more absorbent diapers and the use of recycled plastic packaging. They were also reminded that: almost nowhere in America were we anywhere close to running out of landfill space; disposable diapers accounted for only a tiny portion of our waste stream; and the use of cloth diapers has its own negative environmental consequences. By communicating *directly* with consumers, the diaper industry succeeded in placing the controversy in the dumpster – where it belonged.

He who frames the argument often wins it.

—George Will

Pacification: Compromising with the attackers, by giving in to some of their demands.

This strategy is commonly used to neutralize an adversary while, at the same time, preserving a company's primary business objective. Although there are many situations that will not lend themselves to cooperation, there are times when meeting an adversary half-way can actually produce positive results. Be advised that *pacification* must be approached with great care. Attempting to pacify a group like Greenpeace or Earth First is akin to mud wrestling with a pig – everyone gets dirty, and the pig enjoys the experience.

Corporate executives beware. Do not put *pacification* on the crisis management table unless you see no other option. This strategy will be embraced by every Neville in the room. It's what they live for. Ignore them. Use this strategy sparingly. It may mark you as an easy target for future attacks. Activists have long memories.

A lean compromise is better than a fat lawsuit.

—George Herbert

Preemption: Destroying the news or communications value of an attack in advance of its occurrence; reducing, neutralizing or eliminating its shock value.

While *preemption* can be very effective, it should always be viewed as a high-risk/high-gain strategy. *Preemption* should be executed only if the attackers cannot be stopped through *dissuasion* or some other viable crisis management strategy.

The chemical industry has been in a battle royale with environmentalists since the publication of Rachel Carson's *Silent Spring* in 1962. The battle cry in those days was "cancer!" But as time wore on, science showed that most chemicals were not human carcinogens.

Faced with the devaluation of their call-to-arms, environmentalists sought to open a new front with the publication of *Our Stolen Future,* which promotes the theory that hundreds, if not thousands, of synthetic chemicals may be harming our endocrine systems and robbing us of our fertility. Left unchallenged, the environmental battle cry of the new millennium will be "sperm!" – or something a bit more catchy.

But in the spring of 1996, the chemical industry decided not to be silent. Instead, it worked with journalists, scientists and other key audiences to set the record straight and focus attention on the questionable science behind the theory. By the time the environmentalists hit the book tour circuit, their doomsday predictions had been preempted by the facts, and the immediate impact was minimal.

If the attack of the missing sperm had ended there, this story would have a happy ending. It didn't. Say what you will about activist groups and the foundations that fund them (often with industry money), the fact remains that they possess one attribute that is sadly lacking among the corporations who fund the industry coalitions responsible for stopping the attackers: Tenacity.

They understand *Power Play 9: Never let up. Keep the pressure on.*

After the less than spectacular launch of *Our Stolen Future* – its introduction was authored by then Vice President Al Gore – the industry declared victory and moved on to other issues. The activists regrouped, revised their message, and recruited the U.S. Environmental Protection Agency (which is always looking for new opportunities to regulate) to advance the theory.

Millions of taxpayer dollars are being spent to determine whether our future has indeed been stolen, and the attackers have kicked the butts of several chemicals in the process. Industry is now on the defensive, with little hope of regaining the ground that has been lost.

> Nothing in the world can take the place of persistence. Talent will not; nothing is more common than unsuccessful men with talent. Genius will not; unrewarded genius is almost a proverb. Education will not; the world is full of educated derelicts. Persistence and determination are omnipotent. The slogan 'Press on' has solved and always will solve the problems of the human race.
>
> —Calvin Coolidge

Stultification: Subjecting the attackers and their claims to public ridicule and derision.

Stultification is another high-risk/high-gain strategy. It works best if your adversary's self interest is contrary to the best interests of vulnerable segments of the population, or if the adversary's message flies in the face of conventional wisdom. For example: "Chemicals are threatening our fertility." Sure they are, and that's why the planet is bursting at the seams with people! "Offshore oil platforms destroy the marine environment." Sure they do, and that's why millions of fish and shellfish make their homes under them.

"Aerial pesticide spraying should never be permitted in our communities." That's absolutely correct. It's much better to let children, pregnant women and old people die from malaria and the West Nile virus.

A music licensing agency gets heavy-handed with small businesses. Many complain that fee collection tactics have crossed the line. But the victims aren't the type that evoke public sympathy – that is, until someone discovers that the licensing agency is playing hard ball with the Girl Scouts. Pay up, or stop singing our songs around your campfires! Within days, media ridicule and public protest rain down on the aggressor, creating a chilling effect on those heavy-handed collection tactics.

> Ridicule is man's most potent weapon.
>
> —Saul D. Alinsky

Subordination: Positioning an alleged hazard or risk as trivial, when compared to the personally relevant benefits of a product or an organization.

The risk versus benefit approach is one of the oldest strategies in the crisis management book. Consumers will take benefits into account when a product is attacked – if they are aware of the benefits in advance of an attack. Communicating a benefits message during a crisis is tricky business. Do it wrong, and consumer outrage may increase.

An activist group attacks a new gasoline, claiming it makes people dizzy and nauseous and poses potentially dangerous health effects. The media, hungry to ignite their audience, initially reports each unsubstantiated claim. The affected industries educate reporters about the environmental attributes and long-term benefits of cleaner burning gasoline, comparing these benefits to the product's *true* liabilities – it smells different and costs a little more. Reporters start to question the activists' motives. The result? The group's leader admits to a reporter that the attacks were orchestrated by a corporate competitor.[9] Activist group loses face. Consumer hysteria dissipates...until the next attack.

> People are not interested in my seeds. They're interested in their lawns.
>
> —David Burpee

Vitiation: Positioning the attackers and their allegations as corrupt, faulty, invalid or acting in reckless disregard for the truth.

Motivated adversaries often have a hidden agenda or a pattern of attack. The strategy of exposing the "method to the means" often provides a defense for companies on the receiving end of these attacks. By revealing their corrupt, faulty or invalid information, you can put attackers on the defensive and neutralize their messages.

In some situations, this highly aggressive *vitiation* strategy can be used to position the attackers as the villains.

A national motel chain found itself the target of increasing media attention over "peeping tom" claims. A tabloid broadcaster picked up on an unsubstantiated report from two motel guests, who claimed they discovered multiple holes drilled in the walls, allowing employees to spy on them.

Using investigative techniques, the motel chain learned that the couple had a long history of making false public accusations. When it found out that the tabloid TV host had already taped a segment on the couple and was scheduled to air it within days, the motel chain aggressively presented its evidence and threatened to go public. The company's lawyers also reminded the show's producers of the *New York Times* standard of "reckless or knowing disregard for the truth and wanton and willful indifference to the rights" of an innocent party.

The segment was never aired. The disaster was averted. The attackers disappeared into the night.

The motel chain had understood the stakes. It didn't fall for that *wei-ji* nonsense – crisis as danger and opportunity. The danger of having its reputation ruined was real and immediate. The "opportunity" of getting a fair shake by a television tabloid and its extortionist guests was illusory, at best.

> When you look at the times in history when change was brought about, there were two factors – crisis and leadership.
>
> —Hernando de Soto, author, "The Mystery of Capital"[10]

Chapter 6 Notes

1. Ron Arnold and Alan Gottlieb, *Trashing the Economy: How Runaway Environmentalism Is Wrecking America*, Bellevue, WA: Free Enterprise Press (1993), page 632.
2. William Aiken, "Ethical Issues in Agriculture" in Tom Regan (editor), *Earthbound: New Introductory Readings in Environmental Ethics*, New York: Random House (1984), p. 269.
3. David Foreman, quoted in Gregg Easterbrook, "Everything you know about the environment is wrong," *The New Republic* (April 30, 1990), page 18.
4. Bahgat Eluadi and Adel Rifaat, Interview with Jacques Cousteau, *Novelle Observateur*, November 1991.
5. Pramit Pal Chadhuri, *The Telegraph*, personal communication to editor Paul Driessen, April 7, 1999.
6. John Meredith, "Bio-foods can improve nutrition in America, cut starvation and disease in Africa," *National Policy Analysis* #298 (June 2000), Washington, DC: National Center for Public Policy Research.
7. "Cancer Study Deemphasizes Genes' Role," Rick Weiss, *The Washington Post*, p. A-1, July 13, 2000.
8. "Environmental and Heritable Factors in the Causation of Cancer," Paul Lichtenstein, PhD., Niels V. Holm, M.D., Ph.D., *et al.*, *The New England Journal of Medicine*, Vol. 343, No. 2, July 13, 2000.
9. "Man tied to ethanol firm aided methanol opponent," Nancy Phillips, *Philadelphia Inquirer*, July 30, 1996.
10. Hernando de Soto, *The Mystery of Capital: Why capitalism triumphs in the West and fails everywhere else*, New York: Basic Books (2000).

Part Three

The Pitfalls

7

How to Lose

Every normal man must be tempted at times to spit on his
hands, hoist the black flag, and begin slitting throats.
—H.L. Mencken

The right to speak is of little value if no one is listening.
—Robert Cirino

Where there's smoke, there's probably a smoke making
machine.
—John Fitzgerald Kennedy

During the Gulf War, General H. Norman Schwarzkopf orchestrated a
psychological warfare operation (PSYOPS) aimed at Iraqi troops, before
coalition ground forces entered Kuwait to retake the oil-soaked real estate.
Schwarzkopf's message was plain, simple and personally relevant: "What
you are doing in Kuwait is evil and against your religious beliefs. Get out
or die."[1]

General Schwarzkopf was not only a great military strategist, but also
a great communicator. If Stormin' Norman had allowed public relations
wizards to craft the message, it might have read something like this: "Can't
we all get along? Your unauthorized tour of Kuwait was not well thought
out. If you leave now, you and your neighbors, regardless of their race,
religion, gender or sexual preference, can celebrate the upcoming holidays
in peace."

Far fetched? Read some of the mumbo jumbo that comes out of the U.S. State Department. And, if you think *that's* meaningless drivel, try reading some of the press statements issued by corporate America. Many of them are the product of discussions that sound something like this.

Company CEO: *We know our product isn't hurting babies. All of our research says there is no risk at these levels of exposure. So what's our message to consumers who watch Brian Cross and those environmental extremists lambaste our product?*

Larry, the Ph.D: *We're a science-based company. Let's tell them that, based on hundreds of studies, there is no evidence our product hurts babies, only rats at very high exposures.*

Company CEO: *Why can't we tell them the product is safe? Don't worry, be happy.*

Moe, the Lawyer: *We can't just tell them it's safe. That would put us in a world of hurt. What if someone misuses the product, and a kid gets sick? The lawyers on the other side would have a field day with that statement. We need to give ourselves some wiggle room. Let's tell them that "we pride ourselves on risk management, and the product won't hurt babies if it is used properly."*

Curley, the PR Flack: *Terms like risk management won't get us into any trouble, but let's make sure to include a positive message: "Our product has been used by babies for over 30 years."*

Company CEO: *So what's the damn message? What am I supposed to say on camera, when I'm interviewed by Brian Cross?*

Moe, the Lawyer: *First, you are not doing the interview. Think about your career. We can't risk putting you on camera with that jackal Brian Cross. That's why we hired Larry and Curley. Let one of them do it.*

Company CEO: *So, our product is attacked, and I'm supposed to let Curley defend it? I suppose that will work.*

Moe, the Lawyer: *Curley's the P.R. guy. Brian Cross will understand, and the public won't know the difference. Now, try this message on for size. "We've conducted hundreds of safety studies to better understand our product, using the best risk management in the business, and we believe that our product does not produce adverse health effects in current applications and when used properly by consumers. A baby would have to ingest 500 parts per billion of this stuff before there would be anything to worry about."*

Two days later, Curley and Brian meet for the interview:

Brian Cross: *We're talking about the safety of thousands of babies. Why won't your CEO defend this product?*

Curley, the PR Flack: *Our CEO is at a board meeting. He has a business to run.*

Brian Cross: *So your CEO thinks a board meeting is more important than the health and safety of thousands of babies?*

Curley, the PR Flack: *Our CEO is concerned about babies. His priority today is to protect our stock value. That's why he's at the board meeting.*

Brian Cross: *Can you guarantee that your product isn't going to give kids cancer?*

Curley, the PR Flack: *Our product has been on the market for over 30 years.*

Brian Cross: *Yes, and I'm sure you know that the cancer rate in children has been increasing for the past 30 years.*

Curley, the PR Flack: *I can't comment on that. I don't know where you got that information.*

Brian Cross: *I got that information from the Centers for Disease Control. But you haven't answered my question. Can you guarantee that your product doesn't give kids cancer?*

Curley, the PR Flack: *I can say that we've conducted hundreds of safety studies to better understand our product using the best risk management in the business, and we believe that our product does not produce adverse health effects in current applications and when used properly by consumers. A baby would have to ingest 500 parts per billion of this stuff before there would be anything to worry about.*

Brian Cross: *But you can't guarantee that it's safe, right?*

Curley, the PR Flack: *Well, Brian, you and I both know that there are no guarantees in life!*

Brian Cross: *We're talking babies here, and at least one scientist thinks this product may be giving kids cancer. Dr. Bruce Fernhugger from the group Doctors Against Profits has a lot to say about this product.*

Dr. Bruce: *This product causes cancer in laboratory animals. We all want to do what's right for our children. Do you want to take the chance that this product will give your child cancer? This product should be taken off the shelves and out of our babies' cribs immediately.*

Brian Cross: *Parents, you've heard what the company has to say, and you've heard Dr. Fernhugger's concerns. Now it's up to you. I'll be following this story to bring you future updates.*

Who won that little skirmish in front of ten million households? If you believe the company did, you've either been smoking a controlled substance or you've been spending too much time listening to PR geldings and zero-risk lawyers. The company played the part of a one-legged man in a butt-kicking contest, because it sent a flack to defend its product and because its message had the communications impact of pond scum – or worse.

What did the company's message communicate?

1. Babies are less important than board meetings (stock value and profits come first).

2. We can't guarantee the safety of the product, but we are trying to understand it (we don't completely understand our product).

3. We've done a lot of testing on this product (so, maybe there *is* something wrong with it).

4. If your baby misuses this product and gets 500 parts per billion, start to worry.

5. This product has been in the market for 30 years (so lots of babies could have been exposed).

What did Dr. Fernhugger's message communicate?

1. This product could give your kid cancer.

2. A *good* parent wouldn't take that risk.

3. Better safe than sorry.

4. Ban the product until the company can prove its absolutely safe.

In *Rules for Radicals*, Alinsky writes: "You don't communicate with anyone purely on the rational facts or ethics of an issue."[2]

The fundamental problem with most corporate messages is that they are unemotional and usually mix the two worst ingredients available for concocting a message: weasel words and highly technical science. The weasel words are supplied by you-know-who, and the science is often the only evidence available to defend the product.

What should corporate executives do? First, include some emotion in the message. "We care about kids. We're parents too." Second, abandon the elitist notion that consumers don't recognize a weasel word for what it is. They may not be Yale graduates, but they damn sure understand the difference between "this is a safe product," and "we've conducted hundreds of safety studies to better understand our product, using the best risk management in the business, blah, blah, blah." Third, after you and your team have developed good answers to the tough questions you're likely to get, do the Q&A again as a live-fire exercise, with someone playing the role of a vindictive Brian Cross.

The point? Your mission, should you accept responsibility for message development, is to eliminate, eradicate and erase the weasel words. Force the PR consultants and lawyers to justify their use. If they can't convince you that a weasel is absolutely necessary to protect the company, send them packing.

Improving your message

One relatively painless way to find out if your message is in the weasel-free zone is to put the lawyer or PR consultant in front of a camera for some Brian Cross-style questioning. Instruct the person being interviewed to include the message in every answer, no matter how repetitive it might sound. Instruct the interviewer to ask the nastiest questions possible; the smoking-gun questions that keep you up at night. The objective of the Brian Cross impersonator should be *sweat*! Make that attorney or flack perspire with great profusion. Then, play the interview back and see whether your message passes the red face test.

The person being interviewed will leave the experience with a greater appreciation for what it's like to defend a product on camera and under fire. Chances are there will be far fewer suggested weasel words in future message development sessions.

Incorporating scientific analysis and information in the message is very dicey, and complicated by the need to bring evidence to the table that counters the bogus or misleading claims made by attackers. The fact is, consumers and reporters are complete illiterates when it comes to science and scientific inquiry. Few of them took any science courses after their sophomore year in high school, and almost all have forgotten nearly everything they ever did learn.

A 1999 survey conducted by the National Science Foundation found that only 21 percent of adults provided good explanations for what it means to study something scientifically. Only 13 percent of the respondents were able to define a molecule, and just 11 percent successfully defined radiation. If it makes you feel better, 45 percent of those surveyed answered "true" to the statement, "Human beings as we know them today, developed from earlier species of animals."[3]

Worse yet, a survey published in 1998 by the University of New Mexico
Institute for Public Policy found that 72 percent of the public agreed that
"scientific research is almost always affected by the values held by the
researcher." Sixty-three percent agreed that the "same scientific evidence
can be interpreted to fit opposing views."[4] So, even if consumers were able
to understand a company's research findings, a large majority would believe
the results were tainted by the company's values, or interpreted to coincide
with a corporate agenda.

Ever wonder why anti-business activists constantly yelp in the media
about "industry-funded research"? Now you know. Their yelping reinforces
these attitudes.

Ever wonder why news stories almost never mention the billions of
dollars of foundation and government money that increasingly funds studies
by "independent" researchers, like the ones hired by the attack groups and
government agencies? Such funding is often used to promote policy initiatives with biased research results, and the end game is "science by press
release," to ensure maximum Page One coverage of alarming claims that
have not yet been subjected to peer review.

These facts are the last thing anti-business activists want discussed in
public. But why "investigative reporters" are so reluctant to point out these
incestuous relationships is harder to fathom – unless they too have an axe
to grind or view advancing the attackers' agenda as their "subversive little
mission."

It gets better. The National Science Foundation survey also found that
television is the leading source of information about new developments in
science and technology, followed by books and newspapers.[5] In a 1996
Roper survey, 46 percent of adults said they pay a lot of attention to news
reports about science on evening news shows or programs like "20/20" or
"Nightline." Hold that thought.

A 1997 survey of scientists and reporters, published by the First Amendment Center, found that 48 percent of the scientists and 27 percent of the
journalists said they have hardly any confidence in television reporting.
Confidence in television reporting was the lowest of any news medium.
Thus, the medium most relied upon by the public, as its source of information
about science and technology, is the medium least trusted by scientists and
reporters.

In fact, the news media in general receive very low credibility ratings
from scientists. The vast majority of scientists surveyed either "strongly"
(52 percent) or "somewhat" (39 percent) agreed with the statement, "Few
members of the news media understand the nature of science and technology,

such as the tentativeness of most scientific discovery and the complexities of results."[6] What does this research say about science in the message?

- First, it better be presented in 5th grade terms (not 50 parts per billion or, worse, 50 micrograms per liter).

- Second, the research will be most credible if it is not tied financially, or otherwise, to the company.

- Third, the science message must be coupled with a personally relevant emotional message.

That's a tall order to fill. Corporate executives should not trust themselves (or their consultants) to get the message right. The message and the messenger are everything. Without both, you are a loser. The only way to ensure that a message stands a good chance of neutralizing an attacker's propaganda is to test it on the people who count – your target audience.

There are a number of research techniques available for message testing. Just make sure you hire a qualified research firm to get the job done. My personal preference is Wirthlin Worldwide; the folks who conducted public opinion research and message development for President Ronald Reagan. They wrote the book on a research technique that aids message development and testing, by ensuring that the message resonates with the core values (not simply the opinions and attitudes) of the intended target audience. The technique is complex and time-consuming, but it works – which is more than I can say for most of the alchemy peddled by so-called spin doctors.

Presenting your message

How do you use a message with the media once you've got one? Try this three-part formula for every answer. Lead with the *conclusion*, followed by a brief *explanation*, followed by the *message* (if it hasn't already been delivered in parts one or two).

Question: Is your product safe?

Answer: You bet (conclusion). It has been in the market for 30 years with no problems and we've done safety studies just to make sure (explanation). This company's highest priority is to make safe products that improve the quality of life for all of our kids (message).

Why the conclusion first? It's human nature to lead with the explanation. But in tough interviews, the spokesperson may be interrupted in mid-sentence and never communicate the conclusion. Industry spokespeople suffer from a credibility gap. Leading with the explanation without ever communicating the conclusion may cause the reporter and the audience to believe that you are avoiding the question. Another spin-meister trying to blow smoke up their shorts. No sale.

Why repeat the message with every answer? Quite simple. A spokesperson has two objectives. First, deliver accurate information. Second, deliver that all-important message. Being quoted without the message means you've scored 50% on the test. An "F" by most standards.

In a broadcast interview, message repetition is the only game in town. Fail to deliver the message in a single answer, and you can rest assured that's the one that will find its way to the airwaves. With print journalists this rule can be relaxed a bit. However, a newspaper quote that doesn't include the message is just as ineffective as shooting blanks on the tube.

But, what about spin? Isn't spin the silver bullet in crisis communications? After all, look what it did for Bill Clinton. Business executives should beware of PR industry snake oil salesmen who pitch "spin" every time they walk into a board room. Remove the word "spin" from your vocabulary and replace it with the words "Spin sucks!"

Spin doesn't work. It wasn't spin that kept Bill Clinton's approval ratings high. It was the economy, stupid – combined with the fact that Mr. Clinton's personal behavior was not only consistent with what the voters expected of him, but also consistent with America's cultural values (or lack thereof) at the time. During an appearance on network television, my business partner, Eric Dezenhall, was asked to explain Clinton's approval ratings. Dezenhall's answer was eloquent in its simplicity: "The ratings mean we approve."

The next time someone tells you that spin's the answer, ask yourself whether it worked for Bill Gates, Firestone, DDT, Pee Wee Herman, Union Carbide, Richard Nixon, Alar, the Ford Pinto, Newt Gingrich, or any of the hundreds of other individuals, products and corporations that have been in deep doo-doo at one time or another.

Actually, spin has great entertainment value. Don't you love it when politicians "welcome" FBI investigations into their financial dealings? And when a CEO attempts to redefine the term "child" in response to charges that he's exploiting working children in Bangladesh to make profits – well, that's a real knee-slapper. Just remember when your time comes that the movie "Wag the Dog," with Dustin Hoffman and his virtual war, was entertainment, not reality.

The best way to avoid looking evasive is never to evade. Give a straight answer, in clear and compelling language, and you increase the chances that the public will believe you.

Spin sucks. It undermines your credibility. Whatever the situation, your message should tell it like it is. If Greenpeace is misrepresenting science or just plain lying about your product, say so. A large segment of the consumer population thinks that Greenpeace activists are a wacky bunch of lefties, using environmental issues to achieve their anti-capitalism political agenda. They are joined by Greenpeace founder Dr. Patrick Moore, who was interviewed in 1999 by the magazine *NewScientist*.[7]

Question: *How has the environmental movement got it so wrong?*

Moore: *The environmental movement abandoned science and logic somewhere in the mid-1980s, just as mainstream society was adopting all the more reasonable items on the environmental agenda. This was because many environmentalists couldn't make the transition from confrontation to consensus, and could not get out of adversarial politics. This particularly applies to political activists who were using environmental rhetoric to cover up agendas that had more to do with class warfare and anti-corporatism than they did with the actual science of the environment.*

Question: *But hasn't environmentalism always been about opposing the establishment?*

Moore: *Environmentalism was always anti-establishment, but in the early days of Greenpeace we did not characterize ourselves as left wing. That happened after the fall of the Berlin wall when a whole bunch of left wing activists, who no longer had any role in the peace, women's or labour movements, joined us. I would go to the Greenpeace Toronto office and there would be an awful lot of young people wearing army fatigues and red berets in there.*

So, if one of the founding fathers of Greenpeace can tell it like it is, why can't your company? Here's the typical PR response: "We're a corporation and it's not nice for companies to say that environmental groups have misled the public to achieve their political purposes. It might hurt our image."

Give me a break. The public expects you to defend your product. They assume that if some group attacks your product for no good reason, you are going to set the record straight. When you don't, they assume the attackers must be right. Period.

Getting blindsided on your initiative – inexcusable

In early 2001, hysterical news stories condemned the Bush administration's decision to postpone implementation of rules that would have lowered permissible arsenic levels in drinking water from 50 parts per billion to 10 ppb, until scientists could reexamine whether such a reduction was necessary. The administration was pilloried and excoriated for weeks, thanks to longstanding public anxiety over this well known poison, a well-crafted attack by anti-chemical zealots and liberal congressional Democrats, an unfriendly news media that has roughly a ninth-grade grasp of chemistry and toxicology, and a poorly planned initiative by Team Bush.

The lessons of this communications imbroglio need to be learned by the White House and any other organization involved in high profile public policy initiatives, litigation defense or marketplace assaults.

First, predicting that radical groups will generate well-orchestrated outrage over a hot-button issue like arsenic (or global warming or oil drilling) is not rocket science. You know its coming. The only question is, will you be ready? Set up a rapid education and response group in advance, and staff it with knowledgeable, experienced, articulate people, who know and understand the attack groups, news media, Congress, and independent experts in and out of government. Team Bush needs at least a White House group, and probably smaller groups over at EPA, Interior, Energy, Treasury and other departments. Companies need their own specialized groups.

Second, plan your big initiatives well in advance, and include your most reliable allies in your strategic planning. Churchill would never have planned D-Day without including Roosevelt and Stalin in the process. You and Team Bush need to remember that. Give your key industry, media, congressional and think tank allies advance warning. Brief them on your plans. Seek their advice. Coordinate strategies. Make sure they have speeches, Q&A packets, print and video news releases, sound bites and a counterattack or two ready to go, before you act.

Third, keep your message simple, and maintain that simplicity even in the face of the inevitable attacks on your proposal.

Fourth, frame the issues before the other side does so, and do it in language that the average person can easily understand. Skip the technical mumbo-jumbo and say: "The old standard was in effect throughout the Clinton years, and even before that. The proposed new standard for this chemical is equivalent to emptying two little bottles of common office white-out into a million gallons of water. The old standard is akin to ten bottles of white-out in a million gallons."

Fifth, if your opponents do beat you to the punch, find out what resonates with the public and take immediate steps to reframe the issue in lay terms and to your advantage. Don't get trapped simply responding to questions, claims and cheap shots by the opposition. Say only as much as necessary to deflect charges, and get back to your main message.

Pow! Right in the keester

Now here's the interesting part of this little saga. Other than the Nevilles and some PR witch doctors, the only people who do not expect companies to aggressively defend their products are the attackers. They know there's a Winston shortage in corporate America. The last thing they expect is a load of buckshot in the keester at point blank range.

On rare occasions, a corporate executive will ignore the Nevilles and gets off a good shot. When that happens, most attackers will behave like your standard issue school-yard bully; they turn tail and run. Others will regroup and return later, to launch another assault – but in the meantime, the company has time to prepare better defenses and counterattacks.

Remember when NBC "Dateline" aired its exposé on the GM pickup truck using little rocket motors for special pyrotechnic effects? When GM went public with evidence of NBC's misdeeds, those responsible for the story were left dumbfounded by the company's determination to fight back. They beat a hasty retreat, leaving on-air apologies in their wake. Several of the perpetrators were demoted or lost their jobs – something that should happen far more often in that business.

So if an aggressive response to the media or an activist can vindicate a company under the right set of circumstances, why don't PR consultants recommend it more often? The spin doctors are afraid to go after reporters, because they have to work with those same correspondents on behalf of other clients. How can they *spin* a reporter whom they *shafted* last week?

Taking on an activist group means confrontation. Confrontation violates the Nevilles' public relations code of social hygiene. To them, everything must be nice and puffy. No rough edges. Wouldn't want to offend someone, even if that someone has a stiletto at the client's throat. Let's just serve up some PR spin and hope we can all get along.

> I would freely admit that on this issue [the environment] we have crossed the boundary from news reporting to advocacy.
> —Charles Alexander, Time magazine science editor[8]

> I do have an axe to grind. I want to be the little subversive person in television.
> —Barbara Pyle, CNN environmental director and originator of children's eco-cartoons[9]

Chapter 7 Notes

1. Tom Clancy and General Chuck Horner (Ret.), *Every Man A Tiger*, New York: G. P. Putnam's Sons (1999), page 476.
2. Saul Alinsky, *Rules for Radicals*, p. 89.
3. National Science Foundation , *Survey of Public Attitudes Towards and Understanding of Science and Technology* (1999), Chapter 8, pages 8-11.
4. K.G. Hebron and H.C. Jenkins-Smith, *Public Perspectives on Nuclear Security*, Albuquerque, NM: University of New Mexico Institute for Public Policy (1998), pages 210-11, 213.
5. National Science Foundation, *op. cit.*, Chapter 8, page 8-26.
6. James Hartz and R. Chappell, "Worlds Apart: How the distance between science and journalism threatens America's future," Nashville, TN: Freedom Forum First Amendment Center (1997).
7. Newscientist.com/ns/19991225/drtruth.html.
8. David Brooks, "Journalists and Others for Saving the Planet," *Wall Street Journal*, October 5, 1989, reporting Alexander's remark at the September 1989 conference, Global Environment: Are We Overreacting? sponsored by the Smithsonian Institution.
9. Quoted by Micah Morrison, *American Spectator*, July 1991.

8

Surviving the Media

The old argument that the networks and other "media elites" have a liberal bias is so blatantly true that it's hardly worth discussing anymore. No, we don't sit around in dark corners and plan strategies on how we're going to slant the news. We don't have to. It comes naturally to most reporters.

—Bernard Goldberg, CBS News correspondent[1]

"Edward," Marder said, "we have a problem. *Newsline* is going to run a story on the N-22 this weekend on prime-time television, and it is going to be highly unfavorable."

So begins a crucial scene between an executive of Norton Aircraft and his corporate attorney in Michael Crichton's 1997 bestseller, *Airframe*.

It seems the media plan to call Norton's N-22 airplane a "deathtrap." The executive cuts to the chase: supposing the company lost business as a result of a television report based on an erroneous view – and the reporters were notified in advance that it was erroneous – could the company sue for damages?

The lawyer's answer is stunning.

"As a practical matter, no," says the attorney. Norton would probably have to show that *Newsline* proceeded with "reckless disregard" for the facts known to them.

"Historically," the attorney adds, "that has been very difficult to prove."

The executive is aghast that the television show is not liable for damages. He can't believe *Newsline* can say whatever it wants with impunity. He asks his attorney, "...and if they put us out of business, it's our tough luck?"

The fictional response is factual: "That's correct."

This episode from Michael Crichton's novel, *Airframe*, portrays Norton Aircraft as completely helpless to defend itself against a media exposé that threatens to destroy the company. To find out what happened with Norton and *Newsline*, you'll have to read *Airframe*. To find out how to win a battle with the news media during an attack, read on.

Business spokespersons need not play the role of sacrificial lamb in volatile interviews with the media. By insisting that reporters abide by some simple rules of engagement, a spokesperson can take control of the interview process and greatly increase the likelihood of a more balanced story.

The cornerstone for these rules of engagement is the fundamental truth that in high-stakes situations, to create the perception of a balanced story, reporters may need a company spokesperson more than the company needs them. They need access to the perceived villain. Absent villains to lambaste, news stories risk high ratings on the "yada, yada, yada" scale.

This is not to suggest that the "no comment, no interview" option (often advocated by corporate lawyers) is the solution to hostile media coverage. In fact, reporters love it when a perceived villain goes the "no comment" route. They know that in the court of public opinion, "no comment" means "guilty as charged."

Nor is it to suggest that journalists are always on the attack, and that companies must always engage in combat with the media, rather than working with them.

However, when predators launch an attack, reporters have a fundamental need to fill the "villain void." The Crisis Creation Industry always casts corporations and their executives in the black-hat roles, and many reporters are inclined to follow their lead. But the reporter's need to talk with a corporate spokesperson invests the spokesperson with the power to demand rules of engagement and negotiate the interview environment, before agreeing to participate.

There are fifteen basic ground rules that corporations in high-stakes situations should consider and enforce when a reporter requests an interview during a predatory attack. But enforcing the rules requires a Winston at the helm.

Media Rule 1: Gather intelligence about the reporter's story angle.

Should a corporate executive attend a customer-initiated meeting without first learning the topic? In most companies, an unscheduled meeting called by an important customer would stimulate a lot of soul searching and intelligence gathering.

Why, then, is the landscape littered with the corpses of corporate spokespeople who were sucker-punched in the media by a story angle? The answer is simple. They agreed to star in a Roman tragedy viewed by 30 million people, without first learning their designated role – Caesar. *Et tu, Brute!?!*

When a reporter calls for an interview, particularly when there's a skeleton that's about to leap out of the closet, your first question must be, "What's the story angle?" Your second question must be, "Can you be more specific?"

Most reporters will tell you what they're after. Some will try to camouflage their true intentions. Others will lie. Your response?

First, request a letter from the reporter, specifying the story angle and the reason for the requested interview. No letter? No interview.

Second, ask your communications consultants to use their resources to gather intelligence about the story angle – rapidly. No intelligence? New consultants.

Prior to the interview and based on the intelligence you've gathered, think of the worst possible questions you could be asked, and develop the best possible answers to each one. During the interview, if an underlying premise behind a question is incorrect, challenge it.

Of course, if your company has been gathering intelligence all along – checking out the predators' Web sites, lurking in chat rooms, utilizing list serves, working with allied businesses and grassroots coalitions – there should be no surprises. The company will already know what the reporter's story angle is likely to be. If the CEO and marketing people are in touch with people in the company's front line trenches, they should know if a new product, process, service or initiative is likely to send the environmental or animal rights zealots into a feeding frenzy. If knowledgeable corporate officers and non-coms have prepared brochures, backgrounders, press kits (hard copy and Web site alike) and "dark sites" (hidden URLs) in advance, the corporate spokespersons will be ready to respond at the first sign of trouble. The real problem, in other words, is usually not voracious predators or reporters. The real problem is usually lousy advance work by the corporate chieftains.

It is better to know some of the questions than all of the answers.

—James Thurber

Media Rule 2: Demand the chance to *background brief* the reporter.

Many reporters initiate stories in response to entreaties from attackers seeking to create a crisis catalyst. There's nothing wrong with that. But, unless you put your stick in the spokes, a reporter may never take the time to evaluate the fundamentals of the story being pursued. If a reporter wants to put you on camera or on paper, that reporter had better be prepared to spend an hour listening, on background, to a second opinion. No interest? No interview. In some cases, a background briefing may stop a story in its tracks. In others, an effective briefing may significantly change both the tone and texture of a story. In many instances, simply having a top-notch online press kit – instantly recognizable on your home page, easily navigable and loaded with well-researched backgrounders on all the tough issues facing your company – can obviate the need for reporters to reach the corporate spokesperson at all.

There's another important reason to conduct a background briefing with potentially hostile reporters, or steer them to corporate experts or Web sites. The current standard for media libel and slander requires that the plaintiff (you) prove that a reporter knowingly and recklessly disregarded the truth as it was *known* to the reporter. A background briefing can serve to put a reporter on notice about the facts – if you are prepared to deliver the facts.

Recognize that you may have to force-feed a reporter the facts, particularly during a venomous assault on your company. A few reporters may not want them. Be prepared to deliver box-loads of evidence and testimony to reporters – and their lawyers – to make sure they understand their responsibilities, and your intentions.

Warfare is 90 percent information.

—Napoleon

Media Rule 3: Think twice before you agree to debate an attacker.

In the world in which we live, corporate America is the villain and the attacker is often portrayed by the media as the victim. If you debate someone who has already been designated as the victim *du jour*, be prepared to turn the tables on your adversary. If you are not convinced that you can turn the victim *du jour* into soup *du jour*, don't agree to debate. You will not win!

A friend in the plastics industry agreed to be interviewed by Bryant Gumbel when Gumbel was the host of NBC's *Today*. Mr. Plastics found himself debating two elementary school students. He lost. He didn't do that again.

It's one thing to engage in a rational discussion with someone who disagrees with your views. It's quite a different thing to debate an attacker who is irrational and seeks only to command airtime.

> The American custom is, when you can't beat a man at anything –
> why, the last straw is to debate him.
>
> —Will Rogers

Media Rule 4: Insist on a 24-hour advance review of any document, photo or videotape to which a reporter will expect you to react during an interview.

Want to look like a fool on television? That's easy. Fail to demand this ground rule.

Reporters love to hand an unsuspecting spokesperson a document or photo on camera. They really enjoy showing a video – during an interview – that makes the company look like the devil incarnate.

Go ahead. Sit there and try to read and understand the document, photo or videotape while the cameras are recording every bead of sweat that trickles down your brow, and the road map of blood vessels that has suddenly eclipsed the whites of your eyes. Then, try to respond with just the right tone and sound bite. If you don't look like a fool, you'll certainly look guilty.

If the video in question is purportedly an exposé of your company, its production processes or alleged illegal or unethical practices – insist on seeing the full, uncut version, with original sound. Ask the reporter to identify all the people in the film, and the folks who produced it. If he doesn't know, ask him to find out. Insist on getting sworn statements from the filmmaker and crew about when, where and how the alleged event took place and happened to be filmed.

These requests will not only protect you and your company. They will also raise questions in the reporter's mind regarding the validity and accuracy of the video or other documents. Make the journalist aware that unscrupulous attack groups often try to victimize both companies and the news media, in pursuit of their unsavory agendas. And put the reporter on notice that the legal consequences of reckless reporting can be significant.

No advance review of documents, photos and videos? No interview. Period.

> It is a capital mistake to theorize before one has data. Insensibly, one begins to twist facts to suit theories, instead of theories to suit facts.
>
> —Sherlock Holmes, Sir Arthur Conan Doyle's
> *A Scandal in Bohemia*

Media Rule 5: Always set a time limit for an interview before agreeing to participate.

Imagine sitting in front of a camera for two hours. The lights are throwing off enough heat to melt your polycarbonate lenses. A pit bull reporter is asking the same question over and over again: "When did you stop beating Mother Earth?"

At some point, you *will* give the pit bull the ammunition he needs to complete his story. You'll start asking yourself, "Who am I, and what am I doing here?"

Now, imagine sitting in front of a camera with the lights and the pit bull, as 19 minutes roll by and the pit bull asks, "When did you stop beating Mother Earth?" You respond, "We never started. In fact, our company has always acted responsibly on environmental matters." You then stop the interview.

The pit bull protests. He then is reminded that he agreed in writing to interview you for not more than 20 minutes. End of interview. No blood spilled.

Setting a time limit is among the most important rules in the high-stakes game of crisis media relations. The time limit is your insurance policy. It ensures that you will not be held captive by a camera, or a tape recorder, until you answer the smoking gun question in a way that pleases the pit bull.

Media Rule 6: Evaluate the proposed interview environment. Negotiate changes that will accrue to your advantage.

You are sitting on a straight-backed chair, looking into a camera lens. A black hood extends from the camera and blocks your peripheral vision. A small monitor allows you to see the interviewer – if you look down. But if you look down, you will appear to be avoiding eye contact with the 15 million people who are watching this live interview, and evaluating your credibility. Should they trust someone who can't look them in the eye?

So, you can't see Ted, the star of the show, and you can't see the adversaries who are in a separate studio attempting to convince those 15 million viewers that you are the Saddam Hussein of corporate America. Are we having fun yet?

You can control the interview environment. Don't forget: They probably need you more than you need them. Think about where, and under what circumstances, you want to be interviewed. Should it be live, or taped? A live interview may be an advantage. No editing. Should the interview take place in *their* studio or *your* office? Would it be better for you to do it on location where you can visually deliver a message?

Think about the minor details of the interview environment. The devil *is* in the details!

> Never take anything for granted.
>
> —Benjamin Disraeli

Media Rule 7: Establish the parameters of your expertise. Insist that interview questions remain within those parameters.

You are a toxicologist. You are not a lawyer or a bean counter. Do you really want to respond to questions about your company's long-term profitability? How will it look if a reporter asks you for an opinion on that pesky lawsuit about which you really know nothing? You are an officer of the company. Why don't you know about the lawsuit and the company's financial status? How will your CEO feel if you *do* respond?

If you are thinking about participating in an interview, don't agree until you have clearly established your expertise with the reporter – in writing. Make certain that the reporter understands and agrees to the topics about which you are prepared to talk – the toxicology of your products. Nothing more. Nothing less. Reporters really enjoy dragging spokespersons beyond the boundaries of their expertise. There's nothing like getting a scientist to talk about profits. And getting a Chief Financial Officer to pontificate about science can be really fun. Establish your expertise. Avoid the fun.

At the same time, however, it's also important to help the reporter get the story right. So share the spotlight – refer the reporter to corporate or outside experts who *can* answer the questions, or to a company Web site that addresses the issues. Say simply, "I'm not a scientist, but let me put you in touch with someone who can help you. By the way, our Web site has some excellent material on this topic. Just go to...."

> When you know a thing, to hold that you know it; and when you do not know a thing, to allow that you do not know it – that is knowledge.
>
> —Confucius

Media Rule 8: Secure detailed information about the interview format, *then* decide whether you wish to participate.

"Joining us today on *Ambush* is Max Profit of Acme Chemical Corporation. Call us live at 1-800-RED-NECK to nail Max to the wall with your opinions about the chemical industry." Do you really want to participate in this turkey shoot? Not unless you are in desperate need of professional help. Before you agree to participate in an interview, demand detailed information about the interview format; then verify the information you receive.

Is it a brief stand-up interview for use on the evening news? Or is it a *Meet the Press* format that lasts for 30 minutes? Will there be guests? Who are they? Will there be an audience? Does the audience participate in the interview? Will listeners call in with questions and comments? Will there be more than one interviewer? Who?

Format can make the difference between sweat and no-sweat in a high-stakes interview. Agreeing to an interview without first knowing the format is like jumping into an occupied foxhole behind enemy lines – odds are that the experience will be very unpleasant.

> Little things don't mean a lot; they mean everything.
>
> —Harvey Mackay,
> *Swim With the Sharks Without Being Eaten Alive*

Media Rule 9: Never answer hypothetical questions.

The what-if question by a reporter should set off alarm bells. It forces corporate spokespersons and CEOs to respond to things that haven't happened and may never happen. It boxes you in, by demanding that you pledge in advance – without pausing to think or consult with anyone – how you would respond to a fantasy situation.

If a reporter asks, "Suppose the government changes its pollution standards, and demands that you shut down all your factories, because they pollute too much. Would you then declare bankruptcy, raise prices to pay for new plants, or relocate to foreign countries?" If you try to answer the question with different scenarios, you lose. The headline becomes, your company is considering bankruptcy, price hikes or leaving the country.

The best answer is: "Our plants are safe and comply with all laws. That's a fact, and I can only talk about facts – not speculate about hypothetical guesses that often deal with fiction." Most important, always remember the perspective some journalists bring to the table:

> We in the press like to say we're honest brokers of information, and it's just not true. The press does have an agenda.
>
> —Bernard Goldberg, CBS News correspondent[2]

Media Rule 10: Bring an advocate with you to high-stakes interviews.

The camera is on. The lights are up. The reporter confronts you with photos he claims are proof of your company's guilt. But you have written assurances from the news segment producer that you will be given 24-hour advance inspection of any document, photo or tape intended for use during the interview.

Ground rule broken. Now what?

Even the most experienced spokespersons have trouble engaging in battle when the cameras are on. That's why it is essential to bring an advocate with you to interviews that could get ugly.

When a ground rule is broken, your advocate should turn into an attack dog and stop the interview until things get straightened out. In addition to insisting that all ground rules be respected, the attack dog should remind the reporter that there will be serious legal and professional consequences if the photo ambush portion of the interview is used on the air. (Of course, don't have this fight on camera! And never assume the studio camera is off. Duke it out in another room.)

One final point. Never compromise on established ground rules. Once you violate a ground rule, the reporter will hammer you for your lack of integrity. Once you let the journalist violate your agreement, the journalist will figure anything goes, and you will eat dirt for the rest of the interview. Either way, you lose, and lose big.

The cunning seldom gain their ends; the wise are never without their friends.

—John Pierpont, *The Fox and the Hen*

Media Rule 11: Demand 24-hour advance notice and veto power over any "prop" that a reporter intends to use during the interview.

"Rat scat. Rodent doo-doo. Call it what you will. The Center for Scaring the Public Silly has found rat droppings in most soups sold in supermarkets." And with that said, the reporter puts a can of *your* soup right in front of you – and the 15 million homemakers who are watching you twist in the wind on national television.

The reporter continues, "Can you guarantee that there are no rodent droppings in your egg drop soup?" You respond. "I can tell you that I've checked with the Center and they say they found no material in our soup."

Have you scored a small victory? No! Fifteen million homemakers now visually connect your soup with doo-doo of the rodent variety.

Before you agree to an interview, particularly if a product may be the topic, demand 24-hour advance notice of any prop a reporter intends to use during the interview. If the reporter intends to use your product in a disparaging way, let the negotiations begin.

What if the reporter violates the agreement and puts your product in front of you anyway? Simply pick it up and put it out of camera range. ("Out of sight, out of mind.") Then, because you've prepared for this possibility, you're ready to say something like:

"Brian, you and I both know the Center examined all our soups, and found no rodent droppings in any of them. So your using that can to suggest there's something wrong with our soup – that's a lie, isn't it? Actually, it reminds me of the way NBC reporters put little bombs on the gasoline tanks of GM trucks, to make them explode on cue. Are you trying to give your viewers one more reason to distrust the news media?" Then look right at him, as *he* squirms and tries to come up with a response.

Media Rule 12: Insist on the right to record or videotape an interview, before you agree to participate.

Let's says the ground rules go out the window. Despite the best efforts of your attack dog, the story runs. Your words have been edited to convey a message that you had no intention of sending. And you have no way of proving to your CEO, or that pack of lawyers waiting in your office, that any of this happened. Whoops!

Want to avoid a "he said/she said" battle with an 800-pound gorilla? Demand the right to record (audio or video) the interview, before you agree to participate. Keep your equipment running throughout the entire process. A recording may be your only evidence that a reporter violated ground rules. It could become a powerful negotiating tool with a news organization's general counsel. Your tape may also prove that a reporter acted with malice, or reckless disregard, by intentionally taking your words out of context.

Most reporters feel comfortable with one microphone in the room – *their* microphone. The simple gesture of placing a micro-recorder on the table can throw a reporter off balance. It has a chilling effect on those who would otherwise play loose and free with your words. For the honest, however, recording the interview should cause no discomfort.

One last word. Always inform a reporter that you are recording the interview, whether on the telephone or face-to-face. It can be illegal to secretly record someone.

I never said most of the things I said.

—Yogi Berra

Media Rule 13: Demand 48-hour advance notice of the scheduled broadcast or publication of your interview.

It's been six months since the interview. You feel pretty certain that the story has been abandoned on the cutting room floor. You arrive at your office to find 50 wake-up calls from angry customers, consumer watchdog groups, Wall Street analysts and government regulators – all seeking to turn you into lunch meat. Forgot to set the VCR? Don't worry. Your callers will no doubt give you all the gory details from the lead story on last night's primetime news.

In a crisis, the most important element is time. Knowing when a potentially damaging story is likely to air will provide you with the time to preempt collateral coverage, inoculate customers so they are not caught off guard and prep allied surrogates for follow-up media contact.

Demand advance warning, in return for your participation in an interview. Remind the reporter of your agreement. But don't count on full compliance. Order your consultants to use thei contacts to gather intelligence about program schedules. Tell them that if you get caught between a rock and a hard place, they'll be stuck between a dog and a fire hydrant.

> We should all be concerned about the future because we will have
> to spend the rest of our lives there.
>
> —Charles F. Kettering

Media Rule 14: Gather intelligence about the reporter's style, before you agree to participate in an interview.

You are two minutes into the interview. The reporter is tossing one grenade after another. He sneers. He cajoles. He threatens. His eyes roll. Scenes from *The Silence of the Lambs* keep flashing through your mind.

Fifteen minutes later the interview is concluded. Without saying a word, Hannibal Lecter exits. His producer appears from behind the cameras and says, "You did great. I know a pro when I see one." You respond, "I thought he was going to leap over the table and rip my face off!" She pauses just long enough to say, "Oh, he treats everyone that way."

Bingo. If someone had taken the time to review Hannibal's previous work, you might have decided to bag the interview. Or you may have consulted a media trainer about the best way to defang this reporter.

Another bit of advice: Always assume you are on the record. The public affairs officer for a software and Internet company recalls how a reporter once asked to interview a company executive about general topics.

In the middle of the interview, she asked to take a break, during which she talked informally, off-topic and seemingly off the record. Casually, she slipped in a "killer question" that caught the executive off guard and under the impression that he could speak freely with this "nice, friendly reporter."

When his comments appeared in print, the exec was furious, but the reporter was unapologetic. She later said the key was that she'd never said

"This will be off the record," and this little technique worked every time, except once when an attorney was present during an interview.[3]

Basic rule: It's never off the record – especially when you're dealing with an attack journalist or a zealot-generated conflict.

Bottom line: Never agree to a high-stakes interview until you have gathered intelligence about the reporter's interview style. It's not that difficult. There are broadcast monitoring services that maintain libraries of previous news stories. For a fee, they will provide examples of a reporter's work. If it's a print journalist, do a database search for previous stories. Contact spokespeople who have been interviewed by the reporter in the past. Then, decide how you feel about having your liver next to a side of fava beans.

As the park ranger reminded the hikers, as they headed into bear country:

"The most critical rule for survival in any situation is, never look like food."

Media Rule 15: When you supply the producer or reporter with background photos or video, make sure they all support your message, and don't shoot yourself in the foot.

In the early 1980s, genetic researchers developed an antidote to frost damage, which causes $5 billion to $8 billion in U.S. crop losses every year. Not surprisingly, arch anti-tech Druid Jeremy Rifkin vehemently opposed any field-testing of the technology, even though it involved a naturally occurring bacterium found on many plants. The bacteria had been modified to delete a gene that promotes the formation of ice crystals on plants. No new genetic material would be introduced into the environment. The minimally modified bacteria would simply be sprayed on plants, to prevent frost kills.

After years of protests and legal delays, the researchers finally got their big chance to prove the benefits of this safe, effective new technology on national television. So what did they do?

They had one of their scientists spray these supposedly harmless microorganisms on a plot of strawberries – while he was wearing a bulky "moonsuit," like those used in cleaning up toxic chemical spills.

Talk about shooting yourself in the foot. As journalist Ron Bailey succinctly reported:

That picture said 'these guys are lying' – this stuff is so damned dangerous that you've got to wear moonsuits to use it," despairs Fred Smith of the Competitive Enterprise Institute. By complying with California regulations that unnecessarily required the moonsuit, the biotech industry furnished anti-technology propaganda worth millions to bio-Luddites like Rifkin.[4]

What's the lesson here – besides not trying to be biotechnology innovators in regulation-crazy California? Make sure you're not sending 100-decibel subliminal messages that completely dominate the vital message you're trying to convey.

The American people are a very generous people and will forgive almost any weakness, with the possible exception of stupidity.

—Will Rogers

Communication with the dead is only a little more difficult than communication with some of the living.

—Ashleigh Brilliant,
Chicago Tribune NY News Syndicate, Inc.

Chapter 8 Notes

1. Armstrong Williams, "Media group-think," *Washington Times*, August 24, 2000.
2. Harry Stein, "The media's middle name is not objectivity," *TV Guide*, June 13-19, 1992.
3. Laura Ivey, Public Relations Society of America's Professional Practice Center Online, January 25, 2001.
4. Ronald Bailey, *Eco-Scam: The false prophets of ecological apocalypse*, New York: St. Martin's Press (1993), pages 102-103.

9

Poison in the Well

The Law of Recognition: The more you know, the more
you see. First Corollary: You see only what you are
looking for. Second Corollary: You don't see anything
you are not looking for.

—Anonymous

This is the story of what went on behind a particularly barbed piece of
television journalism. It shines light on the shadowy relationship between
activists, the foundations that fund them, trial lawyers and the news media.
Its focus is a pop culture media icon, Bill Moyers. As the story unfolds,
questions will arise. Does Bill Moyers believe that he is:

- exempt from the rules of professional journalism?

- endowed by the First Amendment with the right to destroy his
  enemies?

- empowered to deny his victims a fair hearing?

Questions.

On March 26, 2001, Public Broadcasting Service (PBS) stations across
the country aired a 90-minute investigative report on the chemical industry
titled "Trade Secrets: A Moyers Report." Most of the same stations also
aired a 30-minute panel discussion that followed. The report targeted the

people who manufacture modern chemicals. It portrayed their industry as having engaged decades ago in a cold, calculated cover-up of deadly health effects linked to certain chemicals, resulting in death and illness for many workers. In other words, the program implied that the chemical industry was guilty of premeditated murder of its own employees.

I know far more about the "Trade Secrets" piece than I ever wanted to know: after the Public Broadcasting Service ran the show, my firm was singled out by Moyers' allies for a particularly venomous attack. Rather than respond in kind, I think it makes more sense to tell exactly what happened and let the reader decide. The facts speak for themselves.

Ten weeks prior to the actual broadcast of "Trade Secrets," a January 15 media advisory was posted on PBS's website to hawk the show. The advisory stated, "Correspondent Bill Moyers and producer Sherry Jones uncover how our health and safety have been put at risk, and why powerful forces don't want the truth to be known." It went on to claim that Moyers' report "is based on a massive archive of secret industry documents as shocking as the 'tobacco papers.'"

The PBS media advisory hit the chemical folks like a two-by-four upside the head. Having your industry compared with the tobacco bad boys will do that.

I first became aware of "Trade Secrets" when a client asked me to try and find out what topics Bill Moyers intended to cover and whether industry representatives would be interviewed to ensure a balanced report.

I had never dealt with Moyers before, but I assumed he was no different from other television reporters I had crossed paths with – folks like Mike Wallace: very tough customers who could nevertheless be trusted to play by the basic standards of professional journalism.

As things turned out, I was right on the tough part.

I told the trade association communicator that I would be happy to make some inquiries, but it would be easier and less costly for the client to ask Moyers directly, the next time he called. My client said the suggestion made sense but, during the many months that Moyers and his associates had been working on "Trade Secrets," they had not called a single chemical industry executive for a response to the "shocking" documents or to request information about past or current safety practices.

What? Something was not right here. Could the Moyers crew have actually conducted an entire investigation without once contacting the target? Walter Cronkite, a journalist renowned for his fairness, once wrote: "In seeking the truth, you have to get both sides of the story."[1]

Dodge and delay

My colleague Sheila Hershow attempted to contact Moyers and his producer Sherry Jones on January 29. Hershow left word through Moyers' assistant that our firm represented a number of chemical industry clients who wanted to know whether "Trade Secrets" would include a response from companies that may be featured in the broadcast.

Prior to joining the firm, Hershow spent nearly 30 years as a broadcast news producer, correspondent and newspaper reporter. She worked as an investigative producer for ABC's "20/20," "PrimeTime Live" and "World News Tonight," winning major awards, including a National Emmy. I figured that Hershow was the right person to represent our clients' interests with Moyers and his associates, since they came from the same world, spoke the same language and probably rattled the same cages at one time or another.

Hershow's efforts to reach Moyers and his producer spanned eight days.

On January 30, Hershow called producer Sherry Jones at Washington Media Associates and left a message. She also left another message with Moyers' assistant, and then called a publicist for Moyers, whose name appeared as a contact on a news release promoting "Trade Secrets."

The publicist told Hershow that she hadn't seen the program yet; it was still in production. Hershow expressed concern about a news release that presented conclusions before both sides of a news story had been interviewed (not the practice at ABC), and voiced similar concerns to Colby Kelly at Moyers' public relations firm, Kelly & Salerno, that same afternoon.

On January 31 Hershow called the two individuals listed on the PBS "Trade Secrets" media advisory. The one she reached disavowed any knowledge of the specific content of the report and told her to contact Moyers directly. Hershow placed yet another call to producer Sherry Jones. Still no luck.

On February 1, Hershow again called Moyers' office, and complained that her inquiries had gone unanswered. She then placed a third call to Sherry Jones and was told she had just missed Jones. Hershow called yet another PBS executive and left a message, asking who at PBS could speak about the mysterious "Trade Secrets" report – the report that no one had seen, but that was explicitly described in a news release and media advisory.

The icon appears

Finally, on February 5, while she was out of the office, Hershow received a voice mail from Bill Moyers, indicating that he had been away the previous week but would be available that afternoon. At 4:20 p.m., Hershow received a fax from Moyers, reiterating that he had been out of the office and had attempted to reach her earlier in the day.

Moyers also requested the names of our clients and stated, "I will certainly advise you if they are identified in the broadcast. We are still working on the program, and as you know from your own experience in journalism, the content of a documentary can continue to change right up until it is finally put to bed."[2]

Moyers was apparently aware of Hershow's background in broadcast journalism. However, he did not respond to questions she had raised about the content and timing of the news release and PBS media advisory, nor did he explain why industry executives had never been contacted to present their point of view and correct inaccuracies.

Subsequently, Hershow sent a faxed memorandum to Moyers: "Thank you for your response to my inquiries. I have advised my clients to contact you directly." And that was *the last direct contact* that anyone from my firm had with Moyers and his associates.

Industry enters the fray

On February 6, Terry Yosie, Vice President of Strategic Communications at the American Chemistry Council, faxed Moyers a letter inquiring about "Trade Secrets." "The American Chemistry Council would like to learn more about the story you are planning to tell, including any information that has already been shared with other parties," he wrote. "The Council expects the story to be accurate, balanced and fair."[3]

Moyers responded on February 8: "We're not finished with the broadcast – it's a work in progress for which I haven't even done the narration – but as a matter of principle I can assure you that it will be accurate, balanced, and fair."[4]

Moyers added that he intended that the final 30 minutes of the program would be a discussion with representatives of the chemical industry, environmental community and public health field, all of whom "will see the film simultaneously prior to the taping."[5]

Yosie and Moyers discussed "Trade Secrets" during a telephone conversation on February 13. Yosie followed up with a letter stating: "It would be inappropriate and unprofessional to have both sides of an issue presented only during a panel segment. Merely having diverse speakers in the final 30-minute portion of the program will not make the entire story balanced."[6]

Yosie also attempted to confirm other information that he believed Moyers shared during their telephone conversation: "You indicated on our telephone call that no individual company or product will be featured during the forty-year time span of coverage. Could you please clarify the specific nature of the information and materials being broadcast?" [7]

Moyers responded on February 28, agreeing to meet with Yosie and his colleagues eye-to-eye, and rejecting the argument that industry should have the opportunity to respond directly to the allegations made in the 90-minute investigative report, prior to broadcast. Moyers added: "Regarding the content of the documentary portion of the broadcast, I would like to clarify your understanding of our discussion on the phone. No individual company or product will be featured during the contemporary reportage of the broadcast. And no brand products will be featured elsewhere in the production." [8]

The message from Moyers to Yosie was anything but clear. Perhaps Moyers intended to say that no company or product would be mentioned in the present tense, but companies whose names or products might be castigated in the past tense would be denied the chance to correct any inaccuracies or to defend themselves prior to the broadcast. It was all very puzzling.

One thing was becoming clear: the industry was being stonewalled by a television reporter, something I had rarely encountered before. We knew the industry would be accused of wrongdoing, that much was clear from the news advisory. But my clients were not being given the chance to correct inaccuracies and defend against allegations of wrongdoing, prior to the broadcast. That was something new. Moyers had not even specified what wrongdoings were to be revealed in "Trade Secrets." It's not uncommon for producers to pussyfoot around the real accusations in advance, but then they hit you with them during an interview. But this time, there was no interview. It was just too bad to be true.

Things went from bad to bizarre. We heard rumors from inside PBS that Moyers was hoping the chemical industry would play dirty, so that he could rally other reporters to his defense. Could this be true? The rumors took on greater significance when media sources told us that Moyers had actually contacted reporters, encouraging them to be on the lookout for dirty tricks by chemical industry officials.

Representatives of the chemical industry met with Moyers and a few of his colleagues at the WNET offices in New York City on March 8 – 39 days after my firm had first attempted to contact Moyers. The industry contingent put information on the table that they hoped would find its way into the 90-minute investigative report and agreed to provide additional information about specific issues of interest to Moyers and his team.

In a letter written the same day, Yosie again challenged Moyers to play by the rules: "We agree with the Society of Professional Journalists code of ethics, stating that journalists should 'test the accuracy of information from all sources and exercise care to avoid inadvertent error' and 'diligently seek out subjects of news stories to give them opportunity to respond to allegations of possible wrongdoing.'"[9]

Moyers took advantage of the industry's offer to respond to his requests for additional information. On March 9, Yosie received a brief letter from Moyers and a *U.S. News & World Report* article on worker safety. Referring to the article, Moyers wrote that it would be "helpful if you could give me the industry's explanation why 'an average of five plant workers have been killed every month in the United States by explosions or leaks of chemicals.'"[10]

Yosie responded. The information in the article was erroneous, and "appears to be based on a report by the U.S. Chemical Safety and Hazard Investigation Board," Yosie wrote. "It is the only report the CSB, as it's known, has issued since it was created.... The CSB withdrew this study in December of last year."[11]

Yosie went on to emphasize: "The American Chemistry Council has further inquired of the CSB if any of the data it has developed could support the claim in the *U.S. News & World Report* article. The CSB response was no."[12]

In fact, industry information showed that chemical industry workers are "four and one-half times safer" than the average for the entire remaining U.S. manufacturing sector, combined.[13]

It is a professional standard that a reporter "test the accuracy of information from all sources and exercise care to avoid inadvertent error."[14] The erroneous worker safety data in the *U.S. News & World Report* article had apparently never been corrected. So, what appeared to be a valid source of information was just plain wrong. Was Moyers and his crew testing the accuracy of "Trade Secrets?" We have no additional evidence that they were.

The plot thickens

On March 13, Yosie penned a letter to Moyers seeking confirmation and clarification of topics discussed during the March 8 meeting at WNET. He informed Moyers that the American Chemistry Council intended to make a full disclosure of all communications with Moyers to PBS. It was clear by then that no amount of cajoling would get Moyers to include the chemical industry's side of the story in his report. Perhaps the powers at

PBS would feel obliged to impose a modicum of fairness and balance on the process. Though Moyers had become a major "sugar daddy" for PBS, it was reasonable to assume that PBS' credibility was worth more than the cash Moyers brought to the table.

Yosie, once again expressed concern about the 90-minute segment of the program: "We are greatly concerned over your continuing insistence that it is sufficient to limit the industry's participation to the final 30-minute panel discussion," he wrote to Moyers. "We seek an accurate, balanced, complete and fair presentation during the 90-minute segment and fail to see how this can be achieved without contacting those individuals or organizations impacted during the first 90 minutes."[15] Yosie also addressed several other topics discussed during the March 8 meeting:

"Both you and your producer Sherry Jones confirmed that the issue of pesticide use will not be featured on the broadcast aside from an infrequent reference to the term 'pesticide.' You also indicated that Jay Vroom, President, American Crop Protection Association, need not appear on the final 30-minute panel. Please inform us if this is not the case."[16]

"On two occasions, February 13 (telephone conversation) and in the March 8 meeting, you disavowed statements made by the Public Broadcast Service (PBS) relative to the 'Trade Secrets' program. On February 13 you stated that you were not consulted by PBS prior to the posting of the news release dated January 15, 2001 on its Web site and were surprised by its appearance. On March 8 you further stated that PBS' reference to the chemical industry as analogous to the tobacco industry 'were not my words.' You also noted that the tobacco industry comparison no longer appeared on the PBS Web site. However, in reviewing the site on March 9, we found the original material unchanged. In addition, the WETA Winter 2001 President's Club Newsletter contains similar language and attributes it to you. We strongly recommend that you and the President of PBS issue an immediate public retraction of this language comparing the chemical industry to the tobacco industry."[17]

On March 15, Moyers responded to Yosie's lengthy letter, stating:

● "We have followed sound journalistic practices."

● "We have thoroughly reviewed the materials you left us."

● "I must correct a misunderstanding on your part. I did not 'disavow' any statements made by PBS relative to the program and I did not tell you that PBS had failed to 'consult' me prior to the posting of the news release. It is true that I was surprised when I read the posted release, but it had been prepared not by PBS but by our promotion agency. What I did tell you is that I had not seen the description prior to the posting and that I had not personally compared the chemical industry to the tobacco industry (although that analogy may not be inapt). As I say, the initial description was prepared and posted by our agency, for which I take responsibility. I am informed by them that it still resides online as an electronic repro-duction of what did appear on January 15, but as I am sure you have noted, a revised updated description was subsequently posted to the PBS Press Room."

In the same correspondence Moyers informed Yosie that he had also selected the questions to be discussed during the final half-hour panel roundtable, including: "What does it mean that each of us has unprecedented combinations of chemicals in our blood? Which are the most dangerous and how can we avoid them? Can we rely on what industry has to tell us? Who should be responsible for protecting the public against unsafe chemicals?[18]

Important questions, to be sure. But what about any baseless allegations and inaccurate information that might have infected the 90-minute "Trade Secrets" documentary? Moreover, Moyers would ultimately select half of the participants and all of the questions to be addressed during the 30-minute panel discussion. Is that stacking the deck?

PBS stands by its sugar daddy

March 15 was a particularly active letter-writing day. Frederick L. Webber, President and CEO of the American Chemistry Council wrote to Pat Mitchell, President and CEO of the Public Broadcasting Service, requesting a meeting to discuss "Trade Secrets." In his letter, Webber said:

"Before airing what has been described as an exposé of the chemical industry, PBS should know that, to the best of our knowledge, neither Mr. Moyers nor his producer, Sherry Jones, contacted any of the targets of this report to give these companies or individuals a chance to respond to allegations and correct possible errors . . . .

"As a result, his report is not based on complete research or a full understanding of all relevant information and perspectives. Thus we fail to see how his investigative report will be fair, accurate, balanced or complete. It should tell more than one side of the story. Our concern is predicated on the standards published by the Society of Professional Journalists that maintain that a journalist should 'diligently seek out subjects of news stories to give them the opportunity to respond to allegations of possible wrongdoing.' What are the principles which Mr. Moyers is following? What are PBS' principles in this regard?"[19]

Webber went on to reiterate a request that had been previously directed to Moyers. He asked the head of PBS to allow all participants in the 30-minute panel an opportunity to view the 90-minute portion of the investigative report 72 hours prior to the taping of the panel.

"Without a prior viewing," wrote Webber, "there can be no conclusion other than that the program is public policy advocacy masquerading as journalism and inherently unfair. A number of other signs have led us to this conclusion:

- "Within an hour of PBS' first Web posting of the announcement of the program the websites of several activist groups announced mature plans for a nationwide anti-chemistry campaign. The groups organizing the campaign announced that Moyers' program would be the centerpiece of their effort...

- "A member company representative has just reported to us that earlier this week plantiff's lawyer William Baggett gave a speech in Lake Charles, Louisiana, in which he claimed that the program will focus on the vinyl industry and he indicated a knowledge of documents to be used in the program. (I might add that the activist Web site activity and Mr. Baggett's speech raise questions as to whether Mr. Moyers has selectively disclosed the content of the program.)"[20]

On March 21, PBS president Pat Mitchell responded to the Webber letter. She refused the request for a meeting due to scheduling difficulties, and ignored Webber's allegations that journalistic standards were not being applied in the production of "Trade Secrets," and that Moyers may have selectively disclosed the content of the program to activists and at least one trial lawyer.

In a display of generosity that can only be described as breathtaking, the PBS CEO told Webber: "I have urged Public Affairs Television to screen the documentary part of the program for you at 9 a.m. on Monday, an hour earlier than the original plan, so that your representatives will have 2½ hours between the screening and their participation in the roundtable discussion portion of the program."[21]

In the midst of all the letter writing, ACC launched a Web site, abouttradesecrets.com, as a counter-measure to the Moyers video, and made journalists and policy experts aware of it.

The Web site featured all ACC communications with Moyers and PBS.

The Web site, and intensifying rumors within the journalistic community, also led to some interesting results.

Poison pill

The morning after Mitchell wrote her generous letter to Frederick Webber, Howard Kurtz, media critic for *The Washington Post*, published an article headlined "Moyers' Exclusive Report: Chemical Industry Left Out." Kurtz wrote: "Bill Moyers, the dogged crusader of public television, is about to air a typically tough exposé on the chemical industry. But unlike the most routine news story, the 90-minute documentary includes not a single comment from the industry under fire. Instead, Moyers has invited two industry officials to play defense in a panel discussion *after* the program."[22]

Kurtz asked the question: "Should industry officials have been allowed to weigh in? 'Sure, we could have interviewed them and cut them down to fit my notion of what I wanted,' Moyers said. 'But that would have been unfair.'"[23]

Moyers' remark about being "unfair" seemed like double-talk. Was it "fair" to expect industry representatives to respond to a 90-minute investigative report covering a forty-year timeframe with roughly 2½ hours preparation and no prior knowledge? And what was that about interviewing industry people and cutting them down to fit *his* notion of what *he* wanted? Is that his usual approach to balanced journalism? And was it "fair" to let avowed enemies of the chemicals industry see portions of his program in advance, and even participate in its development?

That same afternoon, Moyers appeared at the National Press Club for a luncheon in his honor. During his speech, Moyers claimed that he and his producer, Sherry Jones, had been collaborating on "Trade Secrets" for almost two years. Two years for them to collaborate, and 2½ hours for my client to respond. Okay, so I'm nitpicking.

What came next in Moyers' National Press Club address proved even more curious. He proceeded to attack my company.

Remember Sheila Hershow and her eight-day effort to reach Mr. Bill? Well, I can only conclude that Sheila rattled his cage merely by contacting him. In retelling his experience with the chemical industry over "Trade Secrets," Moyers told his Press Club audience: "The first person to contact us was a public relations firm here in Washington noted for hiring private detectives, former CIA, FBI and Drug Enforcement officers to do its investigations."[24]

Moyers was partially correct in this cheap shot. He was wrong to say that we're a public relations firm. However, Moyers was right about who we hire. We do hire *former* law enforcement officials to conduct investigations when our clients are the target of shakedown artists and other low-lifes. And, we're proud of it.

However, I was surprised that Moyers would take umbrage at our investigative tactics, since Andrew Ferguson, an investigative journalist, has written that Moyers, as President Lyndon B. Johnson's press secretary, directed FBI officials to conduct surveillance on the perceived political enemies of LBJ, including Dr. Martin Luther King, Jr. Moreover, the FBI folks he worked with were not in retirement status when he used them.

People who live in glass houses...

In his book *Fools' Names, Fools' Faces*, Ferguson recounts: "As the campaign against King progressed, FBI Director J. Edgar Hoover routinely forwarded to the White House summaries of the King wiretaps, which were placed not only in King's home and office but also in his hotel rooms around the country. The summaries covered not only King's dealings with associates but also his sexual activities. After receiving one such summary, Moyers instructed the FBI to disseminate it widely throughout the executive branch, to Dean Rusk, Robert McNamara, Carl Rowan, and many others. Moyers was also aware at the time of Hoover's efforts to leak King material to the press."[25]

Ferguson also says Moyers and his FBI associates were involved in surveillance operations at the 1964 Democratic convention in Atlantic City. Their targets were dissident Democrats, including Dr. King, who were involved in a credentials challenge to the all-Caucasian Mississippi delegation.

The agent in charge of the bugging operation was Cartha "Deke" DeLouch. According to Ferguson, Moyers and his fellow Johnson aide, Walter Jenkins, succeeded in countering the King Group's maneuvers, allowing the Mississippi Caucasians to take their seats on the convention floor. "Moyers later wrote a note thanking DeLouch for his help. DeLouch replied: 'Thank you for your very thoughtful and generous note concerning our operation in Atlantic City...I'm certainly glad that we were able to come through with vital tidbits from time to time which were of assistance to you and Walter. You know you have only to call on us when a similar situation arises.'"[26]

Ironically, the subject of Moyers' involvement with the FBI surveillance of Dr. King surfaced once again, just a few days after the broadcast of "Trade Secrets," in an April 3, 2001 *New York Times* article by Lynda Richardson. Richardson wrote: "Questioned about his role in the Johnson administration regarding the distribution of classified documents on Martin Luther King Jr., he [Moyers] says he did nothing improper and nobody in the administration leaked files."[27]

I would have added something about "no controlling legal authority," but that's just my opinion.

I was in high school at the time of the King episode, oblivious to the fact that a couple of years later I would find myself in Southeast Asia playing a small role in the bombing of a place called Vietnam.

I do recall watching Moyers on television telling the American people that things were just ducky with the war effort. Richardson quotes Moyers in her April 3 article: "'Did I make mistakes in the White House? Yes, but not about Martin Luther King,' he says, explaining that he wished he had been more prophetic about the Vietnam War. He then proceeds to read aloud, and at length, from a copy of a $9,000 advertisement he placed in *The New Republic* magazine in 1991, his rebuttal to a harsh article about him."[28]

Good for the goose, good for the gander

Moyers asks reporters and the public to evaluate what he may or may not have done in the mid-1960s in the context of history, and that he should be allowed the opportunity to explain and correct inaccuracies. Not only do I have no problem with that – it's what the standards of ethics say journalists are *supposed* to do. I only wish he had provided the chemical industry with the same courtesy in responding to allegations about its behavior during the same time period and in earlier years, when there is evidence that many of those allegations are false or misleading. Does Moyers live by a different set of rules when the shoe is on the other foot?

Unlike the Moyers "Trade Secrets" investigative team, *New York Times* reporter Richardson did what professional reporters do when they're writing a story. She contacted others to check the accuracy of information provided by her original sources, including Moyers. Richardson contacted David J. Garrow, a biographer of Dr. King, who, according to Richardson, "says he got a different response from Mr. Moyers [on the King controversy]. 'Twenty years ago, he very clearly manifested to me guilt over having known contemporaneously what sort of material the FBI was passing around the government about Dr. King.'"[29]

Enough already on Moyers and the FBI. My point? It takes a breathtaking amount of arrogance and some major-league brass yarbles to imply that my company's use of retired law enforcement officials for investigative purposes is unethical, when the accuser has this sort of stuff hanging over his head.

There's one other statement Moyers made during his appearance at the National Press Club that bears repeating. Following his comments about our use of CIA and FBI officials, blah, blah, blah, Moyers observed that, "The founder of the company [meaning Eric Dezenhall, a co-founder of our firm] is on the record in *The Washington Post* saying that sometimes corporations need to resort to unconventional resources. And some of those resources – this is a direct quote – 'include using deceit.' Quote, 'I tell my clients that if you live by the sword you may die by the sword. But if you live by the olive branch, you still may die by the sword.'"[30]

If Moyers had indeed read the October 25, 1999 *Washington Post* article on Dezenhall, he would have discovered that reporter Dwight Thompson wrote: "Dezenhall says he sleeps soundly at night, one reason being that he won't lie or condone lying in any instance."[31] Moyers not only misquoted *The Washington Post*, but did so in a way that materially misrepresented Dezenhall's position, in effect calling Dezenhall a professional liar.

The game continues

Following Moyers' formal remarks at the National Press Club, which were broadcast live over National Public Radio (NPR), moderator Richard Ryan posed questions submitted by reporters. Ryan stated: "I have here a number of questions that deal with the chemical program, as you can well be aware. They all ask why you decided to exclude the industry – shouldn't they have been included? Do you feel that that was wrong now? Do you have regrets? And do you think newspapers might have handled that story differently, since they are instructed to put the opposing view up high in the story?"[32]

The response was classic Moyers. "That's Terry Yosie's spin. He's good at his job. I told him – he said to me yesterday maybe when he gets his next review from his executives that I'll put in a good word for him. I will – he's very good at what he does. But that's not the truth. We didn't exclude the chemical industry from our documentary. We planned a two-hour broadcast in which they would have had – will have – they are coming – a half hour – one quarter of the broadcast to deal with the issues raised by our reporting." Moyers repeated his promise in the question and answer session after his formal remarks: "I do want to say, Terry, that I am a documentarian, and I take too long to tell the story and I take too long to speak, but I promise you you'll have your time, all 30 minutes of it, next Monday night."[33]

So, with just a few well-chosen words, Moyers tried to link the debate over whether he had violated journalistic standards to chemical industry "spin," followed by the unsupportable claim that the chemical industry would have one quarter of the total broadcast to deal with the issues. In fact, when the actual program was broadcast on March 26, the total airtime afforded the chemical industry spokespersons was 13 minutes and 58 seconds.

PBS president Pat Mitchell was at the luncheon. Apparently her busy schedule that precluded a meeting with her counterpart at the American Chemistry Council (ACC) did not prevent her from participating as a cheerleader at the Moyers affair.

David F. Zoll, the top lawyer at ACC, also attended the Moyers event and initiated an impromtu meeting with Mitchell. Later in the day, Zoll penned a letter to Mitchell reiterating his "Trade Secrets" concerns: "...a program purporting to be journalistic in nature is inherently unfair and in violation of the most fundamental canon of journalistic ethics if the target of the program is not given an opportunity to tell its side of the story as part of the process by which the program is created. That is what happened here." Zoll followed with a request: "We ask to see the [Moyers'] video tomorrow."[34]

The ACC general counsel further summarized the dilemma faced by his colleagues: "We face a challenge in responding to your invitation for us to send over any 'information that will contribute to the accuracy of the program' – a program we cannot view and that we know about only through press reports from others who (unlike us) have been favored with advance access to the program material."[35]

The hiatus

Zoll's letter of March 22 was the last recorded written communication between the chemical industry, PBS or Moyers prior to the broadcast. The remaining time leading up to the "Trade Secrets" broadcast was spent selecting the chemical industry's panelists and preparing them to try to respond to the wide range of topics that might, or might not, surface during the 90-minute documentary; the documentary that they would not see until just a few hours before the panel discussion taping.

The American Chemistry Council selected Terry Yosie and Ted Voorhees as its panel representatives. Voorhees, a partner at the Covington & Burling law firm, had detailed knowledge of the allegedly "shocking" documents that Moyers would highlight in the documentary. Those documents were originally obtained through the legal discovery process by none other than William Baggett, the Lake Charles, Louisiana trial lawyer who makes his living suing the chemical industry.

The reader may recall that Moyers had previously selected the issues that should be discussed during the panel roundtable. Moyers also selected the other two panelists for the 30-minute discussion that he said would provide the chemical industry with the fairness and balance it deserved.

Moyers chose Kenneth A. Cook, president of the Environmental Working Group, which also makes its living by attacking the chemical industry, and Dr. Phil Landrigan, a pediatrician and chairman of preventive medicine from the Mount Sinai School of Medicine. In his on-air introduction of Landrigan, Moyers failed to mention that the good doctor is also a long-time activist with Physicians for Social Responsibility,[36] a group of MDs who rarely met a chemical they really liked.

Landrigan was also interviewed in the 90-minute segment of the program and clearly had advance knowledge of the subject matter. The same can be said of Cook, whose organization collaborated with Sherry Jones in the development of "Trade Secrets." But their deep involvement in the production of "Trade Secrets" apparently complied with Moyers' definition of "fairness and balance."

Moyers lets it all hang out

In response to criticism from fellow journalists, Moyers' public relations firm issued a statement and a question and answer sheet through PR Newswire on March 23. The statement quotes Moyers' reaction and reflects his obvious umbrage at the growing challenge to his ethics and professionalism:

> "As usual, the chemical industry is misleading the American people and the press. The American Chemistry Council has known that we designed the broadcast to include industry representatives. Weeks ago we even provided the industry with the very questions to be discussed on the broadcast. When Terry Yosie, the industry spokesman, told me that industry wants to address issues of worker and product safety and the benefits to society of chemicals, I agreed. Mr. Yosie won't tell you that, because Mr. Yosie is trying to defend the industry against the indefensible record in its own documents.

> "I consider myself in good company to be attacked by the industry that tried to smear Rachel Carson when she published *Silent Spring*. As its own documents reveal, this is the industry that kept from its workers the truth about what was making them sick; that opposes the right of citizens to know what is polluting their communities; that manipulated its own science to hide the hazards of chemicals; that spent millions of dollars to buy political influence, carve loopholes in

environmental law, and create a regulatory system that it controls. The people who watch 'Trade Secrets' will decide for themselves who is guilty of malpractice."[37]

I wonder, would Jim Lehrer, Peter Jennings, Tom Brokaw or Mike Wallace issue this kind of statement?

There was once a time when Bill Moyers declared, "A journalist is basically a chronicler, not an interpreter of events."[38]

But that was a long time ago.

The more recent Bill Moyers seems to reflect another famous statement of his: "I own and operate a ferocious ego."[39] No kidding.

Back to the point: what about Moyer's statement?

Were the decades-old chemical industry documents "indefensible?" Sure, if you don't question Moyers' allegations about chemicals, workplace safety and product safety. Was the statement fair? Sure, if you agree with Moyers' refusal to obtain opposing comment in the 90-minute report. Can mules fly? Sure, if Moyers says they can.

And what about Moyers' not-so-veiled attempt to compare himself to Rachel Carson? That's entertainment.

Bill Moyers is no Rachel Carson. She had many critics, but few in her own profession. The vast majority of scientists now acknowledge that Rachel Carson performed an important public service in persuading society to alter and reduce its use of dangerous chemicals – but was wrong about many of her basic conclusions.

As journalist Gregg Easterbrook observes in his monumental work, *A Moment on the Earth*, robins were never "on the verge of extinction," as *Silent Spring* prophesied.

And what about humans in danger? Far from being free of chemicals until the industrial age as Carson implied, humans have been exposed from time immemorial to dangerous chemicals in the air we breathe, the water we drink, the fish and other wildlife we consume, and especially in the form of potent natural insecticides produced by many of the plants we eat.

Rachel Carson also succumbed to twin tendencies common among many ecologists: to observe and analyze natural mutation cycles very selectively, and conclude that the situation is dismal, and rapidly becoming catastrophic.[40]

Unlike Rachel Carson, Bill Moyers has many critics in his own profession. In an investigative article in October 1999, Frank Greve, a Washington reporter for the Knight-Ridder newspaper chain, wrote:

"No TV journalist has reported more aggressively on the influence of money in American politics than Bill Moyers, the anchor of eight hours of hard-hitting, award-winning documentaries on the topic.

"But Moyers has failed to tell one important story about the power of money in public affairs: his own.

"Moyers, 65, a respected figure in broadcast journalism, also is the $200,000-a-year president of a foundation that has pumped more than $15 million into the crusade to change America's campaign-finance laws.

"His triple roles as journalist, advocate and financier have made Moyers one of the nation's most influential champions of tighter restrictions on campaign contributions. In fact, as the Senate began debate on campaign finance this week, Moyers is using his control over money and media to influence public policy in ways that would be the envy of the special interests he deplores.

"His overlapping roles, experts in media ethics say, also pose serious conflicts of interest that Moyers has never disclosed to PBS viewers."[41]

When reporter Greve queried Moyers about his multiple, undisclosed roles, Moyers said, "I practice journalism as a form of public education, and I practice grantmaking as a form of public education. I think a journalist is a citizen and you have to be honest with yourself about what you care about as a citizen as well as what you do as a journalist."[42]

No matter how many times I read that, it never quite says anything. Especially not that Moyers is the money, the message and the messenger.

In his introduction of the "Trade Secrets" panelists, Moyers bowed to the pressure and disclosed that, "the foundation I serve made a small grant to Mr. Cook's organization a few years ago...."[43]

According to public financial records, the Florence and John Schumann Foundation, for which Moyers has served as president, authorized a grant of $225,000 to the Environmental Working Group in 1989, and at least two additional grants totaling $85,000 in 1995.[44]

If those are small grants in Moyers' book, I'm in the wrong business.

On with the show

On Monday, March 26, 2001 the "Trade Secrets" combatants awoke to a *New York Times* review of the 90-minute portion of the program scheduled for broadcast that evening.

Reviewer Neil Genzlinger wrote: "The program tells horror stories of workers who were exposed to fatal risks without being told. It makes a strong case that companies have conspired for decades to hide information and to thwart government regulation with multimillion-dollar lobbying. Appalling stuff. And entirely predictable."

Genzlinger didn't just beat up the chemical industry, however. "There is food for thought, too, in the places Mr. Moyers doesn't go," the *Times* critic wrote. "His program takes the tried-and-true exposé path: the industry is the easy-target bad guy, and everyone else is the victim. How shameless is he? He wraps up the report by invoking that guaranteed tear-jerker, 'the children,' even though practically none of the preceding 90 minutes has involved children."[45]

At roughly 10 a.m. that morning, industry spokespeople Yosie and Voorhees were finally allowed to view, for the first time, the 90-minute segment that they were expected to respond to less than three hours later during the taping of the panel discussion.

What Yosie and Voorhees saw was pretty close to what Neil Genzlinger described in his review. A major segment of the "Trade Secrets" program attempted to portray chemical industry executives as having engaged in the premeditated murder of vinyl industry workers decades earlier.

The report claimed industry knew a chemical called vinyl chloride could cause an array of bad health effects including a rare form of liver cancer, angiosarcoma. It also charged that the chemical industry had tried to cover up the cancer link and had failed to inform regulators about the problem.

To infuse emotion into his documentary, Moyers told the life story of Dan Ross, a vinyl industry worker in Lake Charles, Louisiana, who died of brain cancer in 1990, leaving the clear impression that Ross had been killed by vinyl chloride and by the chemical industry, Ross' employer. William Baggett, Jr. represented the Ross family in litigation against the chemical industry over Ross' death.

The so-called "shocking" documents referred to in the news release promoting "Trade Secrets" came from Baggett's archive. Many of these same documents were the subject of a series of articles in the *Houston Chronicle* in 1998. So much for PBS' claim that Moyers' report "is based on documents never before published."[46]

Ignorance is bliss

Had Moyers been following the ethical code about getting opposing comment advocated by the Society of Professional Journalists, he would have allowed the chemical industry to respond to the allegations contained in "Trade Secrets" *before* it was aired. If he had done so, Moyers would have learned that internationally respected researchers have concluded the evidence does not support a link between brain cancer and vinyl chloride. These researchers include Sir Richard Doll, the epidemiologist who identified the link between cigarette smoking and lung cancer, and Dr. Aaron Blair, the director of the Occupational Epidemiology Division of the National Cancer Institute.[47]

He would have also discovered that the International Agency for Research on Cancer (IARC) carefully studied the health records of more than 12,000 vinyl chloride workers in Europe and concluded in a recent update of that study: "Evidence for an association of brain cancer with VC exposure in the current study was generally negative."[48]

Whether or not Moyers would have factored this information into his report, or allowed it to influence his decision to focus on Ross' death from brain cancer, is anyone's guess, since he and his producer had done a masterful job of isolating themselves from opposing views and contradictory information. They saw only what they were looking for; they did not see anything they were not looking for.

If Moyers, his producer or PBS had obtained opposing comment for the 90-minute segment, they would have also discovered that there is ample evidence that contradicts their allegation that industry failed to tell government regulators about preliminary research results that linked vinyl chloride to liver tumors in laboratory animals.

In its published response to "Trade Secrets," the American Chemistry Council stated: "At a meeting with the National Institute of Occupational Safety and Health (NIOSH) in 1973, NIOSH was informed that European testing had produced tumors in laboratory animals at relatively low levels, down to 250 parts per million. NIOSH also was told that further animal testing would be conducted and epidemiological research was being commissioned to look for possible adverse health effects in vinyl chloride workers."[49]

Had Moyers availed himself of this information prior to broadcast, he might have checked the accuracy of the chemical industry's claim that NIOSH was, in fact, notified. He could easily have discovered that industry had indeed presented the information to government regulators. He didn't, though.

Moyers said those who watch his show will decide for themselves who is guilty of malpractice. So will the people who read this book.

"Trade Secrets" touched on a wide array of subjects beyond vinyl chloride, from benzene to dioxin to industry lobbying practices. Contrary to Moyers' earlier assurances that pesticides would not be a focus of the documentary, several pest control chemicals were mentioned. In fact, an entire segment of the 90-minute report was devoted to worker safety allegations about a chemical called DBCP, which Moyers described as a "little-known pesticide."[50]

Those allegations went unanswered by the chemical industry spokespeople during their 14 minutes of panel response time. They simply had no opportunity to check the facts about DBCP.

Fair and balanced

Chemical industry critics, by contrast, had ample airtime the night of March 26. In addition to placing activists Cook and Landrigan on the 30-minute panel, Moyers interviewed several other chemical industry critics during the 90-minute documentary portion of the program, including: Al Meyerhoff, former attorney for the Natural Resources Defense Council; Sandy Buchanan, executive director of Ohio Citizen Action; and Jacqueline Warren, another former attorney for the Natural Resources Defense Council.

Moyers also interviewed Dr. Michael McCally, a colleague of Landrigan's at Mt. Sinai School of Medicine who is also listed as a member of the Board of Sponsors of Physicians for Social Responsibility, a fact that likewise went unmentioned in the documentary.[51]

Additionally, the "Trade Secrets" production team relied on filmed commentary by Gerald Markowitz, Ph.D. and David Rosner, Ph.D., who Moyers described as "historians of public health in New York...retained by two law firms to study the Ross archive."[52] Moyers failed to mention which law firms had hired the two "historians," or what their interest is in chemicals, the chemical industry and the Ross archive.

Moyers did not acknowledge that Markowitz and Rosner were, at the time, completing a book that would detail the history of the vinyl chloride controversy in the United States. The book title: *Deception and Denial: The Deadly Politics of Industrial Pollution.*[53]

Is it possible that Markowitz and Rosner might benefit financially from their appearance on PBS, through book sales and law firm payments? I'll let the reader decide.

Some of the most critical testimony during the 90-minute documentary came from Richard Lemen, Ph.D., a former deputy director of NIOSH. After retiring from NIOSH, Lemen became a consultant operating out of Atlanta, Georgia. Lemen was also retained to analyze the "secret" industry documents by William Baggett's law firm.

So, almost every "expert" interviewed by Moyers for the 90-minute "Trade Secrets" documentary may have had an axe to grind or bank account to fatten at the expense of the chemical industry. Nonetheless, the industry spokespeople got their 13 minutes and 58 seconds to respond and, by Bill Moyers' standards, that appears to be about as fair as it gets.

Grill Bill

Viewers of the "Trade Secrets" program, regardless of their opinions about the chemical industry, would be justified in posing four questions to Moyers, his colleagues and PBS:

1.   Should industry representatives have been given a chance before the broadcast to respond to the serious allegations of wrongdoing emphasized in the documentary?

2.   Was it fair to deny the industry's spokespersons access to the 90-minute documentary until roughly 2½ hours before they were expected to respond to it?

3.   What did Bill Moyers and producer Sherry Jones have to lose if they had simply adhered to the established standards of journalism?

4.   Were the 2,250,000 American households that tuned in to see "Trade Secrets" well-served by the taxpayer-financed Public Broadcasting Service?

In addition to the criticisms leveled by *The Washington Post's* Howard Kurtz and other reporters, National Public Radio (NPR) ombudsman, Jeffrey Dvorkin, was also critical of Moyers' approach.

In an April 9, 2001, article published in *Current*, a biweekly newspaper that covers public broadcasting, Dvorkin told reporter Karen Everhart, "I found it ["Trade Secrets"] very powerful, tremendously informative and weakened by the fact that it appeared so one-sided." The former NPR news chief said that the journalistic principles of fairness and balance "require a response to any allegations made in an investigation." He added, "[o]therwise a journalist is using his or her program as personal bully pulpit."[54]

Whether it was intentional or not, Dvorkin's use of the term "bully pulpit" resonates with commentary about Moyers' career as a Baptist minister, politician and broadcast journalist. In his book *PBS Behind The Screen*, Laurence Jarvik describes Moyers as "a talented television evangelist but acceptable to progressive, nonreligious public television viewers who prefer sermons couched in the language of pop psychology rather than that of hellfire and damnation; a Baptist minister who hawks tote bags and cassettes instead of prayer handkerchiefs...."[55]

Perhaps Moyers' ministerial training accounts for his zeal against the chemical industry in "Trade Secrets." Clergymen should not share the pulpit with demons.

This speculation is not pointless. The demonization of the chemical industry by "Trade Secrets" will most assuredly have a chilling effect on the already icy relationship between business executives and journalists. Why make an effort to cooperate with the news media when there's a chance you will be subjected to the "Moyers Code of Ethics"?

Who's playing dirty tricks?

Several days following the March 26 broadcast of "Trade Secrets," I was informed that Moyers' ally Kenneth Cook had sent a letter on Environmental Working Group stationery to several chemical industry executives condemning my company's business practices and demanding our firing. He didn't send us a copy. Coward.

Cook repeated Bill Moyers' allegations about our use of retired CIA and FBI officials as private investigators, quoted my business partner Eric Dezenhall, and echoed the claim that Nichols-Dezenhall smeared an opponent by using 'papers apparently retrieved from the trash of one of the preeminent critics' of their client."

Cook went on to write, "I do not think that you or your shareholders condone Nichols-Dezenhall's unsavory behavior, and I expect that you are as surprised as I was to learn of the industry's involvement with the firm. I hope that you will call on the American Chemistry Council to sever its ties with Nichols-Dezenhall and denounce its underhanded tactics."

My colleagues and I did not take kindly to Cook's letter. It put his organization in dangerous legal waters.

Because we're not Nevilles by nature, we contacted some excellent lawyers to explore the possibility of legal action against Cook, the Environmental Working Group, the people who fund them, and Bill Moyers, if he had a hand in sending the letter. This particular firm has an amazing track record litigating libel and slander cases – particularly when the media are involved.

Our otherwise strong case against Cook was undermined by the fact that none of our clients had fired us. Thus, we had suffered no harm, and harm is an essential element in getting into court for any reason.

However, our lawyers did urge us to send Cook a less than light-hearted response to his letter. Here are some excerpts:

"We certainly understand why you want our clients to fire us. We counsel our clients to fight back using all legal means available when they are the targets of unfair and inaccurate attacks by advocacy groups, plaintiffs' attorneys, competitors and biased reporters....

"Over the years on behalf of our clients, we have come up against the Mafia, terrorist groups, violent activist organizations and extortionists, many of whom operate through well-disguised fronts. Working often with the help of law enforcement, we have uncovered a wealth of corruption, fraud and lies – all justified in attacks on our clients under the culturally sanctioned banner of 'the public good.' We don't break the law, we counsel our clients to tell the truth, and have declined business that conflicts with the standards of our clients, the news media and law enforcement. Any statement or any suggestion that our firm has engaged in unlawful or improper conduct is false and defamatory.

"Nichols-Dezenhall aggressively defends the interest of our clients – but we do so within the bounds of the law. All of the tactics we use against our clients' attackers are done with the express intention of having all relevant facts, agenda and funders of our clients' attackers all come out in open court, so that our clients' positions may be vindicated in a public forum. Indeed, we find it curious that EWG and Bill Moyers – self-styled crusaders for disclosure and the public good – feel so threatened by our firm's heavily chronicled track record of exposing hidden relationships, financial *quid pro quo* and the deployment of operatives to attack our clients and their allies.

"If EWG believes that it has credible information that our firm has engaged in illegal or other improper conduct, please provide it to us as soon as possible so that we may respond. Absent such proof, however, it would be irresponsible, false and defamatory for EWG to continue to damage our firm's reputation through sensational allegations about the conduct of its employees.

"Should EWG choose to disregard the information in this letter and persist in spreading damaging statements regarding Nichols-Dezenhall, it will be doing so with the knowledge that it lacks a good-faith factual basis for its conduct. We view such statements as defamatory and to the extent that they are made to our clients, as an intentional and unjustified interference with our business. We are prepared to take all necessary steps to protect our reputation."[56]

As of this writing, we have yet to receive a response from Cook to our letter. However, we remain on the lookout for more notes from Cook, Moyers or their fellow travellers. Only after being advised of the Cook letter did I discover that other people at odds with Bill Moyers have also found themselves the targets of smear campaigns.

CBS "60 Minutes" correspondent Morley Safer was one such individual. In his memoir, *Flashbacks*, Safer charges that Moyers tried to smear him for his August 1965 CBS News report about the burning of a Vietnamese village by U.S. Marines. According to Safer, CBS president Frank Stanton was summoned to a meeting at the White House with Moyers and President Johnson. At the meeting, "Johnson threatened that, unless CBS got rid of me [Safer] and 'cleaned up its act,' the White House would 'go public' with Safer's 'Communist ties.' Johnson claimed that he and Moyers 'had the goods' on me as a result of an investigation launched by the FBI, the CIA, and the Royal Canadian Mounted Police." Stanton didn't flinch. Safer kept his job. The so-called investigation had found nothing.[57]

In *PBS Behind The Screen*, Laurence Jarvik writes: "There is documentary evidence to support Safer's suspicions that Moyers had been an eager adversary. In an undated personal memorandum from Moyers to Johnson, found in a presidential file for August 1965, the young press secretary declares that he has 'been working for the past few days on steps we can take to improve coverage of the Vietnam war.' Moyers had asked for reports from Defense and State Department officials and said he would come to the President with some 'hard proposals.' Although 'we will never eliminate altogether the irresponsible and prejudiced coverage of men like Peter Arnett [later a CNN correspondent] and Morris [sic] Safer, men who are not Americans and do not have the basic American interest at heart,' he pledged to Johnson, 'we will try to tighten things up.'"[58]

I wonder whether Morley Safer and Peter Arnett checked the accuracy of information from their sources, and allowed the subjects of their news stories to respond to allegations of wrongdoing before they aired their, "irresponsible and prejudiced" news stories, as Moyers called them.

My guess is they did.

Mission Accomplished

In spite of Moyer's efforts to stack the deck against the American Chemistry Council, "Trade Secrets" proved to be a mere flash in the pan. The Council's decision to be completely transparent about its dealings with Moyers and PBS produced two very significant results:

1) Moyers' credibility as a journalist was challenged by those in the news business.

2) The collateral coverage that Moyers allegedly coveted, never materialized. No major news organization, print or broadcast, picked up on the story.

Equally important, by agreeing to participate in the 30-minute panel, the ACC spokespeople denied Moyers the grand prize: an opportunity to claim that the industry refused to respond to his allegations. A "no comment" response would have guaranteed a "guilty as charged" reaction from PBS's limited viewing audience.

Dealing with a wolf in journalist's clothing

The rules highlighted in Chapter 8, "Surviving the Media," are effective in dealing with professional reporters – even the nastiest of the lot. However, those rules will not work when you're up against someone who practices the Moyers Code of Ethics. The only rule that will work in this situation is Darwin's rule – survival of the fittest. To survive a "Moyers," the objective must be to create risk for the attacker; legal, financial and professional risk.

How?

Let loose a libel lawyer. At the first hint of a Moyers-style media attack, hire the best libel lawyer money can buy to begin documenting evidence of malice or reckless disregard of the truth. Put the attacker on notice that you intend to record every meeting and every telephone call. Then do it.

Use the libel attorney to communicate your concerns not only to the attacker's legal counsel, but also to lawyers representing others involved in the attack, including the media outlet. Be prepared to threaten legal action, and to back up that threat. While the attacker may believe he's immune to litigation, there is a better than even chance that the broadcast outlet or publication will take the risk seriously.

Follow the money. Use legitimate, legal means to discover who, if anyone, is funding the media attack or those promoting it. If you discover a suspicious underwriter lurking in your attacker's closet, open the door for all to see. Add the name of the funding source to your attorney's target list.

Consider strategies and tactics that will deny the attacker future funding. The one message most of these attack artists understand is, "your bank account is at risk."

Many chemical industry workers and consumers may have been offended by the way Moyers treated their work. Many may have contributed funds to PBS stations. Perhaps they, too, will send a message to PBS next time they're asked to open their check books in support of public broadcasting.

What about the chemical companies and their parent corporations? Some of these companies have been very generous with their funding of PBS programs. Should their generosity match that of Pat Mitchell, the

CEO of PBS who wouldn't give the American Chemistry Council the time of day, much less a reasonable chance to defend the industry?

Last but not least, what about Mutual of America Life, the big insurance company that helped to fund "Trade Secrets?" Should that company's chemical industry customers (and *their* customers) take their business elsewhere?

In May 2001, British pharmaceutical research organizations decided it was time to create risk for those who supported their attackers. The Association of the British Pharmaceutical Industry (ABPI) announced that it might withdraw its business from banks and financial institutions that give in to threats from animal rights activists.

The announcement came in the wake of a decision by the Association of Medical Charities to drop a bank that had severed links with Huntingdon Life Sciences, a drug-testing company. The director-general of APBI told London's *The Daily Telegraph*, "If they [the banks] are not prepared to support a member of our industry, we must ask if they are the people we should rely on for advice and to invest our cash."[59]

If other groups, business coalitions and grassroots organizations were to join an effort like this, the effect could register on the Richter scale.

Are these warrior tactics?

Yes.

Indeed, they are tactics that should be used sparingly, only when the rule of the day is Darwin's rule. But under circumstances like these, it may be essential that they be employed.

Invade the attacker's home turf. Create professional risk for any reporter who lives by the Moyers Code of Ethics. Take your grievances and your side of the story to media critics, ombudsmen, commentators, watchdog groups, academicians at schools of journalism, the Society of Professional Journalists, to those who judge whether a reporter's work merits a Pulitzer, Peabody or any of the other awards for excellence in journalism – and to those who judge whether the work merits an outrageous conduct award for shoddy journalism.

The key to creating professional risk is transparency. Complete disclosure of your communications with the offending reporter is mandatory. Be prepared to acknowledge responsibility for any other actions that have been taken in response to the target reporter's misdeeds. Truth is the only option.

What do you want the critics and other media influentials to do? Precisely what *Washington Post* critic Howard Kurtz did to Bill Moyers. The objective is to convince the critics to question the target reporter's ethics, motives and work product – and to make legitimate print and electronic broadcast outlets very reluctant to deal with their ilk in the future.

Best-case scenario? The attacker receives a very public message from his professional peers: Shame on you! We refuse to associate or work with anyone who has such total disregard for basic standards of fairness, honesty, accuracy and integrity. Shape up. Do right. And come back into the fold as a decent human being and a good reporter.

All armed Prophets have been victorious, and all unarmed Prophets have been destroyed.

—Niccolo Machiavelli

Chapter 9 Notes

1. Quoted at www.dailycelebrations.com/110499 – Walter Cronkite.
2. Memorandum, Bill Moyers to Sheila Hershow, 4:20 p.m., February 5, 2001.
3. http://www.abouttradesecrets.com/letters/2-6Moyersltr2.html.
4. Letter, Bill Moyers to Terry F. Yosie, February 8, 2001.
5. *Ibid.*
6. http://www.abouttradesecrets.com/letters/2-23Moyersltr.html.
7. *Ibid.*
8. Memorandum, Bill Moyers to Terry F. Yosie, February 28, 2001.
9. http://www.abouttradesecrets.com/letters/3-8Moyersltr.html.
10. http://www.abouttradesecrets.com/images/correspondence/Moyers3-9.gif
11. http://www.abouttradesecrets.com/letters/3-15moyers.html.
12. *Ibid.*
13. See "Workplace Safety," American Chemistry Council on its Web site, www.abouttradesecrets.com
14. "SPJ Code of Ethics," Society of Professional Journalists, http://www.spj.org/ethics/code.htm, April 20, 2001.
15. http://www.abouttradesecrets.com/letters/3-13Moyersltr.html.
16. *Ibid.*
17. *Ibid.*
18. http://www.abouttradesecrets.com/images/correspondence/Moyers3-15.gif
19. http://www.abouttradesecrets.com/letters/mitchell.html.
20. *Ibid.*
21. http://www.abouttradesecrets.com/images/correspondence/Mitchell3-21.gif
22. "Moyers's Exclusive Report: Chemical Industry Left Out," Howard Kurtz, *The Washington Post*, Thursday, March 22, 2001; page C01.
23. *Ibid.*
24. Transcript, Moyers Speech, National Press Club Luncheon With Journalist Bill Moyers, Federal News Service, Inc., Thursday, March 22, 2001.
25. Andrew Ferguson, *Fools' Names, Fools' Faces*, New York: Atlantic Monthly Press (1996), page 74.
26. *Ibid.*, page 75.
27. "Public Lives: Away From the TV Fray, Still Landing Punches," Lynda Richardson, *The New York Times*, April 3, 2001.
28. *Ibid.*
29. *Ibid.*
30. Transcript, Moyers Speech, National Press Club Luncheon, March 22, 2001.
31. Dwight Thompson, "Taking On Modern-Day Slingshots," *The Washington Post*, October 25, 1999.
32. Transcript, Moyers Speech, National Press Club Luncheon.
33. *Ibid.*
34. http://www.abouttradesecrets.com/letters/3-22zoll.html.
35. *Ibid.*
36. "PSR Board of Sponsors," Physicians for Social Responsibility, http://www.psr.org/bos.html.

37. Kelly & Salerno Communications, "Bill Moyers Responds to Chemical Industry Attack on Investigative Report Based On Confidential Industry Documents," PR Newswire, 03/23/2001.
38. In www.bartleby.com, Bill Simpson's Contemporary Quotations, 1988: Moyers.
39. *Ibid.*
40. Gregg Easterbrook, *A Moment on the Earth: The coming age of environmental optimism*, New York: Viking Penguin (1995), pages 79-85.
41. "Journalism or favoritism? Moyer reports leave out what some call vital facts," Frank Greve, *The Seattle Times*, October 16, 1999.
42. *Ibid.*
43. *"Trade Secrets,"* Transcript, March 26, 2001 (http://www.pbs.org/tradesecrets/transcript.html).
44. Foundation Center Environmental Grants Database, recipient file of Environmental Working Group, Foundation Center, New York, NY. Moyers' "small" 1989 grant was edged out of first place by only $25,000 as the biggest single grant EWG received that year.
45. *"'Trade Secrets'*: Rendering a Guilty Verdict on Corporate America," Neil Genzlinger, *The New York Times*, March 26, 2001.
46. "'Trade Secrets': A Moyers Report," http://pbs.org/pressroom/2001/winter/releases/tradesecrets.html.
47. "How "Trade Secrets" Got it Wrong: The Story That PBS and Bill Moyers Don't Want You to Hear," American Chemistry Council, March 26, 2001.
48. Ward et al, "Update of the Follow-up of Mortality and Cancer Incidence Among European Workers Employed in the Vinyl Chloride Industry," *IARC Internal Report No. 00/001* (2000).
49. "How "Trade Secrets" Got it Wrong: The Story That PBS and Bill Moyers Don't Want You to Hear," American Chemistry Council, March 26, 2001.
50. *"Trade Secrets,"* Transcript, March 26, 2001.
51. "PSR Board of Sponsors," Physicians for Social Responsibility.
52. *"Trade Secrets,"* Transcript, March 26, 2001.
53. http://www.pbs.org/tradesecrets/program/pop_inter08.html, "Expert Interviews," *"Trade Secrets,"* PBS.
54. "When does the other side get its say? It's after Moyers makes the case against chemical industry," Karen Everhart Bedford, *Current*, April 9, 2001.
55. Laurence Jarvik, *PBS Behind The Screen*, Rocklin, CA: Forum, An Imprint of Prima Publishing (1997), page 57.
56. Letter from Nichols and Dezenhall to Kenneth A. Cook, March 29, 2001.
57. Morley Safer, *Flashbacks: On Returning to Vietnam*, New York: St. Martin's Press (1990), pages 94-95.
58. Laurence Jarvik, *op. cit.,* page 59.
69. "British Research Groups Getting Tough On Banks That Give In To Animal Rights Pressure," *NABR Update*, Vol. XXII, No. 10, May 4, 2001.

10

Ethics Police

The most unethical of all means is the non-use of any means.

−Saul Alinsky

Ethics tell us what we should do, not what we will do. Ethics is a guide to The Good, whatever we conceive that to be. The problem is that different people conceive The Good to be different things. Corporations see The Good as taking reasonable risks to achieve economic growth, technical innovation, public benefit and private profit. Radical ethics see The Good as a world without corporations, technology or risk. Corporate Nevilles succumb to radical ethics to avoid risk. The end result can be the highest risk option of all: Inaction. The boardroom debate goes like this:

Company CEO: *This research scientist from Alchemy College is on TV and in the papers, claiming our product will cause baby boys to develop short stubby...ah...fingers − and you're telling me it's all a lie?*

Larry, the Ph.D: *That's right. This guy's science is garbage. There's not a tox expert in the country who buys his theory.*

Company CEO: *Well, what are we gonna do to stop this jerk before it's too late?*

Moe, the Sales VP: *Who's financing this guy's activities? He's probably on the take. Let's have a private investigator check him out. Use whatever legal means are available to follow the money.*

Curley, a PR Flack: *We can't do that. It would bump right up against our corporate ethics policy. Besides, imagine what the press would do if they found out. Let's issue a statement about our commitment to more research to better understand our product, and we'll throw in some spin about product benefits.*

Company CEO: *Yeh, drive up those benefits. That's the ticket. We don't want to give this character any credibility.*

What did Curly just do? He convinced the CEO not to use legal means to expose a known enemy. He replaced factual opposition research with meaningless hype. He endangered the company. That's not ethical.

The fact is that discussions like this take place every day in company offices and trade association conference rooms. Some folks might think Curly is right. Isn't it unethical to investigate a critic? Well, wouldn't you hire an investigator to expose someone who was falsely accusing your spouse of spreading sexually transmitted diseases to legions of partners? My view? Curly's solution is complete and utter bullshit!

Corporate ethics policies are a guide to The Good. Exposing liars who damage your company is certainly not The Bad.

When an ethics policy is used to obstruct perfectly legitimate decision-making, particularly when a company is being attacked for less than legitimate reasons, then it's time for a real ethics policy. It's also time to remove the obstructionist Ethics Police from the decision-making process.

Surf the Internet for examples of corporate ethics policies and you will come across something called the *Texas Instruments Ethics Quick Test.*[1] According to the company's web site, it "is provided to TI employees on a business-card-sized mini-pamphlet to carry with them." The test poses four questions for employees to consider: "Is the action legal? Does it comply with our values? If you do it, will you feel bad? How will it look in the newspaper?" The test offers further guidance: "If you know it's wrong, don't do it! If you're not sure, ask. Keep asking until you get an answer."

This little test, while perhaps fine for mundane matters, could become a ticking time bomb in a crisis situation. The fourth question – "How will it look in the newspaper?" – has nothing to do with ethics and is an invitation for Nevilles to become Ethics Police.

How will it look in the newspaper if a company uses legal means to investigate a scientist who may be on the take? It probably won't look good. That doesn't mean it's wrong.

Consider what happened to Oracle Corporation when reporters were tipped off that the company had hired a detective agency to investigate

Microsoft's allies. Media coverage was massive, and the focus was on the ethics of the tactic (using private eyes), rather than addressing whether the particular objective sought by Oracle justified the particular tactic employed by the company.

According to *The Wall Street Journal*, Oracle's gumshoes discovered evidence that Microsoft had funded supposedly independent groups to take Microsoft's side in the antitrust battle with the Department of Justice.[2] This evidence was, by and large, lost in the media hand-wringing over corporate spying. Imagine! People who routinely sort through other people's trash, use hidden cameras and engage in other shenanigans to produce *the news* getting all riled up about a company seeking to expose the shenanigans of its fiercest rival.

Interestingly, media reporters were virtually silent about a closely related story. In January 1998, a Sun Microsystems lawyer contacted the head of the Justice Department's Antitrust Division, and offered to set up a "blue-ribbon" panel of antitrust lawyers and economists – all collecting paychecks from the anti-Microsoft factions – to craft a detailed case that the department could bring against their arch rival. The offer was gladly accepted and resulted in a "$3-million tutorial" that Justice found invaluable in framing its case against Microsoft.[3]

Does the Oracle experience mean don't investigate? Not only no, but hell no. What if investigators find that the Alchemy College scientist is being paid by a competitor or professional radicals to use phony research to attack your product? Is it ethical to allow that to happen? Does a publicly traded company have a moral and legal obligation to its stockholders, to protect the value of their stock? Does a company have a moral obligation to its employees and their families, to protect their jobs from predators? To its customers, to safeguard their investments in company products? You bet.

Saul Alinsky taught radicals, "The *end* is what you want, and the *means* is how you get it." His *Rules for Radicals* chapter on the ethics of means and ends became the bible for generations of radicals to come, as you can see by reading the books, articles and Web pages of groups like Earth First, Friends of the Earth, Defenders of Wildlife, the Ruckus Society, Earth Liberation Front, People for the Ethical Treatment of Animals and Wilderness Society. These are not your grandmother's ethics rules, unless your grandmother's last name was Machiavelli.

There are two incontrovertible facts that business people should keep in mind about ethics. First, radical activists have their own radical ethics. Their ethics are incompatible with yours. Second, the public believes corporations are driven by profits, not ethics – and many people believe profits are immoral. It is highly unlikely that they will ever change their minds.

These factoids should be posted on every CEO's office wall, and stapled to the butts of those who constantly cry "ethics" in the midst of a marketplace assault. Read on, until the posting and stapling are completed.

When a company's neck is in a noose and an attacker is about to spring the trap door, that's not a public relations problem. It's a threat to survival. Calling in an ethicist or public relations consultant to loosen the noose is like bringing a butter knife to a gunfight. The outcome is predictable. The aftermath is not pretty.

What's needed in a crisis is a small group of experts and decision-makers who have the *knowledge, resources, authority* and *will* to marshal all company assets for the sole purpose of stopping the attacker. When things go haywire in the corporate world, it's usually because key members of the crisis team do not have the *will* to act.

So, how does a corporate CEO ensure that a company's crisis management team has the *will* to act? How does a CEO distinguish between the ethics that guide attack groups and proper corporate ethics? How does a CEO avoid being paralyzed by wrongheaded Ethics Police? What is the truth about ethics? Here is my realistic assessment of the ethics question, presented for your consideration in eleven Ethics Edicts. Some Edicts apply to corporations, some to radicals and some to both.

Ethics Edict 1: Corporate concern over ethics is a function of battlefield proximity. As the shootin' gets closer, the urge to debate the ethics of returning fire declines precipitously with every step forward.

A sure-fire way to avoid tangled underwear is to appoint a crisis management team with people whose careers, mortgages and children's tuition payments are directly tied to the outcome of the crisis – people who understand that if the company takes the route of the *Titanic*, they'll be on board for the ride.

Business managers, sales directors, product stewards, customer relations executives and, last but not least, CEOs all fall within this category of people who are likely to have a personal interest in the outcome. They're all within spitting distance of the scene of the conflict.

Some may ask, why the CEO?

Take a look at media post-mortems of crises that have spun completely out of control. Who ends up in front of the television cameras looking like a frightened deer in the headlights? Who stands on the trap door at the stockholder's meeting? Who is forced into early retirement? Not the public relations consultant, or the keeper of the corporate ethics code, or the lawyer who preaches "zero-risk" and "no comment."

Then ask: Who has the power to act, and who holds the corporate gold?

Bottom line? The crisis management team must be composed of people who know what's at stake in personal terms – their survival.

But, you ask, what about morality? Moral codes are the regulatory form of ethics. While ethics is concerned with The Good, moral codes deal with Right and Wrong. The best moral code for crisis managers is well known: Thou shalt not kill, steal, lie or covet thy neighbor's property.

Crisis managers also need to know if their decisions will violate laws and regulations. Violating laws and regulations is always bad form, even in a crisis environment. In 1975, the U.S. Supreme Court underscored this point with its decision in *United States v. Park,* which deemed that the most responsible company officials – the chairman, CEO or president – are strictly liable for the illegal actions of a company; a good reason for the presence of an attorney during crisis team deliberations.

As for the publicists, ethicists, lobbyists and all the other "ists," keep them in the closet for consultation on an as-needed basis.

Curiously, the *Park* decision never seems to apply to high ranking officials of government agencies, predator groups, foundations or PR firms, when their underlings, agents, members or grantees engage in unlawful acts – which may include everything from trespass and obstruction to crop destruction by above-ground groups and vandalism, arson and death threats by underground groups.

Ethics Edict 2: Ethics are time-sensitive and perishable.

No, that's not cynical. It's a real-world statement that beliefs about The Good and about Right and Wrong change. Fact: Ethical standards change – depending on people, time, situation and peril. Don't expect otherwise.

What was considered unethical yesterday may well be considered ethical today, and *vice versa.* Anti-business attackers do not apply the ethical standards of the past to tactics that are being considered for the present. And they certainly do not feel obliged to hold today's tactics to some crystal ball notion about the possible ethical standards of the future.

Many industry executives find themselves shackled to the past, not only on ethics, but also on tactics and public policy positions. They hold themselves to the standard that any *means* used today to achieve a specific *end*, must be consistent with past actions and ethics. Moreover, today's tactics must meet a future, ill-defined ethics litmus test. "We sure don't want someone criticizing our tactics ten years from now."

Talk about getting tangled up in your underwear. Face it, any action a company takes that stops the attackers and saves its products from a marketplace assault will be labeled unethical or immoral by someone, at some point in time. That's life. It may not be fair, but it is absolutely predictable.

Moreover, rejecting tactics just because they are inconsistent with what's been done in the past may be tantamount to trading in your pistols and M-16s for a SuperSoaker.® Believe me, that's not right.

The food industry's response to the attack on genetically modified corn, soybeans and other crops in Europe is a classic example of this wacky, self-defeating, almost suicidal approach to crisis management in the face of a frontal assault by direct action predators, who were using every legal (and illegal) weapon in their vast arsenal.

The attackers – a merry band of environmentalists, nutritional neurotics and Luddites – ran around Europe yelling "Frankenfoods!" and questioning the safety of this "mutant American harvest." They were joined and financed by European farmers who apparently believe the cutting edge of technology should be a sickle or scythe, and that U.S. farmers (a.k.a. the competition) are the handmaidens of Satan.

The anti-Frankenfood forces possessed not a whit of scientific evidence to support their claims that genetically modified crops pose a threat to human health or the environment. In contrast, organic farmers, who are beneficiaries of the attacks, use pesticides and fungicides such as rotenone and copper sulfate. These naturally occuring chemicals are much more dangerous to workers and the environment than GM crops. They can threaten farm workers' safety, poison the soil and contaminate groundwater. But that didn't stop the zealots from making doomsday predictions and driving the nutritional nannies of Europe into a frenzied food fight over soybeans and corn.

Most importantly, they did it with a daring, sophisticated battle plan. It was a blueprint for all-out war, hosted on nonprofit Web sites, courtesy of tax-free contributions from foundations, companies, governments and direct mail.[4]

The biotech and food industries' crisis management plans, by comparison, looked like the kind of plays middle school boys scratch out in the dirt, during neighborhood football games.

A radical group called Corporate Watch, a project of the Tides Center, mapped out the locations of GM test sites, labs, company offices, manufacturing plants, storage facilities, ports and other facilities all over England – and posted the information to their www.gm-info.org.uk Web site. The extensive Web library gives radicals dozens of options for legal and illegal "direct action," depending on whether their interests lie in stopping GM foods globally, ending commercial growing of GM crops in the UK, or taking on animal feed, for instance.

The list of actions is breathtaking in its scope, audacity and detail – and includes an entire *Handbook for Action*, for "removing" (*i.e.*, destroying) genetically modified plants in Britain. This "genetiX snowball" guide to locating, spying on, videotaping and destroying GM plant sites is augmented with sample posters, leaflets, briefing materials and "an activist guide to exploiting the media." Like the handbook, posters and other materials, detailed reports on individual GM companies, industry response efforts and many other topics are also available in Adobe Acrobat® and other computer formats. Lists of "local campaign contacts" and allied organizations around the world help ensure that all these efforts really do "snowball."

The eco-militants' investments have already paid big dividends. May Day 2001 events in London caused the city to field 6,000 Bobbies and cost over $29 million in damages and lost business. The skillfully manufactured conflict resulted in extensive, largely one-sided media coverage of the "dangers" of biotechnology and the "unchecked expansion of profit-hungry conglomerates," put the zealots in control of public opinion and generated millions of dollars in new contributions to their cause.[5]

It also underscores, yet again, the results of unleashing such a vast, monied, completely unregulated Crisis Creation Industry on modern society.

Perhaps Greenpeace and its peasant farmer allies will apologize later, when the Europeans discover that their mass hysteria has had the long-term effect of driving the biotech industry offshore to markets that value modern technology and the economic, health and environmental benefits it brings to those who have open minds. Perhaps one day they will also acknowledge that British health authorities first traced that country's rampant foot-and-mouth disease to a small organic-style, family-run farm of the sort that so enamors eco-zealots, where pigs were fed uneaten food from a local army base.[6]

But don't count on it. The Frankenfood fear mongers are already busy organizing radicals from the WTO wars, Brazil's Landless Workers Movement and other protest groups to rant, rage and destroy test crops in Latin America, India and elsewhere. And as Julie Miles, "coordinator" of the Genetically Engineered Food Alert, bluntly told a reporter, even new evidence about the safety of genetically modified crops would most likely not cause her group to change its strident opposition to GM plants.[7]

In spite of these Old-World cultural challenges, food industry executives could have blunted the attack on genetically modified crops if they had heeded Alinsky's admonition that, "In the politics of human life, consistency is not a virtue."[8] Unfortunately, they ignored both Alinsky's warning and the radicals' rapidly escalating marketplace assaults.

What was the most effective consumer message sent by the anti-biotech forces in the battle for the hearts and minds of Europe, and now North America? "They're hiding mutant DNA in your food, so you don't have a choice about eating it." Any crisis manager worth paying attention to knows that *informed choice* is a bedrock value held by most consumers around the world – regardless of their culture. Deny consumers the opportunity to make an informed choice, and they'll make you feel like a prairie dog at a rattlesnake convention. What was needed in Europe was a two-track strategy to blunt the attack.

- First, by the food industry itself: voluntary labeling of food products, combined with a consumer education initiative to raise public awareness about the health, safety, environmental and marketplace benefits of crops produced through biotechnology.

- Second, by respected, independent authorities (scientists, food experts, think tanks, progressive farmers): a concerted effort to question the ethics of the attackers for lying to the public.

This good-cop, bad-cop strategy would have derailed the European food fight. Sure, Greenpeace and the nutritional neurotics would have continued to carp about the technology, but consumers would have *informed choice,* and that's really all they want.

Now, some will say that I am engaging in 20/20 hindsight. To that charge I plead "not guilty." In the early 1990s, my firm helped launch the first gene-altered whole food product: a tomato developed by Calgene, Inc. Calgene's chief executive officer, Roger Salquist, stunned the establishment food industry when he decided to label the tomato, and provide consumers with point-of-purchase brochures describing how it was developed.

The Calgene scientists discovered the gene that causes tomatoes to rot. They simply reversed the gene, extending the tomato's shelf life by several days. This allowed the Calgene tomato to be picked ripe from the vine so consumers could enjoy flavorful, red tomatoes in the dead of winter.

Labeling is still tantamount to heresy to much of the food industry. Food companies have historically fought ingredient labeling tooth and nail, which probably explains why it wasn't done voluntarily in Europe. Salquist was called a loose cannon and a maverick by establishment food mavens. But Roger Salquist succeeded in putting his tomato on supermarket shelves, without setting off widespread consumer protests.

To be sure, Luddites like Jeremy Rifkin, and nose-in-the-air gourmands like Wolfgang Puck, threw tantrums about Roger's tomato, but to no avail, because consumers were offered the opportunity to exercise informed choice. By putting the biotech information in the produce section, Calgene turned the tables on the attackers. The company honored consumers' right to know and offered them a choice of which product to buy – putting the Luddites in the position of denying consumers both of these rights.

Roger Salquist understood that in a marketplace assault, consistency with the past should not be the overriding objective. The primary objective must be to stop the attackers. That is the truly ethical choice.

Not surprisingly, the European "Frankenfood" fight has now been exported to the U.S. and other world markets, where most consumers previously had accepted genetically modified foods. At least one mandatory-labeling bill has been introduced in Congress, regulatory agencies have intervened, and scores of consumer products companies have adopted anti-biotech ingredient policies. And yet, 35 major food industry groups have taken a public position against mandatory labeling legislation, even though a recent survey (by an industry-funded food information group, no less) found that more than half of American consumers said genetically modified foods should routinely be labeled as such.[13]

That certainly is consistent with the past. However, the food groups justified their opposition by claiming that labeling "would result in higher food costs and lower farm prices." They also asserted, "We fully support ...the choice of consumers to purchase products produced without modern technology."[14]

What messages are the food groups really sending to consumers? We oppose telling you what's in your food because it will increase our costs. We support your right to make choices, but we don't believe you have a right to know whether the product you are about to purchase contains genetically modified ingredients. No sale!

What should a label say? It should provide accurate basic information. It could also refer consumers to literature or a Web site for further information that is presented in lay terms and adequately responds to any allegations the Luddites are peddling.

What will happen next? The food groups are likely to get mandatory labeling, whether they like it or not. They may even get a third-party certification scheme – which means the zealots would control the certification process and have yet another vehicle for twisting the facts and raising more cash for their bloated coffers. And instead of being praised as progressive, ethical leaders, champions of informed consumer choice and voices of reason against Rifkin's radical rantings, the industry will be pilloried for having to be forced to do the right thing.

How did American agribusiness respond to the European assault on corn and soybeans? Pretty much the same way it's responding wherever its survival is at stake. Industry looked to the past for a grand strategy that would allow it to export its beans and count them too.

U.S. corporate forces advanced on Europe for the sole purpose of selling regulators on the safety of gene-altered crops. Their theory? If the regulators buy the beans, we can infiltrate the market and win the food fight. As for European consumers, the American bean merchants apparently decided to execute a Mushroom Management Strategy: keep 'em in the dark and throw a little cow manure on 'em every so often.

While this regulatory approach was consistent with what had previously worked in the U.S., it proved disastrous as an export, because European consumers are, quite frankly, different from American consumers. (However, militants, media and politicians in this country are certainly trying their level best to turn every last American into quivering mounds of Euro-Jello.)

For one thing, the Nazis' eugenics programs remain etched in people's collective memories, and many European consumers remember the bad old days when Hitler's mad scientists experimented with an early form of biotechnology in an attempt to create a "master race." Little wonder that some Europeans may not welcome modern gene-tinkering with open arms.

For another thing, Europeans aren't quite as confident as most Americans in their governments' ability to protect them from unsafe food and other products – and rightly so. Ask the families of the 80-some people who died from mad cow disease in Great Britain whether they believe government regulators have the right stuff to protect them from harm.[1] Or those in France whose loved ones died from AIDS transmitted in government-controlled blood supplies.

Third, ask any knowledgeable anthropologist about the strong cultural ties to food in certain European countries. In France, food is the next best thing to sex, or maybe even better. In the U.S., food is what we put in our mouths at half-time or on our way to work.

Fourth, today's basic European genetic stock is a far cry from the one that not so many centuries ago braved storms and adversity in little wooden ships, to launch the age of global exploration and trade. Perhaps the descendents of these hardy souls all emigrated to the United States or perished in two world wars.

Europeans today are now so panicky that the merest whisper of risk sends them diving under the bed covers. "Europe has lost its nerve," says Frank Furedi, a sociologist at Britain's University of Kent. "Every problem, however small, is represented as a major disaster."[2]

Not surprisingly, the continent's politicians are happy to take up arms against a sea of imaginary troubles, now that the old nemesis of Soviet communism is rotting away on that dust heap called "history." But they need a new hobgoblin. "Today," observes German writer Thomas Deichmann, "the easiest way for them to connect with people is to pander to their fears about health."[3]

"The European Commission is obsessed with eliminating every last risk from human life," says Andreas Hansen, a Copenhagen-based pollster and sociologist. "By treating the public like small children, by nannying them all the time, they are making Europeans into people who cannot contemplate risk, however trivial, however theoretical, without panicking." In fact, the EU has made it illegal to sell old plastic sports stadium seats as souvenirs if they contain cadmium – even though a fan would have to devour an entire seat to be poisoned – and banned bananas that have "abnormal curvatures."[4]

Ethics Edict 3: The more strategies on the corporate table, the merrier the debate over ethics.

In the corporate world of crisis management, the third edict on ethics is a serious threat to sanity and survival. Just as a decision is about to be made, there's always some company Neville who stands up and says, "Let's take two steps back, call in a consultant and make sure we've considered the full array of goals, objectives, strategies and tactical options available to us." Ethics Cop on patrol! If others in the room agree, it may be time to order more croissants, because this little game of decision avoidance can lead to a debate that lasts longer than the crisis itself.

For any given crisis, there is probably just one strategy (supported by a few tactics) that is actually capable of achieving the mission. Beware of public relations consultants who bring scores of strategies and tactics to the crisis management table. It's a boilerplate, cover-your-butt technique: "If you don't like Strategy 21(a), how about Strategy 37(b)? We're just chock full of big ideas and 37(b) is a real winner!"

Don't fall for it.

Introducing a gaggle of strategies to a crisis management environment is like bringing a .357 Magnum and an eight-course set of silverware to a gunfight. It's a sure bet the crisis management team will get bogged down in a discussion of pseudo-ethics, precedents and other meaningless jabber, and there's a good chance that, when all is said and done, a butter knife will be selected as the weapon of choice.

Here is some advice for anyone responsible for managing a crisis. If you truly believe a consultant can add something of value (as I would like to think we do on occasion), tell the consultant to present one, and only one, strategy to your crisis team. The one that will work!

Executives often ask how to decide whether the problem they are facing is truly a crisis. It's a fair and important question. Executing crisis management tactics when there is no crisis is not only a waste of valuable resources, but it may also have the effect of *creating* a crisis. That's always considered bad form in a corporation or industry association.

When asked the "what's a crisis" question, I usually put down my croissant, grasp my chin between the thumb and index finger and, after fifteen seconds of contemplation, inform the questioner that a crisis is "an event, hazard, problem, assault or allegation that threatens the survival of a product, company or entire industry."

There is a second litmus test for determining whether a crisis exists: the fourth edict on ethics.

Ethics Edict 4: The less important the mission is to the company, the greater the likelihood of a convoluted, time-consuming, head-spinning diatribe about ethics.

If you are in a crisis management meeting where the participants spend three hours discussing whether a tactic is ethical, moral or a bad precedent, it's not a crisis. It's not even a concern. Grab a croissant and leave.

If the discussion about ethics, morals and precedents lasts two hours, it is probably a public relations problem.

If the discussion about ethics, morals and precedents last five minutes – three of which are spent telling the phony ethics police to "shut up," "sit down" or "take your croissants and get out" – it's a crisis!

If it *is* a crisis, among the most important decisions for the crisis team will be to rapidly define the mission. When the mission is understood, figure out what strategy and which tactics are required to achieve it.

President Roosevelt's World War II Chief of Staff and principal strategist, General George C. Marshall, once observed: "The hardest thing to do is to define the political objectives of war. Once that is done, a lieutenant can lay out an appropriate military strategy." No truer words can be uttered about crisis management. Once the mission is defined, strategies and tactics become fairly obvious, and their implementation can be assigned to the lieutenants.

The predator groups typically frame every new assault around a carefully manufactured "crisis," thus obviating the need to bother with ethical considerations. After all, only their stalwart intervention can save the whales, the elderberry beetle, the children and the planet. So far, they are getting away with it.

Corporations must be far more honest and circumspect. But that doesn't mean they should remain silent about unethical attack group behavior, waste precious time questioning how many corporate ethics police can dance on the head of a pin, or delay in addressing the very real crisis generated by the attacker's shakedown attempt.

The corollary to Edict 4 is the *sine qua non* for the radical attackers – Ethics Edict 5.

Ethics Edict 5: The more important the mission, the fewer the options for effective action, the less concern there will be about ethical considerations.

Why? Good people behave ethically in a crisis. They don't need Ethics Police. They do what is right. They are their own best Ethics Police. Nevilles and capitulation counselors don't trust anyone to behave ethically without their advice. They're wrong. Your people have a strong sense of ethics and they will reject radical ethics once they know what they're up against.

Here's what they should know: Radical ethics begins by assigning "intrinsic value" to "the whole environment, including inanimate objects, rocks and minerals, along with living plants and animals."[15]

In this way, human life is made no better than that of insects: "The life of an ant and the life of my child should be accorded equal respect."[16] It is better that 1,000 humans die of disease than to sacrifice one rat for medical research. "Six million people died in concentration camps, but six billion broiler chickens will die this year in slaughterhouses."[17]

Man is portrayed as the arch villain, the systematic destroyer of all that is good. The radicals become guardians of nature, who preserve Mother Earth by destroying the destroyers and their offensive works. This perverted logic "justifies" threatening rock star Ted Nugent and his family with murder, rape and the destruction of their home, for their pro-hunting philosophies.[18]

It gives animal rights activists a sick rationale for sending threatening letters booby-trapped with razor blades to more than 80 research scientists – and PETA president Ingrid Newkirk license to cheer the violence on, instead of denouncing it: "Perhaps the mere idea of receiving a nasty missive will allow animal researchers to empathize with their victims for the first time in their lousy careers," she wrote to several newspapers.[19]

Radical ethics "justify" PETA's targeting of Edward Walsh and JoAnn McGee, a husband-wife team of scientists at Boys Town National Research Hospital in Omaha, Nebraska, who used to use kittens to study congenital deafness. The two subsequently received death threats, bomb threats and harassing phone calls – some of them directed against their 5-year-old son and Walsh's elderly mother.[20]

In England, this kind of hatred led an animal rights group to publish a "hit list" that included Oxford University professor Colin Blakemore and nine others. The group said the ten would be executed if hunger-striking activist Barry Horne died, because they work with lab animals.[21]

The process is aided further by making the situation as dire and cataclysmic as possible. "[W]e should speak of a single over-arching crisis: the crisis of humankind," says Norman Myers.[22]

The entire planet and all of its species face imminent catastrophe from (choose one or more) global warming, global cooling, chemicals, pesticides, over-population, clearcutting, automobiles, urban sprawl. In this way, even the most extreme acts and questionable practices can be made to appear justifiable, and the radicals can be freed of cords that would otherwise bind them to ethical rules that might prove even a slight obstacle to their holy agenda.

Indeed, the process gradually desensitizes people to the plight of loggers and their families, people forcibly displaced from new tiger preserves, and starving multitudes in Africa. Such desensitization has always been the first step in any program of ethnic, cultural or occupational cleansing.

"Monkeywrenching[23] should not be used when other forms of nonviolent confrontation are in progress, such as blockades or other forms of direct-action civil-disobedience, since it could result in backlash against the protestors or undercut delicate negotiations."[24] Spiking trees, destroying equipment, burning buildings and other forms of "monkeywrenching," say the terrorist sympathizers, are neither immoral nor unethical. They are merely poor choices if they could undermine other pressure tactics.

"I am a product of the Pleistocene epoch, the age of large mammals....
[T]his is my context. I only have meaning *in situ*, in the age I live in, in the
Pleistocene."[25] I seek a return to the world of simpler times, more nature-
centered, untarnished by the stain of man's evil designs. Any tactic that
allows me to reach this pristine state falls within the realm of our ethical
guidelines. Home sweet cave.

Planet Earth is already over-populated well beyond its carrying capacity,
the eco-militants insist. If starving Biafrans and Ethiopians are given food,
they will continue to procreate and cause more environmental devastation
tomorrow. Garrett Hardin's famous lifeboat is already overcrowded and in
danger of capsizing. "Those who hate life try to pull more people on board
and drown everybody. Those who love and respect life use axes to chop off
the extra hands hanging onto the gunwale."[26]

(The inconvenient truth is that birth and fertility rates have plummeted,
and Earth's population may well peak at 8 billion in 2050 and then decline,
predicts American Enterprise Institute scholar Ben Wattenberg, citing UN
studies. Mexico's birthrate has already plunged to 2.1 children per family,
from 6.8 in 1965-70 – and almost every developed country will suffer
severe population losses over the next 50 years. Europe alone could go
from 727 million in 2000 to 556 million, a 24 percent decline that would
strain its vaunted healthcare and pension systems to the exploding point.[27]

"Population bomb" fanatics and their media allies will have an increasingly difficult time keeping these facts buried, but they will no doubt
do their best.)

"Our Earth is being murdered by greedy corporate and personal interests.
The rape of the Earth puts everyone's life at risk due to global warming,
ozone depletion and toxic chemicals. We are but the symptoms of a corrupt
society on the brink of ecological collapse." That's how spokesman Craig
Rosebraugh sought to justify ELF's burning of four new luxury homes in
Long Island, New York's Mount Sinai neighborhood in December 2000.
The new development endangered a drinking water aquifer, he claimed.[28]

On one of the garage doors, the arsonists had scratched, "If you build
it, we will burn it." A few weeks later, another group of ELF terrorists
torched 30 sport utility vehicles in a Eugene, Oregon new car lot. The
SUVs endangered the Earth's atmosphere and energy supplies. In other
words, burning a house or car is morally equivalent to building one.

Or as one of the ELF terrorists put it: "We can no longer allow the rich
to parade around in their armored existence, leaving a wasteland behind in
their tracks. Gas guzzling SUVs are the forefront of this vile, imperialistic
culture's caravan towards self-destruction. Our goal is to cause economic
damage to those who profit from destruction of the natural environment."[29]

Another "puckish" communiqué read: "We are the burning rage of this dying planet. The war of greed ravages the earth and species die out every day. ELF works to speed up the collapse of industry, to scare the rich, and to undermine the foundations of the state.... Together we have teeth and claws to match our dreams. Our greatest weapons are imagination and the ability to strike when least expected."[30]

If anger, outrage and embarrassing hyperbole alone are not enough, the next step is to argue that The System offers no workable alternatives. "Action within the corporate-owned legal system will not be adequate to save the Earth. [Actions like the kind undertaken by the Earth Liberation Front] should be targeted at the corporations most directly responsible for the destruction of the Earth."[31]

Ethics Edict 5 also warns us that radicals can make up the facts as they go along, and push them far enough out into the future that no one can prove them wrong, or even challenge them effectively. If the population bomb doesn't explode in 2002, then surely it will by 2012. If by some miracle global famine is averted in 2013, then surely the immutable laws of Thomas Malthus will bring a famine of biblical proportions by 2023. If we have not exhausted the world's petroleum supplies by 2025, then we will certainly have done so by 2035.

Finally, the Fifth Edict warns us against the endless stream of outrage, simplistic slogans, emotional appeals, phony crises and anti-corporate invective that are the "guts" of environmentalist fund-raising appeals.

Your help is urgently needed "to stop an impending slaughter" of "hundreds of wolves and defenseless wolf pups" in Yellowstone National Park.[32]

Unless you help, "a mile-long concrete pier will cut directly across the path of migrating whales – potentially impeding their progress."[33]

Wildlife experts say both statements are completely false, without a shred of scientific evidence to back them up. Even former Sierra Club board member David Foreman says this "direct mail treadmill" is "a little shabby."[34] National Audubon Society chief operating officer Dan Beard admits that "what you get in your mailbox is a never-ending stream of crisis-related shrill material designed to evoke emotions, so that you will sit down and write a check."[35]

The Sierra Club's Bruce Hamilton says, "I'm somewhat offended by it myself, both intellectually and from an environmental standpoint. And yet, it is what works. It is what builds the Sierra Club." Then, in a marvelous *non sequitur*, he adds: "Unfortunately, the fate of the Earth depends on whether people open that envelope and send in that check."[36]

Watchdog groups, like the American Institute of Philanthropy, are less charitable in their assessment of the Green radicals' grant-generating practices – calling them misleading, unacceptable, excessive, even abusive. Conning school children and little old ladies out of millions of dollars a year deserves that kind of criticism, and more. Carried out by corporations, such misleading advertising and direct mail campaigns would likely result in congressional hearings, Lanham Act investigations by the Federal Trade Commission, mail fraud investigations by the Postal Inspector, and inquiries by state attorneys general.

But the practices continue, driven by the insatiable quest for money, power and influence, and justified for the unethical by *Ethics Edict 5*. It's high time that companies, public interest law firms and citizen groups filed official complaints, legal actions and calls for hearings into these abuses.

Ethics Edict 6: Claim to be snatching victory from the jaws of defeat, and few will challenge the morality of your actions.

Again, not cynicism. Reality. Ever wonder why environmental groups say, "We're losing the battle to save the planet"? *Edict 6* is the answer. An action taken to avert imminent disaster will be subjected to a far more lenient morality test than one taken when victory is all but assured.

It is in the best interest of professional attackers to claim that their cause, whatever it may be, is threatened with imminent defeat by the forces of evil. It is in their best interest to proclaim that they are small but courageous voices, representing Our Earth Mother and The Oppressed, against the massive evil forces of Capitalism. This doomsday demagoguery not only serves to radicalize and mobilize their followers; it also affords the attackers *carte blanche* to engage in tactics that may otherwise be viewed as immoral or unethical.

Free trade. The April 2001 Free Trade Area of the Americas (FTAA) meeting in Quebec was "a return to feudalism," the attackers insisted. "The population has rocks, and they have army tanks. We have scarves soaked in vinegar. They have gas masks. Who will win?" So once more into the breach, as another protester screams, "The fence, it makes us more aggressive than we already are. It makes me feel more violent inside." And the bottles, fires, tear gas, water cannons and rubber bullets continue to punctuate the angry demonstrations.[37]

The savvy radicals who organize these demonstrations know they need to maintain the false image of spontaneous grassroots uprisings of "little people" battling corporate behemoths. In reality, planning for protests like those in Seattle and Quebec often starts years in advance and includes sessions in which foundation-funded trainers indoctrinate naïve high school and college students. The courses teach the novice nihilists how to build human chains, cope with tear gas, and position themselves to ensure coverage by television cameras searching for something more compelling than a bunch of long-winded trade ministers at a plenary session.

As one commentator aptly put it, "this anti-globalization movement is largely the well intentioned but ill informed being led around by the ill intentioned and well informed."[38]

The events were bankrolled to the tune of $250,000 for the Washington, DC World Bank brouhaha, hundreds of thousands for the battle in Seattle and over $2 million for the chaos in Quebec. Once launched, the protests were coordinated on the fly via cell phones by field generals who also used laptops and video gear for instant access to the news media.[39]

One clever tactic developed in Seattle employed a front rank of protesters to absorb the attention of law enforcement officers and TV cameras, while an unseen second phalanx of radicals several blocks behind trashed cars and smashed store windows, unrestrained by the police.

So here we have anti-technology, anti-wealth, neo-barbarian shakedown artists, using opulent budgets and high-tech gadgetry to rid the world of prosperity and technology, prevent ecological Armageddon, and restore mankind and Mother Nature to their former primeval glory. The irony would be delicious, if it weren't so hypocritical and the effects on the downtrodden weren't so devastating.

Recycling. Consider also efforts by environmentalists in the 1980s to impose their recycle-or-die political agenda on what they called "America's throw-away society." How did they force the packaging industry, state and local governments, and individual consumers to embrace recycling as a religion that would not tolerate dissent? Simple.

First, the high priests of recycling charged that Americans were about to lose the battle over garbage and, as a result, future generations of American babies would be buried in trash. Then, to support their doomsday scenario, they perpetrated what historians often call "the big lie," convincing the news media, government officials and consumers that the United States was running out of landfill space. (It wasn't hard to do. Few companies or other experts presented a coherent or effective response to the doomsayers.)

The result? Millions of taxpayer and private sector dollars were spent recycling stuff that had little or no value. Homeowners across the country paid more and used more energy to have their garbage recycled than what it would have cost them to have it sent to a landfill or burned in a modern, non-polluting waste-to-energy plant, to generate electricity.

Were we running out of landfill space? No. There is not a shred of evidence that the country lacked space to manage its garbage.[40]

Could the millions of dollars spent on the recycling religion have been put to better use? A cure for cancer or AIDS? Cleaning up rivers, lakes and brownfields? Sheltering the homeless? Ending malaria and dysentery in developing countries? Certainly.

Have the recycle-or-die activists been held accountable for their big lie? Were they subjected to ridicule and derision? Have they been taken to the whipping post by the media, government officials and contributors who bought the landfill shortage lie lock, stock and barrel? Will they be held to higher standards of proof, honesty and accountability the next time? No, no, no and highly doubtful.

When attackers succeed in positioning themselves as fighting against imminent disaster or defeat, the chances that they will be held accountable for immoral or unethical behavior are greatly reduced. They know it's not going to happen.

That's why the recycle-or-die flim-flam was followed by an even more outrageous environmental scam.

Rain forests. For more than a decade, the environmentally conscious citizens of Mother Earth have been bombarded with doom and gloom predictions about the imminent demise of the Amazon rainforest. Rock stars and celebrities such as Sting, Leonardo DiCaprio, Naomi Campbell, Elton John, William Shatner, Billy Joel, Ricky Martin, Gladys Knight and Stevie Wonder have posed for pious pictures with Greenpeace, the Rainforest Foundation and other fund-raising groups, to preach the gospel of saving rainforests from exploitation and destruction.

A lot of money has been raised on the Amazon rainforest. A lot of publicity has been sucked from a news media all too willing to accept activist claims without question or investigation. According to the *New York Post*, the 10th annual Save the Rainforest rock concert, held in Carnegie Hall, scooped up $2.7 million for Sting's Rainforest Foundation.[41] That's just one concert.

Well, guess what, folks? The rainforest is doing just fine. We're the ones who have been exploited. Two environmental scientists, Dr. Patrick Moore and Philip Stott, decided to find out just how much of the Amazon rainforest had been destroyed and how much time remained before its complete demise. Dr. Moore is a professional forester and a founder of Greenpeace. Stott is a professor of biogeography at London University and the editor of *the Journal of Biogeography*. What did they discover? According to a *New York Post* article by Barry Wigmore, Moore and Stott conclude "the save-the-rainforest movement is wrong: at best, vastly misleading; at worst, a gigantic con."[42]

The two scientists and a television reporter, Marc Morano, calculated that only 12.5 percent of the original Amazon has been deforested, leaving 87.5 percent untouched. And of that 12.5 percent, the scientists concluded, one-third or more is fallow or in the process of regeneration.

In other words, 92 percent of the total Amazon rainforest – the global treasure that's about to be destroyed – is in a pristine or natural state.

The deforestation numbers often cited by concerned "ecologists" like actor Chevy Chase and his wife would earn an "F" on the red-faced test. They are based on worthless extrapolations from one observation in one area of Brazil several years ago – and range from two football fields (2.6 acres) per minute to three football fields (3.9 acres) per second. Even the lower estimate works out to 3,744 acres a day…or 1.3 million acres (the entire state of Delaware) in a single year. At the absurd high devastation rate (123 million acres a year), the entire Brazilian rainforest would be completely denuded in less than nine years.[43]

These scientists also question the veracity of the activist theory that the rainforests are the lungs of the earth, sucking up carbon dioxide and delivering life saving oxygen to our polluted planet.

According to Professor Stott, "This lungs of the earth business is non-sense; the daftest of all theories…. Rainforests actually take in slightly more oxygen than they give out." All old growth forests do so; only young, actively growing forests are actually net consumers of carbon dioxide, and net producers of oxygen – an interesting fact for anyone worried about global warming. Dr. Moore adds that the rainforests "are just about the healthiest forests in the world. This stuff about them vanishing at an alarming rate is a con based on bad science."[44]

There is one question that wasn't addressed by the eco-scientists, Moore or Stott. Where did all that money go? What money? The money raised by the activists from the young children and well-meaning adults who are truly concerned about the environment. That money.

Will the activists ever be called on the carpet for this alleged rainforest scam? Will there be congressional hearings? Will the U.S. Department of Justice follow the cash? Will someone in authority pass moral judgment on the con artists, if in fact they are con artists?

Probably not. The imminent destruction of the Amazon rainforest is now conventional wisdom; a cultural myth that benefits from the protec-tion of *Edict 6*.

Ethics Edict 7: There are only radical ethics in a *jihad*. Achieving victory in a holy war justifies any tactic, no matter how corrupt.

We hate plastics. Let's mislead parents about product safety research, so they'll trash those plastic baby bottles, teethers and toys. What the hell, they can afford it and, if the kid drops a glass baby bottle, let the maid clean it up. Defeating the infidel capitalists justifies any means.

Chemicals are the enemy. Let's exaggerate the risks posed by pesticides. Someone else will worry about how to control those mosquitoes spreading the West Nile virus. Besides, there are too many Americans anyway, and Americans consume too much. Defeating the infidel capitalists justifies any means.

We despise loggers. "The whole damn logging industry should come down with a rare form of cancer."[45] Let's put ceramic and concrete spikes in those trees. (Unlike steel spikes, ceramic and concrete can't be detected by magnetic scanners.) If a lumberjack gets maimed, that's a small price to pay for Mother Nature.

Extremism in defense of nature is no vice. Our goal is to shut down the entire timber industry. "The Northern Spotted Owl is the wildlife species of choice to act as a surrogate for old growth protection, and I've often thought that thank goodness the Spotted Owl evolved, for if it hadn't, we'd have to genetically engineer it. It's a perfect species to use as a surro-gate."[46] Saving forests from infidel capitalists, so that the trees can burn in the next wildfire, justifies any means.

We love bunnies. In fact, we love them more than people. Let's send a hearse to the home of that toxicologist so her kids will see what's waiting for mommy if she continues to experiment on animals. Let's torch another research lab that's finding ways to use fewer animals in research, so we can make all researchers look bad. Let's bomb a few cars and bludgeon a few company execs. Saving animals justifies any means.

We hate free trade. Let's trash downtown Seattle, London and Quebec. Besides, all those Third World types are dead wrong if they think they have some kind of right to stop living like cute primitive peoples, and start living like Americans and Western Europeans, depleting more of the world's vanishing natural resources, and making the global warming problem even worse. Destroying infidel capitalism justifies any means.

I hate technology. I'll send a package-bomb to that advertising executive, because he represents a high-tech corporation. Helping mankind return to simpler times justifies almost any means. Besides, "sober reformists...need immoderates to help make their case; without crazies to which they can appear like moderate alternatives, no one would ever listen to them."[47]

Sierra Club president Adam Werbach titled his 1997 book on grassroots environmental action, *ACT NOW, Apologize Later.*[48] He clearly understands the seventh edict of ethics. I don't know Adam Werbach. And I certainly don't know in what direction his moral compass points. What I do know is that Mr. Werbach and many of his peers play by very different rules than their counterparts in corporate America.

Tell a group of corporate crisis managers to "act now and apologize later." If their legal counsel has a coronary, their ethics expert loses his lunch, and their public relations adviser loses bladder control, it's not because they are bad people. It's because they've been trained in Guilt, Nevillian ethics and Marquess of Queensberry rules of warfare. It's because they do not see the crisis as a threat to their professional survival. From their sheltered, isolated vantage point, it's not a war; it's a public relations problem.

Ethics Edict 8: A cause that is wrapped in moral fabric always has the advantage.

Corporations and radicals both, take note: always clothe your actions in the mantle of morality, and your opponents' in the garments of sin.

Attacks on businesses are always bathed in moral overtones. "We trashed this fast-food restaurant to: a) protect the children; b) defend human rights; c) demand ethical treatment for animals; or d) save the planet." I have yet to hear an activist say, "We trashed this fast-food restaurant because: a) we need publicity; b) we hate capitalism; c) they wouldn't give us money; d) private property sucks; or e) it was a lot of fun."

Companies under attack would do well to heed *Edict 8*. But they rarely do. Instead, corporate decisions are often justified in the context of profits and the bottom line. Wake up, folks. Even in this, the world's most capitalist culture, a huge segment of the U.S. population considers profit-taking to be immoral. Why do you think Governor Gray Davis bellowed "profiteering" – to hide the fact that the real cause of California's 2001 electricity crisis was legislation enacted when he was lieutenant governor and president of the state senate?

So, if your company is trying to defend against a proposed ban on the sale and use of its pesticide product, you had better find that mantle of morality, or be prepared for a hasty retreat.

Where is that mantle of morality? Try running those anti-pesticide zealots up against a human rights issue. More than 2 million people already die from malaria every year in Africa, Asia and Latin America. How many more will die from mosquito-borne diseases if this pesticide is forced off the market? What kind of ethics demand that?

What about the children who have been infected by mosquitoes with equine encephalitis in America's heartland? Or how about the 62 New York residents who contracted West Nile virus from mosquitoes in the fall of 1999, or the seven who died? Will this proposed ban mean that more people – especially children, pregnant women and the elderly – are put at risk?

Environmental groups fought New York City's West Nile virus mosquito control plan, which involved spraying the pesticide malathion over city wetlands. A year later, the anti-pesticide activists opposed the Big Apple's efforts to spray Anvil, a pesticide that can be toxic to fish, when the virus was found in dead birds. According to *The New York Times*, Jay Feldman, executive director of the National Coalition Against the Misuse of Pesticides, opposed the spraying, because "the mayor's constant drumbeat about the safety of this product (Anvil) or any of these products could make people cavalier about exposure."

Feldman was apparently concerned about a public education problem, and theoretical harm to wetlands from a limited and carefully controlled spraying program. Mayor Giuliani, on the other hand, was concerned about more people *dying*. "We catch fish to eat them," he observed. "So we lose a few fish to save human lives. I don't understand."[49]

Anti-pesticide zealots, on the other hand, had this to say. "A person has a much better chance of winning the lottery" than getting West Nile. "These diseases only kill the old and people whose health is already poor." The epidemic is not serious, because it only killed seven people last year, and "after all, more people die of the flu."[50] This from the folks who worry incessantly about phthalates in baby toys, genetically modified seeds, and compounds that may cause agitation, anxiety and sleep difficulties.

Who had the moral high ground in this instance?

Ethics Edict 8 is a major weapon in the arsenal of any party to a conflict. The trick is not to allow it to fall into the wrong hands.

Ethics Edict 9: Politics always determines what is ethical.

Again, not cynical, but factual. Why are people who car-bomb innocent civilians called murderers by some, and freedom-fighters by others? Why was a package bomber called a vicious lunatic by some, and the author of a manifesto whose "principal beliefs are, if hardly mainstream, entirely reasonable" by others?[51] Why are people who burn buildings and destroy years of scientific research branded terrorists by some, but puckish elves or concerned environmentalists by others? *Ethics Edict 9.*

We live in a global economy, not an isolated village. Business is conducted in thousands of towns and cities – from Beijing to Bangor to Buenos Aires. Business decisions will be judged by the people who have real power in these political jurisdictions, and the judges fall within a broad continuum of beliefs and expertise, from village ideologues to village idiots.

A corporate executive who seeks only to avoid conflict and criticism in the global political environment deserves a one-way ticket to that special place where Thorazine is served with every meal, and the dress code requires white gowns and very restrictive jackets. The attackers understand the implications of *Ethics Edict 9*. Business executives, by and large, do not.

Consider what happened at the 1999 World Trade Organization (WTO) meeting in Seattle, Washington. The protesters' objectives were quite simple: disrupt the meeting, scare the bejezzus out of the trade ministers and embolden the faithful.

The attackers knew that destroying private property and battling with police might not go down well with the establishment. They also understood that a few picket signs and a peaceful protest march wouldn't grab headlines and evening news footage. They needed to create a major league ruckus to achieve their ends. And, they did. Here's how Jonathan Dube of ABCNews.com described the scene:

> "The marchers broke the storefront windows of nearly every major downtown store, covered buildings with graffiti and set Dumpsters on fire – often while police watched and did nothing.

> "Rowdy demonstrators hurled bottles and rocks at police, injuring at least two officers. Tear gas and pepper spray wafted through the downtown air.

> "The international trade conference's opening ceremonies were canceled and delegates were furious.

> "A major metropolitan city had been taken over by protesters. The anarchists among them claimed victory – and few could argue. Chaos was everywhere."[52]

So, how were the radicals rewarded for their efforts in Seattle? The trade ministers accomplished nothing. The news media responded predictably with massive news coverage of their shenanigans. The Clinton Administration rebuked the radicals with a "we feel your pain but don't agree with those naughty tactics" message. Seattle's police chief resigned. And, within days of the WTO disaster, legal charges were dropped against more than half of those arrested.

Not bad for a small group of radicals, anarchists and Luddites, whose social agenda would have us return to the good old days when a man's cave was his castle.

How did the attackers prepare for Seattle? Michael Dolan, deputy director of Ralph Nader's Citizens Trade Campaign, spent nine months orchestrating the WTO debacle.[53]

The Ruckus Society and the Rainforest Action Network (RAN) set up a boot camp near Seattle to provide the WTO protesters with "masters-level workshops in non-violent action techniques and civil disobedience, as well as the applied arts of climbing buildings, scouting potential targets, and working with the media."[54] RAN leader Kelly Quirke began his speech to the street crowd with, "Welcome to the revolution!"

They, the Direct Action Network (DAN), Friends of the Earth (FoE) and others devised a command infrastructure that allowed headquarters and field commanders to communicate via cell phones, walkie-talkies and modems with rooftop scouts, to avoid police and coordinate protests for maximum effect.

How did the establishment prepare for the WTO meeting? Clearly, a lot was at stake. It would have been difficult to avoid the warnings of impending disaster. The attackers had been telegraphing their intentions for well over a year. They'd been active in Britain and continental Europe, had a GenetiX Alert Web site in the UK, describing all their best tactics, and had transferred the site to the United States a full year prior to Seattle, to help prepare American and Canadian radicals for the WTO fun and games.

Industry had ample experience dealing with these guys in Europe. The Seattle police were warned about the possibility of violence. U.S. business organizations knew that efforts would be made not only to disrupt the meeting, but also to contaminate WTO deliberations with political mumbo-jumbo that could later be used to erect artificial trade barriers.

What to do? Hundreds of meeting hours and thousands of croissants were consumed deliberating this all-important question. What did the world's most powerful corporations do to protect their backsides in Seattle? They spent millions on irrelevant television ads and hired a public relations firm to orchestrate daily background briefings for reporters who, quite frankly, had only passing interest in what the American business community had to say about the Precautionary Principle, global economics, sustainable development, the balance of trade and doing business with those pesky Chinese.

No, reporters wanted to get pearls of wisdom from the wacky protesters. They wanted to sniff the tear gas, collect those souvenir rubber bullets that the protesters were handing out, see Starbucks™ and McDonalds™ get trashed. Who can blame them? It's what sells.

Did industry have brochures, articles, a list serve or a Web site dedicated to the monarch butterfly hoax and other issues the attackers were using so effectively? No. Did industry express displeasure with the Clinton Administration's milquetoast response to the demonstrations? Not publicly. Wouldn't want to offend anyone in the vicinity of 1600 Pennsylvania Avenue. Did the barons of big business condemn the attackers for destroying private property and disrupting the WTO? Yes.

The National Association of Manufacturers (NAM) issued a statement from Seattle on November 30, 1999, quoting the group's president, Jerry Jasinowski: "There are an awful lot of wild-eyed young people here who seem to be looking for a 'Woodstock experience' rather than engaging in a reasonable debate on the issues. There is absolutely no place for these kinds of violent disruptive demonstrations, and I am saddened that the extremists on the streets are diverting energy away from a serious dialogue on labor standards, environmental issues and other reforms of the WTO."[55]

Should Jasinowski be commended for stepping up to the plate? Without question. The rest of his colleagues were either hiding behind the police, teeing up on the golf course or sipping wine in their Jacuzzis.

However, I would question whether Mr. Jaskinowski was well-served by whoever wrote his press statement. What was the writer attempting to achieve by this press statement? Is it in the best interests of American industry to have the WTO involve itself in disputes over labor standards and environmental issues? What strategic or tactical advantage was achieved by the Woodstock analogy?

Was this statement written by some public relations scribe whose sole purpose was to avoid irritating the "non-violent" protest groups, the Clinton Administration or anyone else who might sit in judgment of industry's behavior in Seattle? You be the judge.

Then take a few minutes to delve into the stories the *Economist* and other periodicals published on the anti-globalization movement. Research the Alliance for Sustainable Jobs and the Environment's Web site at www.asje.org, which reflects the views of a new coalition of militant environmentalists like Earth Firsters and more radical elements of the United Steelworkers of America and other labor groups.

Check out Ralph Nader's Global Trade Watch Web site (www.tradewatch.org) and the National Religious Partnership for the

Environment (www.NRPE.org), which promote narrow definitions of fair trade, human rights, democracy and environmental stewardship.

You will discover that some of these groups (and their comrades in RAN, DAN, FoE and so on) are committed to abolishing the WTO, World Bank, International Monetary Fund, capitalism and corporations. Others seek "less drastic" ends. Abolish intellectual property protections. Use trade protectionism as a perverse form of national sovereignty. Influence or control corporate boards and government agencies. Shake down companies for more money.

Both factions promise a rough road ahead for companies and all who depend on them for goods, services, progress and opportunities.

Groups that routinely attack business and industry justify their actions as part of a greater *jihad* against the forces of evil – a battle for survival. Think about how Greenpeace, Earth First, People for the Ethical Treatment of Animals (PETA), the Animal Liberation Front (ALF), the Earth Liberation Front (ELF), the Northeast Resistance Against Genetic Engineering (RAGE) and other so-called public interest groups communicate their mission to those who follow their lead and contribute cash to their cause. "Save the planet." "Save the children." "Save the Seeds." "Save the Silver Spring monkeys."

In March 2001, ELF claimed credit for a major warehouse fire near Fresno, California, that destroyed a warehouse containing genetically modified cotton seeds. "This seed will no longer exist to contaminate the environment, enrich a sick corporation or contribute to its warped research program," the arsonists ranted in a press release. In other words, they acted to make the world safe for transgenic seeds created by less precise traditional methods.[56]

This is war, folks. The rampaging activists believe it's about battling those profit-grubbing, planet-plundering, animal-molesting, middle-aged alpha-males who spend their time on the golf course dreaming up new ways to victimize Mother Nature, Mother Earth, Mother Jones and all the other helpless mothers on the planet.

Of course, they never have much to say about Third World mothers, who must watch in helpless despair as their infants and children die slow, agonizing deaths from starvation, dysentery, tuberculosis and malaria – courtesy of the virtuous activists' relentless, callous opposition to dams, electrical power, economic development, genetically modified seeds and grains, irrigation, pesticides, and the myriad other benefits that modern industry seeks to bring to these impoverished masses.

Remember, these are the "humanitarians" who fervently, piously believe the teeming masses are a root cause of environmental degradation. The ones the Earth First newsletter was talking about when it lectured: "If radical environmentalists were to invent a disease to bring human populations back to sanity, it would probably be something like AIDS. It has the potential to end industrialism, which is the main force behind the environmental crisis."[57]

Unfortunately, judgments about the ethics of strategies, tactics and consequences are the domain of those sitting in judgment. And those sitting in judgment are the radicals who won the Battle in Seattle.

Ethics Edict 10: If your tactics traumatize the attackers, they will play the radical ethics card against you.

Corporate crisis managers should have *Edict 10* tattooed on whatever body part they stare at most often. They should take comfort in knowing that, when an attack group charges a company with acting unethically, it's a pretty good indicator that the firm has been successful in blunting the attack. Don't worry. Be happy. You've probably won the battle, if not the war.

If the attackers haven't played the ethics card, it may mean that too much time has been spent worrying about what *they* might think, rather than taking the actions needed to survive the attack and kick their butts. If that's the case, corporate ethics will lose and radical ethics will win.

Fortune 500 executives who spend their days trying to get professional attackers to like their companies are in serious need of professional help and a different career. Try pottery, or go to work for the Mother Teresa Foundation.

Don't worry about what the attackers think. Worry about beating them at their own game.

Ethics Edict 11: Win the war, and you will win the ethics debate.

The act of achieving success, in and of itself, will influence future judgments about the ethics of the tactics employed. In other words, don't worry about what journalists, historians or tombstone engravers might say about your ethics. Winners decide what is ethical. So worry about winning the war. An approving historical epitaph will follow.

Can you think of a successful revolutionary leader who's been hanged as a traitor? Of course not. Only losers get hanged. Win the revolution, and you get crowned *El Presidente* or founding father. Put another way, history books and rules of ethics are written by the victors, not the vanquished. Or in the words of Oscar Wilde, "The only obligation we owe to history is to rewrite it."

When professional attackers succeed in driving a product from the marketplace, there is very little chance that they will be judged unethical or immoral, even if they lied about the product, put people out of work, and caused illness, injuries, hunger or deaths. Why? They won.

If attackers engage in an activity that clearly crosses the line, a counterattack must be launched immediately. Charging the attackers with unethical behavior after they have won may make the losers feel better, but it won't turn back the clock, and there's a better than even chance that the losers will be portrayed as whiners.

Never apologize for your tactics, assuming you haven't done anything really stupid. Make sure you're right, then go ahead. Always announce victory, before challenging the attackers' ethics. Point to past examples where the attackers engaged in unethical behavior. Suggest they are doing it again.

What sort of attacker activity clearly crosses the line? Violence. Death threats. Extortion (you pay me or I'll attack your product). Prostitution (you pay me and I'll attack your competitor). Child abuse (your mommy's going to take a ride in a hearse if she doesn't stop experimenting on rats). Fraud (let's release some phony research and watch consumers dump the product). Misrepresentation (let's get an activist to edit a film to look like dolphin slaughter and use it against the tuna fishing industry).

The question is not whether attackers are capable of crossing the line. They cross it. Remember, they play by different rules.

The real question is whether corporate crisis managers have the will to launch a counterattack, using their most effective weaponry during the heat of battle. If they are unduly influenced by conflict-avoiding Nevilles, the attackers will be free to conduct business as usual.

Al Capone once said, "You can get more with a smile, a kind word and a gun, than you can with a smile and a kind word." It's high time corporate executives put away their monogrammed, public relations butter knives and replaced them with crisis management howitzers.

Putting ethics edicts into practice

Now, those who are offended by this advice will whine that it suggests companies should use the tactics employed by their attackers. That's because they may fear a dose of their own medicine.

Business executives must recognize a crisis for what it is. If it's real, their survival is at stake. That's war.

If corporations are to survive the onslaught of attacks in the new millennium, they must start playing by different rules that do not violate the law or true ethical principles. Companies can play by their attacker's rules, or force the attackers to play by industry's new rules.

Forcing the attackers to play by the corporate warrior's rules will not happen until industry and government decide to use existing laws against those who violate them and, where appropriate, to enact laws that protect products from those who play fast and free with the truth to achieve their political ends.

Having spent a good deal of time in various foxholes watching the attackers fire salvos of bull manure at hundreds, if not thousands, of safe products and honest businesses, I can count on my God-given digits the number of times American industry pressed legal action against the aggressors.

Sure, there have been high-profile lawsuits against the news media (General Motors *vs.* NBC, Food Lion *vs.* ABC, Apple Growers *vs.* CBS). However, there have only been a couple of instances where a company filed a legal action against an attacker organization.

In 1997, for example, the New Jersey office of the UK-based pharmaceutical testing company, Huntingdon Life Sciences (HLS), sued People for the Ethical Treatment of Animals (PETA) for infiltrating the company and stealing trade secrets. PETA caved and agreed to return or destroy all of the stolen information. More importantly, PETA was barred from any undercover information-gathering against the Huntingdon lab for five years.[58]

Why does the Huntingdon example stand out? Because it's so rare. Why don't more companies use the judicial system to protect their products, purse-strings and stock portfolios from the likes of PETA and the Rainforest Action Network? Because they confuse the ethics of reasonable debate with reasonable people, with the ethics of survival.

Actual legal action, the threat of legal action, even the predators' legitimate fear of possible legal action would give them pause, and represent a notch in the corporate "win column." Even unsuccessful lawsuits can garner extensive media coverage for your views, open avenues of court-ordered discovery of the predators' internal documents and secrets, and cost the predators' valuable time, money and prestige.

Some corporate attorneys claim the laws are stacked against business. There is more than a modicum of truth to that. But if you cut through all the blue smoke, the reason most companies don't use the courts to protect their people, products and profits is the absence of Winstons in the legal and communications departments.

Corporate lawyers, with some notable exceptions, are masters at playing the zero-risk game. If there isn't a 100 percent chance of victory, they don't want to get anywhere near a judge. And these Harvard and Yale-trained legal eunuchs are often joined at the hip with public relations consultants who whine about bad press at the mere hint of a lawsuit.

The situation would be a lot different if the attorneys' salaries were directly tied to the number of scalps they brought home to the corporate teepee. As for the Chicken Little public relations consultants, Saul Alinsky writes that their influence "is the most subversive and insidious one... Madison Avenue public relations middle-class moral hygiene...has made of conflict or controversy something negative and undesirable. This is all part of an Advertising Culture that emphasizes getting along with people and avoiding friction."[59]

If your public relations flack starts clucking the gospel of Chicken Little in the middle of a crisis, lock him up in his own personal coop until the crisis is over, and then let him loose just long enough to collect for his final invoice.

Corporate executives have a moral and legal obligation to protect the company, its assets and value from harm. While legal action may not always be appropriate in times of crisis, arbitrarily removing it from the arsenal of weapons (because someone has a severe case of "can't we all get along") is unethical and immoral.

Here's an interesting case. *The St. Louis Post-Dispatch* reported in a July 16, 2000 article that "at least 30 incidents of anti-biotech sabotage have occurred in the last year. And that number is likely to jump, as activists race to destroy more crops before the summer growing season draws to a close."[60]

The story goes on to report that vandals attacked a Long Island, New York research farm and "mowed down corn, damaged trucks and spray-painted graffiti on greenhouses. Laboratory officials declined to comment."[61] Great. People whom the FBI classifies as special-interest terrorists draw a "no comment" from their victims. The damage must not have been too serious, even though it involved years of work and millions of dollars in research – or maybe the victims have something to hide.

The *Post-Dispatch* goes on to quote a spokesperson from GenetiX Alert, part of the Bioengineering Action Network that began in the United Kingdom. According to the newspaper, GenetiX Alert is an Internet Web site "that distributes news and *communiques*...about the destruction of genetically engineered crops. The Web site also has tips for activists on finding and destroying their targets, while avoiding arrest."[62]

Is that ethical? No, but it worked.

There's another issue here, as well. Now, this author is not a lawyer and certainly not an expert on First Amendment rights. However, if someone launched a Web site telling people how to vandalize the headquarters of the Natural Resources Defense Council (NRDC) while avoiding arrest, and if said vandalism actually occurred, there's a better than even chance that NRDC's lawyers would seek some kind of judicial remedy.

Even the U.S. Supreme Court recognizes that there is a difference between protected free speech, and shouting "Fire!" in a crowded theater – between railing against a perceived enemy, and inciting a mob to burn, destroy and kill. The courts have also ruled that the publisher of *Soldier of Fortune* magazine was liable for the wrongful death at the hands of a "hit man" who had published an advertisement in the magazine for a professional mercenary, styled as a "gun for hire."[64]

Posting arson instructions, the names and addresses of corporate executives, and veiled or explicit suggestions to "get" the "earth rapers" or "animal abusers" certainly falls into the category of "incitement" to crime, in my view.

Will the biotechnology lawyers take action? Don't bet the farm on it.

They've been too well schooled in the language of preemptive capitulation: "constructive negotiation," "dialogue" and *wei-ji*. They hear only the Siren song of "opportunity" and cannot see the looming danger – that they are setting their industry up as an easy mark for the inevitable next attack.

Ethics police? That's everybody in your company. They know right from wrong. But they need to know what they're up against. They need to know how to fight back. They need to know good crisis management. It's not all that hard.

The idea of crisis management is simple: Win.

That's good ethics.

Chapter 10 Notes

1. http://www.ti.com/corp/docs/company/citizen/ethics/quicktest.shtml.
2. "How Piles of Trash Became Latest Focus In Bitter Software Feud," *The Wall Street Journal*, June 29, 2000.
3. "Beltway vs. Microsoft," *Washington Times* editorial, February 25, 2001.
4. See Tom McClusky. *Putting Our Money Where Their Mouths Are: How WTO's detractors are demonstrating on the taxpayer's dime*, National Taxpayers Union Foundation, Issue Brief #23 (April 14, 2000), www.ntu.org/ntufib123.htm.
5. Jeff Edwards, "The riot stuff: We reveal the 10 groups plotting anarchy on streets of London today," *The Mirror*, May 1, 2001; United Press International, "May Day violence brings chain of charges," May 2, 2001.
6. Joe Murphy (*London Sunday Telegraph*), "British army accused of supplying diseased feed," *Washington Times*, April 30, 2001. See also Dennis Avery, "Europe's foot-and-mouth politics," *Washington Times*, April 3, 2001.
7. "Up with weeds," *Washington Times* editorial, February 24, 2001, citing a report on a decade-long study that was profiled in the February 2000 issue of *Nature*. One is reminded of George Maynard Keynes' famous statement: "In the face of new evidence, I change my opinion. What do you do, sir?"
8. *Rules for Radicals*, page 31.
9. These deaths have traumatized Europeans, even though, from 1995 through 2000, mad cow killed fewer people than die on Europe's roads every day.
10. Carl Honoré, "Europe is freaking out," *National Post*, March 21, 2001, page A17.
11. *Ibid.*
12. *Ibid.*
13. Julie Vorman, "Majority of Americans favor biofood labels – survey," Reuters, February 22, 2001.
14. News Release, "Mandatory Biotech Labeling Bill Would Increase Food Costs, Lower Farm Prices," Grocery Manufacturers of America, January 31, 2000.
15. Carolyn Merchant, *Radical Ecology: The search for a livable world*, New York: Routledge, Chapman & Hall, Inc. (1992), page 75.
16. Michael Fox, vice president of the Humane Society of the United States (not actor Michael J. Fox); incorrectly attributed to PETA founder Ingrid Newkirk, cited in Dan Gabriel, "Radical environmental groups break law to make their points," *Washington Times*, April 19, 2001, page A2.
17. Ingrid Newkirk, quoted in Chip Brown, "She's a portrait of zealotry in plastic shoes," *Washington Post*, November 13, 1983, page B10.
18. Dan Gabriel, *op. cit.*
19. Bill Sizemore, "PETA's Zeal Pushes the Envelope Too Far for Some, *Norfolk Virginian-Pilot*, December 3, 2000.
20. *Ibid.*
21. Teresa Platt and Simon Ward, "Hunger Striker Blows His Horn – Then Quits," Fur Commission USA press release, December 15, 1998.
22. Norman Myers (editor), *Gaia Atlas of Planet Management*, London: Pan Books (1985), page 18.

23. This is the term coined by David Foreman, to connote the wide range of sabotage and eco-terror that he outlines in his book, *Ecodefense: A field guide to monekywrenching*, Tucson, AZ: Ned Ludd Books (1985).
24. Carolyn Merchant, *Radical Ecology*, page 174.
25. Earth First founder Dave Foreman, "Only Man's Presence Can Save Nature," Forum, *Harper's*, vol. 280, no. 1679 (April 1990), page 44.
26. Dana Milbank, "In his solitude, a Finnish thinker posits cataclysms," *Wall Street Journal*, May 20, 1994, page A1.
27. Ben J. Wattenberg, "Burying the big population story," Pfizer Forum, *Washington Times*, May 23, 2001; United Nations Population Division, *Replacement Migration: Is it a solution to declining and aging populations?* (2000); United Nations, *World Population Prospects: The 2000 Revisions* (2001); Nicholas Eberstadt, "World Population Prospects for the 21st Century: The specter of 'depopulation'," in *Earth Report 2000*, Ronald Bailey, editor, New York: McGraw-Hill (2000).
28. "Radical environmental groups break law to make their points," *Washington Times*, April 19, 2001.
29. Doug Saunders, "'Elves' wage terror campaign against urban sprawl," *Toronto Globe and Mail*, April 29, 2001.
30. Earth First, The Radical Environmental Journal online, citing a "communique from the Earth Liberation Front," www.iiipublishing.com/elf.htm.
31. *Ibid.*
32. Defenders of Wildlife funding solicitation, cited by Tom Knudsen, "Green Machine: Mission adrift in a frenzy of fund raising," *Sacramento Bee*, April 23, 2001.
33. Fund-raising mailer sent by Natural Resources Defense Council, *ibid.*
34. *ibid.*
35. Tom Knudsen, "Fat of the Land: Movement's prosperity comes at a price," *Sacramento Bee*, April 22, 2001.
36. Tom Knudsen, "Green Machine," *op cit.*
37. DeNeen L. Brown, "At ground zero, melee of shouting, broken glass, tears: Defiance reigns in Quebec's old city," *Washington Post*, April 22, 2001.
38. Thomas L. Friedman, "Protesting for Whom?" *New York Times*, April 24, 2001.
39. usnews.com/usnews/issue/010430/protest (business and technology), April 30, 2001.
40. See Lynn Scarlett, *et al.*, *Packaging, Recycling and Solid Waste*, Reason Public Policy Institute, June 1997; "Packaging, solid waste and environmental trade-offs," *Illahee*, University of Washington Institute for Environmental Studies, Spring 1994.
41. Barry Wigmore, "Eco-Scientists Deny Amazon's In Danger," *New York Post*, May 30, 2000, page 8.
42. *Ibid.*
43. See Ali Freeman, "Let's Go to the Videotape: Documentary provides balance to counter latest celebrity cause – 'saving' the Amazonian rainforest," *UpDate*, Washington, DC, Competitive Enterprise Institute, August/September 2000, pages 9-11.

44. Barry Wigmore, *op. cit.*
45. Art Wolfe (*Backpacker* magazine wilderness photographer), quoted by Sandra Hines in "Trouble in timber town: A way of life is torn up by its roots," *Columns*, December 1990, page 10.
46. Andy Stahl, staff forester for the Sierra Club Legal Defense Fund, at the Sixth Annual Western Public Interest Law Conference, "Old-Growth's Last Stand," Saturday, March 5, 1988, University of Oregon School of Law, Eugene, Oregon; transcript, pages 13-14. Complete transcript is available from "For the Record," Eugene, Oregon (541-345-6168).
47. Doug Henwood, "World troublemaking organized," *Left Business Observer* #93, February 10, 2000.
48. Adam Warbach, *ACT NOW, Apologize Later*, New York: Harpercollins (1997).
49. "Questions About Where, and Whether, to Spray Pesticides," Thomas J. Lueck, *The New York Times*, July 22, 2000.
50. Angela Logomasini, "Pesticide use debated: Activists on both sides argue impacts of spraying," Blethen, Maine *Morning Sentinel*, December 12, 2000.
51. Alston Chase, "Harvard and the making of the Unabomber," *The Atlantic*, June 2000, citing a 1995 article by *New York Times* environmental writer Kirkpatrick Sale.
52. Jonathan Dube, "Chaos in Seattle," ABCNEWS.com, December 1, 1999.
53. Steven Pearlstein, "Protest's Architect 'Gratified'; D.C.-Based Activist Brought Diverse Groups Together," *Washington Post*, December 2, 1999, page A1.
54. News release, "Activist Bootcamp Near Seattle Attracts Top-Flight Hellraisers from Across U.S., Rainforest Action Network, September 9, 1999.
55. News Release, "NAM to WTO Protesters: Creating Chaos Won't Advance Agenda," National Association of Manufacturers, November 30, 1999.
56. Sam Stanton, "Eco-terrorism group claims Tulare attack – Fire may be ELF's first state foray," *Sacramento Bee*, March 4, 2001.
57. *Earth First!* newsletter, cited in *Access to Energy*, vol. 17, no. 4 (December 1989).
58. Associated Press, "Lab, PETA settle lawsuit over trade secrets," Sonja Barisic, December 15, 1997.
59. *Rules for Radicals*, page 62.
60. "New Breed of Environmental Activists has Research Officials Bracing for Vandalism," Tina Hesman, *St. Louis Post Dispatch*, July 16, 2000.
61. *Ibid.*
62. *Ibid.*
63. Michael Fumento, "Crop Busters," *Reason*, January 2000, available at www.reason.com/0001/fe.mf.crop.html.
64. See Lloyd L. Rich, "Publisher Liability: Incitement & Negligent Publication," The Publishing Law Center (1997), www.publaw.com/negligent.

Part Four

The Outlook

11

Threats of Mass Destruction

> At any given moment in a twenty-four hour day only one-third of the people in the world are asleep. The other two-thirds are awake and creating problems.
>
> —Admiral Hyman Rickover

The groups that profit from attack have spent the past decade developing and field testing several new weapons for the 21st century – weapons designed to drive future corporate targets into full retreat. They are: (1) integrated marketing warfare; (2) the Precautionary Principle; and (3) sustainable development.

If your company is at risk of being targeted by predators in the coming years, your crisis managers should become intimately familiar with these threats.

A. Integrated Marketing Warfare

On March 2, 2000, the Mitsubishi Corporation and the Mexican government announced that they were canceling plans to build what would have been the world's largest industrial salt factory, in Baja, Mexico. Then-president Ernesto Zedillo said his government had withdrawn its support from the venture because it would alter the stunning landscape of the arid desert.[1] Zedillo's announcement was the *coup de grâce* in a campaign by the International Fund for Animal Welfare (IFAW) and the Natural Resources Defense Council (NRDC) that is likely to become the model for attack groups in the 21st century.

The IFAW and its allies had been using traditional tactics in their battle to stop construction of the Mitsubishi salt factory at Laguna San Ignacio. Activists claimed the area was "the last pristine breeding ground of the Pacific gray whale and home to numerous endangered plant and animal species."[2]

During the five-year-long confrontation, nearly one million letters and e-mails were sent to Mitsubishi protesting the salt plant. The results were underwhelming. Mitsubishi didn't budge.

What to do? Recognizing that a tactic that drags on too long becomes a drag,[3] the leaders of the attacking forces decided to give Mitsubishi, one of the world's largest corporations, a dose of its own medicine – marketing. Under the direction of IFAW President Fred O'Regan, the attackers launched a fully integrated marketing campaign aimed at bringing top Mitsubishi executives and Mexican government officials to their knees.

Dubbed "Mitsubishi: We Don't Buy It!," the campaign utilized a full array of marketing techniques including:

- targeted broadcast, cable, newspaper and billboard advertising;
- direct-mail solicitations;
- grasstops and grassroots mobilization;
- media events and story placement;
- celebrity endorsements (Pierce Brosnan);
- Internet communications (www.SaveBajaWhales.com);
- lobbying; and
- investor relations.

By the time Mitsubishi fell on its corporate sword, the marketing-savvy attackers had:

- recruited 34 internationally respected scientists (including nine Nobel Prize laureates) to publicly oppose the salt works;
- mobilized nearly 50 counties and cities to pass anti-Mitsubishi resolutions;
- secured public support for their cause from the California Building and Construction Trades, the AFL-CIO, and the California Costal Commission; and
- convinced 15 mutual funds, with over $13 billion in assets, to publicly reject Mitsubishi stock, until the Baja salt project was deep-sixed.[4]

No fewer than five consulting firms were hired by the activists to organize and execute the anti-Mitsubishi campaign. When all was said and done, *The Los Angeles Times* commented that "...the anti-saltworks campaign broke new ground in environmental activism, developing a multilayered sophistication that is sure to be reflected in future eco-confrontations."[5]

In reality, it wasn't totally new ground. The same tactic had been tried, refined and proven in the IFAW/Greenpeace take-no-prisoners war on Icelandic fishing and whaling industries. (See Chapter 2) But Mitsubishi was a much bigger target, and the eco-radicals felt it was vulnerable, because it was a foreign company that depended heavily on exports, was not used to being attacked in this manner, and would ultimately cave in to continued pressure.

The outcome proved their assessment was right on target. The predator groups issued a news release saying they had brought Mitsubishi to its knees – a claim the company Nevilles never contested – and then proceeded to rub salt into the corporate wounds. When Mitsubishi tried to salvage some Samurai pride, by saying it had bowed out of the salt project due to a corporate commitment to environmental stewardship, IFAW and NRDC hammered the company for disingenuous "greenwashing."

It was another example of how short the honeymoon often is between weak-willed corporations and the environmental attack groups. Indeed, most of these honeymoons rank right up their with legendary Hollywood marriages: Carmen Electra and Dennis Rodman (nine days), Michelle Phillips and Dennis Hopper (eight days), Robin Givens and tennis pro Svetozar Marinkovic (one day).[6]

Mitsubishi II, and beyond

What are the long-term implications of the "Mitsubishi: We Don't Buy It!" attack model? Business Nevilles who respond to marketing warfare with public relations tactics will find themselves on a well-deserved, one-way trip to the corporate salt mine (which won't be located in the Baja).

Company executives with Winston instincts would do well to evaluate the strategies and tactics employed against Mitsubishi, prepare contingency plans for countering a similar assault against *their* corporate interests, and develop strategies and tactics for campaigns against the predators and their supporters. Similar marketing warfare tactics have already been employed against Burger King, Home Depot, Boise Cascade, Staples, Nestle, Freeport McMoRan and other companies, with varying degrees of success. Your organization could be next.

Having initially succeeded in pressuring Home Depot to phase out "objectionable" lumber products, the Rainforest Action Network (RAN) next demanded that Staples office supply stores do likewise with paper products. RAN is battling timber companies and insists that all forest product producers and retailers must comply with *its* very narrow interpretation of what are "sustainable" forestry practices. If RAN has its way, the only products permitted in Staples stores will be those approved by Forest Stewardship Council (FSC), an affiliate of the World Wildlife Fund that has close ties to Hollywood celebrities and receives major funding from big foundations. Of course, RAN is a member of FSC.[7]

IBM, Kinko's and Hallmark are next on their list, and more companies are sure to follow. However, not everything has gone quite the way the eco-radicals planned. Staples did not buckle under (see *Power Rule 5*), and Home Depot discovered that: 1) customers did not want to pay inflated prices for FSC-certified lumber; 2) the supposed demand for these products had been cleverly manufactured by eco-activists through letter writing and e-mail campaigns; and 3) the anticipated supply of certified forest products was illusory, because few producers could meet the strict FSC requirements. So Home Depot quietly backed away from its much-publicized commitment to be ultra-Green.

Many companies and industries have also discovered other significant problems with these pressure group certification initiatives. They ignore sound science and economics. They disregard multiple use, real sustainable development and cost-benefit policies that have been crafted through democratic processes involving a broad spectrum of interested and affected parties – supplanting them with extremely narrow criteria set by an elite few with preservationist and income-generating agendas. They inhibit innovation, impose prohibitive compliance costs on small operators, create trade barriers and cost jobs, especially in developing countries.

The FSC "stamp of approval" guidelines are set by groups that openly and vocally oppose logging, home-building and other economic activities. For them, only one certification system is acceptable – theirs. Only in this way can they control the marketplace, stifle free-market competition, dictate the supply and price of all wood products, and thus more easily control housing markets, urban growth and other economic development that depends on forest products. Last, and not coincidentally, fee-generating certification programs like this often serve as a significant source of income and power for the certifiers and their environmental activist allies.

Quite clearly, manufactured conflicts and crises eventually collapse like the house of cards they are. They collapse more quickly when principled companies, led by type-W managers, confront the attackers and their disingenuous claims. And when consumers, think tanks and grassroots groups take up arms in support of the Winstons, instead of kowtowing to the false prophets of ecological apocalypse, many more Winstons emerge from their foxholes. But one victory does not win a war.

On another battlefield, People for the Ethical Treatment of Animals (PETA) – a group dedicated to ending the use of animals for food, ownership and other human benefit – spent years waging a marketing warfare campaign to get McDonald's to buy eggs only from farmers who give chickens "better living conditions." When McDonald's made some changes in August 2000, PETA declared a one-year moratorium on attacks against the restaurant chain. But it also made eight new demands for more drastic steps that McDonald's must take to improve treatment of chickens, cows and pigs.[8]

On its Web site, PETA warns that if McDonald's does not make significant progress to meet the new demands, "PETA will re-launch its campaign blitz against McDonald's." The same Web site – called meatstinks.com – attacks meat eating as cruel, unhealthy, and a cause of impotence, and blasts Burger King as "Murder King."

Radical predator groups are not the only organizations employing shakedowns. Certain industry groups have also found that these tactics can be highly profitable. The Organic Consumers Association, for instance, has used them successfully against Starbucks, to promote the interests of its organic dairy farmer members. The OCA launched a series of "Frankenfoods" and "Frankenbucks" protests against Starbucks, to force the company to stop serving milk from cows fortified with bovine growth hormones, which are present in lesser amounts in all cows.

Predictably, Starbucks caved in, no doubt hoping the wackos would now leave the company alone. No such luck. Now the OCA, which also includes organic coffee growers in its membership, is demanding that Starbucks pledge never to use genetically modified coffee or other GM ingredients in its products, and to promote organic coffee.[9]

All this should probably come as no surprise. After all, Starbucks stood idly by as the OCA's predatory comrades vandalized downtown Seattle, during the 1999 WTO meeting – and both the Seattle district attorney and Washington attorney general refused to prosecute the anarchists. But why other corporate victims and legal authorities have likewise refused to take action against these criminal tactics and elements is much harder to fathom.

This pusillanimous attitude by corporate and government Nevilles is likely to reap a whirlwind. According to a multi-year research project by food and biotechnology specialists, fear-based marketing by organic retailers is a "major factor driving anti-biotechnology public opinion."

The study reveals disturbing (and mostly hidden) links between organic industry groups and nonprofit environmental and consumer activist groups that attack modern agricultural practices and genetically modified crops, while promoting organic alternatives. These activist groups serve as tax-deductible marketing and propaganda arms of huge and highly profitable companies.

Organizations named in the report include Greenpeace, The Institute for Agriculture and Trade Policy, The Organic Consumers Association, The Center for Food Safety and The Campaign to Label Genetically Engineered Foods. Corporate sponsors who support and direct the efforts of these and other groups include Ben & Jerry's, Patagonia, Whole Foods Markets, Rodale's Organic, Working Assets and Fenton Communications. Should anyone be surprised?[10]

Confronting marketing warfare shakedowns

To the extent that the marketing warfare model is applied by 21st century attackers, businesses must be prepared to respond with the full range of weapons available to them. Strategies and tactics traditionally used to market products must be retrofitted and enhanced for rapid deployment in response to a multi-front, integrated attack.

Publicly traded companies will be particularly vulnerable to adversarial broadsides aimed at undermining investor confidence or exploiting the political sensitivities of mutual fund managers. Those that market directly to consumers should anticipate retail assaults that range from traditional boycotts to in-store confrontations – to sudden, deadly cyber-attacks like the one that used a bogus press release to send the market value of Emulex Corporation plummeting more than $2 billion in just 15 minutes.[11]

Companies that are truly global must be prepared to defend against attacks that are *truly global*. In this century, preparation and planning must be viewed as a cost of doing business.

The predators have turned protests and resolutions at shareholder meetings into an art form, while also focusing increased attention to demands for more "socially responsible" investing by mutual funds and state retirement funds.[12]

A favorite target, naturally, is ExxonMobil. At the oil giant's May 2000 annual stockholders meeting, a priest and nun introduced a resolution urging that the company reduce its focus on fossil fuels and, instead, place greater emphasis on biomass energy, like ethanol. No doubt, their actions were inspired by biblical visions of bioenergy released by a perpetual burning bush that emits no pollutants.

A month earlier, Greenpeace, Ralph Nader's Public Interest Research Group, several like-minded shareholders and a "socially responsible investor" (Trillium Asset Management Corporation) teamed up to embarrass the much more politically correct BP Amoco at its annual shareholders meeting. Claiming that burning fossil fuels will cause "catastrophic" global warming, they offered a resolution insisting that BP Amoco cancel its plans for oil exploration and development in the Arctic and spend the money on expanded solar energy projects.[13]

Both resolutions were soundly defeated, but the activists promised to be back. Indeed, they have since upped their demands a notch: now they want BP to get out of the fossil fuels business entirely. The company also faces shareholder resolutions on human rights in Tibet, for engaging in something called "globalization and corporate power."[14] This is the same BP that has striven so mightily to appease the lunatic fringe, by being more politically and environmentally correct than its corporate colleagues. Peace with honor, peace for our time, anyone?

Meanwhile, Greenpeace has enlisted several celebrities to help promote its call for a boycott against Esso/ExxonMobil, Chevron, Texaco, Conoco and Phillips, out of suspicion that they helped persuade President Bush to oppose the Kyoto Protocol. Their goal is to force the companies to urge U.S. support for the climate treaty.

Environmental shakedown artists have also declared war on banks. The Rainforest Action Network called Citigroup "the world's most destructive bank," because it supposedly supports environmentally harmful development and lending practices that "disproportionately affect low-income people and communities of color." RAN protesters disrupted a shareholders meeting at Carnegie Hall, in support of a credit card boycott against the bank.[15]

The groups and their allies are stepping up the pressure on other fronts, as well. On January 18, 2001, the outgoing Food and Drug Administration published a proposed rule that would empower FDA to release – via the Internet, no less – virtually all trade secrets and confidential commercial information from "investigational new drug" applications involving gene therapy and xenotransplantation. This is information that companies and FDA have traditionally safeguarded as trade secret or confidential commercial information under the Freedom of Information Act, Trade Secrets Act, and Food, Drug and Cosmetic Act.[16]

Strongly supporting the rule are animal rights groups and Public Citizen, which loudly bemoan the fact that the proposal is limited to these two therapies. They would like access to *all* trade secrets and confidential information, so that they can better target their attacks on emerging technologies, the companies behind them, and even the corporations' officers, shareholders and financial institutions. In other words, so that they can create a more target-rich environment. [17]

Animal rights terrorists are no doubt watching eagerly from the sidelines, because the proposed rules would also require disclosure of "sources of cells, tissues or organs" – meaning that researchers would have to identify who their suppliers are, and the criminal elements would have a new list of potential targets. The rule would also give the attack groups new avenues and information with which to pressure companies and FDA regulators, about what gene therapy matters are studied and what products will be produced.

In yet another development, American anti-logging groups are linking up with assorted U.S. timber interests to battle Canada and Canadian lumber companies, and restrict the flow of Canadian forest products into the United States. They claim Canadian products are "unfairly traded" and tree cutting in Canada threatens animals whose habitats straddle the border with the United States.[18] So once again we have the same nonprofit militant groups, supported by the same foundations, using the same divide, deceive and conquer tactics to curtail commercial activities and economic opportunities in another part of the world.

Europe learned in 1939 that serving up the victuals course by course only makes the aggressor stronger, more insatiable, and more convinced of his own strength and his opponents' weakness. Two years later, Joe Stalin discovered that cutting deals with crocodiles can be a risky business – even if you sate the croc's hunger for a time.

Will business ever learn that appeasing shakedown artists, and selling out friends and allies for short-term gain, is a one-way trip into a dangerous swamp? Will it ever realize that the world is quickly running out of places where mining, drilling, timber harvesting, manufacturing and other forms of economic production are permitted? The asteroids beckon, at least until the Greens get wind of your plans.

As energy analyst Robert Bradley observes, "corporations should think very carefully, before embracing…alarmism for short run public relations purposes," for the attackers will merely seize the now-vacated moral high ground and step up their activist agendas, using the companies' own positions and words against them.[19]

In short, stopping the well-financed, sophisticated attackers in this new world order will require more money, time and talent, as well as resources that go well beyond those that have traditionally been used to counter activist assaults. In any marketplace assault, from BP Amoco to Mitsubishi to Starbucks, a company must be willing to match the predators commercial for commercial, direct mail letter for direct mail letter, celebrity endorsement for celebrity endorsement.

A 30-second ad defending your product and revealing the predators' true agenda would neutralize the attackers' media buys and force them to defend their own reputations. And if the extreme Green Earth Communications Office (ECO) can feature Pierce Brosnan, why can't you showcase Clint Eastwood or Arnold Schwartzenegger? There is currently no organization or structure comparable to ECO for mainstream, traditional conservationists, but that does not mean one cannot be created.

The cost may be high, but it is minimal compared to what most companies spend on normal marketing efforts, where producing a single ad can cost hundreds of thousands of dollars. It pales into insignificance, compared to the impact that unwarranted, unchallenged attacks will have on sales and the bottom line.

The question is not whether American companies have the resources and skills required to survive. The question is whether they have the *cajones* to use them.

B. The Precautionary Principle: A 21st Century Trojan Horse

When an activity raises threats of harm to human health or the environment, precautionary measures should be taken, even if some cause and effect relationships are not fully established scientifically.

—Wingspread Statement, January 1998

In spite of their numerous successes manipulating science and regulatory processes to achieve their political agendas, attack groups know that the science-based safety systems employed by businesses and governments will ultimately solve virtually all likely threats to human health and the environment. This fact will undermine even the best laid plans to impose the predators' will on consumers and the marketplace. It is difficult to scare people into giving up their freedom of choice when scientists, physicians, respected officials, and folksy but articulate farmers and loggers are saying the activists are full of hooey.

Faced with certain defeat in the long-term, attack groups apparently concluded that, when science gets in the way of politics, there is but one option left. Return to the good old days, when the absence of science allowed medieval alchemists to convince the ignorant that lead could be turned into gold, and that the discovery of a perpetual-youth elixir was just around the corner.

Those were the good times. Peasants and nobles alike were comfortable in the knowledge that the earth was flat, keeping their pockets full of posies would ward off the Black Death, and the local wizard or sorceress knew what was best for them and their families. No wonder my grandmother always used to say, "The only good thing about the good old days is that they're gone."

Modern-day attack groups spent the final fifteen years of the 20th Century wrestling with the problem of how to keep those pesky scientists at bay, while they went about the business of taking freedom of choice away from consumers, and the power to regulate away from government safety agencies. What they conjured up is nothing short of genius – a 21st century Trojan Horse that is eloquent in its simplicity: the Precautionary Principle.

Who can be against precaution? Isn't "better safe than sorry" what Mom used to say when we were about to do something truly moronic? Aren't "principles" good things? Have you ever heard of a bad principle? Don't most people try to be principled in the way they treat others and the environment in which they live? Surely, this principle of precaution is moral and pristine?

Do the words "evil incarnate" give you pause?

The Precautionary Principle is a political doctrine that subjugates science to partisan values, speculation and good old-fashioned fear mongering, while turning the rule of law on its head and rejecting the modestly successful work of logicians like Aristotle.

The Precautionary Principle also sets up an impossible, even fraudulent balance sheet. In one column, those proposing and opposing a course of action are to list all the potential and hypothetical costs, pains, injuries, perils and negative developments that might plausibly ensue, if the action is permitted. In the other column, they are to list *nothing* – none of the benefits that might result from the activity, none of the harms that might arise because the proposed course of action is *not* taken, and none of the positive and negative consequences of known alternative courses of action.

As devised by the alarmists, predators and shakedown artists, the principle requires that we look to the future. However –

- It never specifies how far into the future we are to look for possible harms – only that it must be far enough that the hypothetical harms cannot be disproven or totally discounted.

- It likewise does not say over what geographic extent we should project the reasonable consequences of an action, or how we are to determine which effects might be due to this particular action, and not some other action.

● Most important, it insists that the matter of deciding how to answer all these questions is to be entrusted only to the alarmists.

Put bluntly, the Precautionary Principle insists that we overturn one of our most cherished and fundamental principles: Innocent until proven guilty. Henceforth, all health, safety and environmental issues must be decided on the basis of Guilty until proven innocent. Henceforth, anyone proposing an activity must demonstrate that it will be completely harmless, and be held strictly liable if any damage occurs.

The Precautionary Principle also enshrines into law Joseph Heller's infamous Catch-22. In the biotechnology arena, the rule works this way: You cannot prove your new genetically modified plant will not harm the environment without field trials – but you cannot conduct field trials until you prove your GM plant will not harm the environment.

According to an activist handbook published as a guide for Luddites wishing to spread the gospel of precaution, there are at least six major components of the Precautionary Principle that should concern business leaders, scientists, government officials and consumers:[20]

1. "Taking precautionary action before there is scientific certainty about cause and effect."[21]

Sounds simple enough. But there is a problem. As any high school science student knows, it is impossible to prove that something is absolutely safe. There will always be some degree of uncertainty. So, all that an attacker has to do is claim that a product or an activity may cause some health effect, or some environmental problem, and it's off to the precautionary races. The attacker doesn't have to prove that the alleged hazard is real. That wouldn't be much fun. But it sure is fun to watch scientists try to prove something is safe, when it can't be done.

The October 29, 2000 electronic edition of Britain's *Daily Telegraph* featured a story headlined, "Scientists find bras a pain and a possible cancer risk." The article reported that breast cancer levels in Britain are two-thirds higher today than they were 30 years ago, and the scientists who conducted the bra study "say that their findings might prove to support the theories of an American medical anthropologist, Sydney Ross Singer, who has long claimed there is a distinct pattern of risk associated with the length of time a woman wears a bra and her chances of developing breast cancer."[22]

Is it time to deny women the right to wear bras? While there is no scientific certainty that bras cause breast cancer, the potential harm to human health is theoretically significant and the bra manufacturers haven't proven that bras are absolutely safe. Apply the Precautionary Principle. Ban those bras. Sue Victoria's Secret. Better safe than sorry, right?

> "There's the King's Messenger," said the Queen. "He's in prison now, being punished: and the trial doesn't begin until next Wednesday: and of course, the crime comes last of all."
>
> "Suppose he never commits the crime?" said Alice.
>
> "That would be all the better, wouldn't it?" the Queen said.
>
> —Lewis Carroll, *Through the Looking Glass*

2. *"Shifting burdens of proof."*

With the Precautionary Principle, products and activities are presumed dangerous until proven safe – guilty until proven innocent. If a manufacturer cannot prove with certainty that a product is safe, it can be banned from the market and denied to consumers.

Children get cancer. Children play with rubber ducks in the bathtub. Therefore, rubber ducks must be giving children cancer. Infantile logic to be sure, but try proving scientifically that there is zero risk that a rubber ducky will give a kid cancer. Can't be done.

And what if the rubber ducky is made with a material that at extremely high doses has caused tumors in laboratory rats? No more ducky!

Writing in *Reason* magazine, journalist Ronald Bailey observed that the guilty-until-proven-innocent doctrine of the Precautionary Principle is "like demanding that a newborn baby prove that it will never grow up to be a serial killer, or even just a schoolyard bully, before the baby is allowed to leave the hospital."[23]

What if an activist wants a product off the market for purely political reasons, or because a competing company has paid the attacker (or conspired with it) to trash the competition? What if a product poses some theoretical risk to the environment, but offers real and significant health benefits to consumers?

Who decides whether consumers will have access to the product?

Under the Precautionary Principle, the power to choose will be shifted from those who may want to choose to use a product, to those who oppose the product, regardless of their hidden agendas or their real or imagined concerns.

3. *"Seeking out and evaluating alternatives."*[24]

This tenet of the Precautionary Principle requires comprehensive environmental and safety evaluations of alternative products, materials or activities, before a new product or activity can be brought to market. Those responsible for policing the market would also have the power to determine whether consumers *really* need the new product or activity.

Anyone who has been caught between an activist group and an Environmental Impact Statement knows that the process can be exploited endlessly for political purposes. There is always some new, theoretical impact that needs to be evaluated, particularly if the activists don't like you or your new product. The process encourages delay and analysis *ad nauseum*. Add in a requirement that every conceivable alternative must be considered, plus empire-building bureaucrats and a marketplace czar with the power to declare that consumers don't need your product, and you have a recipe for disaster. Paralysis by analysis and strangulation by regulation, I believe they call it.

Forget about new technology. Forget about innovation. Forget about economic expansion and new employment opportunities for the poor. Forget about products that could prevent blindness, reduce malnutrition or even save lives.

"Mr. Edison, you propose to sell your light bulb invention to the public. But your bulb is made of glass. It could shatter and hurt someone. It relies on electricity. Generating electricity may hurt the environment. Besides, can you prove the public really needs your light bulb? There are alternatives. You have to prove the bulb will never shatter, and conduct a comprehensive environmental impact analysis before you can bring the bulb to market. Perhaps you should consider a new and improved candle."

> "You can't move forward, you can't innovate or develop new programs if everyone's saying, 'No, don't, that's bad' all the time."
>
> —Mario Cuomo[25]

4. *"Setting goals."*[26]

Activists are great at goal-setting. They often succeed in imposing zero-tolerance goals on Nevillian diplomats and industry executives. The dolphin-tuna controversy is a case in point. For years, radical eco-pressure groups demanded a zero tolerance standard for "dolphin safe" tuna fishing. Fishermen in the eastern Pacific were forced to avoid the large tuna that swim with dolphins and, instead, focus on baby tunas. In so doing, however, they threatened to reduce future yellowfin tuna populations and catches by as much as 60 percent, because fewer young tuna would mature to breeding age. Even worse, discards of unwanted small tunas, non-food fish, sharks, billfish and turtles rose from 0.1 percent to over 30 percent of the catch.

Eventually, following an intensive educational program by tuna fishermen, in October 1995, five of the largest environmental groups changed their ideological stance and accepted a new definition of "dolphin safe" – one that emphasizes excellence in releasing dolphins unharmed. Greenpeace quickly followed up with a "greenwash" report on the problems with the policy they'd promoted for years, blasting the tuna fishing and processing industries as if they alone were responsible for the fiasco.[27]

In another example, the anti-pesticides lobby has actively influenced negotiations over a legally binding, global treaty on persistent organic pollutants.

Among their goals is eliminating the production and use of DDT, based on precautionary language contained in the 1992 Rio Declaration. Ironically, many chemical companies have endorsed the Rio language.

Sounds reasonable, right? Not so fast. *The Lancet*, Britain's most respected medical journal, editorialized against the anti-pesticide zealots, noting that the risk posed by the Precautionary Principle could well be far greater than any theoretical risk posed by DDT: "Whose health is being protected by this invocation of the precautionary principle?" Lancet asked. "And who will benefit if and when malaria-endemic countries are forced to switch to newer, more expensive insecticides? The answer seems to be that the health of people in poorer countries is being put at a very real risk to protect the citizens of wealthier nations from a theoretical risk."[28]

What may save the world's poor from predominantly white, wealthy environmental activists, who claim to know what's best, is an unwelcome import called the West Nile virus. The anti-pesticide forces have used every tool available, including their beloved Precautionary Principle, to delay, if not stop, the spraying of pesticides to kill mosquitoes that pose a threat to the good citizens of New York City and beyond.

Whoa! That will never do. The response by those at risk was not friendly. Michelle Malkin wrote in *The Washington Times*, "This anti-pesticide patrol claims to work for the most vulnerable members of society. But it is children and the elderly who are most at risk of West Nile-related illnesses that will spread if infected mosquitoes are not controlled. The enviros callously dismiss West Nile symptoms as 'mild.' Tell that to the seven people who died and the 62 people who became seriously ill last year as a result of encephalitis, meningitis and other central nervous system diseases caused by West Nile infections. Tell that to the 17 people who contracted similar illnesses this year..."[29]

The death of millions in a far-away developing country may be an abstraction, harder to grasp perhaps than claims that possibly dangerous chemicals might contaminate (or merely be detectable in) the soil and water in *your* backyard for weeks, months or even years.

But the deaths of Americans with real names and faces, in New York City no less – that is real, immediate, intolerable and a valid reason for putting the Precautionary Principle and theoretical environmental risks in their proper place.[30]

In the hands of reasonable scientists, regulators and corporate officials, caution is a useful, and often used, tool for evaluating environmental problems that may be caused by pesticides and other chemicals.

That's why environmental regulations have huge safety margins built into them.

These precautionary safety margins have lead to safer production processes, better user guidelines and improved disposal practices, to minimize risks to human, animal, plant and ecological health. The key is reliance on flexibility, creativity, fine-tuning and markets to solve the problems.

However, in too many cases, the Crisis Creation Industry and its political and media allies seize on initial findings, distort conclusions, generate unfounded public hysteria, and campaign for immediate regulatory action – based not on the facts and further scientific study, but on the radical activists' hardened ideologies and narrow agendas.

5. Accepting "financial responsibility."[31]

What does financial responsibility mean? According to the Precautionary Principle handbook, it means companies may have to post assurance bonds for products or activities, based on some hypothetical, worst-case scenario.

If a firm wants to build a new gasoline refinery in St. Louis, some "expert" will demand that permits be denied until the company can "prove" it will not blow up some day, killing dozens of local citizens and destroying the Mississippi River and Gulf of Mexico ecosystems.

If the firm can clear that hurdle, it would next have to try to obtain a bond large enough to cover the worst-case damages, as ludicrous as they may be. Normal, market-based insurance policies would not be sufficient. Oh well, who needs gasoline anyway?

Imagine trying to bring a new AIDs drug to market, if the drug may cause nasty side effects in some patients. No bond, no drug.

So much for innovation and progress.

6. "Imposing a duty to monitor, understand, investigate, inform and act."[32]

Under the activists' precautionary manifesto, firms engaged in potentially harmful activities would be required to monitor their effects, with third parties (*i.e.*, activists) performing the verification. The firms would also be required to inform the public and all relevant authorities when an effect is found, and act upon that knowledge – whether or not there is any evidence that the effect is actually harmful.

This new "duty" sounds reasonable. In fact, companies that discover potential adverse effects linked to their products or manufacturing processes are already required by U.S. law to disclose the information to government regulators. The regulators and industry must then decide whether remedial steps are required.

So why should anyone be concerned about this component of the Precautionary Principle? As with many things in life, the devil is in the details.

Who decides what activity or product is potentially harmful? Who decides when, and under what circumstances, a company would be required to inform the public about a potential hazard? If it is discovered that a product causes liver lesions in rats at ten thousand times the dose people are exposed to, will the manufacturer be required to launch an advertising campaign, to inform consumers about this meaningless but scary discovery? Will the answers to these questions change if the activist groups, in effect, are able to usurp the analytical, reporting and protection roles that have traditionally been served by regulatory agencies and scientists?

Will this aspect of the Precautionary Principle serve as a disincentive for companies contemplating new safety research on their products? Imagine what the lawyers would say: "Go ahead, conduct the research, but be prepared to spend millions of dollars informing the public if a mouse dies." Imagine, too, what PETA or the Animal Liberation Front might do, when it discovers that one of your labs is doing such animal research.

A one-way street

What is truly curious about the Precautionary Principle is that it seems to apply only in one direction. If the goal is to prevent harm – and not merely give the predators one more weapon – why do we not demand that the Precautionary pushers post a bond?

Why do we not insist on cautious evaluation of the likely consequences of banning a life-saving pesticide or keeping new products off the market for years?

If a CPR (cardio-pulmonary resuscitation) device could save hundreds or thousands of lives every year, but is kept off the market for several years because Food and Drug Administration (FDA) officials fear its improper use might break a rib and puncture a lung – what are we to tell the hundreds of grieving families whose loved ones died, while "consumer advocates" and regulators fretted about caution, alternatives, proof and corporate financial responsibility?

If the Precautionary Principle's six components are so important, is there any logical reason that they should not be applied to the professional predators, as well? Why should they not be required to prove that their proposed delay or product ban will not cause major adverse health effects or environmental problems? Why are they not obligated to demonstrate conclusively that their agenda will not shift risks from one group of people to another?

Indeed, why should the attackers not be obliged to abide by *all* the cautionary guidelines they seek to impose on governments and corporations?

Hydroelectric dams. Let those who so vehemently oppose building a dam in India's impoverished Gujarat Province, for example, offer truly workable alternatives, fully evaluate the harm that might result from not completing the dam, and post a bond sufficient to pay for any health care costs or deaths that might arise as a result of construction delays.

Tens of thousands of Gujaratis contract dysentery and other diseases every year from drinking contaminated water; thousands of them die, half of them children age five and younger. Thousands more, mostly women and young girls, contract tuberculosis from breathing air contaminated by the cow dung they are forced to burn as cooking fuel. The half-completed Namada River hydroelectric project could provide both power and safe drinking water for Gujarat Province, and yet the NRDC, Friends of the Earth and other Green groups are unbending in their opposition to the dam.

Infant formula. Let UNICEF explain why it refuses to let Wyeth and Nestle donate tons of free infant formula, despite desperate pleas from African hospitals, to prevent babies from being infected by the deadly AIDS virus via breast milk from HIV-positive mothers.

An even-handed Precautionary Principle would compel eco-radicals to reconsider their quarter-century-long boycott of these companies, after some 1.7 million infants had been victimized by HIV-infected breast milk by the end of 2000.[33] It would force them to explain why caution and basic humanity do not demand an end to their opposition to dams and hydroelectric projects that could make local water safe for use in infant formula, even without boiling.

Global warming. Let alarmists prove that their "solution" to the global warming problem will not wreak havoc on the U.S. economy, double gasoline and electricity prices, set minority achievement back a decade or more, and seriously damage our housing, transportation, industrial and recreation infrastructure.

As is too often the case, the illusory "cure" is far worse than the hypothetical disease. Indeed, the proposed Kyoto climate treaty is akin to a classic automobile insurance scam: a policy that costs thousands of dollars a year, carries an exorbitant deductible, provides very limited coverage with numerous fine-print exceptions – and is being peddled to people who don't even own a car.

The treaty would commit the United States to acting by 2012 to reduce "greenhouse gas" emissions (mostly from burning fossil fuels) to 30-40 percent below what we are projected to be using by then in the absence of a treaty.

By contrast, China, India and other developing nations are not bound by the treaty and will not agree to reduce their fossil fuel use voluntarily, even though their greenhouse gas emissions are rapidly reaching the levels of those in the developed world. Like numerous scientists, these countries are not convinced that human factors play more than a minor role (compared to the sun and other natural factors) in a global climate that has warmed and cooled many times in just the past 10,000 years. They also realize that slashing their energy use would hamstring future economic growth and condemn their people to permanent poverty. (By June 2001, the treaty had been signed only by Romania.)

Terrifying predictions that average global temperatures will soar as much as 11 degrees Fahrenheit (5.8° Centigrade) by the end of this century are based on nothing more than a series of worst case scenarios, stacked one on top of the other like a house of cards. These horror movie forecasts by government representatives on the United Nations' Intergovernmental Panel on Climate Change assume that soaring global energy demands will be met primarily by burning fossil fuels, rather than by new technologies, and that air emissions will rise commensurately by a worst-case amount.

The alarmists then plug these numbers into climate models that can't even replicate last year's temperatures. Finally, out of 245 possible outcomes from various climate models, they choose the ones with the highest temperature forecast, and use these projections in press releases that are treated as serious science by the international news media.

When corporations pull stunts like this, they could get prosecuted for fraud or false advertising. When militants, bureaucrats and journalists play fast and loose with the truth, they're applauded for "saving the planet."

Over 17,000 scientists (including hundreds of climate experts) have signed a petition, saying they see "no convincing scientific evidence" that humans are disrupting the earth's climate.[34]

Average global temperatures did rise about a degree between 1860 and 1940, after several centuries of abnormally cold weather, they acknowledge.[35]

But satellite and other temperature data show very little warming since then (about 0.3° C or 0.5° F, according to the United Nations Intergovernmental Panel on Climate Change), and most of this slight warming occurred at night, in mid-winter, in the Earth's coldest regions, like Siberia.

Eleven degrees of transformation

Just 30 years ago, Earth Day crowds in our nation's capital heard a dire warning: "If present trends continue, the world will be about 4 degrees [Fahrenheit] colder for the global mean temperature in 1990, and 11 degrees colder by 2000. This is about twice what it would take to put us in an ice age."[1] Building on this apocalyptic theme, Dr. Doom himself, Stanford's Paul R. Ehrlich, predicted that America would have water rationing by 1974 and food rationing by 1980 – and the oceans could be as dead as Lake Erie by 1979.

Five years later, a worried *Newsweek* story proclaimed, "There are ominous signs that the Earth's weather patterns have begun to change dramatically," and scientists are "almost unanimous in the view that the trend will reduce agricultural productivity for the rest of the century," because average temperatures in the Northern Hemisphere are cooling – possibly sending the world into another "little ice age," like the one that afflicted Europe and North America between 1300 and 1850.[2]

But "present trends" obviously did not continue. Now, just 25 years later, the alarmist prophecies that the earth could *cool* by 11 degrees have transformed into alarmist prophecies that the earth could *warm* by 11 degrees. Steven Schneider, one of the prime ice age alarmists of 1975 metamorphosed into one of the prime global warming alarmists of today. And the science of global warming is more unsettled than perhaps ever before.

One thing has remained constant, however: the theoretical cause of the hypothetical climate catastrophe is the same (fossil fuels), and the proffered solution has likewise not changed one whit (government-driven bans on fossil fuels).

There is also is a strong consensus among many scientists that continued moderate warming would be beneficial for agriculture and society. Warmer temperatures in an atmosphere richer in carbon dioxide would make plants grow faster and need less water.[38]

In this context, a June 2001 announcement by a "panel of top American scientists" under the aegis of the National Academy of Sciences (National Research Council) appears to stand out as a glaring contradiction. As trumpeted loudly by the *Washington Post, New York Times* and other media outlets, the report supposedly "confirms" that "global warming is a real problem and is getting worse." However, these media reports failed to acknowledge some important facts.

The "summary" on which the news stories were based did not accurately reflect the actual report, which stressed the uncertain nature of climate science. For example, the full text noted that 20 years was too short a time for evaluating long-term climate trends, but the summary "forgot" to mention this. The panel was composed of scientists who, while certainly competent, tend to reside mostly in the climate alarmist camp. In fact, the panelists were appointed by former Vice President Al Gore, who is convinced that global warming is so serious that fighting it must become "the central organizing principle for civilization."[39] Neither the summary nor the full report mentioned recent studies by other top scientists whose findings contradict the summary's scary conclusions. On the other hand, the full report does acknowledge a crucial point that was ignored in the summary and most of the news stories:

> "Because of the large and still uncertain level of natural variability in the climate record, and the uncertainties [relating to man-made greenhouse gases], a causal linkage between the buildup of greenhouse gases in the atmosphere and the observed climate changes during the 20th century cannot be unequivocally established."[40]

Virginia state climatologist Dr. Patrick Michaels summed up the NAS report succinctly: "The people on this panel are largely the same ones who produced the United Nations reports, as well as earlier Academy reports. They have been touting big warming for nearly two decades. Reversing course, and saying anything else would have been self-destructive. That's why the contents of this report were so predictable," and why it predicted a warming far in excess of the "very modest" 1.4°C (2.5°F) temperature increase that available evidence and some climate models predict for the next century.[41]

This moderate and generally beneficial temperature change falls well within the range of climate swings that have occurred over the past several thousand years. The NAS/NRC summary ignores this fact and the widespread and potentially catastrophic impacts the Kyoto Protocol itself would have on the United States and world.

The National Center for Atmospheric Research says even "full and perfect compliance" with the Kyoto Protocol would mean the average global temperature in 2050 would be only 0.06° C (0.13° F) lower than it would be in the absence of a climate treaty.[42] Actually stabilizing carbon dioxide and other "greenhouse gases" at current concentrations would require the United States to slash its emissions by 60 to 80 percent below 1990 levels. Meeting that standard would require "19 Kyotos" and send our use of fossil fuels tumbling to somewhere around 1930 levels.[43]

The impact on our economy, lifestyle and productivity would be nothing short of devastating.

According to the U.S. Energy Information Administration, the Kyoto accord would drain as much as *$340 billion a year* from the U.S. economy. Other studies project that the treaty could double fuel prices, cost over 3.2 million U.S. jobs, including nearly 1.4 million in black and Hispanic communities.[44] Since the United States drives nearly one-third of the entire world's economy, any treaty that sends America into a depression would also destroy the hopes and aspirations of developing nations.

But true to form, the energy-suppression militants are determined that only one column in the fraudulent Precautionary Principle's balance sheet for global warming will be considered: the alleged horrors of man-induced catastrophic climate change. As these precautionary activists astutely recognize, no other "crisis" offers the same potential as cataclysmic global warming for curtailing economic growth, changing the way societies produce and use energy, and justifying a powerful system of global government.

Indeed, French premier Jacques Chirac told delegates to the plenary session at the sixth climate change Conference of the Parties (COP-6) in The Hague that the Kyoto Treaty is "the first component of an authentic global governance."[45] Ensconced in the United Nations, fed and nourished with billions in tax dollars, that new global powerhouse would control decisions by nations, states, communities and individuals over economic, employment, transportation, housing and other matters. Chirac's dream is shared by many environmental ministers and their allies. Will their dream become the world's nightmare?

And yet, the Kyoto Protocol on climate change continues to be promoted endlessly by a billion-dollar PR campaign, scientific-bureaucratic-activist self interest, a headline-seeking news media, and self-serving corporations that see new opportunities for government grants, tax breaks and regulations that give them an upper hand over competitors.

"Science, in the public arena, is commonly used as a source of authority with which to bludgeon political opponents and propagandize uninformed citizens. This is what has been done with both the reports of the IPCC and NAS. It is a reprehensible practice that corrodes our ability to make rational decisions. A fairer view of the science will show that there is still a vast amount of uncertainty – far more than advocates of Kyoto would like to acknowledge – and that the NAS report has hardly ended the debate. Nor was it meant to."

—Richard S. Lindzen, member of
NAS panel on climate change[46]

"To capture the public imagination,...we have to offer up some scary scenarios, make simplified dramatic statements, and make little mention of any doubts we might have. Each of us has to decide what the right balance is between being effective and being honest."

—Stephen Schneider, climate scientist and activist[47]

A beautifully crafted wooden horse

In addition to its adverse policy implications, the Precautionary Principle poses yet another significant threat to industry, because it is a stealth weapon, a Trojan horse. Consumers are unaware of its potential for abuse, and are thus inclined to embrace its "better safe than sorry" mantra when confronted with alarmist claims about product safety and environmental protection.

Wirthlin Worldwide, the opinion research firm, published a report in February 2000, highlighting the susceptibility of Americans to Precautionary Principle rhetoric. Wirthlin's surveys found that 69 percent of adults felt that activist groups are justified in urging consumers to discontinue use of a product "as a precautionary measure," even in the face of FDA and industry assurances that no threat exists. Three out of four (77%) Americans agreed that, "when it comes to environmental pollution, any amount of potential health risk should not be tolerated."[48] QED, say the eco-alarmists.[49]

That was before the electricity and natural gas crisis hit California and many other parts of the United States, however. The obvious question is, how would American consumers respond after watching their natural gas and electricity prices skyrocket 300-400 percent between January 2000 and March 2001, because environmental restrictions prevented the construction of more generating plants and production of adequate supplies of natural gas? The question was answered by a March 2001 *Time*/CNN poll, which found that only 48 percent of Americans would be willing to pay a paltry 25 cents more for a gallon of gasoline, even if the tax was intended to help prevent global warming.[50]

Another obvious question is, how do people who worry incessantly about "potential health risks" get out of bed in the morning, take showers, get into their cars, cross the street or climb a ladder? Annual injuries and deaths from these everyday activities number in the millions.

The February 2000 Wirthlin researchers also interviewed U.S. Congressional staff, to gauge their reaction to the Precautionary concept. Two-thirds of the staffers agreed that an overly cautious precautionary approach would likely result in regulations that make no sense from a cost/benefit point of view, and that the resulting regulations might do more harm than the risks they are supposed to prevent. Asked the same questions, 81 percent of industry executives agreed that the Principle would likely produce regulations that make no sense; 73 percent said the regulations would do more harm than good.[51]

Given the nature of the threat, it is telling that, of those surveyed, only three percent of industry executives and nine percent of Congressional staffers demonstrated top-of-mind awareness of the Precautionary Principle by name.[52] Adding insult to ignorance, many of the public relations Nevilles providing counsel to corporations have advocated what is best described as a Gates of Troy strategy: "Nice horse, come on in." Rather than taking on the activists, rather than engaging in conflict, the Nevilles have convinced many of their corporate patrons to embrace the Principle.

As a result, several industry groups have actually endorsed the Precautionary Principle, as interpreted and imposed by the radical attack groups – creating a glorious opportunity for the predators to execute a divide and conquer strategy: "Mr. CEO, why won't you endorse our Principle? Your counterpart in Europe has. Why should American babies be subjected to more risk than European *bambinos*?"

With industry disinterested, divided and defensive, activists have made significant progress toward infecting international treaties, national laws and a variety of regulations with Precautionary Principle language.

The 1987 Second North Sea Conference Ministerial Declaration, known as the London Declaration, included the following language: "To protect the North Sea from *possibly* damaging effects of the most dangerous substances, a *precautionary* approach is necessary, which may require action to control inputs of such substances *even before a causal link has been established by absolutely clear scientific evidence.*" (Emphasis added.)

A more expansive version of the Principle was adopted in the 1989 final report of the Nordic Council's International Conference on the Pollution of the Seas. The Council concluded that the Precautionary Principle must be enforced to "safeguard the marine ecosystem by, amongst other things, eliminating and preventing pollution emissions where there is *reason to believe* that damage or harmful effects are *likely* to be caused, *even where there is inadequate or inconclusive scientific evidence to prove a causal link between emissions and effects.*" (Emphasis added.)

The Precautionary Principle at work

International protocols. The first international diplomatic initiative to regulate the trade of pesticides was the 1991 Bamako Convention on the Ban of the Imports into Africa and the Control of Trans-boundary Movement and Management of Hazardous Wastes Within Africa. The anti-pesticides zealots succeeded in convincing the diplomats to embrace the Precautionary Principle. The negotiators agreed: "Each party shall strive to adopt and implement the preventive, precautionary approach to pollution problems, which entails, *inter-alia,* preventing the release into the environment of substances which *may* cause harm to humans or the environment, *without waiting for scientific proof regarding such harm.*" (Emphasis added.)

It is quite possible that those who negotiated the Bamako Convention have blood on their hands. Since 1991, millions of Africans have succumbed to diseases transmitted by mosquitoes and other insects. How many died because they did not have access to the pesticides covered by the Bamako Convention? How many died because they could not afford the much more expensive, much less effective alternatives to those pesticides?[53]

At the 1992 Rio de Janeiro global environmental summit, attending countries adopted Principle 15 of the Rio Declaration: "In order to protect the environment, the precautionary approach should be *widely* applied by states, according to their capabilities. When there are threats of serious or irreversible damage, *lack of full scientific certainty* shall not be used for postponing *cost-effective measures* to prevent environmental degradation." (Emphasis added.)

Companies seeking to appease environmental activists endorsed the Rio Declaration. The language *seemed* reasonable. The appeasers focused on the words "cost-effective measures." They believed "cost effective measures" meant protecting jobs, profits, markets and products. But the attackers are not bound by the carefully negotiated wording of international treaties. They don't play by the same rules. As a result, several major American industries have been victimized by the Precautionary Principle.

For example, the European Union (EU) has banned imports of U.S. and Canadian beef, claiming that hormones used to fatten cattle may cause damage to human endocrine systems. The FDA has declared that the scientific evidence shows that hormone residues in beef are safe, and the World Trade Organization (WTO) has ruled that the ban is unjustified. But the ban is still in place, thanks to the European Union's most effective protectionist weapon, the Precautionary Principle.

Ironically, the European farmers protected by the ban on North American beef may have been raising and marketing cattle that posed a quantifiable threat to the health of European citizens. Various forms of mad cow disease (bovine spongiform encephalopathy or BSE) occur naturally in cattle, goats, sheep, elk and deer, and have infected these animals periodically for centuries. There is growing evidence that BSE may be linked to the deaths of dozens of beef eaters in Britain and other EU countries.

The disease agent has not been found in dairy products or in beef or sheep muscle meat, meaning it is safe to eat those products. However, the brains, eyes, spinal cords, bone marrow and intestines of infected animals can carry the disease agent. None of these items are part of the American diet, by and large, but some of them were certainly an accepted part of the Euro diet until recently.

Moreover, BSE can be spread by giving cattle and sheep "feed" derived from these animal parts – a practice that has been outlawed in the United States for years, but not in Europe. Only belatedly did continental European governments take action on this truly serious threat. Simply put, if certain European governments had been more concerned about their own agricultural practices than about small amounts of hormones in U.S. cattle, some of the mad cow victims might be alive today.

The agricultural biotechnology industry is another American enterprise that has been assaulted by activists wielding the Precautionary Principle. The attack started in Europe and has spread globally. This promising technology has the potential to significantly increase food production, and reduce the tragic incidence of blindness caused by insufficient Vitamin A in diets, while also reducing the need for water and pesticides. But it is gravely threatened by trade protectionists, acting in cahoots with precautionist Luddites and eco-anarchists.

Even more seriously, for the first time, U.S. officials have surrendered to pillagers brought in by the Trojan horse. On January 29, 2000, representatives from 130 countries endorsed the Cartagena Protocol on Biosafety.

The protocol establishes rules governing international trade in genetically modified organisms (GMOs). After opposing import restrictions for more than a year, U.S. diplomats were forced to retreat. The final treaty allows a country to unilaterally ban GMO imports if the country believes there is not enough scientific evidence showing the product is safe. This arbitrary standard was advocated by the European Union, which repeatedly cited the Precautionary Principle as the authoritative precedent.

Writing about the various international initiatives to regulate biotechnology, Dr. Henry I. Miller, MD, the founding director of the FDA's Office of Biotechnology, and Competitive Enterprise Institute analyst Gregory Conko observed:

> "Focusing mainly on the possibility that new products may pose theoretical risks, the Precautionary Principle applied to agricultural and food biotechnology ignores very real, existing risks that could be mitigated or eliminated by those products. If the Precautionary Principle had been applied decades ago to innovations like polio vaccines and antibiotics, regulators might have prevented occasionally serious, and sometimes fatal, side effects by delaying or denying approval of those products. But that precaution would have come at the expense of millions of lives lost to infectious diseases."[54]

Vinyl plastic. Companies that make the compounds used to soften vinyl plastic (polyvinyl chloride) have also been victimized by attackers exploiting the Precautionary Principle. Led by Greenpeace, which has been engaged in a decade-long holy war against vinyl (because it is made with chlorine), European activists lobbied government officials and product manufacturers to ban vinyl toys and baby products, because the vinyl softeners (phthalates) might pose a very slight theoretical risk to children.

The anti-vinyl forces succeeded in convincing Greens Party elected officials and their socialist brethren to support the toy bans as a precautionary measure. With pressure mounting from the activists, the news media and government, several toy manufacturers and retailers decided to flee rather than fight. Vinyl toys were pulled from the shelves.

In December 1999, the attackers managed to secure a temporary ban in Europe, prohibiting the use of phthalate softeners in vinyl toys and other products intended to be placed in the mouths of children under three years of age. They accomplished this stunning victory without credible evidence that phthalates, which had been used in a wide array of products for almost 50 years, had harmed a single child.

On March 3, 2000, the European Commission decided to prolong the temporary actions taken against vinyl toys and other childcare articles.

The decision was criticized by the chairman of the Commission's own Scientific Committee on Toxicology, Ecotoxicology and the Environment.

How did Europe's phthalates industry respond? While some of the phthalate-producing companies fought to defend their products, others joined with European chemical manufacturers in an appeasement strategy that endorsed the Precautionary Principle. Thus, the same weapon employed to kill phthalates was embraced by many of its future victims.

Bill Durodié, a research fellow for the European Science and Environmental Forum, observed that the European toy ban "was a significant victory for the politics of emotionalism over reasoned debate and shows that many, including some scientists and industrialists, are guilty of seeking to legitimate their authority by pandering to consumer fears, under the guise of protecting health."[55]

The next group of victims may be very large, indeed. Radical activist groups like the disingenuously named Health Care Without Harm have now called on hospitals to phase out vinyl blood bags that store 12 million units of blood a year in the United States. Vinyl is the preferred container, because it safely stores red blood cells for twice as long as the next best alternative. In a nation and world faced with chronic shortages of blood, the HCWH campaign makes no sense at all, and both FDA and the medical community have concluded that the bags are safe. Yet the activists demand that the bags (and vinyl products that account for 25 percent of all medical devices) be taken off the shelves, claiming vinyl might release chemicals into the blood and could potentially harm blood recipients.[56]

The Precautionary Principle has slowly, but surely infected the cultural mainstream in the U.S. and Canada, as well. Gradually, the idea is taking hold among consumers that any risk is too much to tolerate. Recent actions by government regulators appear to place risk avoidance above all other considerations.

For example, the U.S. Consumer Products Safety Commission (CPSC) intervened in the phthalates in toys controversy. After studying the activists' allegations that phthalates posed a threat to American toddlers, the CPSC released a report in December 1998 that concluded, "generally, the amount ingested does not even come close to a harmful level."[57] Then, to the dismay of industry, CPSC chairwoman Ann Brown, never one to dodge a television camera, ignored her own findings and publicly suggested that, *as a precaution,* toy manufacturers should avoid using phthalates in products intended for young children.

Chairwoman Brown and her merry band of government bureaucrats later pressured crayon manufacturers to remove talc from their products, after eco-activists generated media reports claiming the talc contained asbestos fibers. Laboratory analyses of the supposed killer crayons showed they did not contain asbestos fibers. But science doesn't stand a chance when precaution dominates the regulatory process, and the desire to see one's face on the "Today" show takes precedence over the truth.

The CPSC is not the only U.S. regulatory agency guilty of subjugating science to the Precautionary Principle. The Food and Drug Administration exacerbated a nationwide shortage of blood in 2000, when it banned donations from people who traveled to England during the mad cow crisis – and pressured pharmaceutical companies to recall plasma products – purely on the theory that the disease might by transmitted by those life-saving products.

There is no scientific evidence that mad cow disease is linked in any way to human blood or plasma. By applying the Precautionary Principle in this instance, the FDA is subordinating the obvious and quantifiable risk that hemophiliacs and others will die if they cannot get a blood trans-fusion or medicines that are made from human plasma – to the unproven, theoretical risk that donated blood and plasma might carry the mad cow disease agent. Some argue that the FDA action is reasonable, in light of past cases of people getting AIDS from contaminated blood. However, no one (including FDA) knows how BSE is transmitted. It is therefore impossible to prove the disease can *not* be transmitted via blood or plasma – which means theories about possible harm once again trump realities of actual, demonstrable benefits.

Pesticides and beyond. The Environmental Protection Agency offers ample evidence of the Precautionary Principle run amok in its administration of the Food Quality Protection Act, the Federal Insecticide, Fungicide and Rodenticide Act (FIFRA), and other laws and regulations pertaining to the use of pesticides.

With the encouragement of the Environmental Working Group (EWG) and other anti-pesticide zealots, the EPA has been systematically taking action to restrict consumer access to pesticides that for decades have been used to rid America's homes of termites, asthma-causing cockroaches, mosquitoes and other unwelcome guests. With the spread of West Nile virus and other pest-borne illnesses, only time will tell whether the EPA and EWG will be held accountable for their indiscriminant and one-sided use of the Precautionary Principle.

Will advocates of the Principle limit their lobbying activities to the federal level of government? Not according to the leaders of the Massa-chusetts Precautionary Principle Project, a joint effort of the Clean Water Fund, Lowell Center for Sustainable Production, and Science and Environ-mental Health Network. The Project's November 2000 newsletter claims so-called Campaign Option Groups (COGs) are already:[58]

- drafting state legislation that would incorporate the Principle in state statutes;

- exploring avenues for advancing the Precautionary Principle through case law;

- developing ideas and opportunities for judicial and legislative actions to incorporate precaution in judicial reviews, such as shifting burdens of proof and changing standards of judicial review; and

- drafting model municipal ordinances and health regulations to promote the Principle.

As activists arm their *better safe than sorry* doomsday weapon at international, national, state and local levels of governance, many corporate executives remain ambivalent about whether the Precautionary Principle is a friend or a foe. Their public relations Nevilles continue to preach appeasement, arguing that companies have no choice but to endorse the Principle and bring the Trojan horse through their corporate gates. They are all deserving of a Neville Chamberlain award. Their naivete is breathtaking.

Other business leaders, those who recognize a Trojan horse when they see one, have formed a coalition of industry executives, scientists and policy mavens to confront the Precautionary Principle head on. They are fighting an uphill battle, however, and may suffer marketplace losses from deadly predatory fire, as well as from the *friendly fire* of the Nevilles and appeasers, who won't think twice about taking pot shots at those seeking to block their retreat.

Those fighting to stop the spread of the Precautionary Principle know from first hand experience that it will be used to erect artificial trade barriers, politicize the regulatory process, stifle innovation, restrict consumer choice, and undermine mainstream science.

Perhaps even worse, it all but ensures massive transfers of wealth, power and technology to predators, appeasers and nations that employ the Principle in pursuit of their own agendas.

A way out of the box

Does this litany of wrongs mean the Principle has no value whatsoever? No. In the words of the Social Issues Research Center in Oxford, England: "If we apply the Precautionary Principle to itself – by asking what are the possible dangers of using the principle – we would be forced to abandon it very quickly."[59]

What should industry and its allies do to slay the Principle once and for all? First, the stakeholders must use their full arsenal of scientific, communication, government relations and litigation resources, to raise awareness that the science-based regulatory system is already embedded with precaution to the core. The system works extremely well, as evidenced by the quality of life and life expectancy we enjoy in the 21st Century. So do the many different insurance policies that are readily available on the open market, to cover *real* risks.

Second, make sure consumers are better prepared to understand and evaluate science when they are exposed to it. If people were more science-literate and more familiar with the scientific method, they would be less vulnerable to the mumbo-jumbo claims of the fear mongers in their midst. Given the failure of our educational system to adequately teach science to two generations of students, this task will take decades and a huge commitment of public and private resources to complete. Nonetheless, if industry and its allies fail to serve as catalysts for this massive undertaking, the damage inflicted by ignorance, and by those who exploit it, will far exceed the cost of getting this important job done.

Third, expose the true agenda of those who advocate the Precautionary Principle for all to see. It's all about power and politics; it has nothing to do with the health and safety of people or the planet. Shedding light on this corrupt and shameful agenda during scientific forums, government hearings, industry gatherings and stockholder meetings, on the Internet, through litigation and regulatory challenges and, whenever possible, through the news media will ultimately destroy the Principle and banish those who advocate it to the lunatic fringe.

Finally, use the Precautionary Principle against the predators. Press for enactment (even if only in a few friendly jurisdictions) of laws requiring that caution be used to evaluate the costs and likely unintended consequences of *not* introducing a new technology. Help minority groups and citizens in developing countries educate the media, courts and legislatures about the harm caused by the attackers' use of the principle to thwart progress, keep life-saving genetically modified foods out of the market-place, prevent energy development and ban the use of disease-fighting pesticides. Assist them with legal actions, to impose precautionary principles on attack groups and government regulators, and compel development opponents to post bonds covering the costs and consequences of their dilatory tactics.

Rather than attempting to define the undefinable, policymakers should search for ways to weed out the more ridiculous claims made by environmentalists, consumer activists and others, the application of which would be a disaster for us, as it would be for our children and our children's children . . .Who knows? Maybe it will return policymaking on such issues to the rule of law and the rule of reason.

—Julian Morris[60]

For radical environmentalists, 'sustainable development' means don't use it today, and the Precautionary Principle means don't produce it tomorrow.

—Fred Smith, Competitive Enterprise Institute[61]

C. Sustainable development: Another Trojan Horse

Sustainable development is a notion of discipline. It means humanity must ensure that meeting present needs does not compromise the ability of future generations to meet their own needs.

—Gro Harlem Brundtland,
former Prime Minister of Norway[62]

Who could possibly argue with those sentiments? Who could possibly be in favor of non-sustainable development? What could possibly be wrong with a concept that promises a happy, mutually reinforcing, synergistic synthesis of economics, environment and equity? Actually, there are several fundamental problems.

1. A vague definition masking a coercive agenda

First and foremost is the *definition*. No one knows or agrees on what the concept actually means. Indeed, as former California community organizer John Callewaert bluntly told attendees at the 1999 National Town Meeting for a Sustainable America in Detroit, "sustainable development is a nebulous ideal we hope to move toward, even if we do not know what it is."[63]

The forest products industry, for example, argues that its modern timber cutting practices are clearly sustainable, since it always plants new trees, maintains forest health, protects sensitive areas, and is careful to prevent soil erosion. But environmental and "social justice" groups, which continue to play a dominant (and dominating) role in the sustainable development movement, insist that timber companies and retail lumber outlets should sell only "certified" products that meet the extreme standards they have set through their Forest Stewardship Council. Other greens, naturally, want no timber harvesting at all. (See the previous discussion of Home Depot and the FSC's "sustainable forestry practices" certification program.)

Maurice Strong, secretary-general of the United Nations' 1992 Rio de Janeiro Conference on Environment and Development (whose vast wealth derives from hydroelectric power in Canada) reveals an even broader, more coercive agenda.

"It is clear that current lifestyles and consumption patterns of the affluent middle class – involving high meat intake, consumption of large amounts of frozen and convenience foods, use of fossil fuels, appliances, home and work-place air-conditioning, and suburban housing – are not sustainable. A shift is necessary toward lifestyles less geared to environmental damaging consumption patterns."[64]

Echoing Strong's sentiments, Worldwatch Institute president Lester Brown wrote: "Building an environmentally sustainable future requires restricting the global economy, dramatically changing human reproductive behavior, and altering values and lifestyles. Doing this quickly requires nothing short of a revolution."[65]

In other words, beneath the altruistic-sounding euphemisms of the basic definition, lies a radical agenda aimed at sharply reducing or even eliminating what activists define as unsustainable production and consumption.

In their view, the world faces an imminent apocalypse – caused by over-population, resource depletion, species loss, global warming and general environmental degradation – and only drastic measures will avert the crisis.

Life-enhancing benefits of modern science, technology, housing and civilization must be curtailed.

For, as former Vice President Al Gore argued in his book, *Earth in the Balance*, only "sacrifice, struggle and a wrenching transformation of society" can save us, and it is pure "appeasement" to suggest otherwise.[66]

"But 'glory' doesn't *mean* 'a nice knock-down argument,'" Alice objected.

"When I use a word," Humpty Dumpty said in a rather scornful tone, "it means just what I choose it to mean – neither more nor less."

"The question is," said Alice, "whether you *can* make words mean so many different things."

"The question is," said Humpty Dumpty, "which is to be master – that's all."

—Lewis Carroll, *Through the Looking Glass*

2. Undemocratic process to transform society

The second problem is the *process* used to determine what is, or is not, a sustainable practice. The Rio conference resulted in a 40-chapter, 300-page treatise, known as *Agenda 21*, covering virtually every facet of human life, and offering hundreds of specific recommendations as to what we must do to achieve a sustainable world.[67] The process followed since then has been a carefully designed, top-down program to "educate" people about the wisdom of ecological central planning, and why and how we must dramatically alter our lifestyles.

Agenda 21 lists numerous policies that can be implemented at the local, state, national or international level, without the need for new legislation (or oversight by elected legislators). Similarly, President Clinton's Council on Sustainable Development also focused heavily on executive orders, regulatory edicts and other initiatives that can be implemented without new legislation and often in spite of intense opposition by members of Congress, local communities, minorities and other interest groups who will be adversely affected by the actions. These initiatives included national monuments and other land withdrawals, anti-sprawl land-use policies, extensive "public awareness" campaigns, classroom materials for children, new college courses that stress "growing social and global crises," and councils of "key stakeholders."

Their purpose is to prevent resource development, limit growth, "protect and enhance biodiversity" (more deliberately vague terms), and force societies and individuals to shift to organic farming, multiple housing units, bus and rail transportation, restrictions on the use of private property, primitive technology, and related components of "sustainable, responsible international citizenship" and life styles. Their goal is to achieve a utopian vision of how society should be organized in the future, and how people should live.[68]

As is the case with nearly all the activists' programs, behind the sustainable development movement lurks a deep distrust, even hatred of business, consumers, free markets, individual freedom and private property as the source of progress, human betterment and environmental improvement. Indeed, the activists view economic progress itself with suspicion and even alarm, since it generates increased consumption by the "haves" and an expectation of increased prosperity and consumption by the "have-nots."

In the attackers' view, fairness and equity must be grounded in an egalitarian agenda, administered by them and focused on managing resources, development and society, so as to share the (eagerly) anticipated scarcities. Their agenda includes "global tax equity," to combat "unfair and harmful tax competition" among nations, and a fee on all currency transactions.

Led by the European Union and Organization for Economic Cooperation and Development, this "global tax equity" or "tax harmonization" movement seeks to achieve three things. Reduce national sovereignty. Force all countries to have the same high tax rates. And eliminate the temptation for companies and individuals to invest in more competitive economies, where profits are taxed at lower rates. In effect, the EU and OECD are admitting that their growth-strangling, high tax welfare states are not "sustainable" without such an international agreement.[69]

The tax on currency transactions is another clever strategy designed to generate a steady flow of revenue for already affluent NGOs. The arrangement would become yet another vibrant profit center for the Crisis Creation Industry, the last unregulated bastion of rampant Capitalism.

3. Regulators and NGOs in charge

The third problem, of course, is the *people* who will get to decide what is sustainable, and what is not. The Rio conference, United Nations and White House Council on Sustainable Development all agreed that government agencies and non-governmental-organizations (NGOs) would play the lead roles in defining, planning and implementing sustainable development programs.

Only fully "accredited" international NGOs and carefully selected "stakeholder councils" will coordinate and participate in the decision process. But the process is no longer a traditional public hearing – with a wide range of witnesses, offering their comments, concerns and insights. Rather, it is a carefully orchestrated presentation of the government-NGO position, followed by "consensus-building" sessions, conducted by trained facilitators and designed to achieve largely pre-determined results. It reflects the view of these elite organizations that only they can adequately perceive the crisis that looms just ahead, and only they have the wisdom and commitment to properly manage resources, development, society and individual choices.[70]

During the National Town Meeting for a Sustainable America, for instance, advocates of sustainable development gave speeches and presented multi-media programs, often singling out certain companies as being enlightened or socially responsible for having accepted the activists' visions and agendas. Few of those businesses were willing to challenge the pseudo science or coercive actions that are the foundation of sustainable development – out of fear that they might jeopardize the environmentally friendly image they have so carefully cultivated.[71] One has to wonder how long *this* honeymoon will last, before the eco-radicals assail these businesses for greenwashing.

Businesses and individuals that challenge the activists' vision and agenda were not even invited to participate in the town meetings. Indeed, many of them were pilloried as greedy, self-serving polluters, whose views and interests are irrelevant, or even detrimental, to the discussion.

Senator Chuck Hagel (R-NE), Congressman John Dingell (D-MI) and many others have frequently raised serious concerns that sustainable development initiatives, treaties on biodiversity and global warming, and assorted other global governance programs infringe on the national sovereignty of the United States and other countries. That these concerns are hardly misplaced can be seen in comments by John Gummer, a member of Britain's Parliament, former Secretary of State for the Environment in the United Kingdom, and a European Union Delegate to the U.N. Convention on Climate Change:

> "I have got my national sovereignty constantly being attacked by the United States. Your pollution is changing my climate. I'm not having you telling me that I've got no say in what you do. You are changing my climate. My constituency will be underwater because of your pollution. Don't talk to me about national sovereignty. The United States has got to realize that it lives in the world. It is not the United States' world. It's our world: the world of poor people and rich people alike. The United States' sovereignty is of no account in a world that is being destroyed by the United States' pollution...."[72]

4. Taxpayer and foundation funding

In response to prodding and financial incentives by the United States, Canada, European Union, United Nations, World Bank, private foundations and NGOs like the Sierra Club, more than 130 countries have created new bureaucracies to implement *Agenda 21* and related sustainable development initiatives. It is, by now, hardly surprising that these programs are lavishly funded by the twin money trees of wealthy foundations and tax-supported government agencies. Thus, problem number four is the bottomless *budget*.

Government funding for sustainable development efforts has come from the U.S. Departments of Agriculture, Energy and Interior, Environmental Protection Agency and White House – directly or through intermediaries like the National Science Foundation and Smithsonian Institution. Former President Clinton's Council on Sustainable Development created the model for developing public policy by "consensus." Consisting of cabinet-level government appointees, executives from selected environmental and social organizations, and a few "socially responsible" businessmen, it consumed millions of dollars over an eight-year period, identifying *Agenda 21* policies that could be implemented without additional legislative authority.

Just how much money was spent, which groups got it and how it was used has been hard to ascertain. However, some have expressed hope that the George W. Bush Administration will be able to answer these questions.

Interesting things have also happened at the equally secretive foundation level. For example, Ron Arnold discovered that the Forest Stewardship Council was funded to the tune of some $575,000 by a series of grants from the MacArthur and Surdna Foundations, between 1993 and 1998. Other foundations gave the FSC an additional $925,000 in 1996-1998 through various intermediaries.[73]

More intriguing, says Arnold, a Wallace Global Fund grant reveals that the supposedly independent FSC's efforts are actually coordinated by MacWilliams Cosgrove Snyder, the same PR firm that produced the "Search and Destroy Strategy Guide," which recommended and outlined a "smear campaign" against the wise use movement. It is this same FSC that helps ensure that retailers sell only "certified" forest products that meet the activists' extreme sustainable development criteria.[74] Some of these retailers have been counseled in this abject surrender by none other than the capitulation counselors at Edelman Public Relations.[75]

Canada, home of UN-reformer Maurice Strong and "unified one world order" Prime Minister Jean Cretien, has sponsored and played major roles in a number of "sustainable planet" summits and conferences. It has talked of implementing an international tax on world money transactions, to help fund "a new world vision," and Strong's home province of Manitoba has hosted a conference on sustainable development for a new world agenda.[76]

5. Progress or deterioration?

What all this means is that, on the basis of alarmism, pseudo science and brilliant public relations by a host of activist groups – and without any conscious decisions by U.S. or other citizens – the world is being nudged toward their vision of central planning. This time, the rationale is ecological, rather than economic.

Worse, we are being guided in this process by a well-funded army of unelected, unaccountable bureaucrats, who act behind closed doors, masking their true agendas and concealing what will happen to the millions of people whose livelihoods depend on activities that the activists decree are not sustainable.

Over 170 years ago, the great English politician and historian Lord Thomas Macaulay asked, "On what principle is it that, when we see nothing but improvement behind us, we are to expect nothing but deterioration before us?" This question should be inscribed in stone (or spray painted) on the walls of every apocalyptic organization, for it is even more relevant and incontestable today.

The prophets of doom who promote sustainable development as a central organizing principle for mankind have repeatedly predicted mass starvation, energy and resource depletion, and environmental catastrophe. Not only have they been consistently wrong on all these dire predictions, but they have studiously and stubbornly ignored the vital roles played by human ingenuity, innovation and entrepreneurship – what myth-slayer Julian Simon called "the ultimate resource" – in solving even the most vexing resource and environmental problems.[77]

Competitive Enterprise Institute president Fred Smith points out that, since 1950, improved plant and animal breeds, expanded availability of new agri-chemicals, innovative agricultural techniques, expanded irrigation, and better pharmaceutical products have all combined to spur a massive expansion of world food supplies. Since 1974, Asian rice yields have risen nearly 40 percent, yields of wheat and other grains have increased by similar amounts, and the nutritional levels of a majority of people throughout the world have also risen, in spite of rapid population growth.[78]

Indeed, in the developed world, food *surpluses* have become a more common and complex problem than food shortages. Modern packaging has greatly reduced food spoilage, transit damage and disease-causing bacteria; increased the shelf life of numerous products; and enabled businesses to expand food distribution across regions, nations and even oceans. Meanwhile, in much of the Third World, antiquated farming methods (which activists laud as sustainable) continue to result in shortages and malnutrition, political institutions continue to obstruct the distribution of food, and an absence of refrigeration and packaging still results in widespread spoilage, Smith notes.

Furthermore, this amazing progress has been accompanied by reduced pollution and environmental stress. If we still had to use 1950s technology to feed the world's current population at today's nutritional levels, Smith observes, we would have to plow under an additional 10 to 11 million square miles, almost tripling the world's agricultural land demands, which now stand at 5.8 million square miles. This is land that would then be rendered unavailable for wildlife habitat, recreation and other uses.

In the United States alone, production of our 17 most important food, feed and fiber crops rose from 252 million tons in 1960, to 700 million tons in 1999. This amazing feat, moreover, was accomplished using 10,000,000 fewer acres than were cultivated in 1960.[79] In other words, modern farming practices sent yields per acre soaring, allowing America to utilize vast areas for wildlife and other purposes.

The message of optimism is the same virtually everywhere we look.

In 1947, the world's proven reserves of crude oil totaled 68 billion barrels; over the next 50 years, we consumed 783 billion barrels – and still had proven reserves of 1,050 billion barrels at the end of 1998! The world's proved natural gas reserves totaled 1,041 trillion cubic feet (tcf) in 1966; 32 years later, we had used up 1,883 tcf – and still had untapped proven reserves of 5,145 tcf.[80]

What about fears that we would soon run out of copper, because we were using so much for communication lines? We switched to fiber optic cables made of silica, the earth's single most abundant element.

How did all this happen? As Julian Simon and Fred Smith have emphasized over and over, it's a natural outgrowth of our most important renewable, sustainable resource: human ingenuity. To cite just one example, advanced computers and algorithms like those that mapped the human genome now promise to make it vastly faster and easier to analyze entire subsurface rock formations – and pinpoint oil and gas deposits with uncanny accuracy.[81] In league with drilling and other technologies that are improving at almost the speed of light, this revolutionary new method will again put the lie to apocalyptic warnings that we will soon run out of petroleum.

Brain power is the ultimate resource because no mineral or other natural resource has any value (and thus no one has any incentive to find and produce it), until human genius finds economic uses for it. History proves that this genius flourishes best in a climate of freedom and opportunity. One would therefore expect that the most successful and productive nations ought to be those with the greatest economic and political freedom – and indeed that is the case.

The most prosperous countries in the world continue to be those with the most economic and political freedom, lowest taxes and lowest barriers to foreign trade. It is these open economies that have consistently higher per capita income, faster growth rates and better economic opportunities than do those with restrictive policies. They also have more money and resources to spend on human health and environmental protection.[82]

The least prosperous nations are the socialist dictatorships and kleptocracies so beloved by those same anti-capitalist activists. Often, they are also the countries with the worst social unrest, most savage ethnic cleansing, most rampant AIDS epidemics, filthiest air and water, and gravest threat of mass hunger, starvation and disease. Thus, by making economic development difficult or impossible, the militant environmentalist NGOs are prolonging these problems and contributing to the disintegration of countries like Indonesia.

Of course, all this flies in the face of the rigid ideologies and dooms-day predictions by neo-Malthusians such as Lester Brown, Paul Ehrlich and Maurice Strong, who have repeatedly predicted catastrophes that never arrived.

But the radical activists have never curbed their "facticidal" impulses, or let facts get in the way of emotion, ideology and their eternal quest for money and power. Nor are they about to do so now.

Our world will only get better, unless those who fear and loathe energy and technology continue to get the upper hand. Even cursory research provides ample evidence that the depth and intensity of the radicals' antipathy toward energy development actually has little to do with concern about the environmental impacts of fossil fuels.

The true reasons are perhaps revealed in the viscerally negative reactions of well known activists to the unexpected (and later disproven) announcement by two research physicists in 1989 that room temperature (cold) fusion could be a new, inexhaustible supply of cheap energy.[83]

- Jeremy Rifkin, Foundation on Economic Trends: "It's the worst thing that could happen to our planet." It would give people an infinite ability to exhaust the planet's resources, destroy its fragile balance, and create unimaginable human and industrial waste.

- Paul Ehrlich, Stanford University biologist: Given our society's dismal record in managing technology, the prospect of inexhaustible fusion power would be "like giving a machine gun to an idiot child." It won't be "a panacea" (as though anything ever is), and by the time fusion could make a difference, thirty years down the road, the world will have long since succumbed to over-population, famine, global warming and acid rain.

- Barry Commoner, Queens College, New York: Fusion could be a "dangerous distraction" from efforts to develop safe, proven, decen-tralized technologies like solar power.

It's hardly surprising, then, that some "deep ecologists" have argued that federal mileage and air pollution standards are disastrous laws, because they make driving cheaper and easier to justify on environmental grounds. Had these laws not been enacted, they say, cars and trucks would still be horrible polluters, and smog would by now be so hideous and deadly that cities would have no choice but to ban automobiles altogether.[84]

It should come as no surprise, then, that the BANANA zealots[85] are pressing forward with major initiatives on the Precautionary Principle, sustainable development, climate change, pesticides, chemicals, plastics and an encyclopedia of other alarmist topics.

Their tactics include lobbying, boycotts, street theater, shareholder actions and cyber-attacks, to name just a few. Among their allies are foundations, PR firms, Hollywood, the United Nations, European Union and many agencies of the U.S. government. To build on their recent successes in Seattle, Quebec and Washington, DC, the activists are training new regiments of radicals in Europe, Canada, the United States and even Brazil – in anti-business, anti-trade ideology and the fine arts of raucous protests, cyber technology, how to conduct running street battles[87] with the police, and how to commit arson and other acts of eco-terror.

So the bad news is, companies and CEOs can look forward to much more of the same – on an even more intense level, from a growing horde of savvy, well-organized, well-heeled, politically powerful predators, who will use every weapon in their arsenal.

The good news is, companies and CEOs don't have to just sit back and take it, or engage in pre-emptive appeasement. They, too have a well-stocked arsenal, if they choose to use it – and many potential allies, if they choose to ask for help.

"Would you tell me, please, which way I ought to walk from here?" said Alice.

"That depends a good deal on where you want to get to," said the Cat.

"I don't much care where," said Alice.

"Then it doesn't much matter which way you walk," said the Cat.

"– so long as I get somewhere," Alice added as an explanation.

"Oh, you're sure to do that," said the Cat, "if only you walk long enough! In that direction," the Cat said, waving its right paw round, "lives a Hatter; and in that direction," waving the other paw, "lives a March Hare. Visit either you like; they're both mad."

"But I don't want to go among mad people," Alice remarked.

"Oh, you can't help that," said the Cat; "we're all mad here. I'm mad. You're mad."

"How do you know I'm mad?" said Alice.

"You must be," said the Cat, "or you wouldn't have come here."

—Lewis Carroll, Alice in Wonderland

The last century witnessed many tyrannies imposed in the name of justice, religion and the betterment of man and society. Is this new century to witness new tyrannies imposed in the name of "environmental justice" and saving the earth from mankind's "industrial follies"?

— Rev. Dr. R. Thomas Coleman and Fr. Robert A. Sirico[86]

Chapter 11 Notes

1. Mary Beth Sheridan and James F. Smith, "Mexico Deep-Sixes Plan for Baja Lagoon Saltworks," *Los Angeles Times*, March 3, 2000.
2. Michael P. Shea, "Beating Mitsubishi," *Campaigns & Elections*, July 2000.
3. Saul Alinsky's seventh rule of power tactics, *Rules for Radicals*, page 127.
4. *Ibid.* Many of these scientists have worked closely with radical environmental groups for many years, as have various California city councils. All can usually be counted on to toe the Green line. Pierce Brosnan, Cindy Crawford, James Cromwell, Woody Harrelson, Ed Begley, Jr. and some 1,500 other Hollywood celebrities are affiliated with the Earth Communications Office (ECO), which produces "public service" messages and helps slip Green messages into scripts and other materials. Most of the mutual funds are dominated by eco activist organizations; the Global Environment Fund, for example, is largely the Pew Charitable Trust, and the "socially responsible" Calvert social index fund has lost its investors some 18 percent since its inception.

   It is another example of radical Green agendas enjoying phony "public" support that is actually a mile wide and a half-inch deep. However, this eco-propaganda machine is highly effective, largely because it can trot out these "experts" on a moment's notice, secure in the knowledge that the news media will treat them as independent, credible and "not in the hip pockets" of corporations. Traditional conservationists have no comparable vehicle. See Ron Arnold and Alan Gottleib, *Trashing the Economy: How runaway environmentalism is wrecking America*, Bellevue, WA: Free Enterprise Press (1993), pages 626-627.
5. James F. Smith, "Activists Break New Ground to Help Shake Off Saltworks Project." *Los Angeles Times*, April 23, 2000.
6. Walter Scott, "Personality Parade," *Parade*, June 10, 2001.
7. Capital Research Center, "Environmentalists target retail stores to pressure timber industry," January 26, 2001, www.green-watch.com/StaplesRAN.html; Ron Arnold, *Undue Influence*, pages 290-297; Sean Paige, "Bringing the battle to the suburbs," *Washington Times*, December 19, 2000.
8. PETA news release, "PETA gives McDonald's a break today: One-year moratorium on 'Unhappy Meal' declared after fast-food giant makes major improvements in treatment of chickens," September 6, 2000.
9. Steven Milloy, "Organized organic crime," *Washington Times*, March 27, 2001.
10. Graydon Forrer, Alex Avery and John Carlisle, *Marketing and the Organic Food Industry: A history of food fears, market manipulation and misleading consumers*, The Center of Global Food Issues at the Hudson Institute, Indianapolis, IN (September 2000). Copies of the report are available upon request and can also be found on the web at www.nomorescares.com/news/organic.htm .
11. Public Relations Society of America, "The Emulex hex: Newswires under scrutiny," *Public Relations Tactics*, January 2001, pages 18-19.

12. The U.S. Securities and Exchange Act has guaranteed shareholders with a $2,000 stake in any publicly traded company the right to file so-called "shareholder resolutions." By law, companies must include these resolutions as ballot questions in their annual reports to shareholders. Even if a resolution fails to pass, if it garners at least 3.5 percent of the vote, the companies must offer it on the ballot the following year.

13. Lisa Buckingham, "Greens take on BP Amoco: Environmental lobby wins shareholders support," *The Guardian*, January 27, 2000.

14. Rainforest Action Network news release, Tuesday, April 17, 2001.

15. *Ibid.*

16. King & Spalding, Comments on FDA proposed rule, "Docket number 00N-0989: Availability for public disclosure and submission to FDA for public disclosure of certain data and information related to human gene therapy or xenotransplantation/information collection requirements," April 18, 2001.

17. Public Citizen's Health Research Group, Comments on FDA proposed rule, Docket number 00N-0989, April 18, 2001.

18. Carter Dougherty, "Greens, lumber team in trade fray," *Washington Times*, business section, March 20, 2001.

19. Robert L. Bradley, Jr., "Clement Maitlin's overview," Letters, *Oil & Gas Journal*, October 2, 2000, page 10.

20. Joel Tickner, *et al., The Precautionary Principle In Action: A Handbook*, Science and Environmental Health Network, Washington, DC (2000).

21. *Ibid.*

22. "Scientists find bras a pain and a possible cancer risk," Oliver Poole, *Daily Telegraph*, October 29, 2000.

23. "Precautionary tale; environmentalist concept of the Precautionary Principle," Ronald Bailey, *Reason*, April 1, 1999.

24. Joel Tinkner, *et al., op cit.*

25. David Shaw, *The Pleasure Police: How Bluenose Busibodies and Lily-Livered Alarmists Are Taking All the Fun out of Life*, New York: Doubleday (1996), page 44.

26. Joel Tinkner, *et al., op cit.*

27. Teresa Platt, "Totems, Taboos, Sacred Cows and Tunafish," Fishermen's Coalition article reprinted at www.furcommission.org/resource/perspect7.htm (December 1997).

28. *Lancet* editorial, "Donor responsibilities in rolling back malaria, *The Lancet*, vol. 356, No. 9229, August 12, 2000.

29. Michelle Malkin, "Anti-Pesticide Pests," *Washington Times*, October 13, 2000.

30. There are nine disease-carrying rats in New York City for every human being – and animal rights activists are trying to convince authorities to ban traps, as cruel and inhumane.

31. Joel Tinkner, *et al., op cit.*

32. *Ibid.*

33. Alix M. Freedman and Steve Stecklow, "As UNICEF battles baby-formula makers, African infants sicken," *Wall Street Journal*, December 5, 2000;

284 **Rules for Corporate Warriors**

Henry J. Kaiser Family Foundation, "Global Challenges: UNICEF, infant-formula makers mired in ethical, political controversy," Kaiser daily HIV/AIDS Report, December 5, 2000, www.report.kff.org/archive/aids.

34. Oregon Petition Project on global warming, Oregon Institute of Science and Medicine, www.oism.org/pproject.
35. See for example, Wallace S. Broeker, "Was the Medieval warm period global?" *Science*, Vol. 291, pages 1497-99; H. H. Lamb, *Climate History and the Modern World*, New York: Routledge (1985); and Brian Fagan, *The Little Ice Age: The Prelude to Global Warming, 1300-1850*, New York: Basic Books (2000). Recall, too, that when Leif Ericson colonized Greenland in 1000, it really was green and he could actually grow crops and raise sheep in areas that today are covered by ice and snow.
36. Kenneth E.F. Watt, former University of California professor of zoology and environmental studies, speech in Washington, DC during Earth Day rally, April 25, 1970. See http://www.free-market.net/forums/spotlight9802/messages/571648057.html.
37. "The Cooling World," *Newsweek*, April 28, 1975. See also Brian M. Fagan, *The Little Ice Age: The Prelude to Global Warming, 1300-1850*, New York: Basic Books (2000).
38. See www.GreeningEarthSociety.org and www.co2science.org (the nonprofit Center for the Study of Carbon Dioxide and Global Change, located near Phoenix, Arizona).
39. Al Gore, *Earth in the Balance: Ecology and the human spirit*, New York: Plume (1992).
40. National Academy of Sciences, National Research Council, *Climate, Climate Forcings, Climate Sensitivity, and Transient Climate Change* (2001), page 17. See also Richard S. Lindzen, "Scientists' report doesn't support the Kyoto Treaty," *Wall Street Journal*, June 11, 2001. Lindzen is a professor of meteorology at the Massachusetts Institute of Technology and was a member of the NAS panel on climate change.
41. Patrick J. Michaels, "Postscript: National Academy report on global warming," Cato Institute, Washington, DC, June 7, 2001.
42. Martin Parry et al, "Adapting to the inevitable" *Nature* Vol. 395, page 741 (1998). Noted in S. Fred Singer, *Hot Talk, Cold Science: Global warming's unfinished debate*, Oakland, CA: Independent Institute (1999), page 67.
43. Intergovernmental Panel on Climate Change, *Climate Change: The IPCC Scientific Assessment*, Cambridge University Press (1990) and subsequent 1992 and 1995 supplementary reports. See also Patrick J. Michaels and Robert C. Balling, Jr., *The Satanic Gases: Clearing the Air about Global Warming*, Washington, DC: Cato Institute (2000); S. Fred Singer, *The Scientific Case against the Global Warming Treaty*, Fairfax, FA: Science and Environmental Policy Project (1997); S. Fred Singer, *Climate Policy – From Rio to Kyoto: A Political Issue for 2000*, and Beyond, Palo Alto, CA: Hoover Institution (2000).
44. *Impacts of the Kyoto Protocol on U.S. Energy Markets and Economic Activity* (available at www.eia.gov/oiaf/Kyoto/pdf/sroiaf9803.pdf) and Management

Information Services, Inc., *Potential Economic Impacts of the Kyoto Climate Change Protocol on Blacks and Hispanics in the U.S.*, Washington, DC (2000).

45. Jack Kemp, "Global government in retreat," Copley News Service (www.copleynews.com), December 6, 2000.

46. Richard Lindzen, "Scientists' report doesn't support the Kyoto Treaty," *Wall Street Journal*, June 11, 2001.

47. Jonathan Schell, "Our fragile Earth," *Discover*, October 1987, page 47. Cited in Ronald Bailey, *Ecoscam: The False Prophets of Ecological Apocalypse*, New York: St. Martin's Press (1993), page 171.

48. "The Precautionary Principle: Throwing Science Out With The Bath Water," Wirthlin Worldwide with Nichols-Dezenhall, *Issue Perspective*, February 2000.

49. *Quod erat demonstrandum*, "which was to be proved" – a notation added at the end of a analytical problem, to indicate it had been solved correctly.

50. Jeffrey Kluger, "A climate of despair," *Time*, April 9, 2001.

51. *Ibid.*

52. *Ibid.*

53. Richard Tren and Roger Bate, *When Politics Kills: Malaria and the DDT Story*, Washington, DC: Competitive Enterprise Institute (2000).

54. Julian Morris, *et al.*, *Rethinking Risk And The Precautionary Principle*, Oxford: Butterworth-Heinemann (2000), page 100.

55. *Ibid.*; Bill Durodié, *Poisonous Propaganda: Global echoes of an anti-vinyl agenda*, Washington, DC: Competitive Enterprise Institute (1999).

56. Angela Logomasini, "Blood supply besieged," *Washington Times*, August 10, 2000.

57. "CPSC Releases Study on Phthalates in Teethers, Rattles and Other Children's Products," *NEWS from CPSC*, December 2, 1998.

58. Massachusetts Precautionary Principle Project, Newsletter, November 2000.

59. "Destructive precaution," H. Sterling Benett, *National Post*, Toronto, Canada, November 20, 2000.

60. "Rethinking Risk And The Precautionary Principle," Julian Morris et al, Butterworth-Heinemann, Oxford, pp. 19-20, 2000.

61. Fred L. Smith, Jr., speech at Warren Brooks memorial dinner, Washington, DC, May 24, 2001.

62. Quoted in Henry Lamb, "What's Wrong with Sustainable Development?" *eco-logic* online, January 15, 2001, www.eco.freedom.org/el/20010102/susdev.shtml.

63. Michael Barkey, "Sustaining Radicalism: Eric Voegelin meets Al Gore," Acton Institute, Grand Rapids, MI (1999).

64. Michael McCoy, "Trekking to the summit," *Earth Summit in Focus, No. 2*, United Nations Conference on Environment and Development (1991), page 2. See also Ronald Bailey, "Who is Maurice Strong?" *National Review*, September 1, 1997, pages 32-37.

65. Lester Brown, *World Without Borders*, New York: Vintage Books (1972), page 308.

66. Albert Gore, Jr., *Earth in the Balance: Ecology and the Human Spirit*, New York: Plume (1992), page 274.

67. Agenda 21, United Nations Conference on Environment and Development (1992), available at www.igc.apc.org/habitat/agenda21.
68. See James M. Sheehan, *Global Greens: Inside the International Environmental Establishment*, Washington, DC: Capital Research Center (1998), pages 13-16, 91-103; Jacqueline R. Kasan, "Doomsday every day," *ecologic*, Fall 1999, pages 2029; Terry L. Anderson and J. Bishop Grewell, *The Greening of Foreign Policy*, Bozeman, MT: Political Economy Research Center (2000).
69. Daniel Mitchell, "OECD's perpetual tax grab," *Washington Times*, December 7, 2000. Daniel Mitchell, "OECD's glass house," *Washington Times*, December 8, 2000. Walter Williams, "Global tax thuggery of OECD," *Washington Times*, December 29, 2000.
70. Michael Barkey, *op cit.*; Henry Lamb, *op cit.*; Jacqueline Kasen, *op cit.*
71. *Ibid.*
72. 1997 Conference of the Parties on global climate change, Kyoto Japan. Quoted in interview with Sovereignty International, available in *eco-logic* online, January 2001, at http//sovereignty.net/p/clim/glummer97/htm.
73. Ron Arnold, *Undue Influence*, pages 290-292.
74. *Ibid.*, page 296.
75. Malcolm Wallop, "Memo to Business: The Greens intend to place profits on the endangered list," *Investor's Business Daily*, January 8, 2001, page A24.
76. Carl Teichrib, "Canada's role in sustainable development," *eco-logic*, Fall 1999, pages 6-8.
77. See Julian Simon, *The Ultimate Resource 2* (revised edition), Princeton, NJ: Princeton University Press (2000); Julian Simon and Herman Kahn, *The Resourceful Earth: A response to Global 2000*, New York: Basil Blackwell, Inc. (1984); Julian Simon, *Population Matters: People, resources, environment and immigration*, New Brunswick, NJ: Transaction Publishers (1990).
78. Fred L. Smith, Jr., "The bankruptcy of collectivist environmental thought," paper presented at Mont Pelerin Society meeting, Santiago, Chile (November 2000), pages 46-49.
79. *Ibid.*
80. Robert L. Bradley, Jr., *Julian Simon and the Triumph of Energy Sustainability*, Washington, DC: American Legislative Exchange Council (2000), pages 28-32.
81. Lynn Cook, "Extreme exploration: Chroma Energy is ferreting out oil and natural gas reserves with the kind of algorithms that mapped the genome," *Forbes*, May 28, 2001, pages 186-188.
82. James Gwartney, Robert Lawson, *et al.*, *Economic Freedom of the World 2001 Annual Report*, Vancouver, BC: Fraser Institute, (2001); Gerald P. O'Driscoll, Jr., Kim R. Holmes and Melanie Kirkpatrick , *The 2001 Index of Economic Freedom*, Washington, DC: Heritage Foundation (2001).
83. Paul Ciotti, "Fear of fusion: What if it works?" *Los Angeles Times*, View section, April 19, 1989.
84. Gregg Easterbrook, *A Moment on the Earth: The coming age of environmental optimism*, New York: Viking Penguin (1995), pages 192-193.

85. Build Absolutely Nothing Anywhere Near Anything.
86. R. Thomas Coleman and Robert Sirico, "Environmental Injustice," *Detroit News*, December 18, 2000. Rev. Dr. Coleman is a founder of the African-American Institute for Racial and Social Justice in Muskegon, MI; Father Sirico is president of the Acton Institute for the Study of Religion and Liberty in Grand Rapids. Both are signatories to the Cornwall Declaration on Environmental Stewardship, which emphasizes mankind's central place in the world's natural order, our obligation to be wise stewards of the environment and the Earth's natural resources, and the need to emphasis people and humanity in our economic and environmental decisions.

12

The Coming Combat

We must make this an insecure and uninhabitable place
for capitalists and their projects. This is the best contribution we can make towards protecting the earth.

—Dave Foreman, co-founder, Earth First[1]

By foreseeing them at a distance ... the evils that might
arise from [human affairs] are soon cured; but when, from
want of foresight, they are suffered to increase to such a
height that they are perceptible to everyone, there is no
longer any remedy.

—Niccolo Machiavelli

Modern corporations have brought untold wealth, health, prosperity,
opportunity and hope to billions of people. And yet, companies, officers
and CEOs are under constant attack by regulators, politicians, the news
media and professional predators. They are held accountable for all manner of
infractions, major and minor, real and imaginary, based on long established
legal principles and on strained interpretations of complex, convoluted
new laws and regulations.

Peter Huber describes their predicament in his book *Hard Green* as,
"The only soup that is just right is the one not yet on the table."[2] Clearly,
the goal of these attackers is not to achieve solutions, but to perpetuate
grievances. Unfortunately, too many companies fall right into their traps.

In response to attacks, CEOs and middle managers alike often behave like victims, complaining bitterly about forces they cannot control – while taking too little responsibility for their predicament, and surrendering their own substantial power to determine their fates. They forget that, in the political arena, in this world where only the fittest survive, they must set aside their comfortable roles as problem solvers, and become front-line warriors.

As ex-leftist radical David Horowitz writes in *The Art of Political War*, "Politically, it is better to be seen as a peacemaker, than a warmonger. But it is not always possible. If forced to fight, then fight to win."[3]

This means, first of all, that you must understand and adopt five principles of political war, if your company is to be one of those survivors.

1. Politics is war conducted by other means.

If war is political relations conducted by other means, it is also true that the politics of extremist pressure groups is all-out guerrilla warfare disguised by a thousand pieties, moral claims and euphemisms. Unfortunately, most corporations have shown little capacity for successfully waging war against their most virulent, vicious adversaries. A combatant who employs conventional tactics and strategies against a guerrilla force will lose. Period. Vietnam taught us that lesson. Ignore it at your own peril.

Despite television and Hollywood portrayals of corporate executives to the contrary, business ethics and Higher Authorities demand that only legal measures be employed.

The harsh reality is that communicating more effectively, "finding common ground" or even prevailing in debates are useless, almost suicidal strategies in conflicts with predatory extremists. Their purpose is to geld, blackmail or destroy capitalism, technology, progress and your company. Just like the Viet Cong three decades ago, activists know they don't really need to destroy a business, cause significant damage or win on the factual merits. They simply need to destroy their corporate target's will to fight back.

Willie Sutton is credited with the famous quote, "I rob banks because that's where the money is." The Willie Sutton rationale drives today's NGO, regulatory attackers and other shakedown artists. (One report had Reverend Jesse Jackson replying when asked why he focused on telecommunications mergers, "It's where the most money was.")[4] Each victory, each shakedown gives them more money, influence and power – and positions them to ratchet their demands up a notch when they go after their next target, or come back to you for more loot.

This is out and out political warfare, and the CEOs' goal must be to destroy the attacker's effectiveness and fighting ability. Most corporate commanders understand this and would be quick to summon their companies to combat. But they often find their battle cries drowned out by the Siren songs of PR firms and corporate Nevilles, who so sanitize the retelling of how they secured "peace for our time," that their fables bear little resemblance to the actual battlefield carnage.

As this book demonstrates, companies have many effective weapons in their arsenal. Business executives need merely learn how to use them, be resolved to do so when the need arises, and ensure that everyone associated with their companies are not only well tutored in the strategies and tactics of self-defense and counter-attack, but also have the *cajones* to use them.

2. The best defense is a good offense.

Just as the French waited behind their "impregnable" Maginot Line for the Germans to attack – and then got outflanked and destroyed – so is a purely defensive strategy the surest route to corporate defeat. Company officers must learn the importance of good intelligence, the positive impact of ideology, and the need to win ideological wars, not just marketplace battles.

Spy on your adversaries. The Russians do it. The Americans do it. The Vatican does it, and so do the Israelis and the French. More importantly, the activists spy on you. Return the favor. Just do it legally. Read the attacker's materials, have trusted officers and employees join their organizations, browse their Web sites, lurk in their chat rooms and attend their meetings. Utilize list serves, online libraries and "members only" sections of Web sites. Plant moles in their organizations.

Read analyses by groups that track the extremists. Study the issues and the attack groups' portrayals of them. Do everything legal to determine where the next attacks are likely to come from, what tactics will be used, which predator groups will be arrayed against you, and how best to respond to the emerging threat. If you believe this activity requires too much time and energy, you're a dead man walking. Knowing the enemy is a cost of doing business in today's culture of attack.

To survive, companies must be prepared to launch pre-emptive strikes, or at least counterattacks, fast and powerful enough to turn the tide of battle. By discrediting the radicals in advance and launching a furious first strike or counterattack, your company can define the issues, seize the moral high ground, shape the agenda, demonstrate that it is protecting the most vulnerable in society against predatory extremists, and secure real peace on your terms. Next time, the wounded predators may go elsewhere, in search of easier prey.

3. Politics is a war of position.

In political conflicts, the one who ultimately convinces the most people that it will best protect their interests wins the battle. This is the most important principle of political warfare.

Define and position your company as the provider of essential services, products and benefits to the largest constituency possible. Link your agenda, products and services to the interests of women, children, the oppressed, disadvantaged and impoverished. Form fighting coalitions – and support and nurture their long-term efforts – for each issue that confronts you.

Strip away your opponents' phony mantle of virtue, and expose the callous predator beneath. Show that they are well-funded, savvy aggressors, who mangle the truth, hide their true agendas beneath clever euphemisms, keep their well-heeled funding sources a closely guarded secret, have little regard for people, and believe they have the right to make decisions for everyone.

How does a company win this positioning war? By applying the same strategies and tactics used to market products and services – but adapted for guerilla warfare against both powerful mechanized forces and well-armed hidden adversaries.

This requires going beyond your company's self interests and expanding into the broader context of what's best for your industry, allied constituent groups, consumers and society. If your company is battling PETA over its beef with beef, for instance, make sure your response focuses on consumer choice, and product benefits. Remind your audience that Americans enjoy the safest food supply in the world, and show them why. If appropriate, deliver a stinging message that annexes the adversaries to the lunatic fringe. Always seek opportunities to align your company with individuals and groups that are part of the mainstream of society: ranchers, agricultural groups, nutrition experts, and even supportive consumer groups.

4. Position is defined by fear and hope.

"Those who provide people with hope become their friends," Horowitz notes; "those who inspire fear become enemies."[5] My corollary? Offer hope to your employees, investors, customers and consumers generally. Create fear in the hearts of your enemies. Position your company as the provider of safe, life-enhancing products. Humanize the issues that matter to real people, personalize them, and make them real, graphic and urgent.

The facts are mostly on your side. Demonstrate with hard evidence that those who are attacking your company are extremists, who should inspire fear in your audience. Drive up the costs of the predators' demands by making them personally relevant to customers, clients, consumers, constituents, communities and families – and to the media, politicians, community leaders and clergy. Show how the poor and downtrodden have been or will be victimized.

Your business makes peoples' lives longer and more productive. Be proud of that accomplishment. Let the world know you are proud of it, and why.

At the same time, be honest and pragmatic about your corporate image. It should be built around tangible, easily understood results of how your industry has improved health, extended life, promoted democracy and opportunity, and created prosperity for many millions.

Encourage your allies to remind the public that the predatory attackers vigorously oppose this progress and improvement, and promote policies that mean continued poverty, disease and death for millions. They propose visions and "solutions" that fail miserably, but always promise a utopia that's just over the next horizon (or the one after that).

They take no personal risks, impose numerous risks on others, create nothing, and are almost never held accountable for the damages, misery and deaths they may cause.

To top it off, they often carry out these campaigns using tax dollars, allegedly abusing their nonprofit, tax-exempt status, by engaging in, promoting and supporting activities that are clearly not educational – but involve lobbying, pressure-tactic shakedowns and "direct action" assaults on companies, products, research facilities and personnel.

Demonstrate that consumers and the less advantaged are the real victims of extremist policies and tactics. Better yet, enable your many, diverse, non-corporate allies to do so. This will demonstrate that your attack or counterattack is not only fully justified self-defense – but also protection of society's most defenseless.

Don't talk about costs, profits, patent life or even jobs. Drawing a lesson from Archer Daniels Midland's advertisements with David Brinkley, talk about *people's lives* and how your company improves them.

Be imaginative in finding ways to give a platform to our nation's and world's poor, powerless, disenfranchised, ignored and forgotten.

It's been said that, to make an omelet, one must break some eggs. But, after all these years, all these broken eggs, all this misery, all these deaths – where are all the omelets the eco-anarchists promised us? There are no omelets, just the putrid results of their pillaging:

- Low income people whose promised jobs and health insurance disappeared because of a phony "environmental justice" campaign that stopped the construction of new manufacturing plants, and thus could not afford to see a doctor and did not recognize the warning signs of breast cancer or pneumonia, until it was too late.

- Indian and African mothers whose children died from dysentery and tuberculosis, because Green extremists prevented construction of dams that would have brought them clean water and electricity.

- African children who carry the AIDS virus, transmitted through their mothers' breast milk, because extremists made infant formula unavailable – and fought projects that would have purified local water and made it safe for use in formula.

- Families who lost their homes, possessions, heirlooms and loved ones in California and New Mexico fires, because radical government land managers ignored weather forecasts and started a fire, issued edicts prohibiting people from clearing flammable brush from around their homes to protect "endangered" kangaroo rats, or prohibited the removal of overgrown, dead and diseased trees. (In 2000 alone, over 65,000 fires in 13 western states burned over 7 million acres.)[6]

- Twenty-nine pilots and crew members who died since 1983 in crashes of logging helicopters that eco-fundamentalists have forced the timber industry to use, as an alternative to roads and trucks through forest lands.[7]

- Families of the three women who drowned, because callous government ideologues refused to let their community repair a dangerous earthen dam, claiming bushes at the base of the dam might someday become habitat for the endangered elderberry beetle.[8]

Promote the production, broadcast and distribution of documentaries and news segments that challenge environmental extremists, their tactics and the policies they advocate. A good example is the CEI tape of television journalist John Stossel interviewing powerful, authoritarian bureaucrats, in the wake of disastrous fires that killed people and destroyed dozens of homes. "All 600,000 species of beetles should be protected?" Stossel asked – and a smug Fish and Wildlife Service bureaucrat responded, "If we can."[9] (But at what price, for what benefits, who gets to decide, and will it be a democratic process that addresses competing needs and interests?)

Drop talk about the expense and technical difficulty of meeting higher Corporate Average Fuel Economy (CAFÉ) standards. Instead, explain why consumers place fuel economy well below other considerations when choosing a car, and emphasize the energy, environmental and societal costs of horse-blinder policies that focus so narrowly on this single approach to a valid policy goal.

Through your non-corporate allies, refer families, clergy and newspaper editorial writers to the *USA Today* study and other research reports, showing that CAFE standards have resulted in smaller, lighter, less safe cars that have been responsible for 25,000 to 46,000 deaths since the late 1970s. Urge them to demand that Consumers Union and *Consumer Reports* address this issue honestly, instead of ignoring car size and weight as critical components of the safety issue.

The Insurance Institute for Highway Safety and many automotive experts put vehicle size and weight among the most important considerations. Consumers Union, however, seriously misleads its readers, by saying absolutely nothing about these factors in selecting a safer car or light truck.[10]

Modern technology, free trade and globalization have greatly improved the lives of millions, especially in underdeveloped nations. This progress is clearly their best chance to fight starvation, disease, illiteracy, child labor and prostitution, pollution, environmental degradation and premature death.

Nevertheless, during the World Trade Organization talks in Seattle, widespread theatrics and vandalism (mostly by middle-class white kids) pressured industry, government and the WTO into numerous concessions – stalling or derailing progress for the poorest of the world's poor. A major reason the radicals won is that the banks, businesses, politicians and trade groups were oddly (if not predictably) silent, invisible or ineffective. As a September 23, 2000 *Economist* editorial observed:

> "These outbreaks of anti-capitalistic sentiment are meeting next to no intellectual resistance from official quarters. Governments are apologizing for globalization and promising to civilize it. Instead, if they had any regard for the plight of the poor, they would be accelerating it, celebrating it, exulting in it – and if all that were too much for the public, they would at least be trying to explain it.

> "Yet even under these wonderful circumstances, politicians in Europe and America are wringing their hands about the perils of globalization, abdicating their duty to explain the facts to voters, and equipping the anti-capitalists with weapons to use in the next fight.

> "Companies, too are bending to the pressure, modest as it might seem, and are conceding to the anti-capitalists not just specific changes in corporate policy, but also large parts of the dissenters' specious argument."[11]

Why and how can anyone who professes to care about the poor allow this to happen? Every case has a human face. Tell the human tragedies. Show whose side your company is on. Show you care. Make these people's lives and needs an integral part of your corporate philosophy and daily practices. Don't let predators put garage sale price tags on people's lives. Now, that's what I call corporate ethics.

5. Your weapons are symbols that evoke fear and hope.

Corporate CEOs, media relations personnel, technicians and attorneys too often speak in long-winded technical terms and statistics. Resist the temptation. In media interviews and public forums, it is concise, carefully crafted statements that get through, and don't get left on the cutting room floor. (Details and analyses are important, to back up your conclusions. But save them for some other time and place, such as company and allied groups' Web sites, brochures, articles, op-eds, advertorials and press kits.)

So whatever you say, keep it simple and short, and say it loud, clear and often. Persuade and win people over with images, symbols and messages that:

- Define yourself, your company and the issue in ways people understand;
- Humanize, personalize and dramatize the issue;
- Focus on your two or three core messages;
- Repeat them over and over;
- Convey your positive messages, while painting your radical opponent's message in stark, unsavory terms; and
- Give people hope, while inspiring in them a dread of your opponent's political agenda.

You have 8 to 30 seconds to reach the average person, who often will not even be interested in the issue or what you have to say. In this brief news flash, you have to get their attention, make them trust you, persuade them that you're reasonable, and win them over. Don't waste the opportunity. Covering too many points is as bad as providing too much boring detail: your message will be diffused, and nothing will get through. So make the one point that counts the most, make it over and over again, and let your audiences know how they can get more information: your corporate Web site, an 800 number or independent experts, for example.

As Horowitz observes: "The audiences that will determine your fate are audiences that you will first have to persuade.... With these audiences, you will never have time for real arguments or proper analyses. Images – symbols and sound bites – will always prevail."[12]

Position yourself on the side of children, the poor, the downtrodden, working Americans, minorities, the world's disenfranchised masses who never had a chance or a hope. Speak directly to people about things they intuitively understand: the concrete lives of their fellow humans. Demonstrate with hard evidence that you care, and that the other side is cold, callous and mean-spirited.

Have confidence in facing your enemies. Never suppose the enemy's firepower is greater than your own. Never allow yourself to be psychologically beaten in advance by an opponent who knows how to fight

With steady commitment to principles, as evidenced by your actions, convince people that your policies and programs flow from concern for them – and from deep concern about your opponents' agendas. Show that your intentions are noble, your opponents' intentions crass and rooted in disdain or hatred for people, especially those who have the least.

Mobilize your allies' fire-power to attack the attackers. This will help you avoid coming across as hard-edged, scolding or sanctimonious. At the same time, though, when it is appropriate, express a little well-chosen outrage at the attackers' distortions, pressure tactics and disregard for people's lives and livelihoods. Never fail to condemn the terrorism and other crimes that have become the hallmark of eco-anarchists who detest science, debate, democracy, the rule of law and other keystones of modern civilization.

These broad strategies, while aimed at the general public, will bolster customer and shareholder confidence in your company and your resolve to stand up to attackers.

And now, a few tactical suggestions.

Arm your employees and stockholders.

Any predatory attack is bound to damage employee morale. These are your front-line communicators, and they need a clear sense that: company leadership is hanging tough, there's a credible message and a plan, you're forging ahead, and you're in it for the duration. Use your company Web sites, newsletters, shareholder materials and other means to educate, prepare, arm and energize your employees and stockholders in the strategies and tactics of self-defense, attack and counterattack.

Choose the appropriate spokesperson. Your messenger is at least as important as your message, particularly with broadcast media. At the risk of being age-ist or otherwise politically incorrect, this means chubby, gray-haired, middle aged white guys will often not be your best representatives. Spend as much time choosing and training your spokespersons, as you do refining your message and building your network of allies.

Wrap your messages in a principle.

When all is said and done, what does your company really stand for? Find a principle that defines who you are and stick with it. It's principles – not logic – that shape minds and motivate. Identify your principle and articulate it proudly.

Utilize the legislative and regulatory hearing process.

Work with friendly federal and state officials to make more aggressive and effective use of government hearing processes. Frame issues and shape agendas. Seize the moral high ground. End government funding and protection of attack groups.

Press congressmen, legislators and regulators to invite witnesses who support science, technology and progress. Persuade them to question radical group witnesses thoroughly, under oath and penalty for perjury, to ensure that their testimony and answers are factual and honest.

Build networks and cultivate relationships –

With the media. Get to know reporters who cover your issues, before you meet them in the heat of battle. Find potential allies – editors, business and environmental journalists, and investigative reporters – who are true professionals, still have open minds, and don't simply shill for the predators. Ensure that they receive a steady flow of accurate information that buttresses your integrity – while undermining your opponents' credibility. Do this yourself and through independent third party organizations, which you can support with grants and by giving them access to your data, research and other resources.

Arrange editorial board meetings, facility tours, press briefings, and regular "gaggles" with reporters, where they can ask questions and address emerging issues. Reward journalists who live by the Society of Professional Journalists' code of ethics and are prepared to take the time to investigate both sides of your issues. Give "exclusives" and "backgrounders" to editors and journalists who consistently demonstrate balanced reporting.

Cooperate with independent writers and television/video producers who have demonstrated a willingness to challenge the radicals – John Stossel, Ronald Bailey, Bill O'Reilly and others. Do the same with newspaper columnists and correspondents. Get to know them personally, watch their programs, and support their work directly, through think tanks and with advertising.

Urge reporters to challenge the validity and accuracy of any film or video footage they receive from attack groups, and to demand that the activists provide: full, unedited source tapes, complete with sound; the names and affiliations of all people featured in the unedited footage; and sworn statements from the producer and crew, attesting to where, when and under what circumstances the film or video was shot. Be prepared to meet the same requirements. Only in this way will reporters avoid being conned into becoming propaganda tools for the Crisis Creation Industry.

Return fire immediately if you are attacked in the print, broadcast or online media. If you have been gathering intelligence regularly, or a long-anticipated report is involved, you'll rarely get caught flat-footed by a media feeding frenzy precipitated by attack groups. Your mission, just like the Boy Scouts, is to be prepared so you won't be blindsided or allow the "sky is falling" crowd to "spin" the issues and rule the headlines and airwaves.

But even if it's an unexpected breaking story or a true sneak attack, never allow the predators to savage you and your company. Pound them with heavy return fire, using your phone, fax, e-mail, company Web site, allied groups and every other resource at your disposal to launch an immediate counterattack, respond to distortions and false allegations, and get "the other side of the story" out while it's still part of the first day's news. Add wit and good visuals to your comments, to ensure greater interest in them.

Be bold, and mighty forces will come to your aid.

—Goethe

With market-oriented think tanks, in the United States and overseas. They can provide research, present a credible independent voice to views similar to your own, influence opinion and political leaders, and promote responsible social and economic agendas. These institutes have extensive networks among scholars, academics, scientists, journalists, community leaders and politicians. With your encouragement, they can help you counter the negative attacks the predators will inevitably launch against you – and drive home the negative consequences these extremist groups will inevitably cause for vast legions of people.

Key U.S. think tanks focusing on national and/or international issues include the Committee For A Constructive Tomorrow (CFACT); Cato, Claremont, Competitive Enterprise, Frontiers of Freedom and Heartland Institutes; Heritage Foundation, Hoover Institution, Hudson Institute, Media Research Center, National Center for Policy Analysis, National Center for Public Policy Research, Pacific Research Institute and Reason Public Policy Institute. The Capital Research Center and Center for the Defense of Free Enterprise track corporate, government and foundation grants to radical groups, and promote people-focused, market-oriented solutions to complex environmental and economic problems. CFACT and other think tanks are also building chapters on college campuses and are active overseas.

The Leadership Institute and Institute for Humane Studies teach moderate college students and young professionals how to work more effectively with the media and Capitol Hill. The Mackinac Institute, State Policy Network and other think tanks address statewide topics.

Access to think tanks in foreign countries is facilitated by the Atlas Economic Research Foundation.[13] Its broad network includes the Fraser Institute and Atlantic Institute for Market Studies in Canada, Institute for Economic Affairs in Great Britain, IEA-Ghana, Liberty Institute in India, Hong Kong Center for Economic Research, Korea Center for Free Enterprise, Institute for Public Affairs in Australia, and Libertad y Dessarrollo, Instituto Liberal, Instituto Libertad y Democracia, and Fundacion Republica in Latin America. All these organizations promote sound science, market-based economic and environmental measures, intellectual property rights and global free trade.

With organizations and people who support your views, whose political and economic interests depend on your continued prosperity, who believe deeply in progress, humanity and the system that brings wealth, opportunity, health and technology to billions. Educate them, learn from them, show you care, adopt their causes and persuade them to adopt yours.

Grassroots NGOs like the Alliance for America, Foundation for Biomedical Research, National Animal Interest Alliance and American Land Rights Association can be especially important allies. So can clergy, academics, local business leaders, independent scientists, and respected spokespersons for the poor and disadvantaged.

Utilize their opinions, political influence and economic pressure, to identify, publicize and ridicule the predators. Promote and support campaigns that –

- Encourage and buy from companies that refuse to kowtow to the predators. Let their sales clerks, store managers and corporate officers know why you shop there. Rally people to write op-eds and letters to editors, send e-mails to friends and use other tactics to expand the campaign.

- Boycott the eco-radical boycotters, and the craven companies that cave in to the attackers. Let *their* officers and personnel know why your grassroots supporters refuse to buy their products. Tell their friends, neighbors, fellow congregants and newspaper editors why they have taken this principled stand.

Join forces with others to help build and support an organization comparable to the Earth Communications Office (ECO) to recruit, mobilize and activate celebrities who support traditional conservation efforts, property rights, local control, science and technology, and free enterprise. Orchestrate forums and platforms to present their views. Make it easy for them to deliver their messages, and urge them to become more involved in public policy debates.

This new weapon would change the dynamics of the policy debate, encourage others to step forward, and make it less acceptable and less politically correct for Hollywood liberals to support extremist causes.

Above all else, stop providing aid and comfort to your enemies. There's a word for that in the military. It's called "treason." So, get a grip on your company's grant-making policies before more of your profits end up in the wrong hands.

With conservative legal organizations, like the Institute for Justice and Landmark, Mountain States, Pacific, Southeast, Southwest and Washington Legal Foundations. All utilize litigation, regulatory appeals and other legal mechanisms to address regulatory, business opportunity, constitutional and similar issues.

Civil actions by these organizations – and by corporations and trade associations themselves – could help hold predator groups and overzealous regulators accountable for the deliberate and unintended consequences of their actions.

In cases involving mail fraud, Lanham Act violations, conspiracy and RICO violations, false statements in hearings, terrorism, threats and intimidation, personal injuries, property damage and wrongful death, it may also be appropriate to seek redress through district attorneys, state attorneys general, the U.S. Department of Justice or the International Court of Justice.

Legal actions will break the attackers' momentum, and force them to expend time, money and energy dealing with matters outside their experience: attacks and counterattacks on *them*, defending *their* ethics and morality, and attempting to rehabilitate *their* reputations. Even ultimately unsuccessful actions can generate press coverage for your company and position, put the attack groups on notice, hurt their credibility and fund raising, and encourage citizen groups to file their own lawsuits and be more effective activists.

Become the media.

Where you can't get an even shake with the print and electronic media, become your own media outlet, by publishing newsletters and flyers, building and publicizing valuable Web sites, hosting meetings and public forums, and launching mass media campaigns of radio and TV advertising, op-eds, Web bulletins and advertorials. Consider reinforcing these programs with a billboard campaign – putting your favorite anti-humanity quotations of earth and animal rights militants in big, bold letters, where everyone can see them, juxtaposed with pictures of burned out laboratories, blind or starving children, and malaria-ridden adults.

Your company Web site, in particular, can be a vitally important resource for reporters and editors, community leaders and concerned citizens. It will educate on a continuing basis, provide instantaneous research assistance, help ensure that your corporate viewpoint is represented in stories, and keep unfounded rumors and misinformation from spreading. Your site can be especially valuable in a crisis if it includes up-to-date information, frequently asked questions, special press sections, and contact information grouped by topics and fields of expertise.[14]

Online information can also offset the need to get someone on the telephone, especially in the evening or over the weekend, or when reporters or investors need immediate answers to breaking news stories. All this should be obvious, which makes it hard to understand why many companies still lag behind.

A recent survey found that newspaper and magazine journalists and editors increasingly use the Internet to add breadth and depth to articles, locate photographs and other images, and even find or develop story ideas.[15] These findings underscore the importance of building extensive, informative, easily navigable online corporate press centers.

Make sure they include downloadable images in several file formats, and materials that will be useful to journalists: press releases and legal or financial documents, for instance.

Convert important surveys, reports and news releases to Adobe Acrobat files and load them on your sites. People can readily access these documents (software is available for free download) and, most importantly, they cannot alter the documents.

Lurk in chat rooms and utilize list serves, to learn what predators are up to and how other companies are responding. Launch your own cyberadvocacy programs, to augment your blast-faxes and phone calls. Create "dark" web sites, ready to launch and promote at a moment's notice, in the event of a crisis or attack. Post video clips, animations and photographs on your sites, along with audio commentaries, charts and analyses, interviews and horror stories. Armed with the facts, expose the predators' hidden agendas, inhumane actions and attitudes, cozy relationships with bureaucrats and terrorists, lies and misrepresentations, and secretive arrangements with foundations, companies, scientists, PR firms and others.

For more ideas, read *The Net Effect* and *Public Relations on the Net,* and join the Public Affairs Council and similar organizations that utilize "cyberactivism" via the Internet to reach target audiences.[16]

Educate the urban cargo cults.

During World War II, aboriginal people in New Guinea helped Allied troops by clearing air strips in the jungles, so airplanes could land with food, weapons and materiel. The aborigines received some of these supplies as payment, and quickly grew dependant on them. When the war ended, however, the planes stopped coming. Increasingly desperate, the natives formed "cargo cults" that hacked out new landing strips, just as they had during the war. They prayed to their gods – thinking this would bring new planeloads of supplies. To no avail.

A quarter century later, half a world away, new cargo cults took root and began to dominate political thought. Western society had changed, and most of its population now lived in big cities. More dependent on energy, raw materials and agricultural products than any previous society, these urbanites are clueless about where their most basic necessities actually come from.

They cannot begin to grasp the vast expertise, raw materials and manufacturing processes involved in making even a simple wood-and-graphite pencil.[17] They assume every price spike and supply interruption is due to a corporate conspiracy. They are ripe for exploitation by the Crisis Creation Industry and its constant appeals for precaution, preservation and sustainable development.

Winning the battle means making these city slickers as knowledgeable about the true sources of their prosperity and life styles, as they are about driving a car or surfing the Internet. Educate them about your production and manufacturing processes. Extol your products' benefits. Emphasize the true costs of listening to the attack groups.

How? By terminating your support of anti-industry environmental groups – and channeling that money to think tanks and grassroots organizations that support your views. By taking your message to classrooms and your company Web site, with brochures, videos, and the vast array of other communication technologies and opportunities.

Demand accountability.

Civil fines and penalties, even criminal sanctions, now apply to minor oil spills and even the most far-fetched claims of injury from perfectly safe products. But stupid, reckless, even deliberate and malicious acts by predators and regulators are routinely ignored by journalists, law enforcement officials and legislators alike.

The far-flung empire of extremist attack groups is the last unregulated, unaccountable big business in America. The time has come to subject it to the rules of law and civilized behavior that govern other businesses and citizens in our society. Recruit your employees, shareholders, customers and allies to help launch a multi-pronged campaign that will make the Crisis Creation Industry accountable at last.

Emphasize that your company supports freedom of speech, assembly and peaceful protest. However, it will not tolerate threats, physical or psychological intimidation, arson, assaults on people or any similar criminal tactics. These actions cross the line between free speech and incitement to (or complicity in) riot, extortion, terrorism and other illegal acts.

Join the Sierra Club, Greenpeace, PETA and other attack groups and use their magazines, mailings, Web postings and list serves to learn more about their philosophies, tactics and coming assaults. Utilize the Freedom of Information Act, litigation discovery and other legal processes to ferret out still more information.

Press district attorneys, state attorneys general, the U.S. Department of Justice and other officials to investigate and prosecute wrongdoing by predators, under tax, criminal, RICO (Racketeer Influenced and Corrupt Organization) and other statutes.[18]

Insist that the U.S. Postal Service crack down on fraudulent fundraising by extremist environmental groups, just as it has in the case of televangelists, corporations and other organizations that have engaged in such abuses.

Petition the Internal Revenue Service to revoke the privilege of donor-contribution deductibility [501-(c)(3) status] of any nonprofit organization that recommends, organizes or accepts responsibility for unlawful acts. Request that these organizations be required to reorganize under the political activism tax exemption [501-(c)(4) status]. Insist that any tax-exempt organizations perpetrating unlawful acts be legally sanctioned.

Demand that the FBI, IRS and other law enforcement officials crack down on "cyberspace slumlords." These entities host or maintain Web sites that list the names and addresses of people targeted by terrorists, offer online guidance on how to commit arson and avoid prosecution, and urge or suggest illegal "direct action" against companies, research laboratories and individuals. They also support and promote other activities that are illegal or not in accord with the groups' nonprofit, tax-exempt status.[19]

Demand permanent termination of all such sites, and the imposition of fines, imprisonment and other penalties as may be appropriate.

Speak out, gather signatures and write articles in support of eco-terror legislation. Petition for bigger law enforcement budgets, tougher penalties, heavier fines and longer prison terms for arson, sabotage and other crimes against facilities, equipment, research programs, private residences, or individuals and their families.

Insist that Congress create a *national clearinghouse on environmental crimes.* This will make it easier for local, state, federal and private law enforcement officials to track criminal activity and crime sprees, profile individual eco-terrorists, and evaluate patterns and methods.

Take pictures and post them on your Web site any time protesters engage in trespass, harassment, intimidation or theft. (Send a copy to Mom and Dad, who probably had no idea how their child was spending spring or summer break.) Then have the perpetrators arrested, finger printed, mug-shot and prosecuted.[20]

You'll make some hooligans think twice about doing it again, help build a portfolio of potential suspects for acts of more serious eco-terror, and dissuade many from engaging in more serious crimes.

Seek disbarment for attack group attorneys, and civil or criminal penalties for any organization's officers and directors who fail to stop or report illegal activities that they knew about or reasonably should have known about. (In other words, hold them to the same standards of conduct that now apply to corporate executives.)

Demand prosecution and severe penalties for any nonprofit member, officer or board member who contributes to the delinquency of minors, by recruiting or inciting them to engage in illegal actions, such as arson, crop damage or smashing windows.

A court gets tough with eco-terrorists

In a victory for the forces of law, sanity and civilization, self-proclaimed eco-anarchist Jeffrey Michael Luers was sentenced to 22 years in prison for arson, criminal mischief, and manufacturing and possessing a destructive device used in a June 2000 fire at Eugene, Oregon's Romania Chevrolet truck dealership. The fires caused "only" $40,000 in damage, but Lane County Circuit Court Judge Lyle Velure ruled the arsons could have posed a significant risk to individuals in the neighborhood and to those who discovered and fought the fire.

Luers claimed he set the fires because he was frustrated about the growing ecological destruction of the planet. County law enforcement authorities said they took the incidents very seriously, were "not going to tolerate terrorism" and hoped the stiff sentence would "send a message" to other would-be terrorists. They also pointed out that Eugene has become a haven for anarchists, some of whom were among the rioters during violent protests at the December 1999 World Trade Organization meeting in Seattle.

Several days before Luers' trial began in March, the Romania truck lot was hit again, and 30 sport utility vehicles were damaged or destroyed, causing about $1 million in damage. Although no suspects have been named, Earth Liberation Front spokesman Craig Rosebraugh claimed ELF had torched the SUV's because they threaten the environment.

Obviously unable to distinguish between free speech and violent crime, University of Oregon sociology professor Michael Dreiling asserted that the "exaggerated sentencing" meted out by the court "clearly reflects a no-tolerance standard for political dissent." Luers' lawyer argued for a lighter sentence and said Luers would appeal.[21]

Pressure local, state and federal law enforcement authorities to place a much higher priority on investigating and stopping eco-terror, by devoting more time to these crimes, setting up investigative task forces, offering rewards and imposing stiffer penalties for anyone convicted of these crimes.

Seek compensatory and punitive damages for lost business, costly delays, property damage, illness, injury, wrongful death, and harm to your employees and customers as a result of extortion, mail fraud, false advertising, terrorism and other actions by predator groups. Corporate officers and private citizens have paid severe penalties for such activities. There is no reason why Greenpeace, Earth First, PETA and similar groups should not be held to the same standards.

Choose your test case carefully. Seek remedy only for damages you have actually sustained. Seeking in court to stifle the free speech rights of your opponent is wrong and could even subject you to penalties if you try it. If you have suffered real harm, your company can help true justice by bringing legal action against the proper defendant. You may find help from legal foundations and grassroots citizen groups.

Band together with other potential eco-terror targets, to develop improved security measures and offer substantial rewards for the arrest and conviction of perpetrators of arson, extortion and other offenses.

Launch a campaign to compel the predator groups (and their sugar daddies) to abide by the same moral and ethical guidelines that businesses follow. Present them with a code of ethics, similar to the Sullivan and CERES Principles on humanitarian and environmental issues – and a pen to sign it.

Insist that they publicly reject violence, and condemn and root out extremists within their ranks who engage in or promote criminal acts. Insist that they refuse to offer a public forum to any group or individual who promotes unlawful acts.

Frame the issues to buttress your position. Do so at every opportunity – from talk shows and news releases to congressional testimony. Put the predators on the defensive. As Eldridge Cleaver used to say, "If you are not part of the solution, you are part of the problem." Stress that any organization that fails to condemn and root out the violence is implicitly condoning and supporting it.

Challenge obscene class action lawsuits. Hundreds of Massachusetts Mutual Insurance policyholders did just that recently – sending vigorous objections to the judge overseeing a settlement between the company and class-action attorney Gary Duncan.

The settlement, under the Truth in Lending Act, would have given one named plaintiff (now deceased) $250,000 and a second one $100,000. The rest of the "injured parties" would have gotten nada, zip. But Duncan would have pocketed a cool $5 million in immediate cash and $250,000 a year for the rest of his life. When all hell broke loose, Duncan actually gave in and withdrew the settlement, sniffing that he just couldn't believe he was being "portrayed as a villain."[22]

Go after the deep pockets – the foundations and other big contributors that back these predator groups – when they knew or had reason to know that their money was supporting organizations that engage in unlawful activities.

Bars that give more liquor to inebriated patrons, companies that sell dangerous products, landlords who allow drug dealers to use their buildings, corporate officers who fail to report violations – all are held accountable under well established legal principles. White supremacists have been sued successfully for depriving people of their civil rights.

There is no reason why deep-pocket supporters of unlawful acts should be held to a lesser standard. Ted Turner's foundation has routinely given the Ruckus Society substantial grants. Ruckus trained many protesters at the Seattle WTO riots. If any of them smashed the windows of Seattle retailers such as Starbucks, there is no reason why Mr. Turner should not become a defendant for any involvement in the group's unlawful acts.[23]

If individuals affiliated with the Forest Stewardship Council, Friends of the Earth, Greenpeace or Rainforest Action Network (RAN) are, in fact, convicted of serious crimes, there is no reason why the W. Alton Jones, Goldman, MacArthur and Pew Foundations should not be vulnerable to lawsuits seeking damage awards if their actions contributed to unlawful acts.

These foundations gave millions of dollars to these four attack groups between 1996 and 1999. The Richard & Rhoda Goldman Fund alone gave $1 million to RAN in September 1997. These and other grants enabled RAN (for example) to jump-start major protests that progressed to the WTO riots and continue today.[24]

Security specialist Edward Badolato emphasizes the vast national and international breadth of this conspiracy. Leftist, anti-West, anti-corporate radicals from Europe and the United States are sharing highly professional technology and techniques for encryption, anonymous Web-surfing, arson, fundraising, "safe houses" and "clean rooms," to minimize the risk of leaving evidence behind or being caught, alleges Badolato.

He also says the Clinton-Gore administration "was very quick to intervene on behalf of environmental groups to keep government investigations of their activities to a minimum." These past failures are being redressed, however, and government agencies have begun to increase their counter-terror efforts significantly. Make sure they continue to do so.

As Badolato observes, there are four keys to combating the eco and animal rights terrorists.

- Never make a deal with them or give in to their extortion and intimidation.

- Maintain a full-court press against them, with every civil, criminal, tax, financial and immigration law available to you.

- Force these organizations to comply with the rule of law – to the letter of every law.

- Participate in national and international cooperative efforts to break up these groups and incarcerate any members convicted of criminal offenses.[25]

Yes, all this will take time, money, effort and commitment. However, the tab for these efforts pales in comparison to the cost of many marketing and advertising campaigns – or the costs these predators and terrorists are exacting on your business every day. Moreover, there may be a surprising number of enterprising lawyers and organizations who are willing to pursue cases like these, because of the potentially large payoffs involved – to say nothing of the public interests to be served in bringing these radicals and their financial backers to justice.

At the very least, your efforts will result in negative publicity for the attackers, tarnish their image, reveal their true agendas, and force them to divert time, staff and money to defend against your counterattack. With a little luck, you will prevail in some cases, the idea will catch on, and a modicum of balance and accountability will be restored to our political and legal systems.

> Fascism and Nazism systematically downgraded the role of reason, logic and intelligence in human behavior, stressing instead its irrational and emotional components. Life, according to these ideologies, defies rational explanation. Truth is elusive and ordinary minds are incapable of understanding anything in depth. What is needed is intuition, instinct and emotion as the means of mobilizing and binding the masses. What is also needed is *action*: the simple and unambiguous assertion of one's power, force and strength against all perceived corruption and evil. In a chaotic universe, only the superior *will* can prevail. Political action – particularly of a violent nature – has value in and of itself: it is an exhibition of one's strength, an imposition of one's will, a demonstration of one's superiority. Violent action, in a word, is its own justification.
>
> — Mostafa Rejai[26]

Monkeywrenching is more than just sabotage, and you're goddam right it's revolutionary. This is jihad, pal. There are no innocent bystanders, because in these desperate hours, bystanders are not innocent.

—Mike Roselle, Earth First! co-founder,
director, Rainforest Action Network[27]

Serve up some gander sauce.

Why should the attack groups continue to have the field all to themselves?

Corporate warriors can borrow some of their favorite tactics and serve up some flavorful sauce for the eco-radical ganders.

Shareholder resolutions. Instead of letting annual corporate meetings be hijacked by activist resolutions, offer some provocative resolutions of your own.

Mobilize market-oriented activists who own sufficient shares of stock in your company to introduce resolutions that:

- Require the corporation to prosecute protesters who trespass on company property, harass or intimidate employees, steal merchandise or equipment, or try to extort money from the company.

- Restrict corporate relationships and funding only to nonprofits that formally endorse a set of principles that condemn: 1) violence against people and property; 2) the misuse and distortion of science; 3) the misuse, distortion or one-sided application of the so-called Precautionary Principle.

- Require that the company stop doing business with any financial institution or vendor that provides any kind of support to NGOs that have engaged in unjustified attacks on the company.

Insider information and influence. Basic membership in environmental attack groups offers a number of benefits other than just access to valuable information and opportunities to ask embarrassing questions that challenge agendas and group-think.

You may even be able to offer resolutions demanding that the organizations renounce violence, reveal questionable funding practices and work with law enforcement officials to arrest and prosecute eco-terrorists.

Counter protests. Environmental activists and protesters are used to having extensive, favorable media coverage of their news conferences and other staged events. Counter protests can change the dynamics and disrupt the radicals' agenda, give the media new people and issues for stories, and focus attention on sound science and responsible land and resource management.

Counter Protests R Us

The goal of counter protests is not just to generate positive media coverage for your company's point of view, or even negative coverage for the attack groups. Counter demonstrations can also steal the radicals' thunder, keep them from scoring points off you, or prevent them from getting their message out with the attention, spin and glowing reviews they seek.

As the Conservation And Reinvestment Act neared a Senate vote in September 2000, environmental groups rallied on the Capitol steps, to support the bill's billions of dollars in off-budget (hidden) appropriations for federal acquisition of private property.

Opponents called CARA the Confiscation And Redistribution Act – pork-barrel spending designed to take private property (often against the owners' will) and turn it over to government land managers who had allowed millions of acres to burn in wildfires.

Grassroots opponents donned jail-bird costumes, complete with balls-and-chains labeled "CARA" (to emphasize that landowners are often prisoners on their own land) and gave out pork rinds. Competitive Enterprise Institute staff handed out fact sheets and explained that, despite its good intentions, the legislation would undermine true conservation.

Tourists enjoyed the protest, as did media covering the event. The jail birds and anti-CARA views received extensive coverage and, in the end, the Senate voted against the legislation and approved only a much smaller authorization.[28]

Derail the gravy train.

Reveal and oppose further government, corporate and foundation funding of radical groups. Embarrass the groups and their sponsors publicly (directly or through allied groups), by linking the funding to misdeeds and undesirable consequences.

Let your employees know that the Supreme Court's *Beck* decision allows them to withhold the portion of their union dues that is dedicated to political efforts, or insist that it go to a selected charity, instead. Take maximum advantage of any opportunity that arises to generate financial or public relations nightmares for attack groups and their funding sources.

Kangaroo court

In February 1996, House Democrats staged a "hearing" at which a completely one-sided parade of speakers was to promote the Clinton Administration's environmental agenda. However, a strategically positioned National Center for Public Policy Research (NCPPR) staffer changed both the dynamics and media coverage of the event.

Television cameras could not record statements by Secretary of the Interior Bruce Babbitt or other "witnesses" without also including the costumed staffer's huge kangaroo head. The media were thus forced to explain why a kangaroo was in the "courtroom" and include NCPPR information in their coverage. When Democrats tried to have the 'roo expelled, Capitol Hill police told them he'd waited in line just like everyone else and had a right to be there.[29]

Play your trump card.

Empower "real people" who can dramatically underscore and denounce the harm inflicted on them by the radical attackers. Their message: Kill this project, this company, this technology – and you kill my chance for a better life.

Inuit Eskimos in Alaska's Arctic National Wildlife Refuge lack running water and basic sanitation. Infant mortality is high and cases of sometimes-fatal hepatitis-A are not uncommon.

For years, animal rights activists have attacked their traditional source of income – trapping seals and other animals for their pelts. Now radical environmentalists are pummeling them for supporting oil development on tribal lands and elsewhere in the desolate refuge.

Other North Slope Eskimos have benefited greatly from petroleum operations, and Gwich'in Indians hundreds of miles to the south have been supported financially by Green pressure groups for opposing oil development. Not surprisingly, the ANWR Eskimos are angry and resentful about "being held as economic hostages" by disingenuous attack groups and ill-informed opponents – when 80 percent of them favor development. [30]

Throughout the West, small family-owned ranching and logging operations have been driven to the brink of ruin by anti-everything pressure groups and eco-terrorists. When University of Washington horticultural labs were destroyed, researchers still got paychecks.

When ranchers, timber companies and car dealers lost millions of dollars in equipment and merchandise to arsonists, no one guaranteed their employees a paycheck or came to their aid. Some simply went on welfare, declared bankruptcy or moved.

This is your trump card. Your critics will not attack these people. So be daring and imaginative in finding ways to give them a platform. Do everything in your power to include our nation's and world's poor, powerless, ignored and forgotten in every debate. Make their names, faces and heartrending stories an integral part of every political battle.

Actually bring them to the next WTO, World Bank, forest management or oil development summit. Not just here in the States, but overseas as well.

Help people whose lives have been disrupted or destroyed by militant environmentalists to appear as witnesses at your next press conference or congressional hearing. Enlist the aid and expertise of people like Ingmar Egede and his Greenland-based International Training Center of Indigenous Peoples.[31] If you can't bring them in as live witnesses, make sure they appear on videotape.

Put them and their stories on the Internet. Feature them in television and radio spots, on talk shows, and in op-eds. Make sure they meet legislators, journalists, clergymen, and other potential allies, so they can explain their plights and views in person.

But don't just try to trot them out when you need help – or expect them to be happy to see you if you forgot about them after they helped you out of your last scrape. Many of them are highly skilled, accomplished, articulate and charismatic. They can be invaluable allies, and you can be their lifeline.

Work with them on a continuing basis, sustain them through slow periods, and retain their services whenever possible – as consultants, organizers, speakers and featured personalities. Your friendship, commitment and support will be repaid many times over.

Valediction

Conventional wisdom and capitulation counselors constantly preach that attacks by predatory extremists are no more than honest disagreements over legitimate grievances.

The solution, they say, is "better communication," "constructive engagement," "mutually beneficial relationships" based on "mutual trust."

They keep harping on *wei-ji*, the Chinese notion of crisis as danger and opportunity. They continue to ignore the danger and urge you to "take advantage of the opportunity to become a better, more socially responsible company."

BUNK! These PR flacks should be defrocked for gross professional incompetence. What they are feeding you is the same stuff Third World families burn in their cooking fires.

The fact is, their Chinese is better than their Greek. When the bard Homer wrote about the first Trojan Horse, he showed he understood attacks. His advice about crisis was crystal clear:

"This choice is left to you – fight or die."

When Winston Churchill viewed the Nazi war machine from across the English Channel, he understood that his problem was not poor communications, insufficient constructive engagement or a need for dialogue. It was an enemy bent on Great Britain's conquest or annihilation. It was a question of survival – his people's survival as a free nation.

That, in the simplest possible terms, is the question you face: Your company's survival. The free-market world's survival.

Will you succumb to the soft, seductive voices that urge "peace, dialogue, mutual trust"? Or will you recognize that your company's only real choice is between war and dishonor?

Will you capitulate? Or will you be guided by Churchill's reflections on having emerged from the darkest hours into the early dawn of a day that would eventually bring victory to his beleaguered nation?

> Now, this is not the end. It is not even the beginning of the end. But it is, perhaps, the end of the beginning.
>
> When I warned that Britain would fight on alone whatever the French did, their generals told their prime minister and his divided cabinet, "In three weeks, England will have her neck wrung like a chicken." Some chicken; some neck.
>
> –Winston Churchill[32]

Chapter 12 Notes

1. David Foreman, *Ecodefense: A field guide to monkewrenching*, Tucson, AZ: Ned Ludd Books (1987).
2. Peter Huber, *Hard Green: Saving the environment from the environmentalists – A conservative manifesto*, New York: Basic Books (1999).
3. David Horowitz, *The Art of Political War – And Other Radical Pursuits*, Dallas: Spence Publishing Company (2000), page 8.
4. Noah D. Oppenheim, "Follow the Money: The Jesse Jackson story," *The Weekly Standard*, April 2, 2001. Unauthentic Willie Sutton quote: Paul F. Boller, Jr. and John George, *They Never Said It*, New York: Oxford University Press (1989), page 121.
5. David Horowitz, *The Art of Political War*, page 12.
6. Robert H. Nelson, "Forest fires scorch seven million acres," *Environment & Climate News*, November 2000.
7. "Lives lost to environmental lobbies," *Environment & Climate News*, November 2000.
8. National Center for Public Policy Research, *National Directory of Environmental Victims* (2000), page 15.
9. Competitive Enterprise Institute, *Talking about Overregulation*, Kent Washburn, producer (1997).
10. See for example "Getting there safely: How to select a safer car, and how the experts can make auto travel safer," *Consumer Reports*, April 2000, pages 22-25. Contrast this to the Insurance Institute for Highway Safety's Web site guide (www.iihs.org) on shopping for a safer car. See also "Death by the Gallon," *USA Today*, July 2, 1999; Sam Kazman, "Testimony before the Transportation Research Board on the Effectiveness and Impact of Corporate Average Fuel Efficiency Standards," Competitive Enterprise Institute, February 6, 2001.
11. "The Case for Globalisation," *The Economist*, September 23, 2000, pages 19-20.
12. David Horowitz, *op cit.*, page 15.
13. Use the Atlas Foundation's "virtual phone book" at www.AtlasUSA.org, for easy access to market-oriented think tanks throughout the United States and world. Information about many US think tanks can also be found at www.heartland.org.
14. A good example of an online press kit dealing with especially volatile and often misunderstood issues can be found at www.furcommission.com/resource/presskit.htm.
15. Sixth annual Middleberg/Ross Media in Cyberspace survey, summarized in "Create an online press center that will keep reporters coming back," Ragan's *Media Relations Report*, October 2, 2000.
16. Daniel Bennett and Pam Fielding, *The Net Effect: How cyberadvocacy is changing the political landscape*, Merrifield, VA: e-advocates Press (1999); Shel Holtz, *Public Relations on the Net: Winning strategies to inform and influence the media, the investment community, the government, the public and more!* New York: AMACOM Publications (1999).

17. See Leonard Read's famous "I, Pencil" monograph (available through the Foundation for Economic Education or FEE at www.fee.org/about/ipencil.html) or go to www.generalpencil.com for interesting facts and photographs about the many complex steps involved in making common yellow wooden pencils.

18. Anyone providing information that leads to a conviction under RICO and certain other federal statutes is entitled to as much as 40 percent of the amounts ultimately recovered in fines and penalties.

19. Cyberspace slumlords offer free Internet hosting and services to radical and eco-terrorist organizations, enabling them to organize criminal and other activities. They typically claim they have no knowledge of or control over their tenants' unlawful activities, and "do not endorse their actions, opinions or expressions." Most of the cyber slumlords and their tenants are 501-(c)(3) nonprofits and thus are supported by taxpayers through tax-exempt status granted to them by the IRS. An example is Enviroweb.org, which is part of the EnviroLink Network and is home to some of the most radical anarchists and eco-terrorists on the Net. Envirolink was designed and built by students at Carnegie Mellon University in Pennsylvania – another example of tax and tuition money at work.

20. New York City slashed its crime rate in large part because Mayor Rudy Giuliani went after the nuisance crimes and thus cleared the streets of troublemakers who often were involved in more serious crimes, as well. The same methods and dynamics are likely to apply to your situation.

21. Associated Press, "Anarchist sentenced to more than 20 years in prison for arson," June 12, 2001 (Dateline: Eugene, OR).

22. Michael Katz, "Hush Moncy," *Forbes*, March 19, 2001.

23. Turner Foundation, Forms 990, 1994-2000, grant recipient lists.

24. Christopher Morris, Capital Research Center, "Sources of eco-radical funding," remarks at the Frontiers of Freedom conference on "Eco-Terrorism and Extremism: The costs imposed on Americans," Hart Senate Office Building, June 13, 2001; Internet search engine at www.green-watch.com; Teresa Platt, "Extremists Get $ Millions, Donor Gets Complaints," Alliance for America, www.allianceforamerica.org/Oldweb/1297003.htm (September 10, 1997). The Goldman Foundation's award notification mysteriously disappeared from its Web site at www.goldmanprize.org shortly after Platt and various organizations severely criticized the grants. For a detailed report by one of the RAN organizers on their "successful" riots in Seattle, go to www.co-intelligence.org/WTOblowbyblow.html.

25. Edward Badolato, Counterterrorism and Security Education and Research Foundation, "Combating eco-terrorism," remarks at the Frontiers of Freedom conference on "Eco-Terrorism and Extremism: The costs imposed on Americans," Hart Senate Office Building, June 13, 2001. Personal communication, June 14, 2001.

26. Mostafa Rejai, *Political Ideologies A Comparative Approach*, Armonk, NY: M. E. Sharpe, Inc. (1991), page 62.

27. Mike Roselle, "Forest Grump," *Earth First! Journal*, vol. 16, no 2, Yule, December 1994 / January 1995, page 23.

28. David Riggs, Competitive Enterprise Institute, personal communication, May 17, 2001.

29. David Ridenour, National Center for Public Policy Research, personal communication, June 7, 2001.

30 Deroy Murdock, "Eskimos: Open ANWR Now: Their desire to open ANWR deserves the immediate attention of policymakers and journalists alike," *National Review Online*, May 17, 2001; Jonah Goldberg, "Ugh, Wilderness! The horror of ANWR, the American elite's favorite hellhole," *National Review*, August 17, 2001.

31. Egede and his center teach indigenous people about the international treaty process, promote sustainable use of whales and other wildlife resources, and work to bridge the chasm between indigenous and western cultures. See www.maninnature.com and its "voices of sustainability" lecture series.

32. Winston Churchill, speech at the Lord Mayor's Day luncheon, London, November 10, 1942.

Bibliography
and
Resources

Bibliography
and Suggestions for Further Study

Adler, Jonathon H., editor; *The Costs of Kyoto: Climate change and policy and its implications*; Washington, DC: Competitive Enterprise Institute (1997).

Adler, Jonathon H., editor; *Ecology, Liberty and Property: A free market environmental reader*; Washington, DC: Competitive Enterprise Institute (2000).

Alinsky, Saul; *Rules for Radicals: A Pragmatic Primer for Realistic Radicals*; New York: Vintage Books (1971).

Anderson, Terry L. and Peter J. Hill, editors; *Environmental Federalism*; Lanham, MD: Rowman & Littlefield (1997).

Anderson, Terry L. and Donald R. Leal; *Free Market Environmentalism*; San Francisco: Pacific Research Institute (1991).

Arnold, Andrea; *Fear of Food: Environmentalist Scams, Media Mendacity and the Law of Disparagement*; Bellevue, WA: Free Enterprise Press (1990).

Arnold, Ron; *Ecology Wars: Environmentalism As If People Mattered*, Bellevue; WA: Free Enterprise Press (1987).

Arnold, Ron; *EcoTerror: The violent agenda to save nature – The world of the Unabomber*; Bellevue, WA: Free Enterprise Press (1997).

Arnold, Ron; *Trashing the Economy: How runaway environmentalism is wrecking America*, Bellevue, WA: Free Enterprise Press (1993).

Arnold, Ron; *Undue Influence: Wealthy foundations, grant-driven environmental groups, and zealous bureaucrats that control your future*; Bellevue, WA: Free Enterprise Press (1999).

322 **Rules for Corporate Warriors**

Bailey, Ronald, editor; *Earth Report 2000: Revisiting the True State of the Planet*; New York: McGraw Hill (2000).

Bailey, Ronald; *Eco-Scam: The False Prophets of Ecological Apocalypse*; New York: St. Martin's Press (1993).

Bailey, Ronald, editor; T*he True State of the Planet*; Washington, DC: Competitive Enterprise Institute (1995).

Bast, Joseph L., Peter J. Hill and Richard C. Rue, *Eco-Sanity: A commonsense guide to environmentalism*; Lanham, MD: Madison Books (1994; second edition 1996).

Beckerman, Wilfred; *Through Green-Colored Glasses: Environmentalism Reconsidered*; Washington, DC: Cato Institute Press (1996).

Bennett, Daniel and Pam Fielding; *The Net Effect: How Cybertechnology is Changing the Political Landscape*; Merrifield, VA: e-advocates Press (1999).

Bennett, James and Tom DeLorenzo, *The Food and Drink Police:America's Nannies, Busybodies and Petty Tyrants*; New Brunswick, NJ: Transaction Publishers, Inc. (1999).

Boorstin, Daniel J.; *The Image: A guide to pseudo-events in America*, New York: Vintage Books (1992).

Bradley, Robert L. Jr.; *Julian Simon and the Triumph of Energy Sustainability*; Washington, DC: American Legislative Exchange Council (2000).

Breyer, Stephen; *Breaking the Vicious Circle: Toward effective risk regulation*; Cambridge, MA: Harvard University Press (1993).

Clausewitz, Carl von; *On War*; Princeton, NJ: Princeton University Press (1976).

DeLong, James V.; *The New Criminal Classes: Legal Sanctions and Business Managers*; Washington, DC: National Legal Center for the Public Interest (1997).

DeSoto, Hernando; *The Mystery of Capital: Why capitalism triumphs in the West and fails everywhere else*; New York: Basic Books (2000).

Dezenhall, Eric; *Nail 'Em: Confronting high profile attacks on businesses and celebrities*; New York: Prometheus Books (1999).

Easterbrook, Gregg; *A Moment on the Earth: The coming age of environmental optimism*; New York: Viking Books (1995).

Editors (unnamed), *The Right Guide* and *The Left Guide*; Ann Arbor: Economics America, Inc. (1998).

Fagan, Brian; *The Little Ice Age: How climate made history, 1300-1850;* New York: Basic Books (2000).

Fink, Steven; *Crisis Management: Planning for the Inevitable*; AMACOM – American Management Association (1999).

Folsom, Burton; *Empire Builders: How Michigan entrepreneurs helped make America great*; Traverse City, MI: Rhodes & Easton (1998).

Frieden, Bernard J.; *The Environmental Protection Hustle*; Cambridge, MA: Massachusetts Institute of Technology (1979).

Fumento, Michael; *Polluted Science: The EPA's Campaign to Expand Clean Air Regulations*; Washington, DC: American Enterprise Institute (1997).

Fumento, Michael; *Science Under Siege: Balancing Technology and the Environment*; New York: William Morrow and Company, Inc. (1993).

Goklany, Indur M.; *Economic Growth and the State of Humanity*; Bozeman, MT: Political Economy Research Center (2001).

Ghyczy, Tiha von and Bolko von Oetinger and Christopher Bassford; *Clausewitz on Strategy: Inspiration and Insight from a Master Strategist*; New York: John Wiley & Son, Inc. (2001).

Hagen, Eric W. and James J. Worman; *An Endless Series of Hobgoblins: The Science and Politics of Environmental Health Scares*; Irvington-on-Hudson: Foundation for Economic Education (1995).

Holtz, Shel; *Public Relations on the Net: Winning strategies to inform and influence the media, the investment community, the government, the public and more!* New York: AMACOM – American Management Association (1999).

Horowitz, David; *The Art of Political War – And other political pursuits*; Dallas: Spence Publishing Company (2000).

Howard, Philip; *The Death of Common Sense: How law is suffocating America*; New York: Random House (1994).

Huber, Peter; *Galileo's Revenge: Junk Science in the Courtroom*; New York: Basic Books (1991).

Huber, Peter; *Hard Green: Saving Environmentalism from the Environmentalists: A conservative manifesto*; New York: Basic Books (1999).

Isaac, Rael Jean and Erich Isaac; *The Coercive Utopians: Social Deception by America's Power Players*; Washington, DC: Regnery Gateway (1983).

Johnson, M. Bruce; *The Attack on Corporate America: The corporate issues sourcebook*; Miami: Law and Economics Center, University of Miami School of Law (1978).

Jones, Laura, editor; *Global Warming: The science and the politics*; Vancouver, BC: Fraser Institute (1997).

Karliner, Joshua; *The Corporate Planet: Ecology and politics in the age of globalization*; San Francisco: Sierra Club Books (1997).

Kaufman, Wallace; *No Turning Back: Dismantling the fantasies of environmental thinking*; Lincoln, NE: iUniverse.com (2000).

Lomborg, Bjorn; *The Skeptical Environmentalist: Measuring the real state of the world*; Cambridge: Cambridge University Press (2001).

Marzulla, Nancie G. and Roger J. Marzulla; *Property Rights: Understanding government takings and environmental regulation*; Rockville, MD: Government Institutes (1997).

Merchant, Carolyn; *Radical Ecology: The search for a livable world*; New York: Routledge, Chapman & Hall, Inc. (1992).

Michaels, Patrick J. and Robert C. Balling, Jr.; *The Satanic Gases: Clearing the air about global warming*; Washington, DC: Cato Institute (2000).

Miller, Henry I; *Policy Controversy in Biotechnology: An insider's view*; Stanford: Hoover Institution (1997).

Milloy, Steven; *Science without Sense: The risky business of public health research*; Washington, DC: Cato Institute (1995).

Milloy, Steven and Michael Gough, *Silencing Science*, Washington, DC: Cato Institute (1999).

Moore, Patrick; *Green Spirit: Trees are the answer*; Toronto: Hushion House (2000).

Narayan, Deepa; *Voices of the Poor: Can Anyone Hear Us?* Oxford: Oxford University Press (2000).

National Center for Public Policy Research; *National Directory of Environmental Regulatory Victims*; Washington, DC (1998. 1999, 2000).

Neal, Mark and Christie Davies; *The Corporation under Siege: Exposing the devices used by activists and regulators in the non-risk society*; London: Social Affairs Unit (1998).

Oliver, Daniel T.; *Animal Rights: The Inhumane Crusade*; Bellevue, Washington: Merril Press (1999).

Park, Robert L.; *Voodoo Science: The Road from Foolishness to Fraud*; Oxford: Oxford University Press, 2000.

Ray, Dixie Lee, with Lou Guzzo; *Environmental Overkill: Whatever happened to common sense?* Washington, DC: Regnery Gateway (1993).

Ray, Dixie Lee, with Lou Guzzo; *Trashing the Planet: How science can help us deal with acid rain, depletion of the ozone and nuclear waste (among other things)*; Washington, DC: Regnery Gateway (1990).

Regan, Tom, editor; *Earthbound: Introductory essays on environmental ethics*; Prospect Heights, IL: Waveland Press (1984).

Ries, Al and Jack Trout; *Marketing Warfare*; New York, NY: McGraw-Hill Book Company (1986).

Rosenberg, Nathan and L.E. Birdzell; *How the West Grew Rich: The economic transformation of the industrial world*; New York: Basic Books (1986).

Sanera, Michael and Jane S. Shaw; *Facts Not Fear: A Parent's Guide to Teaching Children about the Environment*; Washington, DC: Regnery Publishing (1996).

Satel, Dr. Sally, MD; *PC, MD: How Political Correctness Is Corrupting Medicine*; New York: Basic Books (2000).

Scarlett, Lynn and Jane S. Shaw; *Environmental Progress: What Every Executive Should Know*; Bozeman, MT: Political Economy Research Center (1999).

Schall, James Vincent; *Religion, Wealth and Poverty*; Vancouver, BC: Fraser Institute (1990).

Schoenbrod, David; *Power Without Responsibility: How Congress abuses people through delegation*; Cambridge, MA: Yale University Press (1995).

Sheehan, James; *Global Greens: Inside the International Environmental Establishment*; Washington, DC: Capital Research Center (1998).

Simon, Julian; *The Resourceful Earth: A response to Global 2000*; New York: Basil Blackwell (1984).

Simon, Julian; *Population Matters: People, resources, environment and immigration*; New Brunswick, NJ: Transaction Publishers and Cato Institute (1990).

Simon, Julian; *The Ultimate Resource 2: Natural resources, pollution, world's food supply, pressures of population growth. Every trend in material human welfare has been improving and promises to continue to do so, indefinitely*; Princeton, NJ: Princeton University Press (1998).

Sowell, Thomas; *The Vision of the Annointed: Self-congratulation as a basis for social policy*; New York: Basic Books (1995).

Stauffer, Dennis; *Mediasmart: How to handle a reporter (by a reporter)*; Minneapolis, MN: MinneApplePress (1994).

Stein, Harry; *How I Accidentally Joined The Vast Right-Wing Conspiracy (and found inner peace)*; New York, NY: Delacorte Press (2000).

Tsu, Sun; *The Art of War: A New Translation*; Boston & London: Shambhala (2001).

Vazsonyi, Balint; *America's Thirty Year War: Who Is Winning?* Washington, DC: Regnery Publishing (1998).

Weaver, Paul H.; *The Suicidal Corporation*; New York: Simon and Schuster (1988).

Werbach, Adam; *Act Now, Apologize Later*; New York: Harper Collins (1997).

Whelan, Robert, Joseph Kirwan and Paul Hafner; *The Cross and the Rain Forest: A critique of radical Green spirituality*; Grand Rapids, MI: William B. Eerdmans Publishing Company and Acton Institute (1996).

Williams, Walter E.; *Do the Right Thing: The people's economist speaks*; Stanford, CA: Hoover Institution Press, No. 430, (1995).

Williams, Walter E.; *More Liberty Means Less Government: Our founders knew this well*; Stanford, CA: Hoover Institution Press, No. 453, (1999).

Yandle, Bruce; *Bootleggers, Baptists and Global Warming;* Bozeman, MT: Political Economy Research Center (1998).

VIDEOTAPES

Aquariums Without Walls; Paul Driessen, producer; Irving, TX: Exxon Company, USA (1988).

Science Under Siege; Kent Washburn, producer; Washington, DC: Competitive Enterprise Institute (1996).

Talking about Overregulation ; Kent Washburn, producer; Competitive Enterprise Institute, Washington, DC (1997).

Against Nature; Martin Durkin producer, London: Channel 4 Television Corporation (1997).

Resources

Selected Think Tanks

Accuracy in Media
4455 Connecticut Ave NW, Suite 330, Washington DC 20008 202-364-4401 www.aim.org
American Council on Science and Health
1995 Broadway, 2nd Floor, New York, NY 10023, 212-362-7044, www.acsh.org
Atlas Economic Research Foundation
4084 University Drive, Suite 103, Fairfax, VA 22030, 703-934-6969, www.atlasusa.org
Capital Research Center
1513 - 16th Street NW, Washington, DC 20036, 202-483-6900, www.capitalresearch.org
Cato Institute
1000 Massachusetts Avenue NW, Washington, DC 20001, 202-842-0200, www.cato.org
Center for the Defense of Free Enterprise
12500 NE Tenth Place, Bellevue, WA 98005, 425-455-5038, www.cdfe.org
Citizens for a Sound Economy
1250 H Street NW, Suite 700, Washington, DC 20005, 202-783-3870, www.cse.org
Claremont Institute
250 West First Street, Suite 330, Claremont, CA 91711, 909-621-6825, www.claremont.org

Committee For A Constructive Tomorrow
PO Box 65722, Washington, DC 20035, 202-492-2737, www.cfact.org
Competitive Enterprise Institute
1001 Connecticut Avenue NW, Suite 1250, Washington, DC 20036,
202-331-1010, www.cei.org
Consumer Alert
1001 Connecticut Avenue NW, Suite 1128, Washington, DC 20036,
202-467-5809, www.consumeralert.org
Defenders of Property Rights
1350 Connecticut Avenue NW, Suite 410, Washington, DC 20036, 202-
822-6770, www.defendersproprights.org
The Fraser Institute
1770 Burrard Street, 4th Floor, Vancouver, BC V6J 3G7 Canada, 604-
688-0221, www.fraserinstitute.ca
Frontiers of Freedom Institute / People for the USA
12011 Lee Jackson Memorial Highway, Third Floor, Fairfax, VA 22033,
703-246-0110, www.ff.org
Heartland Institute
19 South LaSalle, Suite 903, Chicago, IL 60603, 312-377-4000,
www.heartland.org
Heritage Foundation
214 Massachusetts Avenue NE, Washington, DC 20002, 202-546-4400,
www.heritage.org
Hoover Institution
Stanford University, Stanford, CA 94305, 650-723-0603,
www-hoover.stanford.edu
Hudson Institute
Herman Kahn Center, 5395 Emerson Way, Indianapolis, IN 46226,
317-545-1000, www.hudson.org
Institute for Energy Research
6219 Olympia, Houston, TX 77057, 713-974-1918, www.institutefor
energyresearch.org
Institute of Economic Affairs
2 Lord North Street, Westminster, London, SW1P 3LB, UK, 44-020-7799-
8900, www.iea.org.uk
Institute of Public Affairs (publisher of *NGO Watch*)
410 Collins Street, Level 2, Melbourne, Victoria 3000, Australia, 49-008-
627-727, www.ipa.org.au
Leadership Institute
1101 North Highland Street, Arlington, VA 22201, 703-247-2000,
www.leadershipinstitute.org
Mackinac Center for Public Policy
Post Office Box 568, Midland, MI 48640, 989-631-0900,
www.mackinac.org

Media Research Center
325 S. Patrick Street, Alexandria, VA 22314, 703-683-9733, www.media research.org
National Anxiety Center
9 Brookside Road, Maplewood, NJ 07040, 973-763-6392, www.anxiety center.com
National Center for Policy Analysis
12655 N. Central Expressway, Suite 720, Dallas, TX 75243, 972-386-6272, www.ncpa.org
National Center for Public Policy Research
777 North Capitol Street NE, Suite 803, Washington, DC 20002, 202-371-1400, www.nationalcenter.org
National Foundation for Energy Education
Post Office Box 8186, Reston, VA 20191, 703-860-0951, www.nfee.org
Pacific Research Institute for Public Policy
755 Sansome Street, Suite 450, San Francisco, CA 94111, 415-989-0823, www.pacificresearch.org
Reason Public Policy Institute
3415 South Sepulveda Boulevard, Suite 400, Los Angeles, CA 90034, 310-391-2245, www.reason.org, www.rppi.org
State Policy Network
6255 Arlington Boulevard, Richmond, CA 94805, 510-965-9700, www.spn.org
Statistical Assessment Service, 2100 L Street NW, Suite 300, Washington, DC 20037 202-223-3193 www.stats.org.
Toward Tradition
Post Office Box 58, Mercer Island, WA 98040, 206-236-3046, www.towardtradition.org

Selected Grassroots Groups

American Land Rights Association - Land Rights Network
Post Office Box 400, Battle Ground, WA 98604, 360-687-3087, www.landrights.org
Legislative office: 508 First Street SE, Washington DC 20003, 202-210-2357
Alliance for America
Post Office Box 449, Caroga Lake, NY 12032, 518-835-6702, www.allianceforamerica.org
Blue Ribbon Coalition
4555 Burley Drive, Suite A, Pocatello 83202, 208-237-1008, www.sharetrails.org
National Animal Interest Alliance
Post Office Box 66579, Portland, OR 97290-6579, 503-761-1139, www.naiaonline.org

Selected Legal Foundations

Landmark Legal Foundation
3100 Broadway, Suite1110, Kansas City, MO 64111, 816-931-5559,
www.landmarklegal.org
Mountain States Legal Foundation
707 17th Street, Suite 3030, Denver, CO 80202, 303-292-2021,
www.mountainstateslegal.org
Pacific Legal Foundation
10360 Old Placerville Road, Suite 100, Sacramento, CA 95827, 916-362-2833,
www.pacificlegal.org
Washington Legal Foundation
2009 Massachusetts Ave NW, Washington, DC 20036, 202-588-0302,
www.wlf.org

Selected Web Sites

www.AtlasUSA.org – Atlas Economic Research Foundation's directory
of U.S. and overseas think tanks.
www.heartland.org (links) – Heartland Institute's database of policy think
tanks
www.policyexperts.org – Heritage Foundation's database of U.S. policy
experts
www.spn.org/directory – State Policy Network's database of state-focused
think tanks.
www.TruthAboutTrade.com
www.JunkScience.com
www.greeningearthsociety.org
www.greenspirit.com – Dr. Patrick Moore's inspired website.
www.globalwarming.com
www.john-daly.com
www.nichols-dezenhall.com
www.RulesForCorporateWarriors.com

Index

Index

pollution, 2, 78, 140, 262, 279
polycarbonate, 36
Pombo, Richard, 11
population, human, 5-6, 129, 217, 218, 277
positioning, 292, 297
Post Dispatch, 233
power corrupts, 21
Power Plays, 76, 80-108
–brass knuckles, 80-83
–enjoy the experience, 88-90
–execute the unexpected, 83-87, 128
–exploit your strengths, 87-88
–keep pressure on, 103-104, 138
–locate and lock onto target, 104-108
–make them sweat your threat, 93-94
–new plays from the bench, 90-93
–scorn and ridicule, 97-103
–turn enemy rules into weapons, 94-97
Power Strategies, 128-141
–annexation, 128-129
–Balkanization, 129-131
–cauterization, 131
–differentiation, 132
–diffusion, 132-133
–dissuasion, 133-134
–diversion, 134-135
–expiation, 135
–fraternization, 136
–inoculation, 136-137
–pacification, 137
–preemption, 138-139
–stultification, 139
–subordination, 140
–vitiation, 140-141
PR Newswire, 187
practice interviews, 149
Precautionary Principle, 227, 249-271, 310
–duty to monitor, inform and act, 256
–evaluating alternatives, 253
–financial responsibility, 255
–fraudulent balance sheet, 256-264
–scientific certainty, 251-252
–setting goals, 253-255

Precautionary Principle (continued)
–shifting burdens of proof, 252
–theory versus reality, 264-269
preemption, 138-139
preemptive capitulation, 68, 234
preservationists, 1, 5
Prisoners of Hate, 56
Private Ryan, 45
profits, 43, 66, 121, 148, 205, 224
progress, scientific and technological 2-5, 253, 276-278
props (for interview), 161, 166
propaganda as science, 262
prosecuting criminal actions, 85, 305-306
prove product safety, 251-252
Prudhoe Bay oil field, 92
psychological profile, 54-57
psychological warfare, 93, 145
psychopathic element of crusade, 129
Public Affairs Council, 303
Public Broadcasting Service (PBS), 173-175, 176-177, 179, 180-181, 186, 189, 190-193, 196-198
–executives, 174-175, 179-182, 186-187, 193, 198
–funding, 179-180, 193, 197-198
–media advisories, 174-176, 179, 187, 190
Public Citizen, 19, 115, 247
public hearings, 274-275
Public Interest Research Groups (PIRGs), 11, 18
Public Relations on the Net, 303
Public Utilities Commission, 45
Puck, Wolfgang, 210
Pyle, Barbara, 155

Quebec, Ontario, 219-220
Quirke, Kelly, 227

Rabinowitz, Dorothy, 134
Racketeer Influenced and Corrupt Organization (RICO), 301, 304, 316
radical ethics – see ethics, radical